CISCO CERTIFIED NETWORK ASSOCIATE

Cisco CCNA Test

Yourself Practice

Exams

D1361791

Cisco CCNA Test Yourself Practice Exams

Syngress Media, Inc.

Osborne McGraw-Hill
Berkeley New York St. Louis San Francisco
Auckland Bogotá Hamburg London Madrid
Mexico City Milan Montreal New Delhi Panama City
Paris São Paulo Singapore Sydney
Tokyo Toronto

Osborne McGraw-Hill
2600 Tenth Street
Berkeley, California 94710
U.S.A.

For information on translations or book distributors outside the U.S.A., or to arrange bulk purchase discounts for sales promotions, premiums, or fund-raisers, please contact Osborne/**McGraw-Hill** at the above address.

Cisco CCNA Test Yourself Practice Exams

1234567890 AGM AGM 90198765432109

ISBN 0-07-212052-5

Publisher
Brandon A. Nordin

Associate Publisher and
Editor-in-Chief
Scott Rogers

Acquisitions Editor
Gareth Hancock

Editorial Management
Syngress Media, Inc.

Project Editor
Emily Rader

Editorial Assistant
Tara Davis

Technical Editors
Neil Lovering
John Dyer

Copy Editor
Nancy Faughnan

Proofreaders
Rhonda Holmes
Karen Mead

Computer Designers
Michelle Galicia
Gary Corrigan

Illustrators
Beth Young
Robert Hansen

Series Design
Roberta Steele

FOREWORD

From Global Knowledge

At Global Knowledge we strive to support the multiplicity of learning styles required by our students to achieve success as technical professionals. In this series of books, it is our intention to offer the reader a valuable tool for successful completion of the CCNA Certification Exam.

As the world's largest IT training company, Global Knowledge is uniquely positioned to offer these books. The expertise gained each year from providing instructor-led training to hundreds of thousands of students worldwide has been captured in book form to enhance your learning experience. We hope that the quality of these books demonstrates our commitment to your lifelong learning success. Whether you choose to learn through the written word, computer-based training, Web delivery, or instructor-led training, Global Knowledge is committed to providing you the very best in each of those categories. For those of you who know Global Knowledge, or those of you who have just found us for the first time, our goal is to be your lifelong competency partner.

Thank you for the opportunity to serve you. We look forward to serving your needs again in the future.

Warmest regards,

Duncan Anderson
President and Chief Executive Officer, Global Knowledge

About Syngress Media

Syngress Media creates books and software for Information Technology professionals seeking skill enhancement and career advancement. Its products are designed to comply with vendor and industry standard course curricula, and are optimized for certification exam preparation. Visit the Syngress Web site at www.syngress.com.

About the Contributors

Melissa Craft (CCNA, MCSE, CNE-3, CNE-4, CNE-GW, MCNE, Citrix) is a consulting engineer for MicroAge, a dynamic systems integration company in Phoenix, AZ. Melissa handles internetwork systems design for complex or global network projects, concentrating on infrastructure and messaging. She has a bachelor's degree from the University of Michigan. During her career, she has obtained several certifications: CCNA, MCSE, CNE-3, CNE-4, CNE-GW, MCNE, and Citrix. She is a member of the IEEE, the Society of Women Engineers, and American Mensa, Ltd.

Glenn Lepore (CCNA) is a senior network engineer with Niche Networks, LLC, in Herndon, VA. He has over 13 years experience in LAN and WAN design, installation, and troubleshooting. His background includes frame relay, X.25, TCP/IP, IPX, and SNA. His experience includes Novell and UNIX administration, Web page design, and Internet service provider (ISP) network operations. He is a CCNA, and is working toward CCIE certification as well as MCSE.

Glenn Pritchard (CCNA) is a Senior Network Consultant for Niche Networks, LLC. He has over 15 years experience designing and implementing large scale global networks. He specializes in requirements analysis, network management, and application performance analysis modeling. He has implemented many military-based satellite and WAN networks used for defense communications. Mr. Pritchard is currently producing training materials for several large ISPs and teaching several Cisco product classes to customers nationwide. He is also a CCNA.

Josh Ament (CCNA, MCSE, CNA) is an owner and senior consultant for Dexi, a consulting firm based in Southern California. He has extensive experience in UNIX, Windows, and Novell-based operating systems. He specializes in network design, configuration, and implementation. Mr. Ament currently holds Microsoft, Novell, and Cisco certifications.

Kevin E. Greene currently works in the telecommunications industry as a network security professional. He holds a Master of Science degree in Information Systems and a Bachelor of Science degree in Management Information Systems from the New Jersey Institute of Technology. In addition, he has attained CheckPoint Firewall-1 certification as a System Engineer and System Administrator.

Amar Reddy works for USWeb/CKS, Inc., as a Senior Engineer in the New York/New Jersey area. He has worked in the telecommunications, pharmaceutical, and finance and banking industries. He has a wide range of experience in data communications, including designing wide area networks and high-speed switching and network management systems for major organizations. Mr. Reddy holds a Masters degree in Computer Science with Networking specialization from City University of New York–College of Staten Island, New York.

Technical Editors

Neil Lovering is a CCIE-certified (#1772) network consultant and Cisco-certified instructor (#95010). He has helped with many large and small network design and optimization projects throughout the United States and Canada, specializing in OSPF configuration and migration. He has taught thousands of students over the last few years how to configure Cisco routers and switches, design and troubleshoot complex networks, and earn various Cisco network certifications. Mr. Lovering authored the first in a series of Cisco-based computer training courses offered through Global Knowledge, has coauthored many Cisco-related technical books, and has been the technical editor on others.

John Dyer is a partner at Niche Networks, LLC, in Herndon, Virginia. He has 13 years of experience in systems integration and networking in the information technology industry, including design and installation of LAN/WAN infrastructures, network management, and network security platforms. Mr. Dyer is a Cisco Certified Instructor teaching Introduction to Cisco Router Configuration, Advanced Cisco Router Configuration, CiscoWorks, and Managing Cisco Switched Internetworks.

ACKNOWLEDGMENTS

We would like to thank the following people:

- Richard Kristof of Global Knowledge, for championing the series and providing us access to some great people and information.

- All of the incredibly hard-working folks at Osborne/McGraw-Hill: Brandon Nordin, Scott Rogers, and Gareth Hancock, for their help in launching a great series and being solid team players. In addition, Tara Davis and Emily Rader, for their help in fine-tuning the book.

- Bridget Robeson, managing partner of Niche Networks, LLC, for all her help.

CONTENTS AT A GLANCE

Part 12
Test Yourself: Practice Exam 2

Part 13
Test Yourself: Practice Exam 3

CONTENTS

Part 3
IP Addressing

Part 4
The TCP/IP Protocol Suite

Part 5
IP Routing

Part 6
IP Configuration

Part 7
Configuring Novell IPX

Part 8
Basic Traffic Management with Access Lists

Part 9
Wide Area Networking

Part 10
Virtual Local Area Networking

We built this book for a specific reason. Every time we asked Cisco technicians and CCNA candidates what they wanted in their study materials, they answered, "More questions!" Based on that resounding request, we built a book full of questions on the CCNA exam, so you can test yourself to your heart's desire.

In This Book

This book is organized in chapters, according to topics tested on the CCNA certification exam. We cover each of the exam topics in a separate module of questions and answers, and we also have three separate "Test Yourself" Practice Exams.

The Q&A Modules

You will find one Q&A module for each exam topic, from Internetworking to Virtual Local Area Networking. Each question section has between 38 and 40 original questions, followed by an answer section that has full explanations of the correct choices.

Each module is divided into categories, so you will cover every topic tested by Cisco. Each topic is a heading within the chapter, so you can study by topic if you like. Should you find you need further review on any particular topic, you will find that the topic headings correspond to the chapters of Osborne/McGraw-Hill's *CCNA Cisco Certified Network Associate Study Guide.* Want to simulate an actual exam? The next section, "The Test Yourself Practice Exams" explains how.

In addition, throughout the question and answer chapters, we have sprinkled helpful notes in the form of Q&A scenarios that detail problems and solutions in a quick-read format, as shown in next.

QUESTIONS AND ANSWERS

I am running RIP across a 64 Kbps WAN link. The updates are taking up too much bandwidth. What should I do?	Change the update period to a slower amount than the default 30 seconds.
How do I get my workstations to receive their IP addresses via DHCP on a different subnet than the DHCP server?	On the router that connects the two network segments, enter an IP helper address and point it to the DHCP server.

The Test Yourself Practice Exams

If you have had your fill of exam questions, answers, and explanations, the time has come to test your knowledge. Or maybe you are starting with one of the Test Yourself exams to see where your strengths and weaknesses are, so you can review only certain topics. Either way, turn to the final three modules of the book, the Test Yourself practice exams. These modules actually simulate the exams. We have given you three practice tests, with the number of questions corresponding to the actual exam in random order. Lock yourself in your office or clear the kitchen table, set a timer, and jump in.

The Global Knowledge Web Site

Global Knowledge invites you to become an active member of the Access Global web site. This site is an online mall and an information repository that you'll find invaluable. You can access many types of products to assist you in your preparation for the exams, and you'll be able to participate in forums, online discussions, and threaded discussions. No other book brings you unlimited access to such a resource. You'll find more information about this site in "About the Web Site," at the end of the book.

How to Take a Cisco Certification Examination

This section covers the importance of your CCNA certification and prepares you for taking the actual examination. It gives you a few pointers on methods of preparing for the exam, including how to study, register, what to expect, and what to do on exam day.

Catch the Wave!

Congratulations on your pursuit of Cisco certification! In this fast-paced world of networking, few certifications compare to the value of Cisco's program.

The networking industry has virtually exploded in recent years, accelerated by nonstop innovation and the Internet's popularity. Cisco has stayed at the forefront of this tidal wave, maintaining a dominant role in the industry.

Since the networking industry is highly competitive, and evolving technology only increases in its complexity, the rapid growth of the networking industry has created a vacuum of qualified people. There simply aren't enough skilled networking people to meet the demand. Even the most experienced professionals must keep current with the latest technology in order to provide the skills that the industry demands. That's where Cisco certification programs can help networking professionals succeed as they pursue their career.

Cisco started its certification program many years ago, offering only the designation of Cisco Certified Internetwork Expert, or CCIE. Through the CCIE program, Cisco provided a means to meet the growing demand for experts in the field of networking. However, the CCIE tests are brutal, with a failure rate over 80 percent. (Fewer than five percent of candidates pass on their first attempt.) As you might imagine, very few people ever attain CCIE status.

In early 1998, Cisco recognized the need for intermediate certifications, and several new programs were created. Four intermediate certifications were added: CCNA (Cisco Certified Network Associate), CCNP (Cisco Certified Network Professional), CCDA (Cisco Certified Design Associate), and CCDP (Cisco Certified Design Professional). Two specialties were also created for the CCIE program: WAN Switching and ISP Dial-up.

We would encourage you to take beta tests when they are available. Not only are the beta exams less than the cost of the final exams (some are even free!), but also, if you pass the beta, you will receive credit for passing the exam. If you don't pass the beta, you will have seen every question in the pool of available questions and can use this information when preparing to take the exam for the second time. Remember to jot down important information immediately after the exam, if you didn't pass. You will have to do this after leaving the exam area, since materials written during the exam are retained by the testing center. This information can be helpful when you need to determine which areas of the exam were most challenging for you as you study for the subsequent test.

Why Vendor Certification?

Over the years, vendors have created their own certification programs because of industry demand. This demand arises when the marketplace needs skilled professionals and an easy way to identify them. Vendors benefit because it promotes people skilled in their product. Professionals benefit because it boosts their career. Employers benefit because it helps them identify qualified people.

In the networking industry, technology changes too often and too quickly to rely on traditional means of certification, such as universities and trade associations. Because of the investment and effort required to keep network certification programs current, vendors are the only organizations suited to keep pace with the changes. In general, such vendor certification programs are excellent, with most of them requiring a solid foundation in the essentials, as well as their particular product line.

Corporate America has come to appreciate these vendor certification programs and the value they provide. Employers recognize that certifications, like university degrees, do not guarantee a level of knowledge, experience or performance; rather, they establish a baseline for comparison. By seeking to hire vendor-certified employees, a company can assure itself that, not only has it found a person skilled in networking, but it has also hired a person skilled in the specific products the company uses.

Technical professionals have also begun to realize the value of certification and the impact it can have on their careers. By completing a certification program, professionals gain an endorsement of their skills from a major industry source. This endorsement can boost their current position, and it makes finding the next job even easier. Often, a certification determines whether a first interview is even granted.

Today, a certification may place you ahead of the pack. Tomorrow, it will be a necessity to keep from being left in the dust.

Signing up for an exam has become more effortless with the new Web-based test registration system. To sign up for either of the CCNA exams, access http://www.2test.com and register for the Cisco Career Certification path. You will need to get an Internet account and password if you do not already have one for 2test.com. Just select the option for first time registration, and the Web site will walk you through that process. The registration wizard even provides maps to the testing centers, something that is not available when calling Sylvan Prometric on the telephone.

Cisco's Certification Program

As mentioned previously, Cisco now has six certifications for the Routing and Switching career track, and four certifications for the WAN Switching career track. While Cisco recommends a series of courses for each of these certifications, they are not required. Ultimately, certification is dependent upon a candidate passing a series of exams. With the right experience and study materials, each of these exams can be passed without taking the associated class. The following table shows the various Cisco certifications and tracks.

Track	Certification	Acronym
Routing and Switching: Network Support	Cisco Certified Network Associate	CCNA
Routing and Switching: Network Support	Cisco Certified Network Professional	CCNP
Routing and Switching: Network Support	Cisco Certified Internetwork Expert (Routing and Switching)	CCIE-R/S

Track	Certification	Acronym
Routing and Switching: Network Support	Cisco Certified Internetwork Expert (ISP Dial Technology)	CCIE-ISP Dial
Routing and Switching: Network Design	Cisco Certified Design Associate	CCDA
Routing and Switching: Network Design	Cisco Certified Design Professional	CCDP
WAN Switching: Network Support	Cisco Certified Network Associate—WAN switching	CCNA-WAN Switching
WAN Switching: Network Support	Cisco Certified Network Professional—WAN switching	CCNP-WAN Switching
WAN Switching: Network Support	Cisco Certified Internetwork Expert—WAN Switching	CCIE-WAN Switching
WAN Switching: Network Design	Cisco Certified Design Professional—WAN Switching	CCDP-WAN Switching

The following illustration shows Cisco's Routing and Switching track, with both the Network Design and Network Support paths. Candidates can pursue either the Network Design path to CCDA and CCDP, or the Network Support path to CCNP and CCIE.

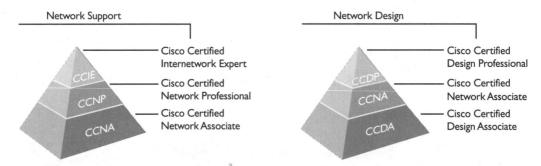

The following table shows a matrix of the exams required for each Cisco certification. Note that candidates have the choice of taking either the single Foundation R/S exam, or the set of three ACRC, CLSC, and CMTD exams—all four exams are not required.

Exam Name	Exam #	CCNA	CCDA	CCNP	CCDP	CCIE
CCNA 1.0	640-407	x	x	x	x	
CDS 1.0	9E0-004		x		x	
Foundation R/S	640-409			x	x	
ACRC	640-403			x	x	
CLSC	640-404			x	x	
CMTD	640-405			x	x	
CIT	640-406			x		
CID	640-025				x	
CCIE R/S Qualifying						x
CCIE Lab						x

You may hear veterans refer to this CCIE R/S Qualifying Exam as the "Cisco Drake test." This is a carryover from the early days, when Sylvan Prometric's name was Drake Testing Centers, and Cisco had only the one exam.

In addition to finding the technical objectives that are being tested for each exam, you will find much more useful information on Cisco's Web site at http://www.cisco.com/warp/public/10/wwtraining/certprog.

You will find information on becoming certified, exam-specific information, sample test questions, and the latest news on Cisco certification. This is the most important site you will find on your journey to becoming Cisco certified.

When you find yourself stumped answering multiple-choice questions, you can use your scratch paper to write down the two or three answers you consider the strongest, and then underline the answer you feel is most likely correct. Here is an example of what your scratch paper might look like when you've gone through the test once:

21. B or <u>C</u>

33. <u>A</u> or C

This is extremely helpful when you mark the question and continue on. You can then return to the question and immediately pick up your thought process where you left off. Use this technique to avoid having to reread and rethink questions.

You will also need to use your scratch paper during complex, text-based scenario questions to create visual images to better understand the question. For example, during the CCNA exam you will need to draw multiple networks and the connections between them. By drawing the layout while you are interpreting the answer, you may find a hint that you would not have found without your own visual aid. This technique is especially helpful if you are a visual learner.

Computer-Based Testing

In a perfect world, you would be assessed for your true knowledge of a subject, not simply how you respond to a series of test questions. But life isn't perfect, and it just isn't practical to evaluate everyone's knowledge on a one-to-one basis. (Cisco actually does have a one-to-one evaluation, but it's reserved for the CCIE Laboratory exam, and the waiting list is quite long.)

For the majority of its certifications, Cisco evaluates candidates using a computer-based testing service operated by Sylvan Prometric. This service is quite popular in the industry, and it is used for a number of vendor certification programs, including Novell's CNE and Microsoft's MCSE. Thanks to Sylvan Prometric's large number of facilities, exams can be administered worldwide, generally in the same town as a prospective candidate.

For the most part, Sylvan Prometric exams work similarly from vendor to vendor. However, there is an important fact to know about Cisco's exams: they use the traditional Sylvan Prometric test format, not the newer adaptive format. This gives the candidate an advantage, since the traditional format allows answers to be reviewed and revised during the test. (The adaptive format does not.)

To discourage simple memorization, Cisco exams present a different set of questions every time the exam is administered. In the development of the exam, hundreds of questions are compiled and refined using beta testers. From this large collection, a random sampling is drawn for each test.

Each Cisco exam has a specific number of questions and test duration. Testing time is typically generous, and the time remaining is always displayed in the corner of the testing screen, along with the number of remaining questions. If time expires during an exam, the test terminates, and incomplete answers are counted as incorrect.

At the end of the exam, your test is immediately graded, and the results are displayed on the screen. Scores for each subject area are also provided, but the system will not indicate which specific questions were missed. A report is automatically printed at the proctor's desk for your files. The test score is electronically transmitted back to Cisco.

In the end, this computer-based system of evaluation is reasonably fair. You might feel that one or two questions were poorly worded; this can certainly happen, but you shouldn't worry too much. Ultimately, it's all factored into the required passing score.

You will know you are coming up on a series of scenario questions, because they are preceded with a blue screen, indicating that the following questions will have the same scenario, but different solutions. You must remember the scenario will be the *same* during the series of questions, which means you do not have to spend time reading the scenario again.

It is extremely helpful to put a check next to each objective as you find it is satisfied by the proposed solution. If the proposed solution does not satisfy an objective, you do not need to continue with the rest of the objectives. Once you have determined which objectives are fulfilled you can count your check marks and answer the question appropriately. This is a very effective test-taking technique!

Many experienced test takers do not go back and change answers unless they have a good reason to do so. Only change an answer when you feel you may have misread or misinterpreted the question the first time. Nervousness may make you second-guess every answer and talk yourself out of a correct one.

Question Types

Cisco exams pose questions in a variety of formats, most of which are discussed here. As candidates progress toward the more advanced certifications, the difficulty of the exams is intensified, both through the subject matter as well as the question formats.

True/False

The classic true/false question format is not used in the Cisco exams, for the obvious reason that a simple guess has a 50 percent chance of being correct.

Instead, true/false questions are posed in multiple-choice format, requiring the candidate to identify the true or false statement from a group of selections.

Multiple Choice

Multiple choice is the primary format for questions in Cisco exams. These questions may be posed in a variety of ways.

"CHOOSE THE CORRECT ANSWER."   This is the classic multiple-choice question, where the candidate selects a single answer from a list of about four choices. In addition to the question's wording, the choices are presented in a Windows "radio button" format, where only one answer can be selected at a time.

"CHOOSE THE THREE CORRECT ANSWERS."   The multiple-answer version is similar to the single-choice version, but multiple answers must be provided. This is an "all-or-nothing" format; all the correct answers must be selected, or the entire question is incorrect. In this format, the question specifies exactly how many answers must be selected. Choices are presented in a check box format, allowing more than one answer to be selected. In addition, the testing software prevents too many answers from being selected.

In order to pass these challenging exams, you may want to talk with other test takers to determine what is being tested and what to expect in terms of difficulty. The most helpful way to communicate with other CCNA hopefuls is the Cisco mailing list. With this mailing list, you will receive e-mail every day from other members discussing everything imaginable concerning Cisco networking equipment and certification. Access http://www.cisco.com/warp/public/84/1.html to learn how to subscribe to this wealth of information.

Make it easy on yourself and find some "braindumps." These are notes about the exam from test takers, which indicate the most difficult concepts tested, what to look out for, and sometimes even what *not* to bother studying. Several of these can be found at http://www.dejanews.com. Simply do a search for CCNA and browse the recent postings. Another good resource is at http://www.groupstudy.com.

In addition to gathering enough reading material for the CCNA exam, we strongly recommend you spend plenty of time using the *Personal Testing*

Center included in the *CCNA Cisco Certified Network Associate Study Guide*, Second Edition (Osborne/McGraw-Hill, 1999) to simulate the actual testing environment. As we indicated earlier in this section under "Question Types", the Cisco exam questions are not simple multiple choice. Understanding the various types of questions that you will see during the real exam is a very important feature of the *Personal Testing Center*.

"CHOOSE ALL THAT APPLY." The open-ended version is the most difficult multiple-choice format, since the candidate does not know how many answers should be selected. As with the multiple-answer version, all the correct answers must be selected to gain credit for the question. If too many answers are selected, no credit is given. This format presents choices in check box format, but the testing software does not advise the candidates whether they've selected the correct number of answers.

Freeform Response

Freeform responses are prevalent in Cisco's advanced exams, particularly where the subject focuses on router configuration and commands. In the freeform format, no choices are provided. Instead, the test prompts for user input and the candidate must type the correct answer. This format is similar to an essay question, except that the response must be very specific, allowing the computer to evaluate the answer. For example, the question

Type the command for viewing routes learned via the EIGRP protocol.

requires the answer

SHOW IP ROUTE EIGRP

For safety's sake, you should completely spell out router commands, rather than using abbreviations. In the above example, the abbreviated command SH IP ROU EI works on a real router, but might be counted wrong by the testing software. The freeform response questions are almost always commands used in the Cisco IOS.

Even though the CCNA certification is not required for CCIE certification, it is recommended that the CCNA certification be completed first. The CCNA test covers a lot of the same subjects as the CCIE test, and gives you some basic groundwork for getting to the next level of certification.

Fill in the Blank

Fill-in-the-blank questions are less common in Cisco exams. They may be presented in multiple choice or freeform response format.

Exhibits

Exhibits accompany many exam questions, usually showing a network diagram or a router configuration. These exhibits are displayed in a separate window, which is opened by clicking the Exhibit button at the bottom of the screen. In some cases, the testing center may provide exhibits in printed format at the start of the exam.

Scenarios

While the normal line of questioning tests a candidate's "book knowledge," scenarios add a level of complexity. Rather than just asking technical questions, they apply the candidate's knowledge to real-world situations.

Scenarios generally consist of one or two paragraphs and an exhibit that describe a company's needs or network configuration. This description is followed by a series of questions and problems that challenge the candidate's ability to address the situation. Scenario-based questions are commonly found in exams relating to network design, but they appear to some degree in each of the Cisco exams.

Exam Objectives for the CCNA

Cisco has a clear set of objectives for the CCNA exam, upon which the exam questions are based. The following list gives a good summary of the things a CCNA must know how to do.

1. Identify and describe the functions of each of the seven layers of the OSI reference model.

2. Describe connection-oriented network service and connectionless network service, and identify the key differences between them.

3. Describe data-link addresses and network addresses, and identify the key differences between them.

4. Identify at least 3 reasons why the industry uses a layered model.

5. Define and explain the 5 conversion steps of data encapsulation.

6. Define flow control and describe the three basic methods used in networking.

7. List the key internetworking functions of the OSI network layer and how they are performed in a router.

8. Differentiate between the following WAN services: frame relay, ISDN/LAPD, HDLC, and PPP.

9. Recognize key frame relay terms and features.

10. List commands to configure frame relay LMIs, maps, and subinterfaces.

11. List commands to monitor frame relay operation in the router.

12. Identify PPP operations to encapsulate WAN data on Cisco routers.

13. State a relevant use and context for ISDN networking.

14. Identify ISDN protocols, function groups, reference points, and channels.

15. Describe Cisco's implementation of ISDN BRI.

16. Log into a router in both user and privileged modes.

17. Use the context-sensitive help facility.

18. Use the command history and editing features.

19. Examine router elements (RAM, ROM, CDP, show).

20. Manage configuration files from the privileged EXEC mode.

21. Control router passwords, identification, and banner.

22. Identify the main Cisco IOS commands for router startup.

23. Enter an initial configuration using the SETUP command.

24. Copy and manipulate configuration files.

25. List the commands to load Cisco IOS software from flash memory, a TFTP server, or ROM.

26. Prepare to backup, upgrade, and load a backup Cisco IOS software image.

27. Prepare the initial configuration of your router and enable IP.

28. Monitor Novell IPX operation on the router.

29. Describe the two parts of network addressing, then identify the parts in specific protocol address examples.

30. Create the different classes of IP addresses [and subnetting].

31. Configure IP addresses.

32. Verify IP addresses.

33. List the required IPX address and encapsulation type.

34. Enable the Novell IPX protocol and configure interfaces.

35. Identify the functions of the TCP/IP transport-layer protocols.

36. Identify the functions of the TCP/IP network-layer protocols.

37. Identify the functions performed by ICMP.

38. Configure IPX access lists and SAP filters to control basic Novell traffic.

39. Add the RIP routing protocol to your configuration.

40. Add the IGRP routing protocol to your configuration.

41. Explain the services of separate and integrated multiprotocol routing.

42. List problems that each routing type encounters when dealing with topology changes and describe techniques to reduce the number of these problems.

43. Describe the benefits of network segmentation with routers.

44. Configure standard and extended access lists to filter IP traffic.

45. Monitor and verify selected access list operations on the router.

46. Describe the advantages of LAN segmentation.

47. Describe LAN segmentation using bridges.

48. Describe LAN segmentation using routers.

49. Describe LAN segmentation using switches.

50. Name and describe two switching methods.

51. Describe full- and half-duplex Ethernet operation.

52. Describe the network congestion problem in Ethernet networks.

53. Describe the benefits of network segmentation with bridges.

54. Describe the benefits of network segmentation with switches.

55. Describe the features and benefits of Fast Ethernet.

56. Describe the guidelines and distance limitations of Fast Ethernet.

57. Distinguish between cut-through and store-and-forward LAN switching.

58. Describe the operation of the Spanning-Tree Protocol and its benefits.

59. Describe the benefits of virtual LANs.

60. Define and describe the function of a MAC address.

Studying Techniques

First and foremost, give yourself plenty of time to study. Networking is a complex field, and you can't expect to cram what you need to know into a single study session. It is a field best learned over time, by studying a subject and then applying your knowledge. Build yourself a study schedule and stick to it, but be reasonable about the pressure you put on yourself, especially if you're studying in addition to your regular duties at work.

One easy technique to use in studying for certification exams is the 15-minutes per day effort. Simply study for a minimum of 15 minutes every day. It is a small, but significant commitment. If you have a day where you just can't focus, then give up at 15 minutes. If you have a day where it flows completely for you, study longer. As long as you have more of the "flow days," your chances of succeeding are extremely high.

Second, practice and experiment. In networking, you need more than knowledge; you need understanding, too. You can't just memorize facts to be effective; you need to understand why events happen, how things work, and (most importantly) how they break.

The best way to gain deep understanding is to take your book knowledge to the lab. Try it out. Make it work. Change it a little. Break it. Fix it. Snoop around "under the hood." If you have access to a network analyzer, like Network Associate's Sniffer, put it to use. You can gain amazing insight to the inner workings of a network by watching devices communicate with each other.

Unless you have a very understanding boss, don't experiment with router commands on a production router. A seemingly innocuous command can have a nasty side effect. If you don't have a lab, your local Cisco office or Cisco users group may be able to help. Many training centers also allow students access to their lab equipment during off-hours.

Another excellent way to study is through case studies. Case studies are articles or interactive discussions that offer real-world examples of how technology is applied to meet a need. These examples can serve to cement your understanding of a technique or technology by seeing it put to use. Interactive discussions offer added value because you can also pose questions of your own. User groups are an excellent source of examples, since the purpose of these groups is to share information and learn from each other's experiences.

And not to be missed is the Cisco Networkers conference. Although renowned for its wild party and crazy antics, this conference offers a wealth of information. Held every year in cities around the world, it includes three days of technical seminars and presentations on a variety of subjects. As you might imagine, it's very popular. You have to register early to get the classes you want.

Then, of course, there is the Cisco Web site. This little gem is loaded with collections of technical documents and white papers. As you progress to more advanced subjects, you will find great value in the large number of examples and reference materials available. But be warned: You need to do a lot of digging to find the really good stuff. Often, your only option is to browse every document returned by the search engine to find exactly the one you need. This effort pays off. Most CCIEs have compiled six to ten binders of reference material from Cisco's site alone.

Scheduling Your Exam

The Cisco exams are scheduled by calling Sylvan Prometric directly at (800) 204-3926. For locations outside the United States, your local number can be found on Sylvan's Web site at http://www.prometric.com. Sylvan representatives can schedule your exam, but they don't have information about the certification programs. Questions about certifications should be directed to Cisco's training department.

The aforementioned Sylvan telephone number is specific to Cisco exams, and it goes directly to the Cisco representatives inside Sylvan. These representatives are familiar enough with the exams to find them by name, but it's best if you have the specific exam number handy when you call. After all, you wouldn't want to be scheduled and charged for the wrong exam (for example, the instructor's version, which is significantly harder).

Exams can be scheduled up to a year in advance, although it's really not necessary. Generally, scheduling a week or two ahead is sufficient to reserve the day and time you prefer. When scheduling, operators will search for testing centers in your area. For convenience, they can also tell which testing centers you've used before.

Sylvan accepts a variety of payment methods, with credit cards being the most convenient. When paying by credit card, you can even take tests the same day you call—provided, of course, that the testing center has room. (Quick scheduling can be handy, especially if you want to re-take an exam immediately.) Sylvan will mail you a receipt and confirmation of your testing date, although this generally arrives after the test has been taken. If you need to cancel or reschedule an exam, remember to call at least one day before your exam, or you'll lose your test fee.

When registering for the exam, you will be asked for your ID number. This number is used to track your exam results back to Cisco. It's important that you use the same ID number each time you register, so that Cisco can follow your progress. Address information provided when you first register is also used by Cisco to ship certificates and other related material. In the USA, your Social Security Number is commonly used as your ID number. However, Sylvan can assign you a unique ID number if you prefer not to use your Social Security Number.

The following table shows the available Cisco exams and the number of questions and duration of each. This information is subject to change as Cisco revises the exams, so it's a good idea to verify the details when registering for an exam.

Exam Title	Exam Number	Number of Questions	Duration (minutes)	Exam Fee (US$)
Cisco Design Specialist (CDS)	9E0-004	80	180	$100
Cisco Internetwork Design (CID)	640-025	100	120	$100
Advanced Cisco Router Configuration (ACRC)	640-403	72	90	$100
Cisco LAN Switch Configuration (CLSC)	640-404	70	60	$100
Configuring, Monitoring, and Troubleshooting Dialup Services (CMTD)	640-405	64	90	$100
Cisco Internetwork Troubleshooting (CIT)	640-406	69	60	$100

Exam Title	Exam Number	Number of Questions	Duration (minutes)	Exam Fee (US$)
Cisco Certified Network Associate (CCNA)	640-407	44	60	$100
Foundation Routing & Switching	640-409	132	165	$100
CCIE Routing & Switching Qualification	350-001	100	120	$200
CCIE Certification Laboratory	N/A	N/A	2 days	$1,000

In addition to the regular Sylvan Prometric testing sites, Cisco also offers facilities for taking exams free of charge at each Networkers conference in the USA. As you might imagine, this option is quite popular, so reserve your exam time as soon as you arrive at the conference.

Arriving at the Exam

As with any test, you'll be tempted to cram the night before. Resist that temptation. You should know the material by this point, and if you're too groggy in the morning, you won't remember what you studied anyway. Instead, get a good night's sleep.

Arrive early for your exam; it gives you time to relax and review key facts. Take the opportunity to review your notes. If you get burned out on studying, you can usually start your exam a few minutes early. On the other hand, we don't recommend arriving late. Your test could be cancelled, or you may not be left with enough time to complete the exam.

When you arrive at the testing center, you'll need to sign in with the exam administrator. In order to sign in, you need to provide two forms of identification. Acceptable forms include government-issued IDs (for example, passport or driver's license), credit cards, and company ID badge. One form of ID must include a photograph.

Aside from a brain full of facts, you don't need to bring anything else to the exam. In fact, your brain about all you're allowed to take into the exam. All the tests are "closed book", meaning you don't get to bring any reference materials with you. You're also not allowed to take any notes out of the exam room. The test administrator will provide you with paper and a pencil. Some testing centers may provide a small marker board instead.

Calculators are not allowed, so be prepared to do any necessary math (such as hex-binary-decimal conversions or subnet masks) in your head or on paper. Additional paper is available if you need it.

Leave your pager and telephone in the car, or turn them off. They only add stress to the situation, since they are not allowed in the exam room, and can sometimes still be heard if they ring outside of the room. Purses, books, and other materials must be left with the administrator before entering the exam. While in the exam room, it's important that you don't disturb other candidates; talking is not allowed during the exam.

Once in the testing room, the exam administrator logs onto your exam, and you have to verify that your ID number and the exam number are correct. If this is the first time you've taken a Cisco test, you can select a brief tutorial for the exam software. Before the test begins, you will be provided with facts about the exam, including the duration, the number of questions, and the score required for passing. Then the clock starts ticking and the fun begins.

The testing software is Windows-based, but you won't have access to the main desktop or any of the accessories. The exam is presented in full screen, with a single question per screen. Navigation buttons allow you to move forward and backward between questions. In the upper-right corner of the screen, counters show the number of questions and time remaining. Most importantly, there is a 'Mark' checkbox in the upper-left corner of the screen—this will prove to be a critical tool in your testing technique.

Test-Taking Techniques

One of the most frequent excuses we hear for failing a Cisco exam is "poor time management." Without a plan of attack, candidates are overwhelmed by the exam or become sidetracked and run out of time. For the most part, if you are comfortable with the material, the allotted time is more than enough to complete the exam. The trick is to keep the time from slipping away during any one particular problem.

The obvious goal of an exam is to answer the questions effectively, although other aspects of the exam can distract from this goal. After taking a fair number of computer-based exams, we've naturally developed a technique for tackling the problem, which we share with you here. Of course, you still need to learn the material. These steps just help you take the exam more efficiently.

Size Up the Challenge

First, take a quick pass through all the questions in the exam. "Cherry-pick" the easy questions, answering them on the spot. Briefly read each question, noticing the type of question and the subject. As a guideline, try to spend less than 25 percent of your testing time in this pass.

This step lets you assess the scope and complexity of the exam, and it helps you determine how to pace your time. It also gives you an idea of where to find potential answers to some of the questions. Often, the answer to one question is shown in the exhibit of another. Sometimes the wording of one question might lend clues or jog your thoughts for another question.

Imagine that the following questions are posed in this order:

Question 1: Review the router configurations and network diagram in exhibit XYZ (not shown here). Which devices should be able to ping each other?

Question 2: If RIP routing were added to exhibit XYZ, which devices would be able to ping each other?

The first question seems straightforward. Exhibit XYZ probably includes a diagram and a couple of router configurations. Everything looks normal, so you decide that all devices can ping each other.

Now, consider the hint left by the Question 2. When you answered Question 1, did you notice that the configurations were missing the routing protocol? Oops! Being alert to such clues can help you catch your own mistakes.

If you're not entirely confident with your answer to a question, answer it anyway, but check the Mark box to flag it for later review. In the event that you run out of time, at least you've provided a "first guess" answer, rather than leaving it blank.

Take on the Scenario Questions

Second, go back through the entire test, using the insight you gained from the first go-through. For example, if the entire test looks difficult, you'll know better than to spend more than a minute or so on each question. Break down the pacing into small milestones; for example, "I need to answer 10 questions every 15 minutes."

At this stage, it's probably a good idea to skip past the time-consuming questions, marking them for the next pass. Try to finish this phase before you're 50 – 60 percent through the testing time.

By now, you probably have a good idea where the scenario questions are found. A single scenario tends to have several questions associated with it, but they aren't necessarily grouped together in the exam. Rather than re-reading the scenario every time you encounter a related question, save some time and answer the questions as a group.

Tackle the Complex Problems

Third, go back through all the questions you marked for review, using the Review Marked button in the question review screen. This step includes taking a second look at all the questions you were unsure of in previous passes, as well as tackling the time-consuming ones you deferred until now. Chisel away at this group of questions until you've answered them all.

If you're more comfortable with a previously marked question, unmark it now. Otherwise, leave it marked. Work your way through the time-consuming questions now, especially those requiring manual calculations. Unmark them when you're satisfied with the answer.

By the end of this step, you've answered every question in the test, despite having reservations about some of your answers. If you run out of time in the next step, at least you won't lose points for lack of an answer. You're in great shape if you still have 10 – 20 percent of your time remaining.

Review Your Answers

Now you're cruising! You've answered all the questions, and you're ready to do a quality check. Take yet another pass (yes, one more) through the entire test, briefly re-reading each question and your answer. Be cautious about revising answers at this point unless you're sure a change is warranted. If there's a doubt about changing the answer, trust your first instinct and leave the original answer intact.

Rarely are "trick" questions asked, so don't read too much into the questions. Again, if the wording of the question confuses you, leave the answer intact. Your first impression was probably right.

Be alert for last-minute clues. You're pretty familiar with nearly every question at this point, and you may find a few clues that you missed before.

The Grand Finale

When you're confident with all your answers, finish the exam by submitting it for grading. After what will seem like the longest 10 seconds in of your life, the testing software will respond with your score. This is usually displayed as a bar graph, showing the minimum passing score, your score, and a PASS/FAIL indicator.

If you're curious, you can review the statistics of your score at this time. Answers to specific questions are not presented; rather, questions are lumped into categories, and results are tallied for each category. This detail is also printed on a report that has been automatically printed at the exam administrator's desk.

As you leave the exam, you'll need to leave your scratch paper behind or return it to the administrator. (Some testing centers track the number of sheets you've been given, so be sure to return them all.) In exchange, you'll receive a copy of the test report.

This report will be embossed with the testing center's seal, and you should keep it in a safe place. Normally, the results are automatically transmitted to Cisco, but occasionally you might need the paper report to prove that you passed the exam. Your personnel file is probably a good place to keep this report; the file tends to follow you everywhere, and it doesn't hurt to have favorable exam results turn up during a performance review.

Retesting

If you don't pass the exam, don't be discouraged—networking is complex stuff. Try to have a good attitude about the experience, and get ready to try again. Consider yourself a little more educated. You know the format of the test a little better, and the report shows which areas you need to strengthen.

If you bounce back quickly, you'll probably remember several of the questions you might have missed. This will help you focus your study efforts in the right area. Serious go-getters will re-schedule the exam for a couple days after the previous attempt, while the study material is still fresh in their mind.

Ultimately, remember that Cisco certifications are valuable because they're hard to get. After all, if anyone could get one, what value would it have? In the end, it takes a good attitude and a lot of studying, but you can do it!

Part 1

Introduction to Internetworking

Internetworking
Practice
Questions

Q
&
A

The OSI reference model is the foundation for networking as we know it today. Cisco has used it as a mold for their hardware and software development. It has greatly reduced the costs of development and virtually guaranteed interoperability between the products of a variety of vendors. If you do not have a good understanding of the OSI reference model, you will not have a good understanding of advanced networking. The OSI model is the foundation of networking and should not be overlooked.

The Internetworking Model

1. Which group created the OSI reference model?

   A. IEEE

   B. ISO

   C. ARPA

   D. ANSI

2. With which other layers must a layer in the OSI model generally be able to communicate? (Choose all that apply.)

   A. All layers

   B. All higher-level layers

   C. All lower-level layers

   D. Its neighboring layers

   E. Its corresponding layer on the machine with which it intends to communicate

3. What are the most common types of networks? (Choose all that apply.)

   A. Wireless network

   B. Local area network (LAN)

   C. Infrared network

   D. Wide area network (WAN)

4. How many layers does TCP/IP have in its transport model?

    A. 4

    B. 5

    C. 7

    D. 8

The Physical and Data-Link Layers

1. Which of the following would be found at the physical layer? (Choose all that apply.)

    A. Bitstream

    B. Hardware address

    C. Physical address

    D. Transmission media types

    E. Data compression

2. What purpose do voltage levels serve?

    A. To determine positive and negative polarity

    B. To determine who has control of the network

    C. Varies, depending on whether an 0 or a 1 is being transmitted

    D. Defined as part of the OSI reference model

3. Which IEEE standard defines Ethernet?

    A. 802.2

    B. 802.3

    C. 802.6

    D. 802.11

4. What happens when an Ethernet adapter detects a collision? (Choose all that apply.)

   A. The nodes involved invoke a backoff algorithm.

   B. The node that detects the collision floods the network.

   C. The nodes negotiate who should be allowed to transmit.

   D. Nothing happens.

5. Which of the following does Token Ring support? (Choose all that apply.)

   A. Token seizing

   B. Token locking

   C. Multiple token network segments

   D. Beaconing

6. What does FDDI use for fault tolerance?

   A. Beaconing

   B. A star topology

   C. Fiber-optic media

   D. A dual-ring topology

Use the Following Scenario to Answer Questions 7–13

XYZ Company has offices in New York, Chicago, Phoenix, and Los Angeles. The New York, Phoenix, and Los Angeles offices each connect to XYZ Company's frame relay network at 256 Kbps. Each office connects to the Chicago office using only PVCs. The Chicago office has a 384 Kbps connection to the frame relay network.

7. What type of network is this?

   A. LAN

   B. CAN

C. MAN

D. WAN

8. What is the highest guaranteed, combined rate of data transfer that the New York, Phoenix, and Los Angeles offices could transmit to Chicago simultaneously?

A. 192 Kbps

B. 256 Kbps

C. 384 Kbps

D. 512 Kbps

9. What would be the best method of backup if the frame relay network were to fail?

A. Analog modem

B. Cable modem

C. X.25

D. Basic Rate ISDN

10. If New York wants to send data to Los Angeles, what path does it take?

A. New York to Los Angeles

B. New York to Chicago, Chicago to Los Angeles

C. New York to Chicago, Chicago to Phoenix, Phoenix to Los Angeles

D. New York to Phoenix, Phoenix to Los Angeles

11. Why would X.25 be a poor choice for this network? (Choose all that apply.)

A. It is slow.

B. It is limited in speed.

C. It uses cells instead of packets.

D. It performs error checking.

QUESTIONS AND ANSWERS

Shari is configuring the DLCI for a PVC between Portland and Phoenix. The provider gave her two numbers, 12 and 14, and assigned them to the link. Shari arbitrarily used 12 for Portland and 14 for Phoenix. When the link is completely configured, it does not work. Why?	The provider should have specified that the DLCI for Portland was 14 and that the DLCI for Phoenix was 12. The local identifier was wrong and the link did not come up.

12. What information would the frame relay carrier provide to a new subscriber?

   A. FECN

   B. BECN

   C. LMI

   D. DLCI

13. If XYZ Company wanted to do voice, video, and data over the same network lines, which protocol might it consider instead of frame relay?

   A. Dedicated T1

   B. Primary Rate ISDN

   C. X.25

   D. ATM

The Network Layer and Path Determination

1. Which is a feature of network-layer protocols?

   A. The capability to transmit data across a wire

   B. The capability to transmit data through the air

    C. The capability to transmit data between nodes on the same network

    D. The capability to transmit data between networks

2. At which layer of the OSI reference model do routers operate?

    A. Application

    B. Presentation

    C. Session

    D. Transport

    E. Network

    F. Data-link

    G. Physical

3. What purpose do routing protocols serve? (Choose all that apply.)

    A. They maintain a routing table of the network.

    B. They determine where packets should go.

    C. They map out the entire network.

    D. They record MAC addresses.

4. Which of the following are network-layer protocols? (Choose all that apply.)

    A. IP

    B. TCP

    C. UDP

    D. IPX

5. Which of the following are routing protocols? (Choose all that apply.)

    A. RIP

    B. ARP

    C. IGRP

    D. EIGRP

    E. OSPF

The Transport Layer

1. Which protocols operate at the transport layer? (Choose all that apply.)

    A. IP

    B. TCP

    C. UDP

    D. IPX

Use the Following Scenario to Answer Questions 2–5

You are running a simple network at your office in Chicago. The network is connected to the Internet. When you turn a machine on, it gets its IP address from a central DHCP server. You use a Telnet client to get your e-mail via SMTP and do work on your UNIX system. Occasionally you need to FTP a file from a remote site. You also use TFTP to back up copies of your router configuration.

2. Which protocols are connection-oriented? (Choose all that apply.)

    A. DHCP

    B. Telnet

    C. SMTP

    D. FTP

    E. TFTP

3. Which protocol is connectionless?

    A. DHCP

    B. Telnet

    C. SMTP

    D. FTP

    E. TFTP

4. Why is windowing beneficial in this environment?

   A. It allows for more data to be transferred.

   B. It allows for data to be transferred faster.

   C. It allows for better error correction.

   D. It consumes less bandwidth.

5. If you were transferring a large file from a site in Tokyo back to your office in Chicago via FTP, how would a sliding window benefit you?

   A. A small sliding window would allow for more efficient transport of data.

   B. A small sliding window would allow for more data to be transported.

   C. A large sliding window would allow for more efficient transport of data.

   D. A large sliding window would allow for more data to be transported.

Upper-Layer Protocols

1. If you needed to use encryption for all outside communications, at which layer could it take place?

   A. Application

   B. Presentation

   C. Session

   D. Transport

2. Which layers of the OSI reference model are considered part of the lower-layer model?

   A. Application, presentation

   B. Application, presentation, session

   C. Application, presentation, session, transport

   D. Transport, network, data-link, physical

   E. Network, data-link, physical

   F. Data-link, physical

3. What does the application layer do?

    A. It obtains direct user input.

    B. It opens a network connection.

    C. It interacts with applications.

    D. It formats data for use by the receiving station.

4. What occurs at the session layer?

    A. File transfer

    B. Data compression

    C. Flow control

    D. Establishing and maintaining of sessions between two network nodes

Cisco Routers, Switches, and Hubs

1. Cisco IOS does not offer which of the following features?

    A. FTP

    B. Security

    C. Compression

    D. Firewalls

    E. Encryption

    F. CSU/DSU

Use the Following Scenario to Answer Questions 2–6

You are installing a 10BaseT network with 100 network nodes. You want to provide guaranteed 10 Mbps connectivity for each node, but it may be cost prohibitive. The network will be connected to the Internet and will require some security.

2. What type of hardware would you use to provide 10 Mbps throughput to each node?

A. Repeater

B. Hub

C. Switch

D. Router

3. Which piece of hardware would you use to connect to the Internet?

A. Repeater

B. Hub

C. Switch

D. Router

4. Which of the following provide some security and monitoring with your Internet connection? (Choose all that apply.)

A. Authentication

B. Access lists

C. Firewalls

D. Nothing

5. Assuming the use of a Catalyst 1900/2820 switch, what type of forwarding method would be used by default?

A. Fast-forward

B. Fragment-free

C. Store-and-forward

D. Pass through

6. When would you use the store-and-forward method of switching?

A. If the network is goes down

B. When you are connecting a 100 Mbps backbone to 10 Mbps nodes

C. When you want to enable security

D. When you want to back up the network

Configuring a Cisco Switch and Hub

1. What type of media does 100BaseFX use?

    A. Category 3 cable

    B. Category 4 cable

    C. Category 5 cable

    D. Fiber-optic cable

CCNA

CISCO CERTIFIED NETWORK ASSOCIATE

Internetworking
Answers

Q

&

A

The answers to the questions are in boldface, followed by a brief explanation. Some of the explanations detail the logic you should use to choose the correct answer, while others give factual reasons why the answer is correct. If you miss several questions on a similar topic, you should review the corresponding section in the *CCNA Cisco Certified Network Associate Study Guide*, Second Edition (Osborne/McGraw-Hill, 1999) before taking the CCNA Certification test.

The Internetworking Model

1. **B. ISO.** The OSI reference model was developed by the International Organization for Standardization (ISO) in 1984. The standard was created so vendors could develop products that would interoperate on networks. This layered model allowed companies to reduce development costs considerably, since it allowed them to concentrate only on the layers that their product incorporated.

   The OSI reference model is widely accepted in the networking community, and virtually all protocols can be mapped to it in some fashion. It is often the case that layers are combined to simplify a protocol. TCP/IP and IPX are examples of protocols that have fewer layers than the reference model.

2. **D, E.** Its neighboring layers and its corresponding layer on the machine with which it intends to communicate. Every layer must be able to communicate with its neighboring layers (both above and below it in the OSI model). A layer communicates with its neighbors so it can exchange data and use the services of these layers. This is what allows the OSI model to function so well.

   A layer must also be able to communicate with its corresponding layer on the machine with which it intends to communicate so the destination machine can reconstruct the data field. It then passes this data field up to the next layer where the process is repeated. This eventually results in the original data emerging.

3. B, D. Local area network (LAN) and wide area network (WAN). LANs and WANs are the most common networks today. LANs allow the transfer of data within a small group, often a building or workgroup. WANs connect geographically separated locations so that data can be exchanged.

There are also other types of networks, such as campus networks and metropolitan area networks (MANs). Campus networks are in the same geographic area but may be spread throughout many buildings. MANs are spread over a large metropolitan area.

4. A. 4. TCP/IP has four layers in its transport model instead of the seven that the OSI reference model lays out. When compared to the OSI reference model, the TCP/IP model combines the application, presentation, and session layers into a single top layer, called the *application layer,* and combines the data-link and physical layers into a bottom layer, called the *network interface layer.* The network layer is called the *Internet layer.* The transport layer remains the same in both models.

This is meant to show that you don't need to strictly adhere to the OSI reference model. The model is not always followed and layers are often combined. The combined layers simplify the model when similar services are offered at multiple layers.

The Physical and Data-Link Layers

1. A, D. Bitstream and transmission media types. In addition, transmission rates and distance can be found at this layer. The physical layer includes any visible hardware or media.

Hardware addresses and physical addresses are actually the same thing and can be found at the data-link layer. Data compression can be found at the presentation layer or data-link layer. Some services can be placed in different places in the OSI model, depending on the developer of the protocol.

2. C. Varies, depending on whether an 0 or a 1 is being transmitted. The change in the voltage levels is the transmission of binary data, transmitted as

0s and 1s. Physical hardware on the transmitting and receiving sides interpret the voltage changes as a bitstream and reassemble it into layer-2 data and higher. The data is then passed up through the layers and deencapsulated where necessary until it reaches the requesting application. There are other modes of transport besides voltage levels. Fiber-optic transport uses various forms of light to carry data over a line. There are also wireless methods of transport such as laser, satellite, and radio.

3. **B.** 802.3. The IEEE defined Ethernet as standard 802.3 in 1980. 802.3 was based on the Digital, Intel, and Xerox (DIX) version of Ethernet that had been developed in the 1970s. The standard defines the physical layer and the MAC part of the data-link layer. Unlike DIX Ethernet, the IEEE's 802.3 standard does not define the LLC layer of the data-link layer. This is defined in IEEE 802.2 and can be used with various 802.X standards, including 802.3. 802.3 also defines different physical layers, where DIX Ethernet only has one.

   IEEE Ethernet can run on fiber-optic, coaxial, and unshielded twisted-pair cable. It currently runs at speeds of 1, 10, 100, 1000 megabits per second. As bandwidth increases, fewer media types can be used. 100 Mbps no longer supports coaxial cabling. 1000 Mbps originally did not support any media except fiber-optic cables. They have since added Category 5 (CAT-5) cabling to the specifications.

4. **A, B.** The nodes involved invoke a backoff algorithm, and the node that detects the collision floods the network. First, the Ethernet adapter floods the network with enough data that every node is guaranteed to detect it. This is to clear the wire from any use so the fragmented packets can clear.

   Once the flood is over, a backoff algorithm is invoked. This randomly chooses a wait time before it tries to retransmit the data. If it cannot retransmit at the time determined, it calculates a new time. The algorithm generally attempts the backoff up to 16 times before it gives up and reports an error to the host.

5. A, D. Token seizing and beaconing. *Token seizing* uses a method by which nodes on the network can be assigned priorities. If a node with a higher priority than the node that currently has control of the token has data to transmit, it can seize the token for its own use. It raises the priority of the token to its own until it no longer needs to transmit, then it returns the token to its previous priority. *Beaconing* is a method used to trigger a reconfiguration of the network upon a failure detection. If a node detects a failure, it sends out a beacon frame. This causes the network to reconfigure around the failed node.

6. D. A dual-ring topology. The ring consists of two fibers that transmit data in opposite directions. One of the rings is considered the primary ring and used for normal data transmission. The other ring is idle until needed. This is also done with CAT-5 cabling, and is called CDDI, the *C* standing for copper.

When a break in the network is detected, the stations on either side of the fault immediately create a loop by attaching the idle segment to the primary segment. This function is also referred to as a wrap. It brings the network back into a ring topology so it can continue to function. If a second break occurs, the network will fail.

7. D. WAN. This network is dispersed over a large geographic area, making it a WAN. Frame relay is a common WAN protocol that has proven to be more cost effective for businesses than point-to-point links. Frame relay networks are often run by phone companies because they already have the infrastructure necessary to handle the service.

Frame relay usually uses a permanent virtual circuit between the source and destination. A PVC is like having a direct phone line; whenever you pick up the phone, it is already connected to the destination. When talking about frame relay connections, people generally say that they are connecting to XYZ's frame relay cloud. The cloud contains the PVC to the destination or PVCs to the destinations.

8. **C.** 384 Kbps. Chicago has only a 384 Kbps connection to the frame relay network, thus preventing New York, Phoenix, and Los Angeles from using their connections to capacity simultaneously. It is not unusual to run across a home office that has a 1,024 Kbps link with 20 offices connected to the frame relay cloud at 128 Kbps. Mathematically this does not work, but it is often the case that as new offices were added, the network administrator never increased the home offices link size. It is also not necessary for the home office to have enough bandwidth for all the connections, since it is very unlikely that every office would simultaneously be using their connection to capacity.

   Offices will often purchase too much bandwidth, but it is better to lean towards the safe side. Depending on the carrier, it may take weeks to get a bandwidth increase. Generally, it will take weeks or months to get a line initially installed.

9. **D.** Basic Rate ISDN. Analog modems are not reliable and are not capable of very high speeds. Cable modems are generally only used on a public, shared network connected to the Internet, creating no guarantee of service unless special arrangements are made. X.25 is also a PVC connection, so it would make a poor backup.

   A single Basic Rate ISDN would only offer half the bandwidth of the 256 Kbps frame relay link but it would be the best low-cost backup or method of redundancy. Each site would require a line and the home office would require a line for each site. For sites that require higher bandwidths, a good alternative is a second frame relay connection using another service provider.

10. **B.** NewYork to Chicago, Chicago to Los Angeles. Since each office's frame relay connection only goes to Chicago, the data will go from New York to Chicago, and Chicago to Los Angeles. The data will pass over the same wire entering and leaving the Chicago office, but must pass through the Chicago router.

    Unless a logical connection, or PVC, is set up between two offices, it should not be thought to exist. If large amounts of data are sent from

New York to Los Angeles, a logical connection should be established between them. This will cut down on latency and remove the reliance on Chicago to transfer the data.

11. **A, B, D.** It is slow; it is limited in speed; and it performs error checking. X.25 is limited in speed by hardware. These speeds are considerably slower than speeds that can be accomplished with today's networking technology. This limitation alone disqualifies it from consideration by most people. Frame relay is much better equipped to handle today's speed requirements.

 X.25 is also very slow. This is due to a number of factors, including the error checking that it performs at each hop along the way to its destination. When X.25 was first introduced, line quality was poor and it made sense for error checking to take place at each hop. Lines are much better now and error checking can be handled at the receiving end of the transmission rather than along the way.

12. **D. DLCI.** The number is used locally at each end of a connection by the data terminal equipment (DTE) to connect to its neighbor. Each data-link connection identifier (DLCI) is independent of the DLCI on the other end. They may be assigned the same number or two different numbers.

 Each PVC will have its own independent DLCI on each end. For example, the frame relay connection in Los Angeles will have one DLCI for its connection to Chicago, but the Chicago will have three DLCIs for its connections to New York, Phoenix, and Los Angeles. These numbers may all be the same or different. Sometimes they are aligned so that each office has its own DLCI.

13. **D. ATM.** The ATM protocol was designed to transmit voice, video, and data over a single line. The speed of an ATM link can be as low as 1.544 Mbps or as high as 622 Mbps, according to the current specifications from the ATM Forum. It can however, run at speeds of up to 8 Gbps at this time. ATM uses a fixed-length cell to transmit data instead of a packet. The cell is 53 bytes in length, of which five bits are used in the cell header.

ATM can be used as part of a LAN topology as well as a WAN topology. Part of the specification includes ATM over CAT-5 cable to the desktop. ATM also supports VLAN technology, which can significantly reduce the costs of building a LAN or campus network.

The Network Layer and Path Determination

1. **D.** The capability to transmit data between networks. The network-layer protocols have features that allow them to transmit data between different networks through logical addresses that identify each network. Routers operate at this layer of the OSI reference model. Network layer addresses allow for a hierarchical network design. The Internet is based on IP, which is a network-layer protocol. A flat network topology is not practical with a large network.

2. **E.** Network. Routers examine the logical address contained in the header of the data that was applied as a layer of encapsulation. If the address is determined to be on one of the networks connected to the router, it is forwarded on. If the router does not know of a specific network for the destination address, it is either forwarded on to a default path or discarded. Cisco routers do not have a default path unless specified in the configuration.

   It is important to know that routers operate at the network layer, bridges at the data-link layer, and repeaters operate at the physical layer of the OSI reference model. This is one of the foundations of all networking.

3. **A, B.** They maintain a routing table of the network, and they determine where packets should go. Routing protocols maintain a routing table for each protocol throughout the network. They announce all valid networks between routers. When a router receives a packet destined for a particular network, it refers to its routing tables to determine if the network even exists, and if so, what the appropriate next hop (router) for the packet is.

4. **A, D.** IP and IPX. IP uses a 32-bit address for its addressing scheme. IPX uses a combination of the 48-bit MAC addresses and a 32-bit network

address to form an 80-bit address. These addresses are not fixed in hardware and are usually assigned by a person or computer.

IP's use of a 32-bit address has created some problems. The current system is beginning to run low on addresses as the Internet grows beyond what the creators of IP ever imagined. Ipv6 is currently being refined to guarantee that network addresses will never run out.

5. **A, C, D, E.** RIP; IGRP; EIGRP; and OSPF. Routing Information Protocol (RIP), Interior Gateway Routing Protocol (IGRP), Enhanced IGRP (EIGRP), and Open Shortest Path First (OSPF) are all routing protocols supported in Cisco routers. Each differs from the others in the following ways:

   ■ How the table is updated (sending the entire table versus just sending changes)

   ■ How the protocol deals with getting information for a path from multiple routers

   ■ How fast they can converge

   If a routing protocol was not used, all paths would have to be entered statically. Routing protocols keep track of whether the network is up or down and of its changing topology. If a network is small and has a finite number of paths, static routes may be all that are necessary, but for a constantly changing topology, a routing protocol helps greatly.

The Transport Layer

1. **B, C.** TCP and UDP. These protocols are considered part of the transport layer because they determine if the connection is reliable or not. TCP uses a reliable connection, requiring acknowledgements from the receiving side for each packet sent.

   UDP offers no assurances that a packet will be received. It has a considerably lower overhead than TCP and is preferred for certain situations.

2. B, C, D. Telnet; SMTP; and FTP. These are all connection-oriented protocols that run over TCP. Each one requires acknowledgements to function properly. Protocols that require a session to be first established before sending data are connection-oriented. If a connection suddenly fails when using a connection-oriented protocol, it will generally try to re-establish itself for 60 seconds before it times out and reports an error to the user.

3. A. DHCP. The Dynamic Host Configuration Protocol (DHCP) is a connectionless protocol that runs over UDP. This service does not require acknowledgements and is considered unreliable. If a DHCP request is sent out and no reply is received, the machine will continue operation without an IP address. The machine may report this as an error to the user or it may not.

4. B. Windowing allows for data to be transferred faster than if every packet had to be acknowledged before the next one was sent. Windowing allows for more efficient transferring of data and is important in high-latency situations. The end machines automatically adjust the size of the window across connection-oriented links.

Satellite communications has an extremely high latency that would make connection-oriented, large data transfer impractical if not for windowing. Satellite communication is not the preferred medium of data transport in any case, but is required in some cases.

5. C. A large sliding window would allow for more efficient transport of data. Sliding windows help counteract the affects of latency. If each packet that was sent required an acknowledgement before the next packet was sent, it would take slightly more than twice the latency time between Chicago and Tokyo for each packet to be sent.

With a sliding window, data can be sent constantly, with the sending machine only sending up to the size of its window before receiving an acknowledgement. When it receives an acknowledgment, it slides the window over to the last sequence number that was acknowledged. This frees up more space at the end of the sliding window to send more data.

Upper-Layer Protocols

1. **B.** Presentation. Other services that may take place at this layer include compression and data formatting. Encryption can also take place at the data-link and physical layers using hardware connected to the transmission lines. The presentation layer is responsible for converting data into a format that the destination node can read.

2. **F.** Data-link, physical. These layers generally deal with data transport. Lower-layer protocols are more unusual than upper-layer protocols and are often discussed individually.

3. **C.** It interacts with applications. The application layer interacts with software applications that need to communicate across a network. It provides basic services such as file transfer to applications that require it.

   The application layer does not interact directly with the user; rather, the software interacts with the user. It then passes the data onto the application layer.

4. **D.** Establishing and maintaining of sessions between two network nodes. It is also responsible for the termination of sessions when they are no longer needed. The session layer also ties together multiple networking functions that one application may perform simultaneously.

Cisco Routers, Switches, and Hubs

1. **A.** FTP. The only feature not offered by Cisco IOS is FTP. Cisco IOS offers security, compression, firewall, encryption, and CSU/DSU services as well as many other features. The main purpose of Cisco IOS is to provide

the information necessary for Cisco hardware to boot and begin the transport of data. Other features are included with Cisco IOS or can be purchased separately. Cisco IOS can be updated as new releases are provided by Cisco for improvements and security related issues.

Different versions of Cisco IOS are available to fit your needs. Basic Cisco IOS includes IP. More advanced copies include IPX, IBM networking, and voice. As of this publishing, Cisco IOS was at version 12.0.

2. **B.** Hub. To provide each node with shared bandwidth, you would use hubs. Hubs redistribute data onto all ports without analyzing any addressing. Though still very common, hubs are slowly being replaced with switches in some organizations. Hubs still provide adequate service for most networks and save some money.

3. **D.** Router. To connect to the Internet, you would use a router. A router is necessary because it can transmit data based on IP addresses. This is important because of the hierarchical structure that the Internet must maintain. The hierarchical structure allows for addressing, much like the post office. Each IP address contains a network number and a node number.

The network number gets the packet to the correct organization, and then the node routes it to the right node within the organization. Without this structure, it would be impossible to have a network that could handle as many end nodes as the Internet.

4. **B, C.** Access lists and firewalls. You would use a firewall to provide security and monitoring of your Internet connection. Firewalls block your internal network from being touched by the outside. They accept all incoming and outgoing packets and route them to the appropriate outside destination.

Access lists provide some services that a firewall offers, but are mainly limited to blocking the formation of incoming connections. Both firewalls and access lists can be defeated by some hackers.

5. A. Fast-forward. By default, the Catalyst 1900/2820 switch uses the fast-forward method of switching. This efficient method automatically begins forwarding a frame once a MAC address is obtained and is the minimum requirement to do switching.

Fragment-free begins forwarding a frame when it has received 64 bytes of it. This is to reduce the likelihood of a bad packet being forwarded. It is used in environments where it is deemed important to have a clean network.

6. B. When you are connecting a 100 Mbps backbone to 10 Mbps nodes. Store-and-forward adds latency to transmissions by receiving the entire packet and checking for errors. This is important because it allows the switch to slow the speed of a 100 Mbps transmission to 10 Mbps.

Configuring a Cisco Switch and Hub

1. D. Fiber-optic. Fiber-optic cable is often used when electrical interference is likely or when security is a concern. No electrical signal is given off by fiber-optic cable, making it more difficult to eavesdrop.

Part 2

Getting Started with Cisco IOS Software

Cisco IOS
Practice
Questions

Q
&
A

The Cisco IOS software is designed to configure a router to place in your network. In addition, IOS commands allow you to show the status of the router after configuration is complete. In this chapter, we will look at questions that deal with various aspects of the software. We will have questions on the various modes, configuration issues, and status checks. These questions are designed to help you successfully obtain your CCNA certification; however, remember that in the real world you can make use of the HELP command (?) to configure or troubleshoot your router.

User Interface

1. Which prompt verifies that you are in privileged mode?

   A. router>

   B. router#

   C. router(config)>

   D. router(config)#

2. Which command or keystroke is used to go back one step from interface configuration mode to global configuration mode?

   A. EXIT

   B. QUIT

   C. LOGOUT

   D. CTRL-Z

3. In which mode does the IP Packet Internet Groper (Ping) function test for host accessibility?

   A. User EXEC mode

   B. Privileged EXEC mode

   C. Both A and B

   D. None of the above

4. Which command(s) do you use to view the most recent commands you typed during your session?

A. The SHOW command

B. SHOW commands

C. The SHOW HISTORY command

D. VIEW commands

5. Which is the default host name of all routers?

A. Router

B. router

C. ROUTER

D. ROUTERS

6. At which point do configuration commands take effect?

A. When you save the configuration by using the COPY RUN START command

B. When you press the ENTER key after typing in the command

C. When you save the configuration by using the SAVE command

D. When you press SHIFT-S

7. Which is the series of commands to go from user mode to configuration mode if there is no privileged mode password?

A. ENABLE
   CONFIG T

B. PRIVILEGE
   CONFIG T

C. PRIVILEGE
   CONFIG 0

D. ENABLE
   CONFIG 0

8. If you are in configuration mode and you issue the command INT E0, which prompt will result?

   A. router(config-int)>

   B. router(config-int)#

   C. router(config-if)>

   D. router(config-if)#

9. Which is the command to view the configuration saved in NVRAM?

   A. SHOW RUN

   B. SHOW NVRAM-CONFIG

   C. SHOW STARTUP-CONFIG

   D. SHOW CONFIG-NVRAM

10. When entering a password to access privileged mode, what do you see?

   A. Nothing is shown on the screen.

   B. You see your password in encrypted text.

   C. You see xxxxxxx.

   D. You see *******.

Router Basics

Use the Following Scenario to Answer Questions 1–9

You are responsible for maintaining the network for ABC Company, which has 6,000 users. There are three primary sites, with the remaining employees located in two smaller branch offices. The company decides to go with Cisco routers in its network. There are currently two backbone routers in each primary site and one smaller router in each branch office. T1 lines connect the three primary sites. The branch offices are connected to the closest primary site by 56 Kbps lines.

Your network only runs the Internet Protocol (IP). IP is being routed with Routing Information Protocol (RIP) and Open Shortest Path First

(OSPF) in different areas of your network. You have a complaint that network response is slow. Upon investigation, you narrow the problem to a backbone router in one of the primary buildings. You find that the router processor is currently running at 80 percent. Your Fast Ethernet connection to the backbone is also dropping a lot of packets. You determine that a server on your segment is sending out multicast packets and the router is viewing the multicast packets as broadcasts. This is resulting in a broadcast storm. You go to the server and eliminate the multicasts, so the processor utilization drops to four percent.

Just when you thought things were quieting down, you receive another trouble report. Employees in a branch office are unable to access the server on segment 141.154.20.65. You go to the router on which the segment originated and find there has been an access list configured to deny forwarding of this segment. You fix the access list and employees are now able to access the server on this segment. Since you telecommute from home, all of these changes were done remotely by Telnetting into the routers. You have done an excellent job!

1. Because you have to reach the routers remotely, you must be able to Telnet into them. Which is the series of commands to configure a Telnet session with login prompt and password required?

A. LINE VTY 0 4
   PASSWORD *<password>*
   LOGIN

B. PASSWORD *<password>*
   LOGIN
   LINE VTY 0 4

C. LINE TELNET 5 5
   PASSWORD *<password>*
   LOGIN

D. TELNET 5 5
   LOGIN
   PASSWORD *<password>*

2. Which keystroke do you use to suspend a Telnet session?

   A. SHIFT-T

   B. CTRL-SHIFT-T

   C. CTRL-SHIFT-6, then X

   D. CTRL-6, then X

3. Which commands are used to view router statics?

   A. DEBUG commands

   B. STAT commands

   C. VIEW commands

   D. SHOW commands

4. Which command would you use to view information on all protocols running on the router?

   A. SHOW IP PROTOCOLS

   B. SHOW PROTOCOLS

   C. SHOW ROUTING

   D. SHOW IP ROUTING

5. Which command do you issue to view the processor information that reveals the processor was running at 80 percent?

   A. SHOW PRO CPU

   B. SHOW MEM

   C. SHOW MEMORY

   D. SHOW PROC CPU

6. Which command did you issue to show your neighbor routers on your network?

A. SHOW NEIGH

B. SHOW CDP NEIGH

C. VIEW NEIGH

D. VIEW CDP NEIGH

7. When first approached with a network access problem, you checked the status of all router interfaces. Which command did you issue to view the status of your Fast Ethernet 0 interface? (Choose all that apply.)

A. SHOW INT

B. SHOW INTERFACES

C. SHOW INT FA0

D. SHOW FA0

8. After you solved the problem, you wanted to be sure you saved your new running config to memory. What types of memory are used in Cisco routers? (Choose all that apply.)

A. ROM

B. RAM

C. NVRAM

D. Flash

9. Certain commands are not available in older IOS versions; so before you begin, you must check which version you are running. Which command do you issue?

A. DISPLAY IOS VERSION

B. DISPLAY VERSION

C. SHOW VERS

D. SHOW IOS VERSION

Initial Configuration

Use the Following Scenario to Answer Questions 1–7

XYZ Company has 50,000 employees in locations around the world. The corporate headquarters is in London, the North American headquarters in Washington D.C., and the Asian headquarters in Singapore. All three headquarters are connected via T-1 lines. Each regional location manages its own network system. Each of the three networks has IP, IPX, and AppleTalk running. RIP is the dominant routing protocol in use. Cisco routers are used throughout the entire wide area network (WAN). You have been asked to install and configure a router in each regional area. Upon investigation you find that each network has been set up a little differently. In the corporate headquarters, there is a TFTP server that has a configuration for the router already set up. You will need to install router A in London and access the TFTP server for the configuration files. The configuration file to be loaded is named config-1_2.P. The address of the TFTP server is 151.176.21.5. The IOS image is located in ROM. Router B is to be installed in Washington D.C. You find out from the engineer shipping the router that it has been preconfigured in a lab. You only need to install the router and bring it up. The configuration has been saved in the router's NVRAM. The IOS image is located in flash. Singapore will be the location of new router C. This router does not have a configuration completed. You want to initially bring the router up and complete the configuration on the fly.

1. Which is a valid Boot field value for router B?

   A. 0x0

   B. 0x1

   C. 0x2

   D. 2x0

2. Which of the following functions does the configuration register control? (Choose all that apply.)

   A. It sets the console terminal baud rate.

   B. It loads operation software from ROM.

   C. It puts the system into a bootstrap program.

   D. It sets the IOS version setting.

3. Which commands are used to locate the IOS image?

   A. IOS commands

   B. SHOW commands

   C. SYSTEM commands

   D. BOOT SYSTEM commands

4. Router A configuration will not fit into NVRAM. Which is the largest configuration that can fit into NVRAM?

   A. 32,000 bits

   B. 16,000 bits

   C. 32,000 bytes

   D. 16,000 bytes

   E. None of the above

5. Before you TFTP your configuration, you verify that you can reach the TFTP server by PING. When a PING command is successful, what is the screen display?

   A. !!!!!

   B. ....

   C. *****

   D. ^^^^^

6. Which general command would you use to load the configuration file for router A?

A. COPY TFTP CONFIGURATION

B. COPY TFTP RUNNING-CONFIGURATION

C. COPY RUNNING-CONFIGURATION TFTP

D. COPY *<filename>* RUNNING-CONFIGURATION

7. After confirming, you saved the newest configuration to memory. You would like to reboot the router to make sure it comes up correctly. What is the order of events when you power up your router?

A. Test hardware, load IOS image, find CONFIG file

B. Load IOS image, run CONFIG file, test hardware

C. Load IOS image, test hardware, run CONFIG file

D. Load IOS image, test hardware, find CONFIG file

Auto-Installing Configuration Data

1. Which protocol must be present in the network to use the auto-installation feature?

A. TCP/IP

B. SPX/IPX

C. Novell-Ether

D. RIP

2. From where can you enter configurations? (Choose all that apply.)

A. The terminal

B. The TFTP server

C. NVRAM

D. A remote router

3. After installing your router, you realize that a filter on it denies Telnet sessions. In Cisco, what are these filters called?

A. Access filters

B. IP filters

C. Network filters

D. Access lists

4. What router display results in executing the SHOW PRO command?

A. Processor information

B. Protocol information

C. An error message

D. IP information

5. Which command(s) will display the IPX address on interface E1? (Choose all that apply.)

A. SH IPX INT

B. SH INT E1

C. SHOW IPX INT E1

D. SHOW IPX ADDRESS

6. Which command displays IPX routing update packets transmitted or received?

A. SHOW IPX ROUTE

B. DISPLAY IPX ROUTING ACTIVITY

C. DEBUG IPX ROUTING ACTIVITY

D. DISPLAY IPX INTERFACE ACTIVITY

7. Which command can be used to configure a subinterface for modular routers?

A. INT SERIAL0.1
B. INT FA0.1.0.0
C. INTERFACE FASTETHERNET 0 SUB 1.0.0
D. INTERFACE FASTETHERNET 0_1-0-0

8. Which command would you use to display the characteristics of a serial interface?

A. SHOW SERIAL INT
B. DISPLAY INTERFACE SERIAL
C. SHOW SERIAL DISPLAY
D. SH INT S0

9. Which command will display information about ISDN Basic Rate Interface?

A. SHOW ISDN RATE
B. DISPLAY ISDN
C. SHOW INTERFACE BRI
D. SHOW CONTROLLERS ISDN

10. Which prompt is representative of global configuration mode?

A. router(config)#
B. router#
C. router(config-if)>
D. router(config-if)#

11. Which series of commands is used to set the console password when you are in global configuration mode? (Choose all that apply.)

A. LINE CONSOLE 0
   LOGIN
   PASSWORD CISCO

B. LINE CONSOLE 0
   LOGIN
   SET PASSWORD CONSOLE CISCO

C. LINE CONSOLE 0
   LOGIN
   SET PASSWORD CISCO CONSOLE

D. LINE CONSOLE 0
   LOGIN
   SET PASSWORD CISCO CONSOLE 0

CISCO IOS QUESTIONS

12. If the auto-install doesn't provide a host name, what does the router do?

A. It stops the auto-installation process.
B. It sends a DNS request to a name server.
C. It sends out an Address Resolution Protocol (ARP) request.
D. It has no effect on the router.

13. At the end of all access lists, which statement is implicit in the last line?

A. DENY ALL
B. PERMIT ALL
C. DENY ANY TRAFFIC
D. PERMIT ANY

CCNA
CISCO CERTIFIED NETWORK ASSOCIATE

Cisco IOS
Answers

Q & A

The answers to the questions are in boldface, followed by a brief explanation. Some of the explanations detail the logic you should use to choose the correct answer, while others give factual reasons why the answer is correct. If you miss several questions on a similar topic, you should review the corresponding section in the *CCNA Cisco Certified Network Associate Study Guide*, Second Edition (Osborne/McGraw-Hill, 1999) before taking the CCNA Certification test.

User Interface

1. **B. router#.** By default, when you first enter your router you will be in user mode. To go from user mode to privileged mode you have to type **enable**. Often there will be a password to allow you into this mode. When you enter the router for the first time, press the ENTER key at the password prompt. This means no password has yet been configured. From privileged mode you will be able to enter configuration mode in order to configure your router. When you want to configure an interface on your router, you must go from configuration mode into interface configuration mode. To verify you are in configuration mode the prompt is router(config)#. To verify you are in interface configuration mode the prompt is router(config-if)#.

2. **A. EXIT.** If you are in configuration mode, to go to privileged mode, you can type **exit** at the prompt. You can use CTRL-Z to get completely out of configuration mode. This is useful if you are at an interface configuration prompt and want to return directly to privileged mode. Instead of typing exit twice, you can use CTRL-Z. The LOGOUT command takes you out of your session. There is no QUIT command in configuration mode. You can, however, use QUIT in privileged or user modes to logout. Be sure to always notice your prompt. If you try to issue a command that does not work, it is usually because you are in the wrong mode. By using the previously stated commands, you will be able to move between modes.

3. **C. Both A and B.** There are PING (user) and PING (privileged) commands, so PING can be used in both user and privileged modes. The syntax for the PING command is PING [*protocol*](*hostname* | *ip address*). The default protocol parameter is IP. The PING command is a very useful

troubleshooting tool. If you are unable to PING certain segments, you may determine there is a problem with the router configuration. Go into configuration mode and make any necessary changes. Reuse the PING command to test for connectivity. The trace command is also a useful troubleshooting tool. It is used in both user and privileged modes. The syntax is TRACE[*protocol*][*destination*]. The destination can be a host name or IP address. Optional protocols include AppleTalk, IPX and Vines. Be sure to use PING and TRACE if faced with a troubleshooting problem.

4. C. The SHOW HISTORY command. Use this command to view the last ten commands you entered during your session. You can change the buffer size so that you will be able to view more than the last ten. To change the buffer size use TERMINAL HISTORY SIZE *x* command, where *x* is the desired buffer size. This command needs to be executed in privileged mode. You can save typing by using the SHOW HISTORY command and reissue a command that you used previously. You are also able to recall a command and change it slightly to save yourself the time of retyping the entire line. For example, if you want to ping several hosts, you can use the ping function the first time, do SHOW HISTORY, and recall the PING command, changing only the host name. Use CTRL-P to go to the previous command in the history buffer. Use CTRL-N to get to the next command in the history buffer.

5. A. Router. If you connect a terminal to the console port of a new router, you will see the prompt router>. This indicates that the router is in user mode and the host name of the router is Router. It is not recommended that you set the prompt name; the host name will be used. Any of the other answer choices (router, ROUTER, and ROUTERS) could be set as the host name, but are not the default name of any router.

6. B. When you press the ENTER key after typing in the command. If the command entered is not valid, a message appears indicating an error or asking for more specific parameters. There are two configurations on the router, one that is the running configuration, and one that is the saved configuration. To view the running configuration use the SHOW RUN command. This is the configuration the router is using. If configuration changes are not saved, the previously saved configuration becomes the running configuration when the router is rebooted. If you have not saved all configuration changes to the saved configuration, your configuration will be incorrect when you reboot the router. To save the running configuration to nonvolatile RAM (NVRAM), use the COPY RUN START command. The other two answer choices, SAVE command, and a SHIFT-S function, are nonsense.

7. **A.** ENABLE
   CONFIG T

   ENABLE will put you in privileged mode. With no password, press the ENTER key. CONFIGURATION TERMINAL (CONFIG T) will put you in configuration mode. Typing **config ?** displays a list of options. From that list, choose Terminal, and start to configure from there. Answers B and C, which include PRIVILEGE commands, are nonsense. There is no PRIVILEGE command to enter privileged mode. Answer D is incorrect because 0 is not a parameter of the configuration command. Issue commands at the command line or cut and paste a series of commands from any text editor, such as Notepad or MS Word. Make sure when cutting and pasting that all commands are taken. Cutting and pasting can help speed up the process of configuring multiple routers where standards are used.

8. **D.** router(config-if)#. In this example, configure an Ethernet interface where zero is the interface number. As with all configuration, you must be in privileged mode to configure the router or make changes. Answers A and B are incorrect because interface in the prompt is not denoted with *int*, but with *if*. Answer C is incorrect because privileged mode is indicated with the pound sign (#). The greater-than sign (>) represents user mode. No configuration can be executed in user mode. Other router configuration modes include:

   ■ **router(config-line)#**   Line configuration mode, supports commands to configure a terminal line

   ■ **router(config-subif)#**   Subinterface configuration mode, supports commands to configure virtual interfaces on one physical interface

- **router(config-router)#** Router configuration mode, supports commands to configure IP routing protocols. Do not confuse this mode with your router's global configuration mode, also referred to as router config mode.

- **router(config-ipx-router)#** IPX router configuration mode, supports commands to configure IPX routing.

9. **C.** SHOW STARTUP-CONFIG. The complete command is SHOW STARTUP-CONFIGURATION. The configuration stored in NVRAM is the one that runs if the router is ever restarted. It is important to have your most current version of the configuration saved to NVRAM. To save your configuration, just type **copy run start** at the privileged prompt. Answer A is incorrect, because SHOW RUN shows you the currently running configuration of the router. The running configuration is stored in RAM. This may differ from what has been saved to NVRAM, as you may not have yet issued a COPY RUN START command. The complete command for SHOW RUN is SHOW RUNNING-CONFIGURATION. Answers B and D are nonsense answers; there are no SHOW NVRAM-CONFIG or CONFIG-NVRAM commands in the IOS. If you have a new router and never save the configuration to NVRAM, when the router reboots it will enter the setup dialog. You will be able to enter a minimal configuration for the router, but your previous configuration will be lost.

10. **A.** Nothing is shown on your screen. This is an added security system. Answers B, C, and D are nonsense. Passwords are stored in the router's configuration file. You can, however, configure your router to refer to an authentication server instead. To have minimal security on your router you should set passwords for the console and the auxiliary line, and set a VTY, and, of course, an ENABLE password. By default, no passwords are required for the console or auxiliary lines. If you do choose to set up passwords for the console and auxiliary lines, you will have to configure a login as well. Cisco also offers encryption service for passwords. Instead of

seeing the password in text in your configuration files, you will see it is encrypted. This ensures that anyone able to access your configuration files will not also have the password to change configurations. Cisco also recommends that you avoid the Cisco encryption techniques. There are ways to crack simple password encryption in the Cisco router. The ENABLE SECRET PASSWORD command should be used in router configuration mode, not the ENABLE PASSWORD. This password employs the MD6 hashing algorithm, which currently cannot be cracked.

Router Basics

1. **A.** LINE VTY 0 4
   PASSWORD *<password>*
   LOGIN

   The correct way to configure the VTY lines is to enter line mode (LINE VTY 0 4) and set the password (PASSWORD *<password>*) and the login (LOGIN) parameters. Before any Telnet sessions to a router can be accepted, at least one of its VTY lines must be configured. VTYs are virtual terminal sessions and each router has five virtual terminal lines to accept incoming Telnet sessions. You could configure all five. You do not need a password to Telnet to a router. If the router doesn't have a password on the VTY port and there is no LOGIN command, you can get in. If LOGIN is present, but no password, then you cannot log in remotely. If there is no ENABLE PASSWORD or ENABLE SECRET, and someone Telnets to the router, then the console password is used to access privileged mode. However, if you remove the console password too, then Telnet users cannot access privileged mode. In order to Telnet to a router remotely, you must have the IP address of one of its interfaces or know the host name, or the DNS name to be resolved to an IP address. The syntax to initiate a Telnet session is TELNET *<ip address* or *hostname>*. After Telnetting into router, type **exit** or **quit** to exit.

2. **C.** CTRL-SHIFT-6, then X. This is useful in order to leave your Telnet session for a brief time. To return to the session, press the ENTER key on a command line.

3. **D.** SHOW commands. SHOW commands are used to view router statistics and processor information. Before working with the router, become familiar with the various SHOW commands. To view the SHOW commands that are available, use SHOW?. SHOW commands display information on interface status, line protocol status, Internet addresses, ring speeds, IOS versions, processor utilization, MAC address, input queue, output queues, and many other valuable pieces of information. Examples of available options for the SHOW commands are listed here:

SHOW ACCESS LIST	SHOW LANE
SHOW ALIAS	SHOW LINE
SHOW APPLETALK	SHOW LOGGING
SHOW ARP	SHOW MEMORY
SHOW BOOT	SHOW PROCESSOR
SHOW BUFFERS	SHOW PROTOCOLS
SHOW CDP	SHOW RMON
SHOW CLOCK	SHOW ROUTE
SHOW CONFIG	SHOW RUN
SHOW CONTROLLERS	SHOW SNA
SHOW DECNET	SHOW SNMP
SHOW DHCP	SHOW TCP
SHOW FILE	SHOW TRAFFIC
SHOW FLASH	SHOW VERSION
SHOW INTERFACES	SHOW VINES
SHOW IP	SHOW VLAN
SHOW IPX	

This list shows available options, but does not show the proper syntax for these commands. Some commands take additional arguments. There are many more commands that may be useful when trying to identify a problem.

4. **B.** SHOW PROTOCOLS. This command displays all configured protocols on your router. Answer A, SHOW IP PROTOCOLS, displays only the IP protocols running on your router. To configure RIP, use the ROUTER

RIP command in config mode. To turn off RIP, use the NO form of the command, NO ROUTER RIP. To configure OSPF, use the ROUTER OSPF *<process id>* command in config mode. To turn off OSPF, use the NO form of the command, NO ROUTER OSPF *<process id>*. Two other common routing protocols are IGRP and EIGRP. To configure Interior Gateway Routing Protocol (IGRP), use the ROUTER IGRP *<autonomous system>*command in config mode. To turn off IGRP, use the NO form of the command, NO ROUTER IGRP *<autonomous system>*. To configure Enhanced IGRP, use the ROUTER EIGRP *<autonomous system>* command in config mode. To turn off EIGRP, use the NO form of this command, NO ROUTER EIGRP *<autonomous system>*.

5. **D.** SHOW PROC CPU. The syntax for this command is SHOW PROCESSES [CPU]. CPU is an optional argument. This command reveals detailed CPU utilization information. Since the utilization is so heavy, it would not be recommended to run a DEBUG command from this console. Redirect the output so it does not go to the console. SHOW PROC will work, but Answer A, SHOW PRO, will not. SHOW PRO is an ambiguous command because it could mean SHOW PROTOCOL or SHOW PROCESSOR. The SHOW MEM and SHOW MEMORY commands have the same meaning. SHOW MEMORY displays statistics on the memory. The syntax is SHOW MEMORY [*memory-type*][FREE] [SUMMARY]. All of these parameters are optional in using the SHOW MEMORY command.

6. **B.** SHOW CDP NEIGH. The syntax for this command is SHOW CDP NEIGHBORS [*type number*] [DETAIL]. Both arguments are optional. This command identifies from which interface off the router they are, and identifies device ID and host name, if available, as well as the port to which the host name belongs. Cisco Discovery Protocol (CDP) is a good tool to help you understand your network by showing how the routers are connected. In addition, it indicates if some device is not connected, as you will not see it as a neighbor. Unfortunately, this protocol only discovers other Cisco

routers, so if you have any other vendor's routers, they will go undetected. The other answer choices are nonsense. There are no VIEW commands in the IOS command system. The SHOW NEIGH command is a bogus command as well. Be careful, as SHOW NEIGH may seem like a logical choice. You must be familiar enough with the commands to know the difference.

7. **A, B, C.** SHOW INT; SHOW INTERFACES; and SHOW INT FA0. SHOW INT is the short version of SHOW INTERFACES command. This command shows you information on all the router's interfaces, which would include the Fast Ethernet interface. The SHOW INT FA0 is short for SHOW INTERFACES FASTETHERNET 0, which, of course, shows you details of only Fast Ethernet 0 interface. The only one that is not correct is SHOW FA0; you must specify interface before the interface name. The syntax for the SHOW INTERFACES FASTETHERNET command is SHOW INTERFACES FASTETHERNET [*number*], SHOW INTERFACES FASTETHERNET [*slot/port*], SHOW INTERFACES FASTETHERNET [*slot/port-adapter/port*]. If you have a modular router, you will use the *slot/port* parameter instead of the number. This depends upon your router series number. Cisco 7000 series routers are modular.

8. **A, B, C, D.** ROM; RAM; NVRAM; and flash. The types of memory used in Cisco routers include read-only memory (ROM), random-access memory (RAM), nonvolatile RAM (NVRAM), and flash memory. The ROM contains the image the router uses when it is initially booted. The IOS image is usually smaller and lacks the features of the full IOS. The NVRAM is where the startup configuration is stored. This memory does not lose its information when the router is rebooted. This startup configuration is what is shown when you execute the SHOW START command. RAM is where the running configuration is stored. This is lost when the router is rebooted. The routing tables and other tables are also located in RAM. These tables are remade when the router is rebooted. Flash memory is where the operating system software image is held and sometimes executed.

9. C. SHOW VERS. This command is short for the SHOW VERSION command. The SHOW VERSION command shows the software version, the names and source of the configuration files, the boot images, and the configuration of the system hardware. The other answer choices are incorrect because there are no display commands in IOS, nor are there any SHOW IOS commands. The importance of the IOS version is evident in the number and types of commands available. In the older IOS, some commands may differ slightly, while others may not be available at all for usage. Run the highest revision number for any release of IOS software, as it will make configuring and troubleshooting your router easier.

Initial Configuration

1. D. 2x0. If the Boot field value were 0x2 to 0xF, then the router would go through the normal booting sequence. The router would check the configuration for BOOT SYSTEM commands, telling it where to go to boot the IOS image. If this fails, it goes to flash to find the first file. If this fails, it goes to the TFTP server for a default file name. If this fails, it goes to ROM (RXBoot mode). 0x2 to 0xF in binary is 0000 0000 0000 0010 to 0000 0000 0000 1111. The configuration register Boot field is a section of the configuration register. This portion of the register tells the router from where to load the IOS image, if anywhere. The last four least significant bits make up the Boot field. You can use the SHOW VERSION command to view the configuration value. You will also be able to see the value that will be used at the next reboot. If the Boot field value were 0x0 then the router would enter ROM Monitor mode. If the boot field value were 0x1, then the router would enter RXBoot mode.

2. A, B. It sets the console terminal baud rate, and it loads operation software from ROM. Additional functions of the configuration register include selecting a boot source, selecting a default boot filename, and booting from a TFTP server. To change the configuration register you would use CONFIG-REGISTER <*value*> command. The value is the 16-bit configuration register you want to use the next time the router is rebooted.

3. **D.** BOOT SYSTEM commands. These are special commands placed in the router's configuration files. They instruct the router where to go to find and load the IOS image. You will normally want your router to boot from flash memory. Add the BOOT SYSTEM FLASH to your configuration file to achieve this. This command must be entered in config mode. You can also instruct your router to go to a TFTP server to retrieve the IOS image. The command BOOT SYSTEM TFTP *<ipaddress>* accomplishes this. This command must also be entered in config mode. To boot the router from ROM, you would use the command, BOOT SYSTEM ROM. This command must also be entered in config mode. Booting the router from ROM is always a last resort.

4. **E.** None of the above. Flash memory size depends a lot on the model router being used. Lower-end models such as the 2500 series can be equipped with a maximum of 16 megabytes of flash. Higher-end routers such as the 7513 series can be equipped with a maximum of 220 megabytes of flash. To copy the router's running config to the TFTP server, USE COPY RUNNING-CONFIG TFTP. To configure the router from the TFTP server and put the config into the router's RAM, use COPY TFTP RUNNING-CONFIG. To copy the configuration stored in NVRAM to a TFTP server, use COPY STARTUP-CONFIG TFTP. To configure the router with a file from the TFTP server and save it to NVRAM, use COPY TFTP STARTUP-CONFIG.

5. **A.** !!!!!. If a PING is successful, you will see !!!!! on your screen. If the PING is not successful, you will see ....., which would indicate that your request timed out. Always ping your TFTP server before issuing any configuration commands on your router. This will ensure that you are using the correct IP address for the server. It will also verify that you are not experiencing any network difficulties on the server segment. You should also Telnet to the server and verify that you have the correct configuration filename. If you use a wrong filename, it is possible that you will overwrite your current configuration with nothing. Always remember to backup your files, so you will not find yourself in a dead-end situation.

CISCO IOS
ANSWERS

6. **B.** COPY TFTP RUNNING-CONFIGURATION. This command will load the image from the TFTP server. You will be prompted for the IP address of the server and will use 151.176.21.5. You will then be prompted for the name of the file to be copied. You would type in **config-1_2.P**. When you are prompted to confirm, press ENTER. Your file will begin to copy from the server. Be sure that the filename on your server is exactly what you use. If you think you may have made an error in copying over the file, do not reboot the router. This may result in losing any correct running config information. Instead, try to resolve the problem. Get a copy of the config and save it to NVRAM, then you can reboot the router.

7. **A.** Test hardware, load IOS image, find CONFIG file. When the router is first booted it will test all hardware components to ensure everything is working properly. This hardware test includes a test of all router interfaces and memory. The next step is to find the IOS image and load it. Finally, the router needs to find the CONFIGURATION file and apply it so it will work properly on the network. If unable to find a CONFIGURATION file, the router will begin the setup dialog. The router will prompt you with questions and you will supply the answers. This will allow for some minimal configuration to be applied to the router so it will be functional.

Auto-Installing Configuration Data

1. **A.** TCP/IP. The TCP/IP protocol must be running in the network if there is a TFTP server. The TFTP server is accessible by its IP address. It is also possible, but not necessary, to use RIP as a routing protocol. You could use any routing protocol as long as the new router is able to find the TFTP server. In order to copy files to and from a TFTP server, use the following commands:

   ■ To copy the router's running CONFIG to the server, use COPY RUNNING-CONFIG TFTP.

   ■ To configure the router from the TFTP server and put the CONFIG into the routers RAM, use copy TFTP RUNNING-CONFIG.

- To copy the configuration stored in NVRAM to a TFTP server, use COPY STARTUP-CONFIG TFTP.

- To configure the router with a file from the TFTP server and save it to NVRAM, use COPY TFTP STARTUP-CONFIG.

2. A, B, C. The terminal; the TFTP server; and NVRAM. Enter configurations by typing on the command line at your terminal, or you can access configuration files on a TFTP server or in memory. The syntax for the configuration command is CONFIGURE [*terminal | memory | network*]. The terminal can be any machine connected to the router's console port. Memory accesses the commands stored in NVRAM. The network is copying CONFIGURATION files from a certain type of server on your network. In the case of auto-installation, the configuration is done through the network. The router must access the network to reach its CONFIGURATION file. The location of its BOOT files can be configured on the router as well. Once you load the configuration on the router, if the router has to reboot, you can enter a sequence of locations where the router should look for its files. This is accomplished via boot statements.

3. D. Access lists. These are used to control the traffic flow into and out of the router. You can configure access lists to deny Telnet sessions to your router. They can be used to filter out networks in your routing table as well. They can also deny or permit access to individual hosts in your network. The syntax for access lists is ACCESS-LIST <*access-list number*>[PERMIT | DENY][*type wild-mask | address mask*]. Access lists are applied on a per-interface basis. You apply the access list to the interface by using the IP ACCESS-GROUP command. The syntax is ACCESS-GROUP <*access-list number*>. You will also have to identify that the filter is to be applied on inbound or outbound traffic.

4. C. An error message. You will receive an error message if you try to execute SHOW PRO. This is because the router will not be able to determine if you are doing SHOW PROTOCOL or SHOW PROCESSOR. The result will be AMBIGUOUS COMMAND: SHOW PRO. While typing your command you can use the TAB key to complete the full command. For example, if you typed **show pro** then press the TAB key, the command would not fully expand. If you type **show prot**, then press the TAB key, SHOW PROTOCOL will appear on the command line. This helps to save typing and give clarity to the meaning of a command.

5. **A, C.** SHOW IPX INT and SHOW IPX INT E1. The SHOW IPX INT command is short for SHOW IPX INTERFACES. This command will display all interfaces configured with IPX. The display will show IPX address and interface status. The syntax is SHOW IPX INTERFACE [*type number*]. The interface type and the interface number are optional parameters. The SHOW IPX INT E1 command is abbreviated for SHOW IPX INTERFACE E1. This command is the same as answer A, but with the interface type and interface number specified.

6. **C.** DEBUG IPX ROUTING ACTIVITY. This command will show packets going to and from the router. This command and all DEBUG commands are useful troubleshooting tools. The SHOW IPX ROUTE command will display the routing table. It will not, however, show any packets being sent to and from the router. The commands DISPLAY IPX ROUT ACTIVITY and DISPLAY IPX INTERFACE ACTIVITY are bogus. There are no DISPLAY commands in Cisco IOS.

7. **A.** INT SERIAL0.1. The syntax for this command is INTERFACE SERIAL [*port.subinterface*]. The number of ports may start with 0 or 1. Check to ensure you are using the correct numbering sequence. The other answer choices are wrong, because in the command syntax the forward slash (/) is used between parameters, not a dot or a dash. The prefix "sub" is not needed to configure a subinterface. If you are dealing with a 4000 series router, then instead of specifying slot and port information, you would give a number.

8. **D.** SH INT S0. This command is abbreviated for SHOW INTERFACE SERIAL0. This SHOW INTERFACE command for serial interfaces is

the same as those for other types of interfaces. The syntax of SHOW INTERFACES command is SHOW INTERFACES SERIAL [*number*]. This command can be in user and privileged mode. You can use the SHOW INTERFACES SERIAL command to display information about DLCIs if you are using frame relay encapsulation. This command also must be used while in both user and privileged mode.

9. **C.** SHOW INTERFACE BRI. The syntax for the command is SHOW INTERFACE BRI [*number*]. This command has to be executed in both user and privileged mode. For 7000 series routers you would use SHOW INTERFACE BRI [*slot / port*]. This command also is executed in both user and privileged mode. The DISPLAY ISDN command is invalid. Cisco IOS has no DISPLAY commands. The SHOW CONTROLLERS ISDN and SHOW ISDN RATE commands are false.

10. **A.** router(config)#. To enter configuration mode you must first gain privileged access. Global configuration mode refers to the mode where you can configure the global parameters of your router. This is different than configuring the specific interfaces on your router. To go to interface configuration mode, you must type **interface X** at the global configuration prompt. Answer D shows a prompt that is in interface configuration mode. Answer B, the router# prompt indicates privileged mode. Answer C, router(config-if)> is not real, as the > is representative of user mode. In user mode you are unable to reach any configuration command lines.

11. **A.** LINE CONSOLE 0
LOGIN
PASSWORD CISCO

There is no set PASSWORD CONSOLE command in Cisco IOS. To configure a password for the console port you must reach line configuration mode and configure a login. That is why you have LOGIN included in the list of commands. By default there is no password configured for the console port on your router.

12. **B.** It sends a DNS request to a name server. If the TFTP doesn't have a file named HOST NAME-CONFIG, it will send ROUTER-CONFIG, which will allow you to Telnet into the router and make specific changes.

13. **C.** DENY ANY TRAFFIC. At the end of every access list is this implied criteria statement. Therefore, if a packet does not match any of your criteria statements, the packet will be blocked. This is often found to be a trouble spot. Be very careful configuring your access lists. You can often introduce a problem into your network by permitting or denying an incorrect host or network. The syntax to configure an access list is ACCESS-LIST [*access-list number*] [DENY | PERMIT]{*type mask* | *address mask*}. This command is used in global configuration mode. Access lists are applied to the router interfaces after they are configured.

CCNA
CISCO CERTIFIED NETWORK ASSOCIATE

Part 3

IP Addressing

EXAM TOPICS

Classes of IP Addresses

Subnetting and Subnet Masks

Subnet Planning

Complex Subnetting

Configuring IP Addresses with Cisco IOS

IP Addressing Practice Questions

I P is the acronym for Internet Protocol, one of the protocols responsible for addressing networks and nodes. IP is a routed protocol that assigns addresses to nodes in order to route data from a source network and node to the destination network and node. Understanding IP addressing is the key to ensuring that TCP/IP data is routed throughout the internetwork. IP addressing is one of the major topics on the CCNA test (640-407). A CCNA candidate must know how to:

- Discern the class of an IP address

- Use the appropriate default subnet mask for an IP address

- Add subnet bits to the subnet mask

- Determine the number of available addresses for hosts when adding bits to the subnet mask

- Recognize supernetted addresses

- Configure IP addresses on a Cisco router

Classes of IP Addresses

Use the Following Scenario and Illustration to Answer Questions 1–7

Acme Co. has acquired Widget, Inc., and is now merging with it. The management plans to open 22 new sales branches. Acme Co. had two major offices with 500 employees in London and 1,000 in New York. Widget, Inc., had three major offices with 2,000 employees in Phoenix, 500 employees in Los Angeles, and 1,200 employees in Salt Lake City. 14 of the 22 new sales offices will connect to Phoenix; 4 will connect to the London office; and 4 will connect to the New York office. The newly merged IT department has hired you to assist it in selecting and assigning IP addresses.

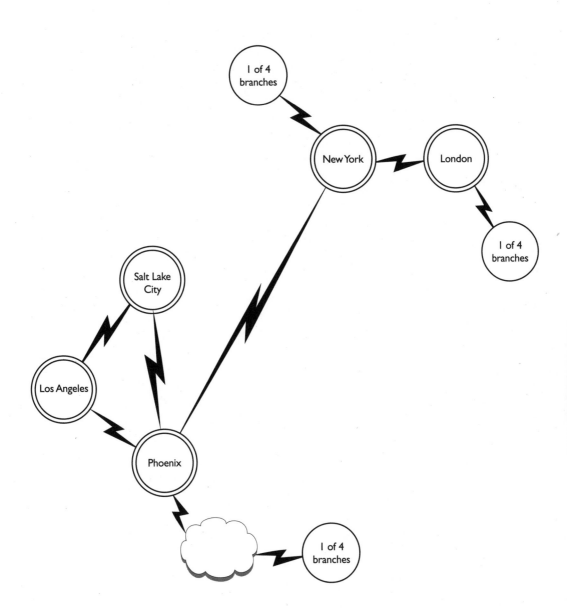

1. When you place a sniffer on the network to view the traffic running across the network, one IP address shows up and the IT department asks what type of address it is. What is it likely to be and why?

   A. 127.0.0.1—loopback

   B. 255.255.255.255—broadcast

   C. 28.190.888.255—directed broadcast

   D. 3.0.0.0—loopback broadcast

2. After explaining directed broadcasts to the IT department, you are asked what the directed broadcast would be to Phoenix from London if the following addresses were being used:

   155.18.88.50, London
   156.18.99.50, New York
   157.18.101.50, Phoenix
   158.18.110.50, Salt Lake City
   159.18.122.50, Los Angeles

   A. 255.17.101.50

   B. 255.255.255.255

   C. 157.18.255.255

   D. 155.18.255.255

3. The IT department has asked what the default subnet mask is for a partner's address of 138.18.11.1. What is it?

   A. 255.0.0.0

   B. 255.255.0.0

   C. 255.255.255.0

   D. 255.128.0.0

4. The IT department is interested in learning how the IP addresses are translated from decimal to binary ones. The IT employees have consulted with you and decided to assign an address of 158.18.200.12 to the router in Phoenix. They would like to know what that address looks like when translated to binary format.

A. 10011110.00010010.11001000.00001100

B. 10011110.00011011.11110010.00001100

C. 01011110.00010010.11001000.00001100

D. 11100001.01010010.11010110.10101101

5. The IT department is very interested in the binary process, but it does not yet fully understand the concept and asks you to do another IP address. The sales branch has been assigned one by an ISP to temporarily connect it to the Internet. It is 220.187.244.25. Convert the address to binary.

A. 11011100.10111011.11110110.01001110

B. 11011100.10111011.11110100.00011001

C. 11100010.10111011.11110110.01011011

D. 01001111.11011101.10010100.01011011

6. The department has decided that for one of the four branches connecting to New York, it wants to use a specific address. The department staff decided to practice the binary decimal conversion and write it down in binary for you and then ask you to translate it to decimal to make sure they did the conversion correctly. The number the department has written is 10011101.00010010.11011100.01100010. What is the decimal equivalent?

A. 157.188.220.12

B. 157.18.200.22

C. 159.18.199.153

D. 157.18.220.98

7. At the IT department's request, you have translated the binary address 11111000.11100000.11111111.11100001, but you inform them that it cannot be used. What is the reason it can't be used?

A. It is a broadcast address and cannot be assigned.

B. It is a Class A address, and Class A addresses can no longer be obtained from InterNIC.

C. It is a Class E address, which is considered to be a research address and not assigned to Internet hosts.

D. It is an address that is assigned to a government agency and is not unique on the Internet.

Subnetting and Subnet Masks

1. Which of the following is a valid Class C subnet mask when using RIP?

A. 255.128.0.0

B. 255.255.255.128

C. 255.255.255.192

D. 255.0.255.128

2. Jacks Properties, Inc., is a homebuilder. The main office is connected to each sales office in the subdivisions being developed. The total number of network nodes is less than 100 for all the offices. Why would Jacks Properties subnet its Class C address? (Choose all that apply.)

A. To optimize network performance by keeping local traffic in each local office

B. To reduce unnecessary traffic on the WAN links

C. To increase traffic across the wide area network

D. To be able to utilize redundant paths

3. Which of the following is the default subnet mask for the address 68.2.0.12?

A. 255.255.0.0

B. 255.0.0.0

C. 255.255.255.0

D. 68.2.255.0

4. How many subnets are created when adding four bits to a Class B address's default subnet mask?

A. 62

B. 14

C. 16

D. 30

5. How many subnets are possible when adding 10 bits to a Class A address default subnet mask?

A. 256

B. 254

C. 1,022

D. None, because the maximum number of bits is six

6. What is the maximum number of bits that can be added to a Class B address's default subnet mask?

A. 8

B. 16

C. 12

D. 14

7. In a Class C address, the subnet mask is 255.255.255.224. How many subnets are available?

A. 6

B. 8

C. 14

D. 16

Subnet Planning

Use the Following Scenario to Answer Questions 1–8

A&A is migrating its existing NetBEUI network to TCP/IP. A&A has 150 network nodes and has noticed that performance is greatly degraded since it was originally installed with 10 nodes. The move to TCP/IP will also be accompanied by the installation of routers and several directly connected networks, in order to isolate some of the network traffic. All new hardware and cabling will replace the existing infrastructure. There are four departments in A&A: Marketing, Administration, Sales, and Service. The Marketing and Sales departments share a significant amount of data. The Administration department, however, has a subdepartment—Payroll—that will require a significant level of security. A&A is a fairly stable company. It has experienced 25 percent or less growth in the number of employees in a 10-year period.

1. If A&A registers a Class C address, which subnet mask will give the company the greatest number of subnets and will be able to address all 150 hosts?

   A. 255.255.255.128
   B. 255.255.255.248
   C. 255.255.255.240
   D. 255.255.255.252

2. If A&A registers a Class C address, which subnet mask will give the company the greatest number of subnets and be able to service 188 hosts (150 existing hosts plus 25 percent growth)?

   A. 255.255.255.192
   B. 255.255.255.224
   C. 255.255.255.240
   D. 255.255.255.248

3. A&A has decided that it will be creating separate network segments for Marketing, Administration, Sales, Service, and Payroll. The Marketing department has 40 hosts, Administration has 32, Sales has 54, and Service has 24. Of the Administration group, 12 are Payroll hosts. Which Class C subnet mask will be able to create the five network segments?

A. 255.255.255.192

B. 255.255.255.224

C. 255.255.255.240

D. None of the above

4. A&A reallocates the Sales and Marketing nodes so that there are 30 Sales nodes on segment 1, 20 Administration nodes + 10 Sales nodes on segment 2, 30 Marketing nodes on segment 3, 14 Sales + 10 Marketing nodes on segment 4, 24 Service nodes on segment 5, and 12 Payroll nodes on segment 6. Which subnet mask for a Class C address will work for this configuration?

A. 255.255.255.128

B. 255.255.255.192

C. 255.255.255.224

D. 255.255.255.240

5. A&A has a Class C address of 200.12.101.0. Using a subnet mask of 255.255.255.224, which is the first available address?

A. 200.12.101.1

B. 200.12.101.32

C. 200.12.101.33

D. 200.12.101.16

6. Using the Class C address of 200.12.101.0 and subnet of 255.255.255.240, which is the highest address that can be used?

A. 200.12.101.255

B. 200.12.101.254

C. 200.12.101.223

D. 200.12.101.238

7. A&A decides to use a mask that will allow all 2,500 remote agents to use the same range of addresses. Which Class B subnet mask will enable at least 2,500 addresses on a single subnet?

A. 255.255.254.0

B. 255.255.248.0

C. 255.255.240.0

D. 255.255.252.0

8. Considering the address 172.10.0.0 with the subnet mask of 255.255.240.0, which is the first range of addresses that can be assigned to a subnet?

A. 172.10.16.1–172.10.31.254

B. 172.10.8.1–172.10.8.255

C. 172.10.16.255–172.10.17.255

D. 172.10.32.1–172.10.63.254

Complex Subnetting

1. Which of the following is the decimal value of the host portion of a Class A address 38.0.53.228 with a subnet mask of 255.255.252.0?

A. 0.228

B. 53.228

C. 1.228

D. 5.228

2. Which of the following subnet masks will not be applicable to a Class C address but can be used with a Class B address?

A. 255.255.255.0

B. 255.255.255.192

C. 255.255.255.240

D. 255.255.255.128

3. Which of the following is a valid address for a Class A address with a subnet mask of 255.255.240.0?

A. 38.255.240.2

B. 38.0.192.0

C. 38.0.240.255

D. 38.255.255.255

4. Which of the following is a valid Class B address with a subnet mask of 255.255.255.224?

A. 18.200.3.55

B. 130.0.0.1

C. 154.255.0.31

D. 147.255.0.48

5. If a host with address 147.254.1.88/26 were to send a broadcast only to the nodes on its own subnet, what would the broadcast address be?

A. 147.254.1.255

B. 147.254.1.127

C. 147.255.255.255

D. 147.254.255.255

6. What does it mean when a network is using an address of 199.200.200.0 with a subnet mask of 255.255.252.0?

A. The network is configured incorrectly.

B. The address has been mistyped; it should be a Class B address, not a Class C address.

C. The network has implemented supernetting.

D. The mask has crossed octet boundaries.

7. What is the basic idea behind variable-length subnet masking (VLSM)?

    A. Subnetting the subnet
    B. Crossing octet boundaries
    C. Subtracting bits from the default mask
    D. Translating to binary

8. Which of the following is the first available address for a Class A address 2.*x.x.x* with a subnet mask of 255.255.255.128?

    A. 2.1.1.1
    B. 2.0.0.129
    C. 2.1.2.3
    D. 2.0.0.1

9. Which of the following addresses is a valid address when using a subnet mask of 255.255.255.192?

    A. 2.0.0.0
    B. 129.1.0.63
    C. 177.255.255.195
    D. 215.1.8.188

Configuring IP Addresses with Cisco IOS

1. Which of the following commands (with IOS 11.2 or greater) will change the router's notation of the subnet mask to use the /24 (number of bits) notation?

    A. router#TERMINAL IP NETMASK-FORMAT DECIMAL
    B. router#TERMINAL IP NETMASK-FORMAT BITCOUNT
    C. router>TERMINAL IP NETMASK-FORMAT HEX
    D. router(config)#TERMINAL IP NETMASK-FORMAT DECIMAL

2. Which of the following will assign the IP address 148.24.58.12 to interface E0?

   A. router>INTERFACE E0 IP ADDRESS 148.24.58.12

   B. router#IP ADDRESS 148.24.58.12 E0

   C. router#IP ADDRESS 148.24.58.12 255.255.0.0 E0

   D. router(config-if)#IP ADDRESS 148.24.58.12 255.255.0.0

3. Whitestone Co.'s network administrator decides to add Cableview's MAIN server to a new DNS server called WHITEDNS, with the address 205.199.52.8, which is on a network segment directly connected to the main Whitestone router. Which command(s) will enable the router to look up name-to-address mappings on the DNS server? (Choose all that apply.)

   A. router(config)#IP HOST WHITEDNS 205.199.52.8

   B. router(config)#IP NAME-SERVER 205.199.52.8

   C. router(config)#IP DOMAIN-LOOKUP

   D. No commands necessary

4. Jerry enters the IP HOST *myserver* 25 108.55.8.202 command on a Cisco router. How can he verify that the command was successful?

   A. He can use the IP DOMAIN-NAME command.

   B. He can issue the IP HOST command again for redundancy.

   C. He can use the SHOW HOSTS command.

   D. He can use the SHOW INTERFACES command.

5. If Kelly wants all host names without a specified domain to be resolved as though typed with the domain name MYDOMAIN.COM, which of the following commands would she choose?

   A. router(config)#IP HOST *hostname.mydomain.com*

   B. router(config)#IP DOMAIN-NAME *mydomain.com*

   C. router(config-if)#IP NAME-SERVER *mydomain.com*

   D. router#IP DOMAIN-NAME *mydomain.com*

IP ADDRESSING QUESTIONS

6. How can you find out the available options for extended Ping?

    A. router>PING HELP

    B. router#PING

    C. router>HELP PING

    D. router#PING; and answer Yes for extended options

7. Which of the following commands will display the routers that are found in the path from the source to the destination host?

    A. router#PING TRACE *host*

    B. router>TRACE ROUTERS *host*

    C. router>TRACE *host*

    D. router(config)#TRACE PING *host*

8. Which of the following commands will establish a connection to a remote host and ensure that all protocol layers are working properly?

    A. TELNET

    B. TRACE

    C. SHOW

    D. PING

IP Addressing
Answers

Q & A

The answers to the questions are in boldface, followed by a brief explanation. Some of the explanations detail the logic you should use to choose the correct answer, while others give factual reasons why the answer is correct. If you miss several questions on a similar topic, you should review the corresponding section in the *CCNA Cisco Certified Network Associate Study Guide,* Second Edition (Osborne/McGraw-Hill, 1999) before taking the CCNA Certification test.

Classes of IP Addresses

1. **B. 255.255.255.255—broadcast.** The most likely address from this set that would show up on a sniffer is 255.255.255.255, which is a broadcast address to all hosts on the local network. The local broadcast address is four octets of 1s: 11111111.11111111.11111111.11111111, written as 255.255.255.255 for convenience. This would probably be followed by a MAC address of FFFFFFFFFFFF, which is also all 1s when converted to binary. Answer A is a loopback address. However, since loopback addresses are used to test the local-host configuration, they would not show up in a sniffer's view of network traffic. Answer C is an incorrect address. Directed broadcasts will begin with the network portion of the address and be completed with all 1s so that a directed broadcast address for network 28.*x.x.x* would look like 00011100.11111111.11111111.11111111, or 28.255.255.255. Answer D is also incorrect because there is no such thing as a loopback broadcast.

2. **C. 157.18.255.255.** According to the list, there is a separate Class B address assigned to each site. Phoenix's Class B address is 157.18.101.50. In this case, then, the only address that is directed to a subnet in Phoenix is 157.18.255.255. The directed broadcast address will be sent to every node on the 157.18.255.255 network. The address in answer A is not a broadcast address. Answer B is a local network broadcast and will not typically cross routers. Answer D is a directed broadcast address to London.

3. **B. 255.255.0.0.** The partner's address is a Class B address because after translating to binary, its leading bits are 10. The network portion of a Class

B address consists of the first two octets. That means that the remaining bits are used for the host address portion. The network portion is then 138.18. To filter out or mask the network portion and allow the host portion of 11.1 to remain, the subnet mask places all binary 1s at a network portion of the address, and places all binary 0s at the host portion. The default subnet mask would be 11111111.11111111.00000000.00000000. This translates directly to 255.255.0.0. Answer A is a Class A default subnet mask. Answer C is the default subnet mask of a Class C address. Answer D is not a valid default subnet mask for any class of address.

4. **A.** 10011110.00010010.11001000.00001100. The decimal form of an IP address is a shorthand notation used because it is easier to remember than the binary form. The binary format is a Base2 system. Each bit represents a power of 2. From left to right in a single octet, the bits decrease in exponents ($2^7\ 2^6\ 2^5\ 2^4\ 2^3\ 2^2\ 2^1\ 2^0$), so each bit represents a decimal number, which is then added to another to equal the decimal for the octet. If each bit is a 1, then the decimal equivalent is $2^7 + 2^6 + 2^5 + 2^4 + 2^3 + 2^2 + 2^1 + 2^0$, which is equal to 128 + 64 + 32 + 16 + 8 + 4 + 2 + 1, and so equals 255. Therefore, the greatest number in any single octet is 255, and the highest address is 255.255.255.255 (which is used as a broadcast address on the local network segment). Referring to our original address, 158.18.200.12, the first octet (158) can be changed to 128 + 0 + 0 + 16 + 8 + 4 + 2 + 0, or 10011110. The second octet (18) is equal to 0 + 0 + 0 + 16 + 0 + 0 + 2 + 0, or 00010010. The third octet (200) is equal to 128 + 64 + 0 + 0 + 8 + 0 + 0 + 0. The final octet (12) is 0 + 0 + 0 + 0 + 8 + 4 + 0 + 0, or 00001100.

5. **B.** 11011100.10111011.11110100.00011001. There is a subtraction method that works well in quickly converting decimal to binary: Take the first octet, 220, place a 1 for every number that can be subtracted from 220 in sequence and a zero for each that cannot. Start with 220 − 128. Since 128 can be subtracted, place a 1 for the first bit of the octet (1*xxxxxxx*). Take the result (220 − 128 = 92), which is 92, and subtract the value of the second bit, 64 (92 − 64 = 28). Since 64 can be subtracted, place a 1 in the second bit place (11*xxxxxx*). The result is 28. When attempting to subtract 32 (28 − 32 = N/A), you realize that you can't because it is larger than 28,

so place a zero in the third bit (110*xxxxx*). Now take 28 and subtract 16 (28 − 16 = 12). Since 16 can be subtracted, place a 1 in the fourth bit place of the octet (1101*xxxx*). The result is 12. Now attempt to subtract 8 from 12 (12 − 8 = 4). Since you can do that, place a 1 in the fifth bit place of the octet (11011*xxx*). The result is 4. The next operation is to subtract 4 (4 − 4 = 0). Since 4 can be subtracted, place a 1 in the sixth bit place of the octet (110111*xx*). Note that the result is 0, which means no other numbers can be subtracted, so place two 0s in the seventh and eighth bit place of the octet. The result is that 220 = 11011100.

6. **D.** 157.18.220.98. You arrive at the decimal figure by adding the decimal value of each bit to each other for each octet. The first octet is 128 + 0 + 0 + 16 + 8 + 4 + 0 + 1 = 157. The second octet is 0 + 0 + 0 + 16 + 0 + 0 + 2 + 0 = 18. The third octet is 128 + 64 + 0 + 16 + 8 + 4 + 0 + 0 = 220. The fourth octet is 0 + 64 + 32 + 0 + 0 + 0 + 2 + 0 = 98.

7. **C.** It is a Class E address, which is considered to be a research address and not assigned to Internet hosts. It cannot be assigned to a network node. The binary address 11111000.11100000.11111111.11100001 does not need to be translated for us to discern to what class of address it belongs. The following table displays the classes of addresses and the corresponding leading bits. To determine that the address is a Class E, review the leading bits. Class E and Class D addresses are not assigned to network nodes. Only Class A, Class B, and Class C addresses are assigned to network nodes.

Class	Leading Bits and Network Portion
A	0*xxxxxxx*
B	10*xxxxxx.xxxxxxxx*
C	110*xxxxx.xxxxxxxx.xxxxxxxx*
D	1110*xxxx*
E	1111*xxxx*

Subnetting and Subnet Masks

1. **C.** 255.255.255.192. The default Class C subnet mask is 255.255.255.0.
   A subnet mask is the default mask plus any added bits. When two bits are
   added to the default mask, the result is 255.255.255.192. This subnet mask
   will provide two subnets and 62 hosts per subnet. The number of subnets
   and hosts is determined by two rules:

   - There can be no subnets whose addresses are all 1s or all 0s

   - There can be no hosts whose addresses are all 1s or all 0s

   Answer A is not a valid subnet mask because it does not start with the
   default mask of 255.255.255.0. Answer B is not a valid subnet mask
   because it adds a single bit to the default mask, and as a result provides for 0
   subnets and becomes unusable. The subnet address could either be a 1 or a
   0 and therefore violates the first rule. Answer D is not a valid subnet mask
   because of the 0 in the second octet.

2. **A, B, D.** To optimize network performance by keeping local traffic in each
   local office; to reduce unnecessary traffic on the WAN links; and to be able
   to utilize redundant paths. Subnetting is used to separate a monolithic
   network address set into multiple subnetworks. Each subnetwork isolates its
   own traffic to its own local network segment. This traffic isolation then
   reduces unnecessary traffic on the WAN links, since local traffic for each
   office's network segment does not travel through the router to the WAN.

   Using subnets means that routers are more likely to be used than
   bridges. Routers are used to route traffic from one subnet to another.
   Bridges are configured with the same subnet on both sides of the bridge;
   they simply forward traffic from one physical segment to the other and
   consider the two segments to be the same logical network. Bridges are more
   difficult to configure with redundant paths than routers are. Answer C is
   wrong because the traffic is reduced over the WAN rather than increased.

3. B. 255.0.0.0. The address 68.2.0.12 is a Class A address since, when translated to binary, the leading bit is 0 in the first octet, and in decimal the first octet is in the range of 1–126. The default mask for a Class A address is 255.0.0.0. Each class of address has a default subnet mask. Class A addresses have the default mask of 255.0.0.0. This determines that the network portion of the address is 68.*x.x.x* and the host portion is *x.*2.0.12. A Class A default mask is 8 bits long and is sometimes written in the format 68.2.0.12/8. Answer A is incorrect because it is a Class B default subnet mask that is 16 bits long. Answer C is incorrect because it is a Class C default subnet mask that is 24 bits long. Answer D does not denote a subnet mask, but rather a host address.

4. B. 14. The Class B subnet mask is 255.255.0.0. This is the same as 11111111.11111111.|00000000.00000000. The 4 additional bits change the mask to 11111111.11111111.|1111|0000.00000000, or 255.255.240.0. At first glance, it appears as though there can be as many as 2^4, or 16, subnets. However, there are two subnets that cannot be used when a subnet is all 1s or all 0s. This means the greatest number of subnets will be 16 − 2, or 14. This reveals a formula for determining the number of subnets: $(2)^{number\ of\ added\ bits} - 2$ = number of possible subnets.

5. C. 1,022. The default subnet mask for a Class A address is 255.0.0.0, or 11111111.|00000000.00000000.00000000. When the 10 bits are added, the subnet mask is 11111111.|11111111.11|000000.00000000, or 255.255.192.0. The possible subnets are $2^{10} - 2 = 1{,}024 - 2 = 1{,}022$. Neither answer A nor answer B is correct. In fact, answer B would be the number of subnets if there were 8 bits added to the default subnet mask. Answer D is incorrect for both Class A and Class B addresses but is correct for Class C addresses.

6. D. 14. The default subnet mask for a Class B address is 255.255.0.0, or 11111111.11111111.|00000000.00000000. The maximum number of bits must allow a host portion that cannot be all 0s or all 1s, which means that the host portion must have at least 2 bits. If leaving 2 bits for a host portion, the subnet mask is 11111111.11111111.|11111111.111111|00. In this configuration, the number of added bits is 14.

7. **A.** 6. The default subnet mask for a Class C address is 255.255.255.0. This means that the subnet bits added are all in the final octet. The binary equivalent is 11111111.11111111.11111111.|111|00000. This demonstrates that 3 bits were added to the default subnet mask. The number of available subnets, then, is $2^6 - 2 = 6$.

Subnet Planning

1. **B.** 255.255.255.248. The subnet mask that will provide the greatest number of subnets and be able to service 150 hosts is 255.255.255.248. The address 255.255.255.248 translates in binary to the following: 11111111.11111111.11111111.|11111|000. This shows that there will be $2^5 - 2 = 30$ subnets. Each subnet will have $2^3 - 2 = 6$ hosts. This provides a total of $30 \times 6 = 180$ hosts on the network. Answer D—which is the greatest number of bits to add to the default mask to obtain a possible subnet mask (255.255.255.252)—only allows 62 subnets with two hosts each, or 124 total hosts, which is not enough. Answer C (255.255.255.240) will have fewer subnets. Answer A (255.255.255.128) is not a viable subnet mask for a Class C address, because having only a single bit added to the subnet mask means there are no subnets that would not be all 1s or all 0s, which would violate the subnet mask rules.

2. **C.** 255.255.255.240. In binary format, this subnet address is 11111111.11111111.11111111.|1111|0000. This allows $2^4 - 2 = 14$ subnets with $2^4 - 2 = 14$ nodes on each. This is a total of $14 \times 14 = 196$ nodes. Answer D allows only 180 nodes in total. Answers A and B allow more hosts but have fewer subnets.

3. **D.** None of the above. No Class C subnet mask will be able to provide 5 or more subnets with 54 hosts on a single subnet. Answer A will create 2 subnets, so it can be rejected. Answer B is promising since it will create 6 subnets. The binary translation of Answer B is 11111111.11111111.11111111.|111|00000. But since there are only 5 bits for the host address, the maximum number of hosts on each subnet are 30, which does not provide enough addresses for the Sales or Marketing departments.

4. **C.** 255.255.255.224. This subnet mask will be the most appropriate for the new configuration, since it provides 6 segments (or subnets) with 30 or fewer nodes on each. Answer A is not a valid subnet mask for a Class C address. This is because it does not have any subnet address that is not all 1s or all 0s. Answer B's subnet mask allows 2 subnets with 62 nodes per subnet. Answer D allows 14 subnets with 14 hosts per subnet.

5. **C.** 200.12.101.33. The first subnet that is usable for 200.12.101.0 using the 11111111.11111111.11111111.|111|00000 mask must have at least 1 bit in it, and the lowest bit value is 32. For the final octet, that value is .|001|xxxxx. The lowest 1 bit value of the host portion is 1. The final octet, then, would be .|001|00001, or 33.

6. **D.** 200.12.101.238. The highest address in the final octet is determined by taking the subnet mask and completing all the highest bits with 1s and the lowest-numbered bit with a 0, because you cannot have subnet bits of all 1s or all 0s. The same thing must be done with the host portion of the address. The result is that the final octet is .|1110|1110, which translates to 238 and makes the highest available address 200.12.101.238 when the subnet mask is 255.255.255.240.

7. **C.** 255.255.240.0. The subnet mask of 255.255.240.0 translates to 11111111.11111111.|1111|0000.0000000. The number of hosts that are

supported on any individual subnet is $2^{12} - 2 = 4{,}094$. Answer B allows 2,046 hosts per subnet. Answer A allows 510 hosts per subnet. Answer D allows 1,022 hosts per subnet.

8. **A. 172.10.16.1–172.10.31.254.** In binary format, the subnet mask 255.255.240.0 translates to 11111111.11111111.|1111|0000.00000000. The first subnet begins with a 1 in the lowest position of the subnet portion. The first host begins with a 1 in the lowest position of the host portion. This makes the first address 172.10.16.1. The last address in this host range still has a 1 in the lowest position of the host range, but all except the lowest bit in the host portion is a 1 bit. That means the final two octets of this range are .|0001|1111.11111110. The result is that the last address in the range is 172.10.31.254.

Complex Subnetting

1. **C. 1.228.** This address crosses the octet boundary with the subnet mask. 11111111.|11111111.111111|00.00000000 is the binary translation of the subnet mask. The address given translates to 00100110.|00000000.001101|01.11100100. The host portion translates back to 1.228.

2. **D. 255.255.255.128.** The subnet mask 255.255.255.128 cannot be used with a Class C address, but it can be used with a Class B address. In binary format, the subnet mask 255.255.255.128 is 11111111.11111111.|11111111.1|0000000 for the Class B address. Because the subnet mask has nine bits for subnetting, it can be used to create 510 subnets. However, for a Class C address, the subnet mask 255.255.255.128 translates to 11111111.11111111.11111111.|1|0000000 in binary. The single bit for the subnet mask cannot create any subnets, since all subnets would be all 0s or all 1s and would violate the rule that no subnet can be all 1s or 0s. The remaining answers are all valid subnets for both Class B and Class C addresses.

3. **C. 38.0.240.255.** In binary format, the subnet mask translates to 11111111.|11111111.1111|0000.00000000. The address 38.0.240.255 is 00100110.|00000000.1111|0000.11111111. This shows that, although an individual octet can be all 0s or all 1s, each portion (network, subnet, and host) is a mixture of 1s and 0s. Answer A has a subnet portion that is all 1s, so it is invalid. Answer B has a host portion that is all 0s, so it is also invalid. Answer D is an all-hosts broadcast address to the 38.0.0.0 network.

4. **D. 147.255.0.48.** The subnet mask is apportioned as follows for Class B addresses in binary: 11111111.11111111.|11111111.111|00000. The address 147.255.0.48 is 10010011.11111111.|00000000.001|10000 in binary, and although some octets are all 1s or all 0s, the network, subnet, and host portion are all combinations of 1s and 0s. Answer A is not a Class B address. Answer B is all 0s for the subnet portion of the address. Answer C is also all 0s for the subnet portion of the address and all 1s for the host portion.

5. **B. 147.254.1.127.** The notation used shows that 26 bits are assigned to the mask of this Class B address, translating to 11111111.11111111.| 11111111.11|000000. The address is 10010011.11111110.|00000001.01| 011000. This means that the broadcast address on that subnet would be 10010011.11111110.|00000001.01|111111, which is 147.254.1.127 in decimal format.

6. **C.** The network has implemented supernetting. Supernetting occurs when an enterprise implements multiple sequential Class C addresses and then removes bits from the default subnet mask. This enables the addresses to be used on the same network segment as though they are Class B addresses. Supernetting fulfills the need to have more addresses per network segment when a Class B address cannot be obtained.

7. **A.** Subnetting the subnet. It takes a standard subnet mask on a single subnet and further divides it into another level of subnet masking. VLSM requires

the transmission of the number of bits used for the subnet mask along with the IP address so that the router can make decisions on how to forward the information. VLSM is recognized by newer routing protocols such as OSPF or EIGRP. VLSM also allows subnets that use all 0s or all 1s in the subnet portion of the address.

8. **B.** 2.0.0.129. The subnet mask translates to this address in binary: 11111111.|11111111.11111111.1|0000000. The first available address will be 00000010.|00000000.00000000.1|0000001, which places a 1 in the lowest value of the subnet portion and a 1 in the lowest value of the host portion. This address translates to 2.0.0.129 in decimal format.

9. **D.** 215.1.8.188. It is the only valid address when a subnet mask of 255.255.255.192 is used. Each of the answers is a different class address, and the subnet mask given is split differently for each one. For answer D, a Class C address, the binary translation is 11111111.11111111.11111111.|11|000000. The address is 11010111.00000001.00001000.|10|111100. Answer A is an address referencing the Class A network only. Answer B is a Class B address that has all 0s for the subnet portion of the address and all 1s for the host portion, since 129.1.0.63 translates to 10000001.00000001.|00000000.00|111111. Answer C has all 1s for the subnet portion of the address since 177.255.255.195 translates to 10110001.11111111.|11111111.11|000011.

Configuring IP Addresses with Cisco IOS

1. **B.** router#TERMINAL IP NETMASK-FORMAT BITCOUNT. The BITCOUNT notation is used for classless IP addressing. This command is issued from the privileged EXEC mode that is designated by the router# prompt. The command defines a global format for how subnet masks will be displayed during the session. The default format is the dotted decimal format. Another option is to use hexadecimal.

2. D. router(config-if)#IP ADDRESS 148.24.58.12 255.255.0.0. The command IP ADDRESS *ip_address netmask* assigns an IP address to an interface. This command must be issued in interface configuration mode. The prompt router(config-if)# denotes that the router is in interface configuration mode. Since each LAN or WAN interface can have a different IP address, the address is applied to the individual interface rather than the network. The way of entering interface configuration mode is to start in privileged EXEC mode and issue the command CONFIGURE TERMINAL. This will change the router into global configuration mode and will display a prompt of router(config)#. From that prompt, type **INTERFACE E0**. The router will then enter interface configuration mode, and the prompt will change to router(config-if)#. At that point, the IP address will be applied to the interface.

3. B, C, D. router(config)#IP NAME-SERVER 205.199.52.8; router(config)#IP DOMAIN-LOOKUP; and no commands necessary. The IP NAME-SERVER 205.199.52.8 will add the WHITEDNS server to the list of DNS servers available to the router. The IP DOMAIN-LOOKUP command enables the router to look up host names on DNS servers. Additionally, the router will look on local network segments if no DNS servers have been identified. However, the IP DOMAIN-LOOKUP command is unnecessary on a Cisco router, because this is already activated by default in the IOS. The DNS server is connected to a network segment that is local to the router in such a fashion that there are several ways that it can be used. First, if the IP DOMAIN-LOOKUP functionality has never been turned off, there are no commands necessary to configure DNS. The router's default configuration is to use the local broadcast address 255.255.255.255 to find a DNS server. If IP DOMAIN-LOOKUP has been toggled off using the NO IP DOMAIN-LOOKUP command, it should be toggled back on with the IP DOMAIN-LOOKUP command issued in global configuration mode, which is denoted by the prompt router(config)#. Adding the DNS server to the list of up to six DNS servers with the IP NAME-SERVER *ip_address* is one way of guaranteeing that the WHITEDNS server will be used.

4. C. He can use the SHOW HOSTS command. This will verify that the IP HOST command added *myserver* to the host cache of the router. The SHOW HOSTS command is issued in privileged EXEC mode. This mode is indicated by the router# prompt and can be entered from user EXEC mode using the command ENABLE. The SHOW HOSTS command will display the contents of the local host cache of the router. Since the IP HOST command adds entries to the local cache, the SHOW HOSTS command can be used to verify that the addition was made. If DNS servers are used, the router does continue to store host name–to–address mappings in the local host cache, and the SHOW HOSTS command can be used to verify that DNS responses are being received correctly from DNS servers.

5. B. router(config)#IP DOMAIN-NAME *mydomain.com.* This command sets the router to automatically assign a host name that is sent without a specified domain name. The IP DOMAIN-NAME command is used to specify a default domain name to be added to any unqualified host names. The result is a fully qualified domain name (FQDN), which is written *server.domain.com.* Many end users will attempt to locate the name of a host on their local network without using anything but the host's name. The way to ensure that the correct or most common domain name is automatically used to complete that host name is to use the IP DOMAIN-NAME *domain_name* command in global configuration mode. Global configuration mode is entered from the privileged EXEC mode by typing the command CONFIGURE TERMINAL. The global configuration mode is indicated by the router(config)# prompt.

6. D. router#PING; and answer Yes for extended options. The way to find out extended Ping options is to type **PING** in privileged EXEC mode and answer Yes for the extended options. Extended Ping can only be issued from privileged EXEC mode. Simple Ping can be issued from user EXEC mode. Extended Ping is an interactive utility that allows the user to stipulate such variables as the number and size of the test packets and timeout values in response to the interactive prompts. Because of the way that the context-sensitive facility works in the Cisco IOS, the extended Ping options are available only from the privileged EXEC mode prompt router#.

7. **C.** router>TRACE *host.* This will display the routers that are encountered in the path between the source router and the destination host. TRACE can be issued from either the user EXEC mode, which is indicated by the router> prompt, or from the privileged EXEC mode, which is indicated by the router# prompt. When TRACE is issued from privileged EXEC mode, it can offer more options; it is then called Extended Trace. The command syntax is TRACE *hostname* or TRACE *ip_address.* The host name can be used if it can be resolved; otherwise the IP address is used. TRACE sends out three test probes per hop to discover the routers in the path to the host or IP address specified. TRACE then lists the IP address of each router, the host name, and return times for each of the test probes. The final IP address or host name should be that of the destination host or IP address specified.

8. **A.** TELNET. The TELNET command establishes a terminal emulation connection to a remote host. This occurs at the application level and establishes that the protocol stack layers are working correctly. The TELNET command can be issued from user EXEC mode, which is indicated by the router> prompt. The syntax of the command is TELNET *ip_address* or TELNET *hostname,* if the host name can be resolved. Since TELNET is the only application-layer command, it is the appropriate answer. Answer B is a network-layer command. Answer C is an IOS command used to display internal router information depending on the command's arguments. Answer D is a network-layer command.

CCNA
CISCO CERTIFIED NETWORK ASSOCIATE

Part 4

The TCP/IP Protocol Suite

EXAM TOPICS

Application-Layer Services

Presentation- and Session-Layer Services

Detailed Protocol Structure

The Network Layer

Operating System Commands

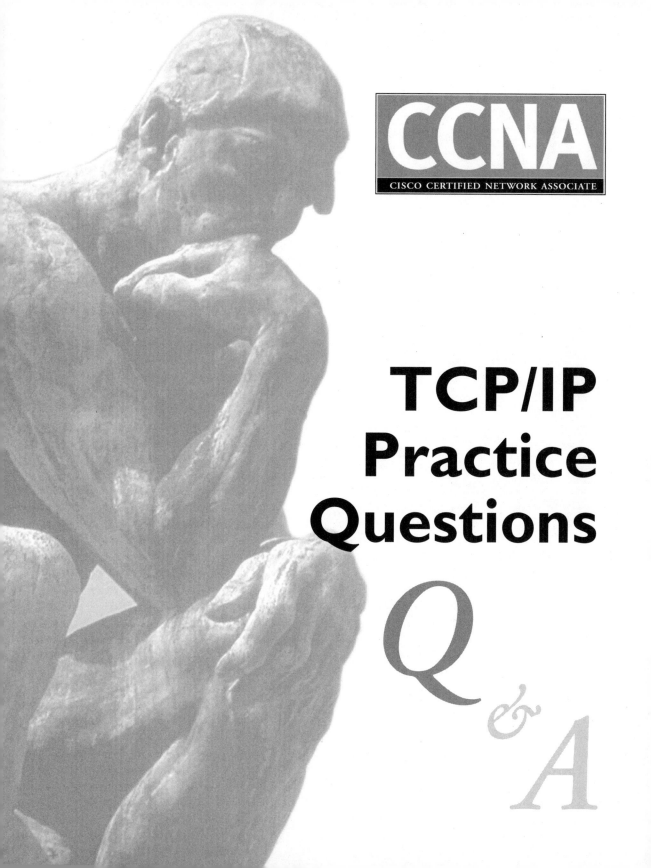

CCNA
CISCO CERTIFIED NETWORK ASSOCIATE

TCP/IP
Practice
Questions

Q
& A

This chapter will review your knowledge of the Transmission Control Protocol/ Internet Protocol (TCP/IP) suite and the Open Systems Interconnection (OSI) reference model. You must have a solid understanding of the various layers of the respective models and how they interrelate. A good understanding of the application layer and its respective tools is essential.

Application-Layer Services

1. When would you use Telnet?

   A. When connecting to a host computer
   B. When attaching a PBX to a data network
   C. When transferring a file to a host computer

2. Which port does Telnet use?

   A. 19
   B. 49
   C. 66
   D. 23

3. How does FTP differ from TFTP?

   A. TFTP is a Microsoft implementation of FTP.
   B. TFTP uses DES encryption algorithms.
   C. TFTP does not support authentication.
   D. TFTP is not interactive.

4. What does SMTP provide?

   A. An e-mail gateway
   B. File transfer
   C. An e-mail attachment manager
   D. A small mainframe terminal program

5. Which layer converts the digital signals in electrical pulses?

   A. Application

   B. Physical

   C. Data-link

   D. Session

6. Which layer sets up and terminates connections between hosts?

   A. Application

   B. Physical

   C. Transport

   D. Session

7. Which layer provides a standard interface for users?

   A. Application

   B. Physical

   C. Transport

   D. Session

8. Which layer provides application management?

   A. Application

   B. Physical

   C. Session

   D. Transport

9. At which layer are hardware addresses translated to network addresses?

   A. Network

   B. Data-link

   C. Application

   D. Transport

TCP/IP
QUESTIONS

10. Which layer provides hardware address mapping?

A. Network

B. Data-link

C. Application

D. Transport

11. At which layer is data encrypted?

A. Network

B. Data-link

C. Presentation

D. Transport

12. Which sequence of layers corresponds to the following three functions of OSI layers, in the correct order?

Converts binary information to electrical pulses to voltage
Provides network topology information and routing decisions
Denotes where a workstation is physically located on a network

A. Application, physical, network

B. Network, transport, physical

C. Data-link, session, physical

D. Physical, network, data-link

Presentation- and Session-Layer Services

1. What is a characteristic of connection-oriented protocols?

A. They are efficient.

B. They are reliable.

C. They are unreliable.

D. They are secure.

2. What is a hazard of RPCs?

   A. They are inefficient.

   B. They are insecure.

   C. They are nonstandard.

   D. They are error-prone.

3. What is one of the most common RPC-based applications?

   A. NetBIOS

   B. SNMP

   C. NFS

   D. XPR

4. At which layer of the OSI model are sockets used?

   A. Layer 1

   B. Layer 3

   C. Layer 5

   D. Layer 7

5. What is a port?

   A. It is hardware contained in the host.

   B. It is a transport-layer reference number.

   C. It is another name for an IP address.

   D. It is a router interface.

6. Which organization maintains the list of well-known ports?

   A. DoD

   B. InterNIC

   C. IANA

   D. IETF

7. Which port must be disabled to disallow FTPs to pass through a router?

A. 21

B. 17

C. 1,024

D. 35

8. What is TLI?

A. It is a proprietary version of sockets.

B. It is similar to NFS.

C. It is another form of ports.

D. It is a programming interface.

Detailed Protocol Structure

1. At which OSI layer does NetBIOS reside?

A. Layer 3

B. Layer 4

C. Layer 5

D. Layer 6

2. What are two of the most common transport-layer protocols for IP?

A. FTP and Telnet

B. ICMP and IGMP

C. TCP and UDP

D. Ping and X Windows

3. When does TCP slow start occur?

A. When TCP is run over an HDLC circuit

B. When TCP terminates the session

C. When TCP does not receive an acknowledgement from a transmission

D. When TCP negotiates a low-speed connection

4. What is the best size for a sliding window?

   A. 10

   B. 1,000

   C. Infinitely variable

   D. 1,024

5. What is a key difference between UDP and TCP? (Choose all that apply.)

   A. UDP is faster than TCP.

   B. UDP has less overhead than TCP.

   C. UDP is less reliable than TCP.

   D. UDP is more efficient than UDP.

6. Your network includes a Dynamic Host Configuration Protocol (DHCP) server and client computers located on separate networks that are connected by a router. What should you configure the router to do?

   A. Use RIP

   B. Use the OSPF protocol

   C. Function as a BOOTP (RFC 1542) relay agent

   D. Forward NetBIOS broadcasts

The Network Layer

1. Why must a router in the network strip off the data-link layer header and trailer information before it can do anything with the packet?

   A. To minimize excess traffic being sent over the network

   B. To expose the portion of the datagram that contains the network-layer information

   C. To reroute the datagram

   D. To perform a CRC check

TCP/IP QUESTIONS

2. Which OSI layer is responsible for packet fragmentation and reassembly?

    A. Layer 2

    B. Layer 3

    C. Layer 4

    D. Layer 5

3. What is an MTU?

    A. Clock speed of a router

    B. Mean time UDP

    C. Maximum transmission unit

    D. Mark Transmission Undelivered

4. For IP, which tool does a host use to identify the destination host's MAC address?

    A. ICMP

    B. RIP

    C. IGRP

    D. ARP

5. How does RARP differ from ARP?

    A. It is more secure.

    B. It does the opposite of ARP.

    C. RARP is the Microsoft implementation of ARP.

    D. RARP is obsolete.

6. At which OSI layer does RARP operate?

    A. Layer 2

    B. Layer 3

    C. Layer 4

    D. Layer 5

7. What is Inverse ARP?

  A. It is the same as RARP.

  B. It is frame relay address resolution.

  C. It is obsolete.

  D. It is ARP for diskless workstations.

8. When an error occurs in an ICMP message, what happens?

  A. The transmitting end is notified.

  B. The packet is dropped.

  C. The RIP tables are updated.

  D. Traps are sent to the management center.

9. Which of the following is a function of ICMP?

  A. It manages networks.

  B. It redirects network messages.

  C. It transports SNMP Gets.

  D. It discovers subnet masks.

10. What is Ping used for?

  A. To connect to remote hosts

  B. To test connectivity between Ethernet workstations

  C. To test connectivity between IP hosts

  D. To transfer small files between hosts

11. What causes ICMP redirects?

  A. The router buffers being full

  B. The router having found a better route to the destination

  C. The end station having experienced an error

  D. A trap having been received by the router

12. What does the transmitting router do when it receives an ICMP Source Quench message?

   A. It aborts the transmission.

   B. It speeds up the transmission.

   C. It slows the transmission.

   D. It sends a warning to the user.

Operating System Commands

1. Which command displays the Windows IP address provided by DHCP?

   A. NETSTAT

   B. PING

   C. RLOGIN

   D. WINIPCFG

T he answers to the questions are in boldface, followed by a brief explanation. Some of the explanations detail the logic you should use to choose the correct answer, while others give factual reasons why the answer is correct. If you miss several questions on a similar topic, you should review the corresponding section in the *CCNA Cisco Certified Network Associate Study Guide*, Second Edition (Osborne/McGraw-Hill, 1999) before taking the CCNA Certification test.

Application-Layer Services

1. **A.** When connecting to a host computer. Telnet is one of the most widely used protocols on the Internet. It was written to support a multitude of terminals and hosts.

2. **D.** 23. Telnet operates using the TCP well-known port 23. Port 19 is used for character generator (chargen). Port 49 is used for TACACS. Port 66 is used for Oracle SQL*NET communication.

3. **C.** TFTP does not support authentication. TFTP is a small subset of the full-featured FTP application. It has no mechanism for authenticating its users and therefore has no security. But its overhead is low since it uses UDP as its transport mechanism. TFTP uses the well-known port 69.

4. **A.** An e-mail gateway. SMTP uses TCP's well-known port 25 for e-mail gateways.

5. **B.** Physical. The physical layer defines the electrical and physical interfaces between user equipment and network-terminating equipment. The issues that need to be addressed at this layer relate to the representation of a 0 bit and a 1 bit, connection establishment, and teardown. This layer provides the link layer with a means of transmitting serial bits.

6. **C.** Transport. The transport layer (Layer 4) is the boundary between the application-oriented protocols and the network-oriented protocols. It provides the session layer with a data transport service that hides the implementation details of the underlying network.

    The function of the transport layer is to fragment higher-layer data into data segments when required, pass these segments to the underlying network layer, and ensure that these segments arrive at the remote end station. The transport layer carries out end-to-end communication. The source transport-layer protocol communicates with the destination transport-layer entity.

7. **A.** Application. The application layer represents the highest layer of the OSI reference model. It provides the user interface to a range of network-wide distributed services. These include file transfer, remote access, and electronic mail. In the case of file transfer, the application layer resolves differences in naming conventions and other differences between systems. Differences in terminal types are resolved at this layer.

8. **C.** Session. The session layer allows remote users to establish multiple connections to remote devices. A session enables two users to organize and manage their data exchange. For some protocols, it is essential that both end systems do not attempt the same operation simultaneously. The session layer can ensure this does not occur through a service called token management. The token is passed from one station to another by the session-layer protocols. The operation can only be invoked by the end station in possession of the token.

9. **A.** Network. IP is at the network, or Internet, layer. It is a connectionless internetwork service that includes provisions for addressing, fragmentation, reassembly, type of service support, and security. IP packets, or datagrams, can be transported over multiple physical networks and are copied by intermediate systems, such as IP routers, from one network to another. IP addresses are independent of the underlying local network hardware addressing scheme. This allows IP addresses to be used in any network and provides a level of abstraction that enables Internet communication to take place over multiple subnetworks.

10. **B. Data-link.** This layer provides an information transfer facility across a physical link. Since the physical layer accepts and transmits a stream of bits without any regard to the actual meaning or the structure of these bits, the data-link layer is responsible for creating and recognizing frame boundaries. Because the underlying physical medium is unreliable, reliability is ensured at this layer, through retransmission.

11. **C. Presentation.** The presentation layer ensures that information from one system's application-layer protocol is readable by the application-layer protocol on the remote system. This layer, unlike lower layers, is simply concerned with the syntax and the semantics of the information transmitted. Sometimes it is necessary to decompress, or decrypt, application information.

12. **D. Physical, network, data-link.** The physical layer defines the electrical and physical interfaces between user equipment and network-terminating equipment. The network layer provides the logical addresses that denote subnets, and provides routing metric values, such as hop count. The data-link layer contains the Media Access Control (MAC) addresses that are used for physical addressing on the network.

Presentation- and Session-Layer Services

1. **B. They are reliable.** A connection-oriented service is like a telephone service. There is a call setup phase. All packets are delivered in order. There is no loss or duplication of data. There is high reliability that the data will be delivered accurately, or retransmitted, in case of error.

2. B. They are insecure. RPCs have no mechanism for authentication; therefore they have been easily exploited as a security hole in systems. Because of low overhead, they are efficient. They are not prone to errors. RPCs were initially defined by Sun Microsystems and are now considered the de facto standard.

3. C. NFS. The Network File System (NFS) developed by Sun Microsystems is the de facto standard for file sharing among UNIX hosts. NFS version 3 is documented in RFC 1813. All NFS operations are implemented as RPC procedures. NFS is a distributed file system for heterogeneous networks. With NFS, a user sees a single local directory hierarchy, even though many, if not most, of the files and directories in that hierarchy, are located on other computers on the network. NetBIOS is a network protocol, and SNMP is a network management protocol. XPR is an X Windows printing application that can take advantage of RPC, but isn't widely used in that way.

4. C. Layer 5. Sockets are an application programming interface (API) that provides a framework for communication between processes that execute either on the same host or across a network. A socket is the basic building block for communication, providing an end point to which a name may be bound. Sockets are created within a communications domain (Internet or UNIX) in the same way that files are created within a file system. Sockets are bidirectional, providing a two-way flow of data between processes that may or may not have the same parent and may or may not live on the same host. Sockets provide a process with a full-duplex byte-stream connection to another process. The application need not concern itself with the management of this stream; these facilities are provided by the transport layer.

5. B. It is a transport-layer reference number. A port is a 16-bit number, used by the host-to-host protocol to identify to which higher-level protocol or application program (process) it must deliver incoming messages. As some higher-level programs are themselves protocols standardized in the TCP/IP protocol suite, such as TELNET and FTP, they use the same port number in all TCP/IP implementations. Those assigned port numbers are called *well-known ports*.

6. **C.** IANA. The well-known ports are controlled and assigned by the Internet Assigned Numbers Authority (IANA) and on most systems can only be used by system processes or by programs executed by privileged users. The assigned well-known ports occupy port numbers in the range 0–1,023. The ports with numbers in the range 1,024–65,535 are not controlled by IANA and on most systems can be used by ordinary user-developed programs.

7. **A.** 21. Port 21 is the well-known port number for FTP. You must disable connections on port 21 to disallow FTP transmissions. Port 20 is also used for FTP. These are the well-known port numbers for FTP. Port 17 is used for the Quote of the Day. Port 1,024 is registered for IANA use. Port 35 is used for private print servers.

8. **D.** It is a programming interface. The transport-layer interface (TLI) is an API developed by AT&T for the creation of distributed applications that can be easily ported to run over different transports.

Detailed Protocol Structure

1. **C.** Layer 5. NetBIOS is a session-level interface that uses alphanumeric strings rather than numbers to identify processes on the network. The current NetBIOS is derived from the NetBIOS introduced by IBM on its first PC LAN network adapter cards.

2. **C.** TCP and UDP. TCP provides reliable, stream-oriented delivery for applications such as file transfers and remote logins. TCP is a sliding-window protocol that takes steps to ensure reliable data transfer, resending if needed, due to network overloads or malfunctions. TCP, one of the most important Internet protocols, is also one of the most complex. Although it often works well unattended, a good understanding of TCP is essential for diagnosing performance problems. UDP provides almost no additional functionality over IP. It performs fast, unreliable, datagram delivery.

3. **C.** When TCP does not receive an acknowledgement from a transmission. TCP uses a concept called *sliding windows.* When an acknowledgement is not received by the transmitting station, TCP assumes that either the network or the end station is congested. It responds by automatically reducing the transmission speed by reducing the window size of data being transmitted.

4. **C.** Infinitely variable. The sliding window algorithm constantly adjusts the size of the windows based on the receiver's ability to receive the transmission.

5. **A, B, C, D.** UDP is faster, has less overhead, is less reliable, and is more efficient than TCP. UDP provides a connectionless datagram service, which means that the arrival of datagrams is not guaranteed, nor in correct sequence. It is considered to be unreliable but best-effort delivery. Used by applications that don't require acknowledgment of receipt of data and that typically transmit small amounts of data at one time. Some examples of applications that use UDP are NetBIOS name service, NetBIOS datagram service, TFTP, and SNMP.

6. **C.** Function as a BOOTP (RFC 1542) relay agent. By configuring the router to use UDP flooding, BOOTP requests will be propagated to other network segments.

The Network Layer

1. **B.** To expose the portion of the datagram that contains the network-layer information. As the data moves through each protocol layer, it is encapsulated in another header. The router must remove that header to see the destination address of the data.

2. **C.** Layer 4. The transport layer can be described as the boundary between the application-oriented protocols and the network-oriented protocols. It provides the session layer with a data transport service that hides the implementation details of the underlying network. The function of the transport layer is to fragment higher-layer data into data segments when required, pass these segments to the underlying network layer, and ensure that these segments arrive at the remote end station.

3. **C.** Maximum transmission unit. This is the upper limit for a frame size. It is dependent on the network transmission medium. Some examples are listed here:

- **Hyperchannel**   65,535 bytes
- **Token Ring (IBM)**   17,914 bytes
- **FDDI**   4,352 bytes
- **Ethernet**   1,500 bytes
- **IEEE 802.3**   1,492 bytes
- **X.25**   576 bytes

4. **D.** ARP. Address Resolution Protocol (ARP), which is for IP addresses on the same physical network, uses the IP address of the target computer to identify its MAC address. For IP addresses on remote segments, ARP will then retrieve the gateway's MAC address. From there, the gateway handles the remote communication activity for the local host. ARP is documented in RFC 826.

5. **B.** It does the opposite of ARP. A Reverse Address Resolution Protocol (RARP) server assigns IP addresses to its clients on the LAN. When you configure a router to use RARP services, it acts as a RARP server. A RARP server supplies clients on the same physical or logical LAN with IP addresses. To use RARP services, you must set up a MAC address–to–IP address mapping table. This table lists the MAC addresses of clients and the corresponding IP addresses that the RARP server assigns to those clients. When a client needs to acquire an IP address, the client broadcasts a RARP request, specifying its MAC address. Upon receiving a RARP request, the RARP server refers to its MAC address–to–IP address mapping table and then sends the client a response packet containing the corresponding IP

address. The client examines the response packet to learn its IP address.
RARP is similar to BOOTP, or DHCP. The command to enable this on a
Cisco router is IP RARP-SERVER *IP-address* <CR>.

6. B. Layer 3. RARP allows a workstation to request its Layer-3 network address.

7. B. It is frame relay address resolution. Inverse ARP enables address
resolution for frame relay or other nonbroadcast interfaces. It is used to
discover the IP address of the station at the remote end of the virtual circuit.
These dynamic IP addresses are then mapped to the frame relay DLCIs.

8. B. The packet is dropped. In the ICMP standard, documented in RFC 792,
errors are not reported on error messages. If they were, during outages the
network could become quickly overloaded with nothing but error messages.

9. B. It redirects network messages. Internet Control Message Protocol (ICMP)
messages, delivered in IP packets, are used for out-of-band messages related
to network operation or misoperation. Since ICMP uses IP, ICMP packet
delivery is unreliable; so hosts cannot count on receiving ICMP packets for
any network problem. ICMP is not used to discover subnet masks. An
SNMP Get uses the UDP protocol but does not specifically contain
network messages. It normally contains Management Information Base
(MIB) network management information from a network component.

10. C. To test connectivity between IP hosts. Ping is one of the most useful
network debugging tools available. In an IP network, Ping sends a short
data burst—a single packet—and listens for a single packet in reply. Ping is
implemented using the required ICMP echo function, documented in RFC
792. Ping places a unique sequence number on each packet it transmits, and
reports the sequence numbers it receives back. Thus, you can determine if
packets have been dropped, duplicated, or reordered. Ping checksums each
packet it exchanges. You can detect some forms of damaged packets. Ping
places a timestamp in each packet, which is echoed back and can easily be
used to compute how long each packet exchange took. This process is called

roundtrip time (RTT). Ping reports other ICMP messages that might otherwise get buried in the system software. It reports, for example, if a router is declaring the target host unreachable.

11. **B.** The router having found a better route to the destination. If a gateway detects that an IP datagram is not using the best route, it forwards the datagram to the gateway that provides the best route and sends an ICMP Redirect message to the source host. The ICMP Redirect message tells the source host the best route to use for datagrams to that destination host. When it receives an ICMP Redirect message, the source host updates its routing table with the new route for that destination host. On IP networks, it is common for devices to send and receive ICMP Redirect messages.

12. **C.** It slows the transmission. When a router does not have enough buffer space to process an incoming IP datagram, it discards the datagram and sends an ICMP Source Quench message to the source host. When a destination host is not able to process incoming IP datagrams that arrive too quickly, it does not receive the datagrams and sends an ICMP Source Quench message to the source host. Depending on the configuration of the gateway or host, it may send ICMP Source Quench messages before it reaches its capacity. If this is the case, the datagram that triggered the ICMP Source Quench message is delivered. If a source host receives an ICMP Source Quench message, it reduces the rate at which it sends IP datagrams to the associated destination host. When the source host stops receiving ICMP Source Quench messages from that destination host, it gradually increases the rate at which it sends IP datagrams to that destination host, until it reaches the normal transmission rate again.

Operating System Commands

1. **D.** WINIPCFG. This application will display the DHCP-assigned IP address to that particular workstation. It will also allow you to release your address and request another.

Part 5

IP Routing

EXAM TOPICS

IP Routing Protocol Basics

Routing Information Protocol (RIP)

Open Shortest Path First (OSPF)

Interior Gateway Routing Protocol (IGRP)

Enhanced IGRP (EIGRP)

Border Gateway Protocol (BGP)

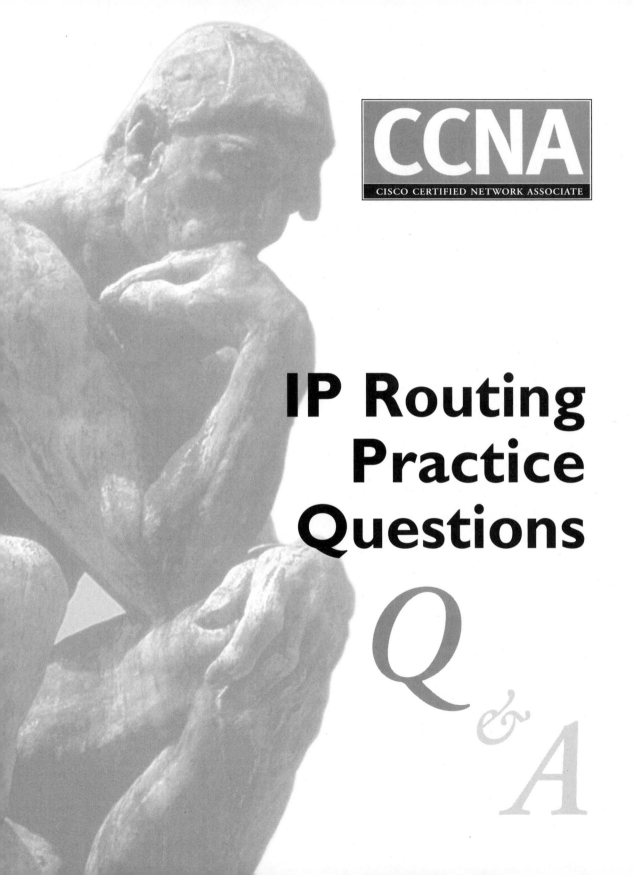

This chapter explores Internet Protocol (IP) routing protocols. Test questions cover such IP routing protocols as Routing Information Protocol (RIP), Open Shortest Path First (OSPF), Interior Gateway Routing Protocol (IGRP), Enhanced IGRP (EIGRP), and Border Gateway Protocol (BGP). We present questions on each protocol with emphasis on RIP and IGRP configuration, as the CCNA exam covers these two protocols in more detail than the others. Scenarios with RIP and IGRP that cover both of these protocols in more detail are included.

IP Routing Protocol Basics

1. At which layer of the OSI reference model does IP routing occur?
   A. Layer 1
   B. Layer 4
   C. Layer 3
   D. Layer 2

2. Which of the following IP routing protocols use the distance vector algorithm? (Choose all that apply.)
   A. OSPF
   B. RIP
   C. IGRP
   D. Static

3. Which of the following protocols uses the link-state algorithm?
   A. Static
   B. OSPF
   C. Dynamic
   D. XNS

Routing Information Protocol (RIP)

1. What is the purpose of an offset list?

A. To filter access to the router

B. To offset an interface using RIP

C. To increase incoming or outgoing metrics identified by RIP

D. None of the above

Use the Following Configuration Files to Answer Questions 2–8

Router A is connected to Router B via Serial 1. Router A also has a connection to the Internet via port Serial 0. The following listings show the network layout.

Router A

```
hostname RouterA
!
interface Ethernet 0
 ip address 192.168.1.1 255.255.255.0
 no mop enabled
 no shutdown
!
interface Serial 0
 description Serial Link to the Internet
 encapsulation hdlc
 ip address 204.59.144.3 255.255.255.252
 no shutdown
!
interface Serial 1
 description Serial Link to Router B
 ip address 172.16.10.3 255.255.255.252
 encapsulation hdlc
 no shutdown
network 192.168.0.0
network 172.16.0.0
!
ip route 0.0.0.0 0.0.0.0 204.59.144.2
```

Router B

```
hostname RouterB
!
interface Ethernet 0
 ip address 192.168.10.2 255.255.0.0
 no shutdown
!
interface Serial 0
 ip address 172.16.10.2 255.255.255.252
 encapsulation hdlc
 no shutdown
!
router rip
network 128.129.0.0
network 192.168.0.0
```

2. Router B is not getting any information from Router A. What is the problem with Router A's configuration?

   A. The static route has an incorrect subnet mask.

   B. The Ethernet interface is not enabled.

   C. RIP has not been enabled.

   D. None of the above.

3. Due to a change on the network, Router A's administrator needs to change the version of RIP on the router to version 2. Router B can't be changed due to network requirements. What changes to Router B's configuration are needed?

   A. RIP needs to be changed to version 2.

   B. RIP needs to be removed and static routes added.

   C. No changes are needed.

   D. RIP needs to be changed on the serial interface to send and receive RIP version 2 packets.

4. What changes could be made to Router A's configuration to accomplish the same goal?

A. Change Router A's interface Serial 1 to send and receive RIP version 1 packets.

B. No changes can be made to Router A's configuration.

C. Remove RIP and use static routes on Router A.

D. Enable authentication on Router A.

5. Devices connected to Router B need access to the Internet. Router A has a default static route to the configured ISP. How can this route be made available to Router B?

A. Redistribute the static route into RIP on Router A.

B. No change is needed, as the route is already advertised by RIP.

C. Add a default network statement to Router A's configuration.

D. None of the above.

6. Authentication needs to be added to the link between Router A and Router B. The link has no type of encryption enabled, and the link is carried by public carrier. What type of authentication is needed?

A. Text

B. Message Digest 5 (MD5)

C. Password

D. 128KB

7. Router B's administrator needs to increase the metric for routes originating at Router A. How would the administrator do this?

A. By creating an access list

B. By enabling BGP

C. By filtering routing updates from Router A

D. By creating an offset list to increase incoming route metrics

8. Users on Router B's network would rather use the other source as the route to the particular IP address block. Without using an offset list, how can this be accomplished?

A. By using OSPF

B. By turning off RIP

C. By creating an access list to block the IP address block advertisement from Router A

D. None of the above

9. Which type of authentication does RIP version 2 support?

A. CHAP

B. Password

C. Simple

D. Text

10. Which version of RIP supports automatic route summarization?

A. RIP version 2

B. RIP version 3

C. RIP version 4

D. None of the above

QUESTIONS AND ANSWERS

Gerald manages an internetwork consisting of three routers and four logical networks. He is using a static routing table. Gerald adds a connection to the Internet. If Router A is connected to B, then to C, then to D, and then to the Internet, Gerald assumes that he can place a single default route on Router D to send everything to the Internet. When the connection goes live, the people connected directly to networks on Router D are able to use the Internet, but no one else can. What is the problem?

Because there are no default routes on Routers A, B, and C, the routers will drop the packets for which there are no existing routes. Then, the Internet cannot be reached. To correct the problem, a default route on C should send all packets to D, a default route on B should send all packets to C, and a default route on A should send all packets to B.

Open Shortest Path First (OSPF)

1. Which of the following RFCs is the most current for OSPF?

   A. RFC 1700

   B. RFC 1267

   C. RFC 2328

   D. RFC 1000

2. Which type of router has interfaces connected to multiple areas?

   A. Area border router

   B. Internal router

   C. Single area router

   D. Backbone router

3. Which group of tests do routers need to pass to become neighbors?

   A. IP address, area ID, subnet mask, and router ID

   B. Area ID, authentication, router ID, and IP address

   C. Router ID, stub area flag, hello and dead interval, and area ID

   D. Subnet and subnet mask, area ID, authentication, hello and dead interval, and stub area flag

4. Which of the following is the first criterion used in determining the designated router?

   A. Router ID

   B. IP address

   C. OSPF priority

   D. MAC address

5. Which of the following is supported by OSPF? (Choose all that apply.)

   A. Redistribution of routes

   B. VLSM

   C. Hop count

   D. Route summarization

Interior Gateway Routing Protocol (IGRP)

Use the Following Configuration Files to Answer Questions 1–8

Router A is connected to Router B via Ethernet 0. Router A also has a connection to the Internet via port Serial 0. The following listings show the network topology as reflected in the router configurations.

Router A

```
hostname RouterA
!
interface Ethernet 0
 ip address 192.168.1.1 255.255.255.0
 no mop enabled
 no shutdown
!
interface Serial 0
 description Serial Link to the Internet
 encapsulation hdlc
 ip address 204.59.144.3 255.255.255.252
 no shutdown
!
interface Serial 1
 shutdown
!
router igrp 200
network 192.168.1.0
!
ip route 0.0.0.0 0.0.0.0 204.59.144.2
```

Router B

```
hostname RouterB
!
interface Ethernet 0
 ip address 192.168.1.2 255.255.0.0
 no shutdown
!
interface Ethernet 1
 ip address 192.168.10.2 255.255.255.0
 no shutdown
!
```

```
interface Serial 0
 ip address 172.16.10.2 255.255.255.252
 encapsulation hdlc
 no shutdown
 !
router igrp 200
network 172.16.10.0
network 192.168.10.0
```

1. Which network(s) will Router B announce to Router A?

A. Network 192.168.0.0

B. Network 172.16.0.0

C. Networks 192.168.10.0 and 172.16.10.0

D. Network 204.59.144.0

2. Which is the Update timer setting for sending routing updates in IGRP?

A. 60 seconds

B. 90 seconds

C. 30 seconds

D. 15 seconds

3. Router B adds a serial port connection to a frame relay network. What would Router B's administrator do to configure IGRP to send information to the router on the other side of the network?

A. Redistribute static routes

B. Use RIP

C. Use the NEIGHBOR command to define the other router

D. None of the above

4. Router A's administrator needs to determine which routes are discovered by IGRP. Which command(s) can be used? (Choose all that apply.)

A. SHOW IP ROUTE

B. DISPLAY IGRP ROUTES

C. SHOW IP ROUTE IGRP

D. SHOW ROUTES

5. Workstations on Router B's network will need access to the Internet connection on Router A. What changes will need to be made to Router A's configuration?

A. The default route will need to be redistributed into IGRP.

B. OSPF will need to be run.

C. A route map will need to be used.

D. An access list will need to be defined.

6. Under which type of routing protocol does IGRP fall?

A. Dynamic

B. DUAL

C. Link-state

D. Dynamic distance vector

7. Router B's administrator needs to add EIGRP to conform to changes being made to the network that is connected to Router B's Ethernet interface. How are routes originating from IGRP distributed into EIGRP?

A. By defining a route map to allow routes to be advertised to EIGRP

B. By enabling EIGRP to take advantage of automatic redistribution

C. By using static routes

D. None of the above

8. Which command would Router A's administrator use to adjust the metrics on routes originating from Router B?

A. The ADJUST METRIC router configuration command

B. The METRIC WEIGHTS router configuration command

C. The ADJUST WEIGHT router configuration command

D. None of the above

Enhanced IGRP (EIGRP)

1. How does EIGRP calculate the best path and achieve convergence?

    A. Distance vector

    B. Shortest Path First

    C. Diffusing Update Algorithm (DUAL)

    D. RIP

2. Which of the following is true of EIGRP?

    A. It allows for automatic redistribution of routes into IGRP.

    B. Its maximum hop count is 15.

    C. It uses more CPU than IGRP.

    D. It does not support VLSM.

3. Which is the metric used by EIGRP?

    A. MED

    B. Path

    C. RIP

    D. Hop count

4. Which statement is true?

    A. EIGRP does not support route summarization.

    B. EIGRP does not support classless interdomain routing (CIDR).

    C. EIGRP supports route summarization.

    D. None of the above.

5. In addition to enabling summarization by default, as in the preceding example, what is another way to summarize routes with EIGRP?

    A. Use the NETWORK command.

    B. Configure RIP.

    C. Use OSPF with EIGRP.

    D. Use the IP SUMMARY-ADDRESS command.

6. Which of the following authentication modes does EIGRP support?

    A. Simple

    B. MD5

    C. Text

    D. None of the above

Border Gateway Protocol (BGP)

1. Which version of BGP is supported in Cisco routers?

    A. Version 2

    B. Version 3

    C. Version 4

    D. All of the above

2. How do you reset a BGP peering session?

    A. You clear IP BGP NEIGHBOR.

    B. You restart IP BGP NEIGHBOR.

    C. You clear BGP ALL.

    D. You reset IP BGP NEIGHBOR.

3. In which of the following instances should BGP traffic be synchronized?

    A. When passing routing information with a peer

    B. When passing routing information from an IGP to another AS

    C. When passing static routes to a peer

    D. None of the above

4. Which of the following commands displays the routes being advertised by an individual AS?

A. SHOW IP ROUTES BGP

B. DISPLAY IP BGP ROUTES

C. SHOW IP BGP AS_NUMBER

D. SHOW IP BGP REGEXP AS_NUMBER

5. Which of the following commands displays information on all BGP peerings?

A. DISPLAY IP BGP SUMMARY

B. SHOW BGP SUMMARY

C. SHOW IP BGP SUMMARY

D. DISPLAY BGP SUMMARY

6. What do AS path filters do?

A. They filter IP address block announcements.

B. They filter routing information from adjacent ASs.

C. They filter AS announcements from adjacent peers.

D. None of the above.

CCNA

CISCO CERTIFIED NETWORK ASSOCIATE

IP Routing
Answers

Q & A

The answers to the questions are in boldface, followed by a brief explanation. Some of the explanations detail the logic you should use to choose the correct answer, while others give factual reasons why the answer is correct. If you miss several questions on a similar topic, you should review the corresponding section in the *CCNA Cisco Network Associate Study Guide*, Second Edition (Osborne/McGraw-Hill, 1999) before taking the CCNA Certification test.

IP Routing Protocol Basics

1. **C. Layer 3.** Routing occurs at Layer 3, the network layer, as opposed to bridging, which occurs at Layer 2, the link layer. While both get information from source to destination, they differ in the way they do this. Routed data will follow a path that is discovered via a routing protocol from the source to the destination. In a bridged environment, if the destination address is not on an originating segment, the data is sent via other interfaces. For routing to occur, it's necessary to have a path from the source to the destination and a means of transport for the information. The optimal path is determined by a routing protocol that uses various algorithms. Bridging does not select an optimal path as it uses link-layer information to transfer information from one internetwork to another.

2. **B, C. RIP and IGRP.** RIP was one of the first routing protocols developed, with variations dating back to the first days of the ARPANET. RIP is based on the routed program, which was developed for use with the Berkeley distribution of UNIX. RIP is still one of the most popular routing protocols with smaller corporate networks. IGRP was developed by Cisco in the 1980s as an alternative to RIP in response to the growth explosion in corporate networks. RIP's limitation on hop count made it necessary for the development of a more robust protocol that could extend networks beyond RIP's 15-hop maximum.

3. **B.** OSPF. The OSPF protocol was developed as a hierarchical routing protocol for use in a single autonomous system (AS). OSPF uses the Shortest Path First (SPF) algorithm to build its routing table so updates are sent to the neighbor instead of sending the entire table. Link-state protocols are less susceptible to routing loops at the expense of more CPU and memory usage, unlike distance vector protocols. The cost of increased CPU and memory requirements should be considered before determining whether a link-state protocol should be used.

Routing Information Protocol (RIP)

1. **C.** To increase incoming or outgoing metrics identified by RIP. Offset lists are used to alter or modify routing metrics as they are advertised to all routers in a network. Many IP routing protocols use offset lists to allow a router administrator to adjust routing metrics that are advertised.

2. **C.** RIP has not been enabled. Since RIP has not been enabled on Router A, the routes will not be advertised to Router B, and routes originating from Router B will not be seen on Router A. To enable RIP on Router A, use the following command in router configuration mode:

   routerA(config)#ROUTER RIP

3. **D.** RIP needs to be changed on the serial interface to send and receive RIP version 2 packets. Cisco routers can run both versions simultaneously. RIP version 2 supports areas such as authentication and variable-length subnet mask (VLSM). By default, Cisco routers can receive both version 1 and version 2 packets, but can only send version 1 packets without setting the configuration to specifically send version 2 packets. This can be

accomplished both globally and on individual interfaces. Router B's administrator can use the following command to set the serial interface to send RIP version 2 packets:

```
router(config)#INTERFACE SERIAL
router(config-if)#IP RIP SEND VERSION 2
```

4. **A.** Change Router A's interface Serial 1 to send and receive RIP version 1 packets. Router A's administrator can use the SEND VERSION command on interface Serial 1 to send and receive RIP version 1 packets from Router B. This will accomplish the same goal. The following commands are used:

```
router(config)#INTERFACE SERIAL 1
router(config)#IP RIP SEND VERSION 1
router(config)#IP RIP RECEIVE VERSION 1
```

5. **A.** Redistribute the static route into RIP on Router A. Redistribution of routes from one routing protocol to another occurs when multiple routing protocols are used. The most common occurrence is when routes from an Interior Gateway Protocol (IGP) are redistributed into an Exterior Gateway Protocol (EGP). In this case the static route on Router A is included in the RIP routing table that is sent to Router B. To redistribute the static route from Router A to Router B, the following commands are used:

```
router(config)#ROUTER RIP
router(config)#REDISTRIBUTE STATIC
router(config)#DEFAULT-METRIC 2
router(config)#PASSIVE-INTERFACE SERIAL 0
```

Make sure that you set Serial 0 on Router A to be a Passive interface, meaning you will prevent Serial 0 from sending routes into RIP.

6. **B.** Message Digest 5 (MD5). Authentication should be considered when there is no security on links. External links should have some type of authentication to prevent hacker attacks. Simple authentication should not be used with public carriers because the password is transmitted with every RIP packet. Authentication is supported only with RIP version 2, covers only RIP updates, and does not protect data other than RIP routing updates. MD5 authentication uses the message digest encryption algorithm and is extremely difficult to crack. To set MD5 authentication, use the following commands in router configuration mode:

```
router(config)#IP RIP AUTHENTICATION KEY-CHAIN [KEY NAME]
router(config)#IP RIP AUTHENTICATION MODE MD5
```

Note that you will need to define the key-chain.

7. **D.** By creating an offset list to increase incoming route metrics. An offset list increases route metrics on incoming or outgoing route announcements. Example: Router B receives route announcements of a certain IP address block from Router A. Router B is also getting the same block from another source such as another router on its Ethernet segment. Since the metric is the same as Router A's advertisement, Router B's administrator could create an offset list to increase the metric on Router A's advertisement to make the other source's advertisement the preferred route.

8. **C.** By creating an access list to block the IP address block advertisement from Router A. Since the address block is being advertised to that of Router B, Ethernet is the preferred route to that segment. Router B's administrator can set an access list to deny the announcement from Router A.

9. C. Simple. This is one type of authentication RIP version 2 supports; another is MD5 authentication. When the AFI field in a RIP header has the code of OxFFFF, the packet contains authentication information. The next field will contain the identifier for simple authentication, which is set for 2. The remaining octets (16) contain the password. Care should be taken when devices such as protocol analyzers can trace simple authentication, as the information is not encrypted. If authentication is needed, consider using a protocol that supports MD5, such as RIP version 2.

10. A. RIP version 2. This version supports automatic route summarization. Routes are summarized by subprefix by the IOS software when crossing network boundaries. The goal of route summarization is to reduce the size of the routing table. RIP version 2 and other protocols support route summarization. When RIP version 2 is enabled, summarization is also enabled by default. RIP version 2 also supports discontiguous subnets. This is accomplished when RIP sends routing updates. RIP also includes the subnet mask in its updates. When your network has disconnected subnets, you will need to disable summarization by using the NO AUTO-SUMMARY command when configuring RIP.

Open Shortest Path First (OSPF)

1. C. RFC 2328. This RFC, authored in 1998, is the most current to cover OSPF. OSPF was originally covered in RFC 1247. Cisco routers support OSPF version 2, which was reflected in RFC 1583.

2. A. Area border router. An area border router (ABR) has interfaces connected to more than one area. The ABR will have one interface that is defined to be the backbone area (Area 0). The ABR will have a separate link-state database for each area it belongs to. Routing information for each area is sent to the other area to ensure proper routing to destinations within that area. When the backbone area receives this information, it passes it on to connected routers.

3. **D.** Subnet and subnet mask, area ID, authentication, hello and dead interval, and stub area flag. Routers sharing a segment can establish a neighbor relationship, which is formed when the following conditions are met:

- Subnet and subnet mask; the routers share subnet and subnet-mask configuration.
- Area ID; the routers belong to same area on the same segment.
- Authentication; authentication is active on both routers.
- Hello and Dead timers are the same in both routers' configurations.
- Stub area flag; flags should be set to zero if the routers are in a stub area.

4. **C.** OSPF priority. When OSPF neighbor routers on a segment establish adjacencies, they must choose a router to become the designated router (DR) and backup designated router (BDR). The DR acts as the central database for routing information exchange. As a result, all routers on the segment will have the same link-state database, with updates being sent by the DR instead of each router sending an update to all neighbors. The DR receives an update, then forwards the change to all routers on the segment. The BDR acts as a hot standby and is prepared to assume the DR's duties in case of a failure.

5. **A, B, D.** Redistribution of routes; VLSM; and route summarization. These are all supported by OSPF. As with most IP routing protocols, redistribution of routes into and out of OSPF is supported. Variable-length subnet masking is also supported by OSPF so the router administrator can divide IP blocks as needed within the network. Route summarization of routes that advertise to OSPF neighbors reduces the size of the routing table.

Interior Gateway Routing Protocol (IGRP)

1. C. Networks 192.168.10.0 and 172.16.10.0. All networks listed by the network command in IGRP will be announced to all peers. Administrators can filter these announcements through access lists that are set as an option in the NETWORK command. Here is an example of an access list:

```
router igrp 200
network 192.168.10.0
network 172.16.10.0 access-list 100 out
access-list 100
permit 172.16.10.0
deny all
```

2. B. 90 seconds. Routes that are not updated by other routers in the network are declared unreachable after three consecutive cycles (270 seconds). If the route is still not updated after seven cycles, the route is dropped from the routing table. The Update timer, as well as other timers used by IGRP for routing updates, are adjustable using the TIMERS BASIC router configuration command.

3. C. Use the NEIGHBOR command to define the other router. The NEIGHBOR command allows IGRP to send routing information to nonbroadcast networks. The administrator would configure the router with the following information (where *xxx.xxx.xxx.xxx* is the IP address of the neighbor router interface):

```
router igrp
neighbor xxx.xxx.xxx.xxx
```

4. A, C. SHOW IP ROUTE and SHOW IP ROUTE IGRP. SHOW IP ROUTE will display all of the routes currently in the IP routing table. Routes are displayed with a code to define the routing protocol that discovered the route. Route entries that are coded with I are routes that are IGRP originated. SHOW IP ROUTE IGRP will display only routes that have been discovered by IGRP.

5. A. The default route will need to be redistributed into IGRP. IGRP supports redistribution of routes from other routing protocols, as well as from static routes. Router A's administrator will use the REDISTRIBUTE STATIC command in IGRP configuration mode to accomplish this. In some cases redistribution is used in conjunction with a distribution list to narrow the scope of addresses to Accept or Deny. In this case, since the route is a default route, an access list is not used.

6. D. Dynamic distance vector. IGRP was developed by Cisco to be the replacement for RIP. One of RIP's disadvantages is the limited hop count. When a route is more than 15 hops to the destination, RIP will declare the destination unreachable. IGRP's default hop count limit is 100, adjustable to a maximum of 255 depending on the size and complexity of the network. IGRP uses a combination of bandwidth, network delay, and reliability to determine the best path to a destination and supports multiple paths to both primary and secondary destinations.

7. B. By enabling EIGRP to take advantage of automatic redistribution. When EIGRP is enabled, automatic redistribution of routes will occur for both protocols. The only requirement needed for automatic redistribution is to make sure that both IGRP and EIGRP are set with the same autonomous system number.

8. B. The METRIC WEIGHTS router configuration command. This command allows the administrator to adjust how IGRP computes metrics to place more emphasis on certain routes. Depending on the type of network topology (an Ethernet network or a network with different types of connections), the adjustments will result in changes to hop count in the case of a single-type network. Care should be taken when adjusting weights, as network performance can be affected.

Enhanced IGRP (EIGRP)

1. **C.** Diffusing Update Algorithm (DUAL). DUAL makes sure that all routes are loop free by allowing all routers to synchronize when a change in network topology occurs. Routes not affected by the topology change are not altered. DUAL determines the best path to a destination based on feasible successors. The successor is a router with the lowest-cost route to a destination that is guaranteed to be loop free. If a successor is not available, DUAL recomputes and chooses a new successor.

2. **A.** It allows for automatic redistribution of routes into IGRP. Automatic redistribution of routes is set as default in both IGRP and EIGRP to allow for routes from both protocols to be redistributed. This allows administrators who are making the transition from IGRP to EIGRP to run both protocols simultaneously while the transition takes place. Redistribution can be turned off if not required.

3. **D.** Hop count. Unlike RIP, which declares routes that are more than 15 hops away as unreachable, EIGRP limits the number of hops in the transport layer and works around this limitation by incrementing the hop count after a packet has been transmitted across 15 routers. This applies only when the route to the destination is an EIGRP-learned route. In RIP the counter increments in the usual way, hence the 15-hop rule.

4. **C.** EIGRP supports route summarization. When two or more networks are defined through the NETWORK command, summarization is enabled by default. Subnets of a major network number are summarized when they cross into another major network. The router administrator, through the NO AUTO-SUMMARY command, can disable summarization. In most cases, route summarization is preferred and will allow the routing table to be smaller, resulting in lower CPU and memory usage.

5. **D.** Use the IP SUMMARY-ADDRESS command. If auto summary is turned off in EIGRP and the router administrator needs to advertise summarized address blocks across individual interfaces, this command is used in interface configuration mode. This will allow the administrator to advertise summarized addresses on certain interfaces, while advertising nonsummarized addresses on other interfaces.

6. **B.** MD5. The message digest algorithm uses an encrypted key to authenticate communications between EIGRP neighbors. Authentication prevents unauthorized access and false advertisement of routes from sources that are not trusted.

Border Gateway Protocol (BGP)

1. **D.** All of the above. When BGP is enabled, it defaults to version 4. When the router administrator configures a neighbor, they will negotiate the version of BGP in which to run. Negotiation continues downward until the routers agree on a version with which to communicate. The administrator can also set the version of BGP. This is accomplished via the NEIGHBOR command using the version option.

2. **A.** You clear IP BGP NEIGHBOR. This command is used to reset the BGP peering session between BGP speakers. Usually a peering is cleared when a change to either router's BGP configuration has been made. BGP peering sessions can be reset two different ways: by the IP address of the peering router using the command CLEAR IP BGP [*IP address*] or by using the command CLEAR IP BGP PEER [*peer name*]. This command is used when a peer group has been defined in the router configuration.

3. **B.** When passing routing information from an IGP to another AS. Information that BGP learns from an IGP is passed to its peers. If this information is not synchronized, the router could receive

traffic-to-destination addresses that may not be available. Synchronization allows the route information to be made available only when the IGP has propagated the route throughout the AS. Synchronization is enabled by default in BGP, but this can be turned off when there is no IGP in use. The command to turn off synchronization is NO SYNCHRONIZATION in BGP configuration mode.

4. **D.** SHOW IP BGP REGEXP AS_NUMBER. The regular expression is a number that matches an AS or part of an AS number. The output that is displayed includes the IP address block, the source AS and source address of the block, as well as other information. You can use wildcards to display AS information on several different ASs with the same numbers. The following illustration shows the result of this command.

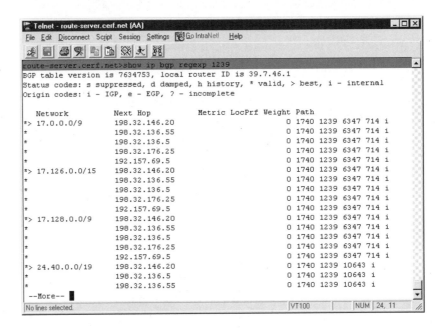

5. **C.** SHOW IP BGP SUMMARY. This command displays the information on all BGP peering sessions. This includes the AS number, the IP address of the neighbor, the length of time the peering has been active, and other information. This information gives a snapshot of all the BGP peerings and can provide information on the status of the peering.

6. **C.** They filter AS announcements from adjacent peers. Administrators can adjust autonomous system (AS) path filters to accept or reject AS announcements from their peers. An example would be an ISP. The Internet today is a vast network of service providers offering access to their customers and peers. A provider can expect to see an AS being announced from several different providers. An AS path filter list can let the administrator decide which path is best for their customers. If AS 500 sees AS 400 coming from three different sources, namely AS 100, AS 200, and AS 300, and wants his customers to use the paths announced by AS 100 and AS 300, the AS 500 administrator can set an AS path filter list to deny AS 400 announcements that originate from AS 200.

Part 6

IP Configuration

EXAM TOPICS

IP Configuration Commands

Configuring Static Routes

Configuring Default Routes

Configuring RIP Routing

Configuring IGRP Routing

IP Host Tables

DNS and DHCP Configuration

Secondary Addressing

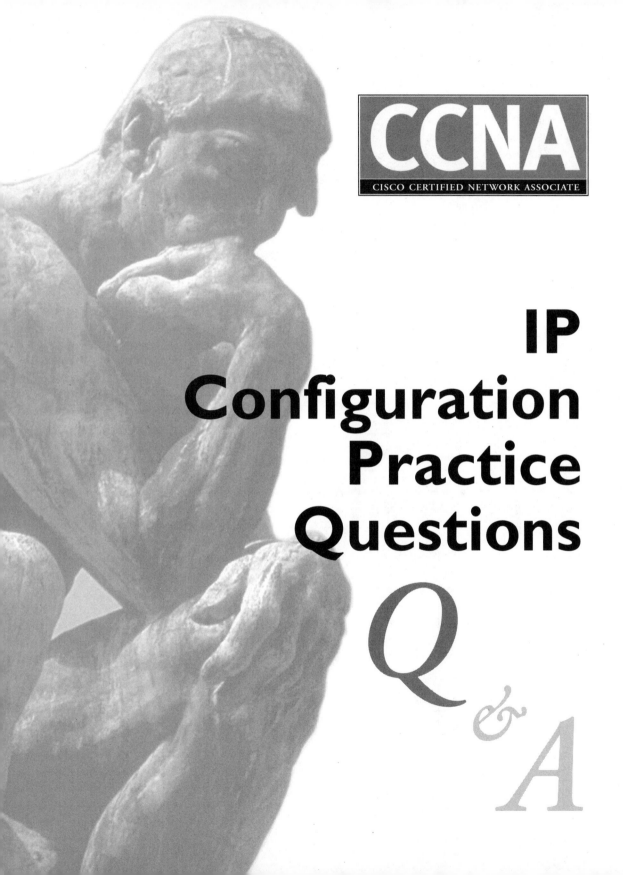

IP
Configuration
Practice
Questions

Q & A

Th<!-- -->he main purpose of this section is to provide problem scenarios that are pertinent to the CCNA examination to help reinforce theory and application of router configuration and installation. The questions in this section provide the framework for familiarizing yourself with Cisco's IOS and configuration commands. It is important to commit these commands to memory; however, it is even more important to thoroughly understand the commands and how they are used for router configuration and setup. Knowing when to use a command—and which command to use—is half the battle. The following section tests how well you understand the IOS and configuration commands. Refer to the following illustration as a framework for all problem scenarios in this chapter.

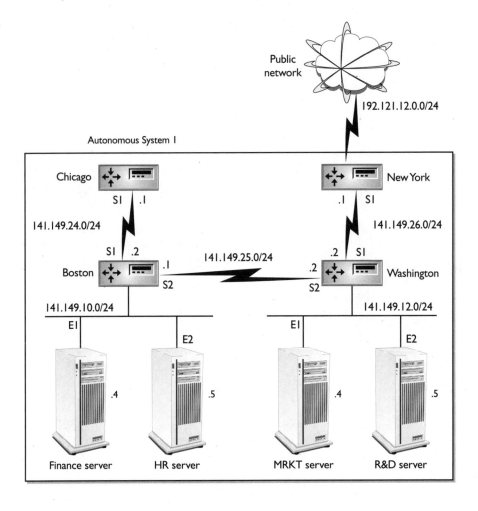

IP Configuration Commands

1. Assuming you are in the global configuration mode of the router, which command will put you in the interface configuration mode of router interface E1? (Choose all that apply.)

   A. INTERFACE ETHERNET1

   B. INT E1

   C. ETHERNET1

   D. None of the above

2. You are now in the interface configuration mode. Which IP configuration command is used to configure the New York interface S1 with an IP address?

   A. IP ADDRESS 141.149.26.1 255.255.255.0

   B. IP ADDRESS 141.149.26.1

   C. IP ADDRESS 141.149.26.0 255.255.255

   D. IP ADDRESS 141.149.26.2

3. In order to set the maximum transmission unit (MTU) size of IP packets sent on interfaces, which of the following configuration commands would you use?

   A. IP *size*-MTU PACKET

   B. *bits* IP MTU SIZE

   C. IP MTU *bytes*

   D. IP MTU *packet size*

4. Which of the following commands removes the IP address from the command found in question 3 of this section?

   A. NO ADDRESS 141.149.26.1

   B. NO IP ADDRESS 141.149.26.1 255.255.254.0

   C. NO IP ADDRESS 141.149.26.0 255.255.255.0

   D. NO IP ADDRESS 141.149.26.1 255.255.255.0

5. In order to restart a disabled interface, which of the following commands must you use in the interface configuration mode?

A. SHUTDOWN

B. NO SHUTDOWN

C. START

D. ACTIVATE

6. To enable IP routing, which of the following commands do you use in global configuration mode?

A. IP ROUTE

B. IP ROUTING

C. IP ROUTE RIP

D. None of the above

7. In order to disable an active interface, which command must you use in the interface configuration mode?

A. SHUTDOWN INTERFACE

B. NO SHUTDOWN INTERFACE

C. SHUTDOWN

D. DEACTIVATE

8. Which of the following commands configures the HR server to be used for the name and address resolution?

A. IP NAME-SERVER HR 141.149.10.5

B. IP NAME-SERVER 141.149.10.5

C. IP NAME-SERVER HR 141.149.10.0

D. IP NAME-SERVERS 141.149.10.5

Configuring Static Routes

1. The Finance employees in Chicago need a static route to the 141.149.10.0
network to access the Finance server. Which command configures that
route in the Chicago router?

A. IP ROUTE 141.149.10.0 141.149.24.2

B. IP ROUTE 141.149.10.0 255.255.255.0 141.149.24.2

C. IP ROUTE 141.149.10.0 255.255.255.0 141.149.24.1

D. ROUTE 141.149.10.0 255.255.255.0 141.149.24.1

Use the Following Scenario to Answer Questions 2–5

Some Marketing employees have moved to Chicago and need static routes
to get to the 141.149.12.0 network to access the MRKT server. In order for
this to be feasible, a static route must first be built in the Boston router.

2. Which command builds the static route in the Boston router to the network
where the MRKT server resides?

A. IP ROUTE 141.149.12.4 255.255.255.0 141.149.25.2

B. IP ROUTE 141.149.12.0 255.255.255.0 141.149.25.2

C. ROUTE 141.149.12.4 255.255.255.0 141.149.25.L

D. IP ROUTE 141.149.12.0 255.255.255.0

3. Which of the following commands removes static routes in the Chicago
router?

A. NO IP ROUTE 141.149.10.0 141.149.24.2

B. NO IP ROUTE 141.149.10.0 255.255.255.0 141.149.24.1

C. NO ROUTE 141.149.10.0 255.255.255.0 141.149.24.2

D. NO IP ROUTE 141.149.10.0 255.255.255.0 141.149.24.2

4. To remove the static route in the Boston router, which of the following commands is used?

   A. NO ROUTE 141.149.12.0 255.255.255.0
   B. NO IP ROUTE 141.149.12.0 255.255.255.0 141.149.25.2
   C. NO IP ROUTE 141.149.12.0 255.255.255.0
   D. NO IP ROUTE 141.149.12.4 255.255.255.0 141.149.25.2

5. In essence, a static route does all the following, except what?

   A. It doesn't provide controlling security.
   B. It doesn't help minimize traffic across the network.
   C. It doesn't provide scalability.
   D. It doesn't provide more than one path to a destination.

Configuring Default Routes

1. Which of the following commands configures the New York router as the default gateway in the Washington router for traffic destined to the Public network when IP routing is disabled?

   A. DEFAULT ROUTE 192.121.12.0
   B. IP DEFAULT GATEWAY 141.149.26.1
   C. IP DEFAULT ADDRESS 141.149.26.1
   D. None of the above

2. Which of the following commands should be used to remove a default route to a specific network from a router entry?

   A. NO IP DEFAULT-NETWORK *IP-address of network*
   B. NO DEFAULT-NETWORK *IP-address of network*
   C. NO IP DEFAULT-GATEWAY *IP-address of router*
   D. A and C

3. Which command routes all traffic out a particular interface S1?

A. IP ROUTE 255.255.255.0 S1
B. IP ROUTE 255.255.255.255 S1
C. IP ROUTE 0.0.0.0 S1
D. IP ROUTE 0.0.0.255 S1

Configuring RIP Routing

1. Which is the command used to associate an attached network with the
RIP process?

A. NETWORK {*network number*}
B. NETWORK {*IP-address*}
C. ROUTER RIP NETWORK {*network number*}
D. None of the above

2. Which command turns off the RIP routing process?

A. ROUTER RIP OFF
B. RIP OFF
C. NO ROUTER RIP
D. RIP ROUTER OFF

3. To adjust routing timers for RIP, which of the following configuration
commands would you use?

A. TIMER BASIC *holddown*
B. TIMER BASIC *valid flush*
C. TIMER BASIC {*specify time*}
D. TIMER BASIC *update invalid holddown flush* {*sleeptime*}

Configuring IGRP Routing

1. Which of the following commands should be used to enable the IGRP
routing process?

A. ROUTER IGRP

B. ENABLE ROUTER IGRP

C. ROUTER IGRP 1

D. ENABLE ROUTER IGRP 1

E. None of the above

2. Which of the following commands associates a network with an IGRP routing process?

A. NETWORK *network-number*

B. NETWORK *IP-address*

C. NETWORK *IP-address address mask*

D. NETWORK *network-id*

3. Which of the following commands associates Washington's directly connected interfaces with the IGRP routing process?

A. NETWORK 141.149.26.0

B. NETWORK 141.149.26.1

C. NETWORK 141.149.25.1

D. NETWORK 141.149.25.0

E. NETWORK 141.149.0.0

4. Which of the following commands defines a neighboring router with which to exchange point-to-point routing information?

A. NEIGHBOR *network*

B. NEIGHBOR *IP-address*

C. NEIGHBOR *IP-address address mask*

D. None of the above

5. Which of the following commands configures the maximum hops for the IGRP routing protocol?

A. METRIC MAXIMUM-HOPS *limit*

B. MAXIMUM-HOPS *hops*

C. METRIC MAXIMUM-HOPS *hops*

D. None of the above

6. Which command is used to remove the NEIGHBOR command in the Boston router for information exchange? (Choose all that apply.)

A. NO NEIGHBOR 141.149.24.0

B. NO NEIGHBOR 141.149.25.0

C. NO NEIGHBOR 141.149.25.2

D. NO NEIGHBOR 141.149.24.1

IP Host Tables

1. Which of the following commands assigns the MRKT server a host name and an IP address?

A. IP HOST 141.149.12.4

B. IP MRKT 141.149.12.4

C. IP HOST MRKT 141.149.12.4

D. IP HOSTS MRKT 141.149.12.4

E. None of the above

2. If a TCP port number is not specified when using the IP host configuration command, which of the following is the default?

A. FTP (port 21)

B. Telnet (port 23)

C. Telnet (port 33)

D. Telnet (port 21)

3. Which of the following commands removes the host name in question 1?

A. NO IP MRKT 141.149.12.1

B. NO IP MRKT HOST 141.149.12.0

C. NO IP HOST MRKT 141.149.12.4

D. None of the above

4. If a host is configured to connect to TCP port 21, which command changes the TCP port back to its default? (Choose all that apply.)

A. IP HOST MRKT 23 141.149.12.4

B. IP HOST MRKT 141.149.12.4

C. IP HOSTS MRKT 23 141.149.12.4

D. None of the above

5. Which is the configuration command that configures multiple IP addresses for a host? (Choose all that apply.)

A. IP HOST *name address1 address2 address3*

B. HOST ADDRESSES 1 2 3

C. IP HOST NAME *address1 address2 ...address^{n+1}*

D. None of the above

DNS and DHCP Configuration

1. To enable the IP DNS-based host name to address translation, which of the following configuration commands would you use?

A. IP DOMAIN-LOOKUP

B. DOMAIN-LOOKUP ENABLE

C. ENABLE IP DOMAIN-LOOKUP

D. NO IP DOMAIN-LOOKUP

2. Which of the following configuration commands specifies a list of default domains to use?

A. IP DOMAIN-LIST *name*

B. DOMAIN-LIST IP *name*

C. IP *name* DOMAIN-LIST

D. None of the above

3. Which of the following configuration commands configures the HR server as a name server and configures its location for lookups?

A. NAME-SERVER HR

B. IP NAME-SERVER 141.149.10.5

C. NAME-SERVER 141.149.10.5

D. NAME-SERVER IP 141.149.10.5

4. Which configuration command configures the R&D server as the destination address used for forwarding User Datagram Protocol (UDP) broadcasts?

A. IP HELPER-SERVER R&D

B. IP HELPER-ADDRESS 141.149.12.5

C. HELPER-ADDRESS 141.149.12.5

D. IP HELPER-SERVER 141.149.12.5

5. Which of the following configuration commands tells the Washington router what protocols and ports to forward when forwarding broadcast packets?

A. IP FORWARD-PROTOCOLS TCP

B. IP FORWARD-PROTOCOLS UDP

C. IP FORWARD-PROTOCOL TCP

D. IP FORWARD-PROTOCOL UDP

6. Which of the following configuration commands removes the IP HELPER-ADDRESS entry from the interface where it was applied?

A. NO IP-HELPER *server-name*

B. NO IP *address*

C. NO IP HELPER-ADDRESS *address*

D. NO IP HELPER-ADDRESS *server-name*

Secondary Addressing

1. Which of the following commands is used to configure a secondary IP address?

A. IP ADDRESS SECONDARY

B. IP ADDRESS *IP-address mask* SECONDARY

C. IP ADDRESS SECONDARY *IP-address mask*

D. None of the above

2. You are in the interface configuration mode of Boston's interface E2. Which command is used to create a secondary IP address of 151.140.44.2/24?

A. IP ADDRESS 151.140.44.2/24

B. IP ADDRESS 151.140.44.2 SECONDARY

C. IP ADDRESS 151.140.44.2 255.255.255.0

D. IP ADDRESS 151.140.44.2 255.255.255.0 SECONDARY

3. Which command removes the secondary IP address from the Boston interface E2?

A. NO IP ADDRESS 151.140.44.2/24

B. NO IP ADDRESS 151.140.44.2 SECONDARY

C. NO IP ADDRESS 151.140.44.2 255.255.255.0 SECONDARY

D. None of the above

4. Which command removes the secondary IP address from the Washington interface E1?

A. NO IP ADDRESS 141.151.12.1 255.255.255.0 SECONDARY

B. NO IP ADDRESS 141.151.12.1 SECONDARY

C. NO IP ADDRESS 141.151.12.1 255.255.254.0 SECONDARY

D. NO IP ADDRESS 141.151.12.0 255.255.255.0 SECONDARY

QUESTIONS AND ANSWERS

I entered a static route that I want to use as a last resort. We are using OSPF, but currently my route takes precedence over OSPF entries. How do I change the configuration?	Change the administrative distance for your static route to any number above 110, which is OSPF's default.
I am running RIP across a 64 Kbps WAN link. The updates are taking up too much bandwidth. What should I do?	Change the update period to a slower amount than the default 30 seconds.
How do I get my workstations to receive their IP addresses via DHCP on a different subnet than the DHCP server?	On the router that connects the two network segments, enter an IP helper address and point it to the DHCP server.
We are using Internet-assigned IPs and are running low on the ones left in our range. We are adding another remote site, and we can't afford to waste an entire subnet. What should we do?	Use IP unnumbered on the two ends of the point-to-point link.
We just added 26 more users on a segment to bring the total to 262 hosts. Am I going to have to add another router to accommodate the new people?	No. Use a secondary IP address on the interfaces connecting each end of the segment.

IP Configuration
Answers

Q & *A*

The answers to the questions are in boldface, followed by a brief explanation. Some of the explanations detail the logic you should use to choose the correct answer, while others give factual reasons why the answer is correct. If you miss several questions on a similar topic, you should review the corresponding section in the *CCNA Cisco Certified Network Associate Study Guide*, Second Edition (Osborne/McGraw-Hill, 1999) before taking the CCNA Certification test.

Refer to the following illustration as you review answers to scenario questions in this chapter.

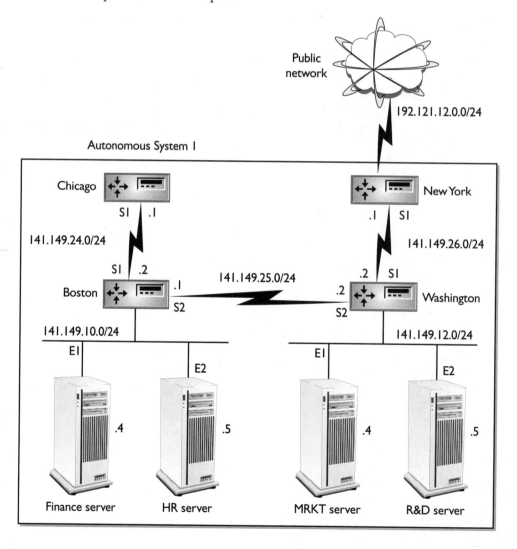

IP Configuration Commands

1. **A, B.** INTERFACE ETHERNET1 and INT E1. In order to configure any router interface you must be in that particular interface. However, the IOS recognizes the command without requiring you to type the command in its entirety. You get the same results by typing **int e1** or **interface ethernet1**. If you are unsure of the correct or proper use of the command, press the TAB key to fill out the rest of the command.

2. **A.** IP ADDRESS 141.149.26.1 255.255.255.0. In Cisco's implementation, the proper way to configure an interface is with both the IP address and the address mask of that interface. Generally, the IP address and address mask will be solely managed by network administrators. In the illustration shown at the beginning of the chapter, the first and second hosts (.1 and .2) are reserved for the WAN interfaces, although other examples you come across may differ. As noted earlier, all interfaces must be configured with both an IP address and address mask (answers B and D). Generally, the network number is not used to configure an interface as in answer C.

3. **C.** IP MTU *bytes*. This command is used within the interface configuration mode to ensure that the command is applied to the desired interface. If an IP packet exceeds the MTU set for the router's interface, the router fragments it. All devices on a physical medium must have the same protocol MTU in order to operate. In this implementation, the word bytes refers to MTU in bytes. Sometimes a router is unable to forward a datagram because it requires fragmentation (the packet is larger than the MTU you set for the interface with the IP MTU command), but the Don't Fragment (DF) bit is set. The router sends a message to the sending host, alerting it to the problem. The host has to fragment packets for the destination so that they fit the smallest packet size of all the links along the path. All interfaces have default MTU packet size. You can adjust the IP MTU size so that if an IP packet exceeds the MTU set for a router's interface, the router fragments it.

4. **D.** NO IP ADDRESS 141.149.26.1 255.255.255.0. Remember that both the IP address and address mask are needed to add and remove the IP address for router interfaces. The other answers are either incomplete or incorrect. In answer B, the mask indicates a 23-bit mask (one bit short of the 24-bit used).

5. **B.** NO SHUTDOWN. Although it's not an IP configuration command, it is important to understand its purpose in configuring routers. After addressing the interface, this command can be used in the interface configuration mode to initialize or start the disable interface. The NO SHUTDOWN command enables all functionality of that specified interface. This command also marks the interface as available. To check whether an interface is enabled, use the EXEC command, SHOW INTERFACES. An interface that has been enabled is marked *up* (given that the physical-layer requirements are satisfied). The SHUTDOWN command is used to disabled a working interface. The other two choices (answers C and D) are not recognized by the Cisco IOS.

6. **B.** IP ROUTING. In order to enable IP routing, you must use the command in its proper format, IP ROUTING. Cisco ships every router with IP routing automatically enabled. Enabling IP routing provides a mechanism for IP datagrams to reach their destination. Without IP routing enabled, the IOS can provide three methods by which the router can learn about routes to other networks: Proxy Address Resolution Protocol (ARP), router discovery mechanisms, or default gateway. If the system is running bridging software, the NO IP ROUTING command turns off IP routing when setting up a system to bridge instead of to route IP packets. The other answers are incomplete or incorrect.

7. **C.** SHUTDOWN. This command disables all functions on the specified interface. This command also marks the interface as unavailable. To check whether an interface is disabled, use the EXEC command, SHOW INTERFACES. An interface that has been shut down is shown as administratively *down* in the display from this command. The other commands are incorrect. The DEACTIVATE command is not recognized by Cisco's IOS. When disabling an interface, you are disabling the interface from the interface configuration mode. Therefore, you may need to specify an interface when issuing the command.

8. **B**. IP NAME-SERVER 141.149.10.5. This specifies the HR server as the name server by associating the host with an IP address. In this example, the HR server has an IP address of 141.149.10.5. You can specify multiple name servers by simply entering other IP addresses sequentially after the first entry. The name server is used for name and address resolution. The other answers are incorrect. In answer A, there is no need to specify both host and IP address; only the IP address is needed to specify the name server. Answer C functions similarly; however, it uses the actual network address instead of the host address. Answer D uses an incorrect command format.

Configuring Static Routes

1. **B**. IP ROUTE 141.149.10.0 255.255.255.0 141.149.24.2. In this scenario, a static route is needed for users in Chicago to access a resource behind the Boston net. This implementation implies that the Chicago net has no direct route to the Boston net. The networks (141.149.10.0) behind the Boston net are not able to send and receive information from the Chicago router. Issuing a static route means having to add a route to a specific network manually—one that may be the only route to that particular network. Using static routes often reduces the overhead associated with route and distance calculations performed by the router. Static routes are always known, which helps reduce the number of places where faults can lie. The other answers are either incomplete or incorrect. The proper format for this command is specification of the IP address and address mask of the destination network and the IP address of the interface to that network. Answer A is a legal command; however, it does not specify the mask of the destination network. Without referencing a mask, the router assumes the entire Class B network is out the serial port. There is only one Class B used in the illustration at the beginning of the chapter. The mask is needed in

case there is a particular subnet of the Class B in question. Answer C specifies the incorrect IP address of the interface. Answer D specifies the wrong IP address interface and an incomplete command.

2. **B.** IP ROUTE 141.149.12.0 255.255.255.0 141.149.25.2. In this scenario a static route is needed for users in Chicago to access a resource behind the Washington net. This implementation implies that the Chicago net has no direct route to the Washington net. The network (141.149.12.0) behind the Washington net is not being propagated to the Chicago router. Issuing a static route requires manually adding a route to a specific network, which is essentially the only route to that particular network. Using static routes often reduces the overhead associated with route and distance calculations performed by the router. Static routes are always known, which helps reduce the number of places where faults can lie. The other answers are either incomplete or incorrect. The proper format for this command is to specify the IP address and address mask of the destination network and the IP address of the interface to that network. Answers A and C do not specify the correct destination network. Answer D does not specify the IP address of the interface to the destination network.

3. **D.** NO IP ROUTE 141.149.10.0 255.255.255.0 141.149.24.2. Adding NO before the command that adds a static route simply removes the static route entry in the router. In answer A, the address mask of the destination network is needed. In answer B, the interface is not correct and answer C has no reference to IP.

4. **B.** NO IP ROUTE 141.149.12.0 255.255.255.0 141.149.25.2. Adding NO before the command that adds a static route simply removes the static route entry in the router. In answer A, the interface to the destination network is needed in addition to adding IP to the command. In answer C, the interface to the destination network is needed. In answer D, there is no reference to the destination network. When configuring static routes, you must specify the network and not the actual host.

5. **C.** It doesn't provide scalability. Although this is not a configuration command, it is important to reemphasize the correct implementation of static routes and know what it can buy you if implemented correctly. One of the drawbacks (if you want to call it that) to static routing is that it lacks scalability. Generally, static routes are easy to implement, given that you are working with a handful of network segments and routers. However, the more network segments and routers you have, the more overhead is involved to enter routes. With static routes, you have more control over the security mechanism for that route or interface to a particular network.

Configuring Default Routes

1. **B.** IP DEFAULT GATEWAY 141.149.26.1. In this scenario, the Washington router has an entry in its configuration that denotes the default gateway with an IP address of 141.149.26.1, which is the address of the next-hop interface from the Washington router. Since IP is disabled, information leaving the Washington net destined for the Public net needs a way to send messages to the particular destination. In Cisco's implementation, the default gateway should point to the IP address of the interface on a router that is directly connected to the router where a default gateway is configured; in this case, the New York and Washington routers, respectively. The other answers are either incomplete or incorrect. Answer A is missing the IP, in addition to specifying the wrong IP address. The network should be specified and not the interface. Answer C uses incorrect format.

2. **A.** NO IP DEFAULT-NETWORK *IP-address of network*. This command simply removes the default route entry in the router for a route to the Public net. In answer B, IP needs to be referenced. In answer C, the gateway command is used instead of the network.

3. **C.** IP ROUTE 0.0.0.0 S1. Using this command specifies that all traffic will be forwarded out of interface S1. The router interface serves as a default gateway router. Typically, this is used when forwarding outbound traffic to the Internet or some other Public network by simply defaulting all traffic out its interface that is connected directly to the outside world. Be careful configuring this entry, you might want to be discreet as to where information is sent on your local nets and WAN interfaces. The other answers are either incorrect or using invalid command format. In answers A and B, mask addresses are used instead of a network number. In answer D, an inverse mask is used, which is incorrect for this implementation.

Configuring RIP Routing

1. A. NETWORK {*network number*}. The command associates a list of networks with a RIP routing process. This is needed in order for routers to know what routes to include in their routing tables and updates. Each entry you specify notifies the router that you want updates and routes to specific networks. Without the proper network entries defined, packets destined for network *x.x.x.x* will not reach their destination because the router may not know where and how to forward the packets, eventually forwarding packets whatever way it can. In most instances, it would certainly be necessary to define the networks to which you are directly attached. In answer B, the network number should be used instead of a specific IP address. In answer C, the command is incorrect, but the network should be referenced in this command.

2. C. NO ROUTER RIP. To disable the RIP process associated with routing you simply insert a NO at the beginning of the ROUTER RIP command. This defaults to IP routing which is enabled when routers are shipped, or to whatever routing mechanism you have defined in your router. If networks are defined for the RIP process, the entries are removed. The other answers are either incomplete or incorrect. The IOS of the router does not recognize OFF in its configuration commands. Usually NO is reserved for the purpose of turning off or disabling a particular process that has been defined in the router.

3. **D.** TIMER BASIC *update invalid holddown flush* {*sleeptime*}. Routing protocols use several timers that determine such variables as the frequency of routing updates, the length of time before a route becomes invalid, and other parameters. You can adjust these timers to tune routing protocol performance to what you desire by making the following adjustments:

- The rate (time in seconds between updates) at which routing updates are sent.

- The interval of time (in seconds) after which a route is declared invalid.

- The interval (in seconds) during which routing information regarding better paths is accepted, as the worse paths are suppressed.

- The amount of time (in seconds) that must pass before a route is removed from the routing table. It also is possible to tune the IP routing support in the software to enable faster convergence of the various IP routing algorithms, and, hence, quicker fallback to redundant routers. The total effect is to minimize disruptions to end users of the network in situations where quick recovery is essential.

Configuring IGRP Routing

1. **C.** ROUTER IGRP 1. In IGRP implementation you must use a process-ID for the IGRP routing process. It is not necessary to have a registered autonomous system number to use IGRP. If you do not have a registered number, you are free to create your own. Cisco recommends that if you do have a registered number, you use it to identify the IGRP process. IGRP sends updates to the interfaces in the specified networks. If an interface's network is not specified, it is not advertised in any IGRP update. The other answers are incorrect. In answer A, the process-ID is omitted. The enable command not recognized in the global configuration mode for this particular process.

2. **A.** NETWORK *network-number*. The command associates a particular Class network with an IGRP routing process. This is needed in order for routers to know what routes to include in their routing tables and updates. Each network entry you specify notifies the router that you want updates and routes to specific networks. If you are using a Class A network you would refer to the network as *x*.0.0.0, Class B *x.x*.0.0 and Class C *x.x.x*.0 (where *x* represents the network number of the IP address). In answer B, the network number should be used instead of a specific IP address. In answer C, the command is incorrect. There is no need to refer to any address mask, because you are using network numbers instead of IP addresses. Answer D, network-ID, should be replaced with network number for correct use of this command.

3. **E. NETWORK 141.149.0.0.** In this scenario, specify the network portion of the Class B (141.149.0.0) to associate the IGRP routing process. This provides routes to the entire network (Boston, New York, and Chicago). If this entry is in each router with a routing associated with it, the entire network is able to exchange routing information and updates.

Defining these networks allows adjacent routers to share routing information about directly connected interfaces and routes to other nodes on the network. A good rule of thumb is to become familiar with each routing protocol and associated configuration commands, and the correct implementation of each in preparation for the CCNA examination. The other answers are either incorrect or incomplete. The network portion of the Class address must be used to associate the corresponding routing process. Simply using the subnet or interface of the router does not properly configure and define the IGRP routing process.

4. **B. NEIGHBOR *IP-address*.** This command is used so that IGRP routing updates can reach nonbroadcast networks, since IGRP is a broadcast protocol. A nonbroadcast network is a network such as classic IP over ATM. Routers within a nonbroadcast network may not dynamically discover their neighbors, since there is no mechanism to broadcast their information across the network. The neighbor command is helpful and allows broadcasting in a nonbroadcast network. Configuring Cisco IOS permits this exchange of routing information to any nonbroadcast network associated with the IGRP

process. This command defines a neighboring router with which to exchange routing information. When using configuration commands, it is important to know the correct format of the command so that the IOS is configured properly.

5. **C.** METRIC MAXIMUM-HOPS *hops.* This command is used to have the IP routing software advertise as unreachable those routes with a hop count higher than is specified by the command. It specifies the maximum diameter to the IGRP network. The *hops* refers to the maximum hop count. The default value is 100 hops, and the maximum number of hops that can be defined is 255.

6. **C, D.** NO NEIGHBOR 141.149.25.2 and NO NEIGHBOR 141.149.24.1. To remove the entry from the router, simply use the NO at the beginning of the command. This does not allow IGRP routing updates to reach nonbroadcast networks.

IP Host Tables

1. **C.** IP HOST MRKT 141.149.12.4. An extension of the IP host command is to associate an IP address with the name of the host. In this scenario, the MRKT server is the host name with an IP address of 141.149.12.4. You can specify any associated IP addresses. You can bind up to eight addresses to a host name. The other answers are incorrect with invalid command format.

2. **B.** Telnet (port 23). By default, TCP port 23 is used in conjunction with the EXEC connect. The other answers are incorrect. The proper TCP port assignment for Telnet is port 23.

3. **C.** NO IP HOST MRKT 141.149.12.4. In order to remove the name-to-address mapping for IP host configuring, add NO to the beginning of the command. Answer A has the wrong IP address and is

missing the HOST portion of the command. Answer B also has the incorrect IP address. When specifying a particular host, you cannot use the network number for name-to-address mapping. The correct implementation is to use the IP addresses other than the ones reserved for network numbers, router ports and broadcast addresses.

4. **A, B.** IP HOST MRKT 23 141.149.12.4 and IP HOST MRKT 141.149.12.4. As mentioned earlier, the default TCP port is 23. If you are changing a particular IP host entry from TCP port 21 without specifying a TCP port, the IOS then defaults to TCP port 23, Telnet. In this example, either specify the default port 23 or simply enter the command with reference to a TCP port, and the configuration will be changed back to its default TCP port assignment of port 23. In answer C, the word host is misspelled.

5. **A, C.** IP HOST *name address1 address2 address3* and IP HOST NAME *address1 address2 ...address^{n+1}*. With the IP HOST command you can specify additional IP addresses for a host (this is optional). Up to eight addresses can be bound to a host name. In answer B, the command is formatted incorrectly. There should be a reference to the IP address of the host. The $n+1$ refers to some integer, where n is less than, or equal to, 7.

DNS and DHCP Configuration

1. **A.** IP DOMAIN-LOOKUP. In order to use host name-to-address translation you must first enable the configuration command, thus providing DNS capability. Once the command has been enabled, the IOS is configured to do address and host translation. The IOS allows DNS configuration, providing the capability to dynamically look up host name-to-address mapping. This is used for connectivity with devices in networks where you don't control the name assignments. This command feature is generally enabled by default. Enable is not used in the global configuration mode to configure router DNS features. The NO IP DOMAIN-LOOKUP simply disables the DNS feature.

2. A. IP DOMAIN-LIST *name*. This command specifies a list of default domains that satisfy a domain name request. The domain name specified is appended to the host name before being added to the host table. A domain name defines a default domain name that the router uses to complete unqualified host names, while a domain list defines a list of default domain names to complete unqualified host names. First tell the IOS to define the domain list and then name the list, where *name* refers to the domain name.

3. B. IP NAME-SERVER 141.149.10.5. In order to enable DNS lookups, you must first start by specifying the location of the name server doing the lookups. If one is not specified, the router makes a broadcast DNS request. When you specify the name servers, you are actually minimizing the amount of broadcast traffic over the network. With this command you can add up to six ($n+1$, where n is less than or equal to 5) name servers. Answer A refers to a particular host and not an IP address. The other answers are incomplete commands, formatted incorrectly.

4. B. IP HELPER-ADDRESS 141.149.12.5. The host address associated with 141.149.12.5 is the R&D host. The IP HELPER command (used at the interface-level command mode) has the IOS forward UDP broadcast, including Bootstrap Protocol (BOOTP) to the specified host address. By default the router does not forward any broadcast-based traffic. To forward a UDP broadcast packet, specify it with the IP HELPER command. An IP HELPER statement forwards selected protocols received on an interface to the specified destination (host or IP address). Other protocols can be forwarded by using the IP FORWARD-PROTOCOL configuration command. The other answers are invalid command formats.

5. D. IP FORWARD-PROTOCOL UDP. This command specifies which protocols and ports the router forwards when forwarding broadcast packets. Dynamic Host Configuration Protocol (DHCP) uses UDP for its transport mechanism, and uses BOOTP protocol for operation purposes. BOOTP encapsulates DHCP information and then is transported over the network by UDP. The IP FORWARD-PROTOCOL command is used in the ·

example to specify forwarding of UDP only. When an IP helper address statement is invoked, UDP packets from certain ports are forwarded by default. Listed below are some of the default UDP ports.

■ TFTP ⇒ port 69

■ DNS ⇒ port 53

■ Time Service ⇒ port 37

■ BOOTP ⇒ port 67 and 68

■ TACACS ⇒ port 49

6. **C.** NO IP HELPER-ADDRESS *address*. This command removes the IP helper address, thus prohibiting forwarding of UDP and BOOTP broadcast packets. The formats of the other answers are invalid. This command should be placed on the interface where it hears broadcast requests from the client. When the broadcast is forwarded, the router changes it to the address specified in the IP HELPER command.

Secondary Addressing

1. **B.** IP ADDRESS *IP-address mask* SECONDARY. Cisco IOS uses secondary IP addressing to support secondary addresses to a single interface. This entire Class B address range is consumed, but you need to add additional users with their own unique IP address. To avoid adding additional internetworking devices such as routers, you can assign secondary IP addresses to allow two logical subnets across the same physical interface. Use the same command format that configures a primary address on an interface and add SECONDARY at the end of the configuration command.

2. **D.** IP ADDRESS 151.140.44.2 255.255.255.0 SECONDARY. Keep in mind that each router that is attached to the same physical subnet as the one that has the secondary address also needs a secondary address on that

same subnet to ensure that each packet can reach its destination. So, it makes sense to implement the scheme in each router attached to the same physical interface in order to provide the reliability and scalability needed for routing across the network. The formats of the other answers are invalid. Use the same command for creating the primary IP address of an interface and add SECONDARY at the end of the configuration command.

3. **C.** NO IP ADDRESS 151.140.44.2 255.255.255.0 SECONDARY. This command removes the secondary IP address from the router. The formats of the other answers are invalid. The same command format used to remove a primary IP address should be used, but SECONDARY should be added at the end of the command.

4. **A.** NO IP ADDRESS 141.151.12.1 255.255.255.0 SECONDARY. This command removes the secondary IP address from the router. The formats of the other answers are invalid. The same command format used to remove a primary IP address should be used, but add SECONDARY at the end of the command.

Part 7

Configuring
Novell IPX

Novell IPX
Practice
Questions

Q

&

A

NetWare is a network operating system offered by Novell. It provides file and printing services as well as application, messaging and other distributed network services. NetWare uses the IPX protocol stack, which includes protocols for the upper-five OSI reference model layers (network, transport, session, presentation, and application). Because of this, IPX can run transparently over nearly any data-link and physical protocol-layer specifications.

IPX Protocol Stack

1. Which of the following transport-layer protocols are correctly matched with their functions? (Choose all that apply.)

   A. SPX provides connection-oriented, reliable delivery services.
   B. IPX provides connectionless, unreliable datagram service.
   C. NetBIOS emulation enables NetBIOS applications over IPX.
   D. SAP advertises services for servers and routers.

2. Which of the following protocols from the IPX protocol stack are matched to their correct OSI reference model layer? (Choose all that apply.)

   A. RIP, transport layer
   B. SPX, transport layer
   C. NCP, physical layer
   D. SAP, network layer
   E. NLSP, network layer

3. If an IPX server uses a link-state algorithm to update the routing table, which of the following is the most likely routing table update protocol used?

A. NLSP

B. RIP

C. SAP

D. IPX

4. Which of the following session-layer protocols are correctly matched with their functions?

A. NLSP dynamically updates routing tables using a link-state algorithm.

B. SAP advertises router and server services.

C. NetBIOS emulation provides addressing and datagram services.

D. SPX creates sessions by exchanging packets.

5. Which of the following is the protocol that provides the network and node address?

A. SAP

B. SPX

C. NCP

D. IPX

IPX Datagram

Use the Following Scenario to Answer Questions 1–11

Desert Dealers, Inc., is a car dealership that has three lots and a main office. As shown in the following illustration, there are 50 employees at the two smaller lots, 75 employees at the largest lot, and 30 employees at the main office.

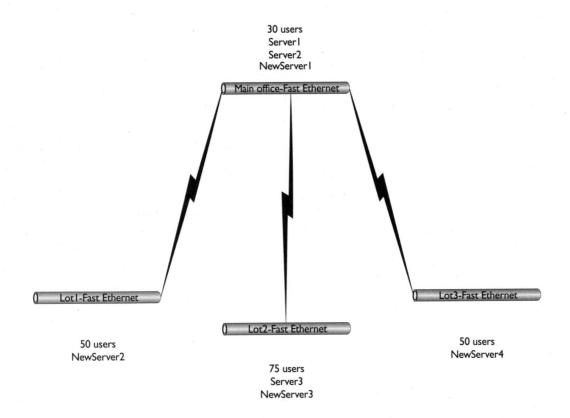

30 users
Server1
Server2
NewServer1

Main office-Fast Ethernet

Lot1-Fast Ethernet

Lot3-Fast Ethernet

Lot2-Fast Ethernet

50 users
NewServer2

50 users
NewServer4

75 users
Server3
NewServer3

Desert Dealers, Inc., has a NetWare network at the main office and one at its largest car dealership. The company has decided to connect all the lots to the main office, install four additional servers, and provide laptops and PCs running Windows 98 to all its employees. Each local network will be upgraded to Fast Ethernet (100BaseT) over Cat5 cabling.

1. Before installing any of the routers and switches, a consultant runs a sniffer on the network at the main office. The sniffer picks up IPX datagrams traversing the single network segment. Which of the following is the value of the transport control portion of any of those IPX datagrams?

   A. 0

   B. 1

   C. 8

   D. 16

2. Prior to installing any routers, the consultant discovers the following information about existing servers:

Location	Server	Network Address	Node Address	Internal Network
Main office	Server1	58fc	0000.8045.1a54	1a00
Main office	Server2	58fc	0100.885a.2cfe	2a00
Lot2	Server3	1a00	23a0.09bc.001d	58fc

From this information, what must be reconfigured before the routers are installed? (Choose all that apply.)

A. Server names

B. The network address of Server3

C. The node address of Server2

D. The internal network address of Server3

3. Desert Dealers, Inc., has suggested the configuration shown here for the old and new servers:

Location	Server	Network	Node Address	Internal Network
Main office	Server1	58fc	0000.8045.1a54	1a00
Main office	Server2	58fc	0100.885a.2cfe	2a00
Main office	NewServer1	58fc	0000.9a8b.333c	3a00
Lot1	NewServer2	58fd	0101.20a8.2545	1a00
Lot2	Server3	58fe	23a0.09bc.001d	1a00
Lot2	NewServer3	58fe	2422.08ac.5577	2a00
Lot3	NewServer4	58ff	003a.9946.bbc3	1a00

Which addresses must be changed in order for this scheme to work correctly?

A. The node address of Server2

B. The node address of NewServer2

C. The network addresses of Server2, NewServer1, and NewServer3

D. The internal network addresses of NewServer2, Server3, NewServer3, and NewServer4

4. Desert Dealers, Inc., uses a unique 10-digit identifier for the location of each office and lot, which ends with the letter *a*. The company would like to use the 10-digit identifier appended with two digits (to ensure uniqueness for internal addresses) as the network address scheme for their network. An example address would be 235500067a01. How well will this work?

A. It will work well, since it provides unique addresses already used by the company.

B. It will not provide unique addresses.

C. It will not be applicable, since the address length is too long.

D. It will cause the node address to be truncated.

5. The network administrator at the main office has reviewed the sniffer's results and asked which part of the address 58fc.0000.8045.0afc.0004 is the node address. Choose the correct answer.

A. 58fc.0000.8045

B. 0000.8045.0afc

C. 8045.0afc.0004

D. None of the above

6. Desert Dealers, Inc., is preparing to document its network. The company has changed its scheme to use repeating numbers for each of the network addresses and repeating letters for each of the server internal network addresses, including all future networks and servers. An example of a network address is 88888888, and an example of an internal network address is aaaaaaaa. What problems might be encountered with this scheme? (Choose all that apply.)

A. The network address that uses all zeroes is invalid.

B. The internal network address that uses all Fs is invalid.

C. The scheme limits the number of servers and networks that can be installed.

D. The network address using all ones is invalid.

7. When the consultant sniffed the main office network, the sniffer picked up the following additional address: 1a00.0000.0000.0001.0004. The network administrator asks what this address is. Choose the correct answer.

A. The address is an error that has been traversing the network.

B. The address is a retransmission due to an error.

C. The address is for a server's internal network.

D. The address is a hello packet to announce a server's presence.

8. The consultant suggested the configuration shown here:

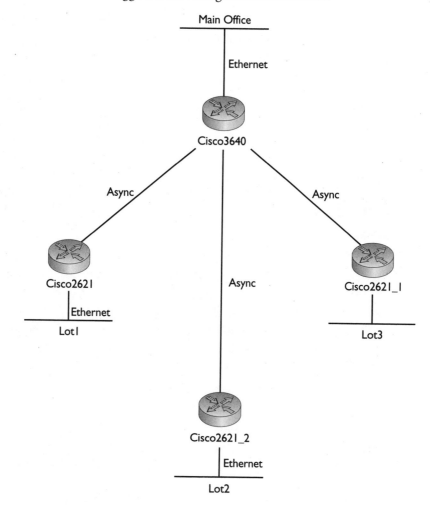

The network numbers that Desert Dealers, Inc., suggested are as follows:

- Main office, 58fc
- Lot1, 58fd
- Lot2, 58fe
- Lot3, 58ff

Are the network numbers suggested by Desert Dealers, Inc., sufficient if the routers will be using only IPX?

A. Yes, because each network has its own network number

B. Yes, as long as the internal network numbers of the servers are unique and different from those on this list

C. No, because the network numbers are the wrong format

D. No, because the network numbers for the async connections are not listed

9. Desert Dealers, Inc., asks for a description of the data transmission from a node (address 8045.1111.1234) at Lot1 (network address 58fd) to a node (address 0000.1234.5888) at the main office (network address 58fc) if the async network address is a1. What is the correct order of the following steps?

A. Data is received by the router's async interface a1.0000.c001.1c33 from a1.0000.ab88.234c.

B. 58fc.0000.1234.5888 examines the data and accepts the packet.

C. Data is sent from 58fd.8045.1111.1234 and received by the router.

D. The router sends the data through Ethernet interface 58fc.0000.c002.1c33.

E. The router examines the packet, determines that it is meant for a different network, and sends it out through interface a1.0000.ab88.234c.

F. The router examines the packet, determines that it is meant for directly connected network 58fc.

10. How many unique network and internal network addresses would Desert Dealers, Inc., require if the following is their final configuration?

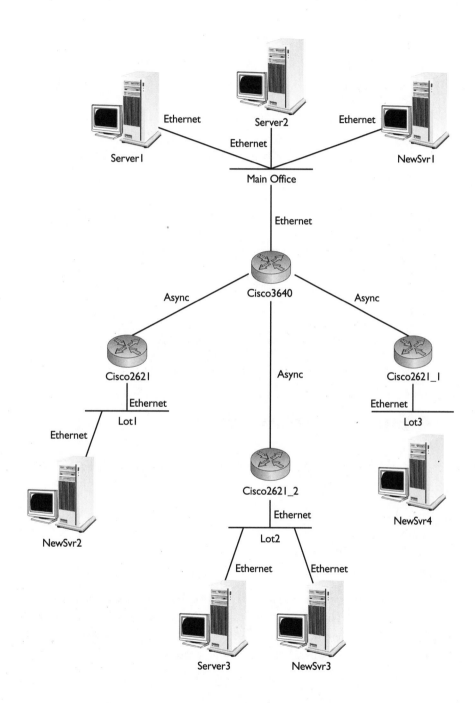

Ethernet

Server2

Ethernet

Ethernet

Server1

NewSvr1

Main Office

Ethernet

Cisco3640

Async

Async

Async

Cisco2621

Cisco2621_1

Ethernet

Ethernet

Lot1

Lot3

Ethernet

Cisco2621_2

NewSvr2

Ethernet

NewSvr4

Lot2

Ethernet

Ethernet

Server3

NewSvr3

A. 10

B. 11

C. 14

D. 18

11. The consultant provides a list of network and internal network numbers. Which is the list he provided if he provided a valid scheme?

A. Ethernet networks e01, e02, e03, e04
   Async networks a01, a02, a03
   Internal networks b01, b02, b03, b04, b05, b06, b07

B. Ethernet networks Ethernet 1, e2, e3
   Async networks a1, a2, a3, a4
   Internal networks i1, i2, i3, i4, i5, i6, i7

C. Ethernet networks e101, e201, e301, e401
   Async networks e102, e202, e302
   Internal networks e103, e104, e105, e202, e203, e303, e404

D. Ethernet networks 58fc, 58fd, 58fe, 58ff
   Async networks 58fa, 58fb, 58fc
   Internal networks 58ea, 58eb, 58ec, 58ed, 58ee, 58ef

IPX Encapsulation Types

1. Which of the following is an encapsulation offered by Cisco for IPX?

A. Arpa

B. DARPA

C. Ethernet

D. IEEE

2. Joe wants to connect two networks with a router that has two Ethernet interfaces. Each network has a NetWare server, one running an Ethernet_II frame type and one running an Ethernet_802.3 frame type. How many network numbers must be used on the network?

A. 1

B. 2

C. 3

D. 4

3. Which Cisco encapsulations are needed on a router connected to a network segment that has a NetWare server running Token_Ring_SNAP and another segment with a NetWare server running Ethernet_II and Ethernet_SNAP? (Choose all that apply.)

A. SNAP

B. Novell-Ether

C. SAP

D. Arpa

4. Network A has two NetWare servers. Svr1 is running Ethernet_802.3, and Svr2 is running Ethernet_802.2. Network B has one NetWare server, Svr3, running Ethernet_802.3. Network C has a client running both Ethernet_802.3 and Ethernet_802.2. Network D has a server, Svr4, running both Ethernet_802.3 and Ethernet_II. All networks are directly connected to interfaces on the router. The encapsulation running on the Cisco router is SAP on all interfaces. Which of the servers will the client be able to contact?

A. Svr1

B. Svr2

C. Svr3

D. Svr4

5. A NetWare server, Svr1, is running Ethernet_802.3 and Ethernet_II frame types. It is connected to LAN1, which is also attached to Router1, which is running Arpa and Novell-Ether encapsulation on its Ethernet 0 interface. Router1 is also attached to LAN2 via the Ethernet 1 interface. Router1 is running SAP and Novell-Ether on the Ethernet 1 interface. Svr2 is attached to LAN2 and runs Ethernet_802.2 and Ethernet_802.3 frame types. Choose the network numbers that can be assigned to LAN1 and LAN2.

A. LAN1: e200 (using Arpa), e230 (using Novell-Ether)
   LAN2: e200 (using Arpa), e230 (using Novell-Ether), e220 (using SAP)
B. LAN1: e200 (using Arpa), e230 (using Novell-Ether)
   LAN2: e220 (using SAP), e230 (using Novell-Ether)
C. LAN1: e200 (using Arpa), e230 (using Novell-Ether)
   LAN2: e221 (using SAP), e231 (using Novell-Ether)
D. LAN1: e200 (using Novell-Ether and Arpa)
   LAN2: e300 (using Novell-Ether and SAP)

6. A client on LAN1 uses frame-type Ethernet_802.2. The NetWare server on LAN2 is using frame-type Ethernet_II. LAN1 is connected to Router 1 via interface Ethernet 0. LAN2 is connected to Router 1 via interface Ethernet 1. Which encapsulations must be run on Ethernet 1 and Ethernet 0 in order for the client on LAN1 to communicate with the NetWare server on LAN2?

A. Ethernet 0, SAP; Ethernet 1, Arpa
B. Ethernet 0, SAP and Arpa; Ethernet 1, SAP and Arpa
C. Ethernet 0, Novell-Ether; Ethernet 1, Arpa
D. Ethernet 0, Novell-Ether and Arpa; Ethernet 1, Novell-Ether and Arpa

SAP and RIP

1. Which three of the following are the types of defined SAP packets?

A. Hello updates
B. Periodic updates
C. Service queries
D. Service responses

2. A client workstation is running on LAN1, which is connected to the Ethernet 0 interface of Router 1. Router 1's Ethernet 1 interface is connected to LAN2, a backbone network containing all the servers on a

network. What allows a client to contact a NetWare server if Get Nearest Server (GNS) queries are broadcasts and not forwarded to all networks?

A. A server must be located on LAN1.

B. The router must be configured to forward all broadcasts.

C. The router listens to SAP queries and distinguishes them from other broadcasts.

D. The router responds to GNS queries on behalf of remote servers.

3. Which of the following are the two fields found in a SAP query packet?

A. Packet type

B. Header

C. Service type

D. Frame Check Sequence

4. Which area of an IPX packet or address denotes whether it is a SAP packet?

A. The node address in the Destination field

B. The source-field network address

C. The socket number in the Source-Address or Destination-Address field

D. The Service-Type field in the data area

5. How often does a server or router broadcast its SAP database contents?

A. Every 60 seconds

B. Every 30 seconds

C. Every 10 seconds

D. Every 120 seconds

6. How many records can a SAP response packet from a Cisco router contain?

A. 1

B. 2

C. 4

D. 7

7. Why would a router not send a RIP or SAP update to the neighbor from which it received the update?

A. Because it has a broken interface

B. To avoid routing loops and unnecessary information transmissions

C. Because it is using half-duplex communications

D. To degrade performance

8. Which of the following are the metrics used by RIP to select the best path? (Choose all that apply.)

A. Hops

B. Bandwidth

C. Ticks

D. Cost

IPX Configuration

Use to the Following Scenario to Answer Questions 1–8

WebSTER Services is a new World Wide Web corporation dedicated to providing Internet connectivity. Because of the amount of incoming traffic, WebSTER plans to install multiple routers and LAN segments to separate the service traffic from corporate data traffic. There will be four segments, each separated by routers. WebSTER will have a NetWare server (Svr2) running both IP and IPX placed on Network 4. This NetWare server's internal network number will be 5. WebSTER also will have a NetWare server (Svr1) running only IPX placed on Network 1 with the internal network number 6. Corporate client computers may attach directly to either Network 1 or Network 2. The following illustration depicts the future WebSTER network:

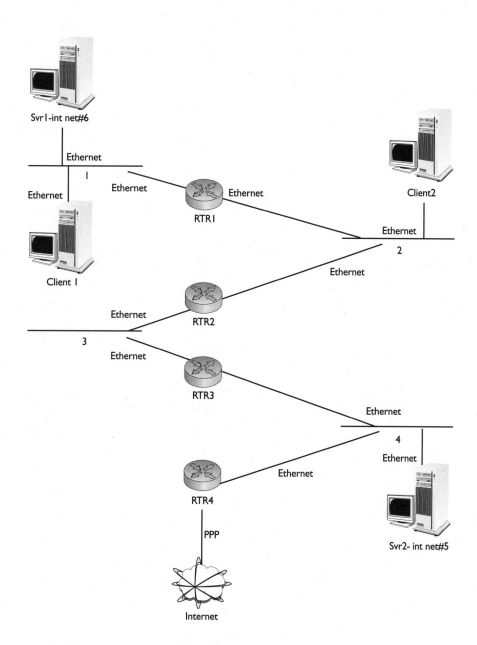

Svr1-int net#6

Ethernet

1

Ethernet

Ethernet

RTR1

Ethernet

Ethernet

Client 1

Client2

Ethernet

2

Ethernet

Ethernet

RTR2

Ethernet

3

Ethernet

RTR3

Ethernet

Ethernet

4

Ethernet

RTR4

Ethernet

PPP

Svr2- int net#5

Internet

1. If the preceding scenario and diagram are all the information given about the network, which of the following need to be defined before configuring the routers and servers? (Choose all that apply.)

   A. Network numbers
   B. Internal network numbers
   C. Encapsulations for each interface
   D. Routing protocols

2. WebSTER states that it is planning to use Ethernet_802.2 on Svr1, and Ethernet_II on Svr2. Clients may use only Ethernet_802.2. Which of the following would be a valid configuration file for RTR3, where Ethernet 0 is connected to Network 3 and Ethernet 1 is connected to Network 4?

   A. Ethernet 0-Network 3, Arpa; Ethernet 1-Network 3, Arpa
   B. Ethernet 0-Network 3, SAP, SNAP, and Arpa;
      Ethernet 1-Network 4, SAP
   C. Ethernet 0-Network 3, SAP; Ethernet 1-Network 4, Arpa
   D. Ethernet 0-Network 3, Novell-Ether; Ethernet 1-Network 4,
      Novell-Ether

3. Which of the following commands will configure RTR1's Ethernet 0 interface, connected to Network 1?

   A. rtr1(config)# IPX NETWORK 2 ENCAPSULATION ARPA
   B. rtr1(config-if)#IPX NETWORK 1 ENCAPSULATION SAP
   C. rtr1#IPX NETWORK 1 ENCAPSULATION NOVELL-ETHER
   D. rtr1(config)#Ethernet 0 IPX NETWORK 1 ENCAPSULATION SAP

4. WebSTER is considering adding Macintosh computers to Network 1. The company needs to communicate with Svr1 via the frame-type Ethernet_SNAP. Which command could be executed on RTR1 in order to add the correct encapsulation on interface Ethernet 0?

   A. rtr1>IPX ROUTING
   B. rtr1#IPX NETWORK 7 ENCAPSULATION SNAP

C. rtr1(config)#IPX NETWORK 7 ENCAPSULATION SNAP SECONDARY

D. rtr1(config-if)#IPX NETWORK 7 ENCAPSULATION SNAP SECONDARY

5. The WebSTER network is installed, with all servers and routers up and running except the last, RTR1. When the network is booted for the first time, the WebSTER administrator immediately goes into privileged mode and types SHOW IPX ROUTE to see the RIP information, but nothing except directly connected route information appears. The WebSTER administrator fears that the router is bad. What else could be the problem?

A. The interface Ethernet 1 is bad, but the rest of the router is fine.

B. The IP information was never entered, so the router will not work.

C. Not enough time has elapsed for RIP updates to be received.

D. The serial interfaces are administratively down.

6. WebSTER decides that it would like to use subinterfaces on RTR4 with two encapsulations, Arpa and SAP. Choose the two commands that will enable SAP on the subinterface of Ethernet 1.

A. rtr4#INTERFACE ETHERNET 1.1

B. rtr4(config)#INTERFACE ETHERNET 1.1

C. rtr4(config-subif)#IPX NETWORK 8 ENCAPSULATION SAP

D. rtr4(config-if)#IPX NETWORK 8 ENCAPSULATION SAP SUBINTERFACE

7. The WebSTER administrator likes the information received from the SHOW IPX INTERFACE command; however, it contains much more information than he wants. Which of the following will give a more concise data output?

A. rtr#SHOW IPX

B. rtr#SHOW IPX INTERFACE BRIEF

C. rtr#SHOW IPX DATA

D. rtr>SHOW IPX INTERFACE SHORT

8. When RTR1 is booted and has been running for a while, the WebSTER administrator enters a command to view the SAP database. Which command does the administrator enter?

A. rtr1>SHOW SAP

B. rtr1#SHOW IPX SAP

C. rtr1#SHOW IPX SERVERS

D. rtr1(config)#SHOW SAP DB

QUESTIONS AND ANSWERS

Why do all the NetWare servers start beeping when I plug my new router into the network?	This is normally caused by a mismatch in network numbers. Check that the network numbers you have configured match the server's configurations.
The router is not listing my servers when I use the SHOW IPX SERVERS command. What is the problem?	Check that the server is using the same frame type as the router interface on the network. If the server and router interface are not using the same frame types, they won't be able to see each other.
Why can't I see any remote networks when I use the SHOW IPX ROUTE command?	Remember that it can take a minute or so for the routes to show up.
How do I configure the clients with their IPX address?	Client addressing with IPX is almost automatic. Normally you just configure the router and servers with the network address and encapsulation. As long as you have the correct encapsulation configured on the clients, they will detect their network number. Of course, the node address is automatically generated from the MAC address in the LAN card.

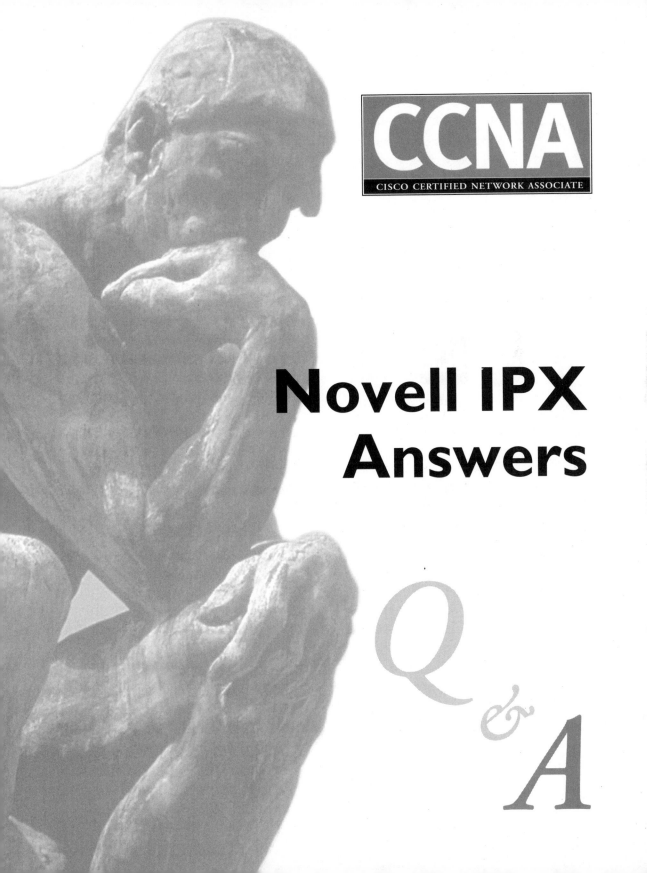

CCNA
CISCO CERTIFIED NETWORK ASSOCIATE

Novell IPX
Answers

Q & A

The answers to the questions are in boldface, followed by a brief explanation. Some of the explanations detail the logic you should use to choose the correct answer, while others give factual reasons why the answer is correct. If you miss several questions on a similar topic, you should review the corresponding section in the *CCNA Cisco Certified Network Associate Study Guide*, Second Edition (Osborne/McGraw-Hill, 1999) before taking the CCNA Certification test.

IPX Protocol Stack

1. **A.** SPX provides connection-oriented, reliable delivery service. SPX (Sequenced Packet Exchange) is a transport-layer protocol. The key to this question is that the testing candidate recognizes which protocols are transport-layer protocols. The only transport-layer protocol listed in the answer options is SPX, which does provide a connection-oriented, reliable delivery service. Answer B, IPX, is a network-layer protocol that provides connectionless, unreliable datagram service. Answer C, Network Basic Input/Output System (NetBIOS) emulation, works at the session layer and allows NetBIOS applications over IPX. Answer D, SAP, works at the session layer and enables servers and routers to advertise their services on the internetwork.

2. **B, E.** SPX, transport layer; and NLSP, network layer. SPX is a transport-layer protocol that provides connection-oriented, reliable delivery. NetWare Link Services Protocol (NLSP) is a network-layer protocol used to dynamically update routing tables on routers and servers. Answer A, RIP, is a network-layer protocol used to dynamically update routing tables based on distance vector algorithms. Answer C, NCP (NetWare Core Protocol), is an upper-layer protocol, with most services being equated to the presentation layer and some services crossing over into both the application and session layers. Answer D, SAP (Service Advertising Protocol), is a session-layer protocol.

3. **A.** NLSP. NetWare Link Services Protocol (NLSP) is a protocol that uses a link-state algorithm to update the routing table. There are two routing

protocols that are part of the IPX protocol stack: RIP and NLSP. RIP (Routing Information Protocol) is an older protocol that uses a distance vector algorithm to update the routing table. NLSP is a newer protocol developed with the link-state algorithm to provide a faster convergence on the internetwork. *Convergence* means the time that it takes for updates to be propagated throughout the internetwork and for the routers to be using the same routing information. Answer C, SAP, is not a protocol used to update routing tables, but rather provides service advertisements. Answer D, IPX (Internetwork Packet Exchange), is not a protocol used to dynamically update routing tables, but rather provides addressing and connectionless, unreliable datagram delivery service.

4. **B.** SAP advertises router and server services. Service Advertising Protocol (SAP) is a session-layer protocol. Each router and server stores SAP advertisements in local databases. In this way, they are able to maintain lists of the services available on the entire internetwork. When clients request services, they send SAP requests to the nearest servers. SAP is a member of the IPX protocol stack and maps to the session layer of the OSI reference model. Answer A, NLSP, is not a session-layer protocol, but it does work at the network layer. NLSP does handle the dynamic updates to routing tables using a link-state algorithm. Answer C, NetBIOS emulation, is a session-layer protocol; however, it does not provide addressing and datagram services. NetBIOS emulation provides the ability to run NetBIOS applications over IPX. Answer D, SPX (Sequenced Packet Exchange), is a transport-layer protocol. SPX does not create sessions by exchanging packets. SPX provides a connection-oriented, reliable delivery service.

5. **D.** IPX. Internetwork Packet Exchange (IPX) is the protocol that provides the network and node address in the IPX protocol stack. IPX maps to the network layer of the OSI reference model. In the OSI reference model, addresses for networks and nodes are assigned. IPX uses the network and node address as a way of identifying where a node is attached to the internetwork. This enables routing of data from a source node to a destination node. Answer A, SAP, provides service advertisements so that clients can locate the services offered by routers and servers. Answer B, SPX, provides a reliable connection-oriented service. Answer C, NCP, provides managed connections and access to services, such as file and print services.

IPX Datagram

1. **A. 0.** Since there is only a single network segment and data does not cross routers, the transport control byte will never be incremented. The transport control byte starts with a zero value and is incremented each time the packet passes a router. The sniffer was placed on the main office network prior to any routers being added to its network, so the transport control byte would be a zero value. The IPX datagram consists of several sections, as shown in following table.

Datagram Section	Size	Function
Checksum	2 bytes	IPX does not use this; it depends instead on the MAC layer to provide checksum error control. This value is typically set to 0xffff.
Length	2 bytes	This identifies the length of the packet.
Transport control	1 byte	Initially this is set to 0 when the packet is generated. Then this byte is incremented each time the packet crosses a router until it reaches 16, at which point the packet is discarded.
Packet type	1 byte	This identifies the packet's protocol.
Destination address	12 bytes	This identifies the IPX network, node, and socket address of the receiving or destination node.
Source address	12 bytes	This identifies the IPX network, node, and socket address of the sending node.

2. **B, D.** The network address of Server3 and the internal network address of Server3. Before the network routers can be installed and the old servers connected on the same internetwork, the network address of Server3 and the internal network address of Server3 must be changed in order to be unique on the future internetwork. Both the network address and the internal network address must be unique on the internetwork. That means that the network address of Server3 (or the internal network address of Server1) must be changed before it is connected via routers to the network

that contains Server1 because Server3's network address (1a00) is not unique. Server1's internal network address is the identical number (1a00). The same change must be applied to the internal network address of Server3 (58fc), since it is the same as the address applied to the network segment containing both Server1 and Server2. Alternatively, the network address can be changed on both Server1 and Server2.

3. **D.** The internal network addresses of NewServer2, Server3, NewServer3, and NewServer4. Since internal network addresses must be unique on the internetwork and these addresses are not, they should be changed. The internal network address is used by NetWare servers as though it is assigned to a virtual network existing logically inside the server. The internal network is considered yet another network segment with its own address. Since network addresses must be unique on the internetwork, the internal network addresses must be unique within the entire set of network and internal network addresses.

4. **C.** It will not be applicable, since the address length is too long. The suggested address is 48 bits in length when translated from hexadecimal to binary format. An IPX network address is 32 bits in length. This means that the network address scheme is too long to be used. When the IPX network address is written, it is usually in hexadecimal format and appears as eight digits in length, consisting of a variation of the numerals 0–9 and the letters *a–f.* On Cisco routers, all leading zeros of a network address are cut from the address and only the remaining digits are used. For example, if the network address is 00000ce3, it would be written on a Cisco router as ce3.

5. **B.** 0000.8045.0afc. The IPX address is written in the following format: *network address.node address.socket number.* The node address itself is a 12-digit hexadecimal address written in three sections of four digits each. When the format is applied to the number given, the network address is 58fc, the node address is 0000.8045.0afc, and the socket address is 0004.

6. **A, B, C.** The network address that uses all zeros is invalid; the internal network address that uses all Fs is invalid; and the scheme limits the number of servers and networks that can be installed. There are several problems with this addressing scheme. It uses two network addresses that are invalid: 00000000 and FFFFFFFF. It also limits the number of networks and servers that can be added to the network. The network address 00000000 is reserved. The network address FFFFFFFF is used for broadcasts. The number of servers that can be installed with this scheme is limited to the number of internal network addresses available. The scheme limits the number of internal network addresses to five: AAAAAAAA, BBBBBBBB, CCCCCCCC, DDDDDDDD, and EEEEEEEE. The number of network segments that can be added to the network is limited to nine: 11111111, 22222222, 33333333, 44444444, 55555555, 66666666, 77777777, 88888888, and 99999999.

7. **C.** The address is for a server's internal network. The first clue to the type of address is the node portion, 0000.0000.0001. This is the node address assigned to an internal network. Each server is considered node 1 on its own internal network. The second clue is the network address portion, since the consultant sniffed the network at the main office, which has the network address 58fc. Server1's internal address was 1a00.

8. **D.** No, because the network numbers for the async connections are not listed. Desert Dealers, Inc.'s suggested network numbers are not sufficient for the internetwork, since there are no network numbers that can be assigned to the async connections. Desert Dealers, Inc.'s network uses only IPX as its protocol, which nominally reduces the possible routing protocols to RIP or NLSP. IPX routing via RIP and NLSP sends data from one IPX network number to the next. When the async connections must pass along IPX data, they must route it using an IPX network number assigned to the async connection.

9. **C, E, A, F, D, B.** Data is sent from the node 58fd.8045.1111.1234 and is received by the router on the 58fd network. The router examines the packet, determines that it is meant for another network for which it has a path, and sends it out the correct async interface (indicated by the network a1) a1.0000.ab88.234c. The next router receives the packet from the async network on interface a1.0000.c001.1c33. It examines the packet and determines that the packet is meant for the directly connected network 58fc. The router sends the data through the Ethernet interface 58fc.0000.c002.1c33. The node on network 58fc (58fc.0000.1234.5888) examines the packet and accepts it. If data is sent from Lot1 to the main office, the source node address is 58fd:8045.1111.1234 and the destination address is 58fc:0000.1234.5888. When the router's Fast Ethernet interface receives the packet, the router knows to send all data to the 58fc destination network through the async interface that is on network a1. The routers only need to find the network address portion of the address in order to route data. Once the data is received by a router directly connected to the network, the node address is used to determine which node should receive the data.

NOVELL IPX ANSWERS

10. **C.** 14. There are 14 unique IPX network and internal network numbers that need to be assigned to this network configuration. Since an internal network number is considered another network number on an IPX internetwork, it is included in the total number of unique network addresses required. Each server requires an internal network number, and there are 7 servers. Each Ethernet network segment requires a network number, and there are 4 Ethernet network segments. Each async network segment requires a network number, and there are 3 async network segments. The total number of unique network numbers is 14.

11. **A.** Ethernet networks e01, e02, e03, e04; async networks a01, a02, a03; and internal networks b01, b02, b03, b04, b05, b06, b07. In this scheme, the Ethernet networks are all labeled with the letter *e* and a two-digit sequence number; the async networks are all labeled with the letter *a* and a two-digit sequence number; and the internal networks are labeled with the letter *b* and a two-digit sequence number. Answer B is incorrect because the scheme does not have enough Ethernet network numbers and has too many async networks. Furthermore, the *i* is not a hexadecimal character. Answer C is incorrect because it contains a duplicate number e202 both in the async network and internal network lists. Answer D is incorrect because it has a duplicate number 58fc in the Ethernet and async lists and does not have enough internal network numbers.

IPX Encapsulation Types

1. **A.** Arpa. The Arpa encapsulation is equivalent to what Novell calls the Ethernet_II frame type. Arpa is used on Cisco routers to ensure that any NetWare server using the Ethernet_II frame type can send data to other networks. Answer B, DARPA, is the acronym for the Defense Advanced Research Projects Agency, not a frame type nor an encapsulation. Answer C, Ethernet, is a physical and data-link–layer protocol specification that is commonly used in conjunction with IPX, but it is not a frame type. Answer D, IEEE, is the acronym for the Institute of Electrical and Electronics Engineers.

2. **D.** 4. There must be four network numbers used on this network due to multiple frame types. The example has LAN1 connected to the router's Ethernet 1 interface, and the router's Ethernet 0 interface is connected to LAN2. There are two physical network segments. However, LAN1 and LAN2 each have two separate, logical networks. The result is that four total network numbers must be assigned to the network segments. Each separate encapsulation type is considered a separate logical network, even if the logical networks use the same physical interface on the router or server. This requires a separate network number for each encapsulation type on each physical network segment.

3. **A, D.** SNAP and Arpa. SNAP on the Token Ring interface, and both SNAP and Arpa on the Ethernet interface. The Cisco router will need to route data from both servers. If the server on the Token Ring network is running the Token_Ring_SNAP frame type, the router will need to use the SNAP encapsulation. If the server on the Ethernet segment is running both the Ethernet_II and the Ethernet_SNAP frame types, the router will need to have the Arpa and the SNAP encapsulation. Since the router already had

the SNAP encapsulation from the Token Ring network segment, it has two encapsulations, Arpa and SNAP.

4. **B.** Svr2. The client will only be able to contact Svr2, on Network A. The router runs only the SAP encapsulation, which is the same as the Ethernet_802.2 frame type. Since the client runs Ethernet_802.2, it can send data to other networks. Svr2 is the only server that is also running the Ethernet_802.2 frame type. On Network A, Svr1 is running Ethernet_802.3 and will not be able to send data through the router. Also connected to Network A, Svr2 is running Ethernet_802.2 and can communicate with the client. On Network B, Svr3 is running Ethernet_802.3 and cannot communicate across the router. On Network D, Svr4 is running Ethernet_II and Ethernet_802.3, and cannot communicate across the router.

5. **C.** LAN1: e200 (using Arpa), e230 (using Novell-Ether); LAN2: e221 (using SAP), e231 (using Novell-Ether). This answer offers unique network numbers and applies separate numbers to each separate logical network. When multiple encapsulations are used on a single interface to a physical network, NetWare views them as separate logical networks. Answer A uses nonunique network numbers (e200 and e230 are used on both LANs). Answer B uses nonunique network numbers (e230 on both LANs). Answer D applies the same network number to two logical networks on each LAN.

6. **A.** Ethernet 0, SAP; Ethernet 1, Arpa. These are the encapsulations that must be run on the router's interfaces. Because the client is using the Ethernet_802.2 frame type, the Ethernet 0 interface must use the same type of encapsulation in order to communicate with the client. The SAP encapsulation is the same as the Ethernet_802.2 frame type. Because the NetWare server is using the Ethernet_II frame type, the Ethernet 1 interface connected to that network must run the same type of encapsulation, which is Arpa. Even when interfaces run different encapsulations, the router will route the data from one network to the other. This means that the client using Ethernet_802.2 can communicate with the server using Ethernet_II via the router.

SAP and RIP

1. B, C, D. Periodic updates; service queries; and service responses. Periodic SAP updates are SAP broadcasts listing the service's name, type, and IPX internetwork address (including the socket number on which this service is listening) for each service. IPX routers listen for these broadcasts and add the advertised services to an internal database. Service queries occur when a NetWare client is initializing and needs to locate a server to connect to. To do this, it sends a SAP Get Nearest Server (GNS) query. SAP responses are packets sent in reply to SAP queries. Each response packet can contain up to seven records.

2. D. The router responds to GNS queries on behalf of remote servers when clients are located on one side of the router and servers are located on another. Because the GNS query is an IPX broadcast packet, it does not travel off the network on which it was generated. In this configuration, clients would be required to be on the same network segment as a NetWare server in order to locate any services on the entire internetwork. But the client will also get responses from routers connected to the same IPX network. To make it possible to locate servers on other networks, IPX routers respond to GNS requests on behalf of remote servers.

3. A, C. Packet type and service type. The SAP query is encapsulated in the data portion of an IPX packet broadcast. It has two 2-byte-long fields, which are packet type and service type, in that order. The packet-type field has the value of 3 for a GNS query. This field value is 1 for a general service query. The service-type field holds the value given to the service type requested. For example, the service type for a NetWare server is 0x0004, but it is 0x0047 for a print server. Service-type values are allocated by Novell.

4. C. The socket number in the Source-Address or Destination-Address field. When the socket number in one of these fields of an IPX packet is set to 0x452, it determines that the packet is a SAP packet. When a router examines IPX packets, it reviews the header of the packet to look at the source and destination addresses. The socket number is part of that address. When the router finds the socket number 0x452 in the Source-Address or Destination-Address field of the IPX packet, it knows that it is a SAP packet and can process it accordingly. Routers place SAP service advertisements in their internal SAP databases and respond to GNS queries on behalf of remote servers.

5. A. Every 60 seconds. IPX routers and servers store the service advertisements in an internal SAP database. Every 60 seconds the router or server will broadcast the contents of that database as the default. On Cisco routers, the default may be changed. Because the router or server is using broadcast packets, the packets are not propagated throughout the network. Instead, the contents of a database are broadcast to neighbors (that is, those that are attached to directly connected networks of the sending server). Since the entire contents are broadcast, new services are propagated throughout the network in a cascading fashion from one router to the next until all routers and servers have been updated with the new services.

6. D. 7. The SAP response is encapsulated within the data field of an IPX packet. The SAP response packet format contains 2 bytes for the packet-type field, 2 bytes for the service-type field, 48 bytes for the server-name field, 12 bytes for the server-address field, and two bytes for the intermediate-networks field. The SAP packet itself is 68 bytes in length, while the data field of an IPX packet can be any size between 43 and 1,500 bytes, depending on the MAC encapsulation. The data field can contain up to 7 SAP responses by repeating the SAP response packet.

7. B. To avoid routing loops and unnecessary information transmissions. The process of not sending these RIP and SAP packet updates back along the paths over which they came is called *split-horizon*. Put another way, a router will not readvertise a service back onto the network from which it was learned. Split-horizon is used with RIP, SAP, and other routing protocols. Its purpose is to avoid retransmitting information onto networks where that information is already known. Split-horizon is a process that is typically used with distance vector routing protocols. RIP is an example of a distance vector routing protocol. SAP uses this process to prevent multiple service advertisements recurring to and from the same network segments.

8. **A, C.** Hops and ticks. These are used to determine the best path to a network. RIP is a distance vector routing protocol. Routing protocols are used to dynamically build routing tables on the routers throughout the internetwork and reduce administration hassles, such as having to statically input routes for each new network segment on each existing router and server. Distance vector routing protocols use a metric. In the case of RIP, this is the distance to the network in terms of hops and ticks, along with a direction, or vector, such as the interface of the next router in the path to the destination network.

The metric is measured in *hops,* which are the number of routers that a packet must pass through until it reaches the destination network, and *ticks,* which indicate the time it takes for the packet to reach the destination network. Ticks are approximately equivalent to one-eighteenth of a second and are the primary metric upon which a route is selected.

IPX Configuration

1. **C, D.** Encapsulations for each interface and routing protocols. To ensure that clients and servers have a path to each other, they must use the same encapsulations that are used on the router interface attached to their network segment. The encapsulation can be the same or different for each interface, and multiple encapsulations can be applied to a single interface. However, these must be the same from the router interface to the client or server in order for a path to reach the other interface of the router. Routing protocols should also be planned for the network in order for the dynamic routing tables to be in place and enable routing functions. Although both answer A and answer B, the network numbers and internal network numbers, need to be defined before the installation and configuration, in the WebSTER case, these numbers have already been defined.

2. **C.** Ethernet 0-Network 3, SAP; Ethernet 1-Network 4, Arpa. The configuration for each interface should be documented. The items that need to be documented for interfaces are the encapsulation and the network number. Each network number is different depending on the encapsulation used. This means that there can only be one encapsulation type per interface, unless more network numbers are assigned. The type of encapsulation used is only required for the Ethernet 1 interface and should be Arpa (since Svr2 is using Ethernet_II frame type). The Ethernet 0 interface could be any encapsulation. Here, the only answer that uses Network 4 on the Ethernet 1 interface using Arpa encapsulation uses SAP encapsulation on the Ethernet 0 interface. Answer A is incorrect because it has a duplicate network number used on Ethernet 1. Answer B is incorrect because there are multiple encapsulations assigned to a single network number. Answer D is incorrect because Arpa is not an encapsulation used on Network 4.

3. **B.** rtr1(config-if)#IPX NETWORK 1 ENCAPSULATION SAP. This command would configure interface Ethernet 0 on RTR1. The IPX NETWORK *network_#* ENCAPSULATION *encapsulation_type* command is used to configure an interface for IPX. This command is an interface configuration command that is indicated by the prompt rtr1(config-if)#. To enter interface configuration mode, you would type the command INTERFACE *interface_#* in global configuration mode. Answer B is correct, because the network number is 1 and the encapsulation needed on that network is SAP, which is equivalent to Frame Type Ethernet_802.2, used on Svr1, which resides on Network 1. Answer A is not correct, because it refers to the Arpa encapsulation and Network 2 and because the command is entered in the wrong mode, global configuration mode. Answer C is not correct, because it refers to the Novell-Ether encapsulation and uses the wrong mode, privileged EXEC. Answer D is not correct, because the command has an additional Ethernet 0 at the beginning and is entered into in global configuration mode.

4. **D.** rtr1(config-if)#IPX NETWORK 7 ENCAPSULATION SNAP SECONDARY. This command could be executed on RTR1 in order to add the SNAP encapsulation on interface Ethernet 0. This IPX

NETWORK *network_#* ENCAPSULATION *encapsulation_type* SECONDARY command is used to add a secondary network to an interface that is already configured for a network. Since RTR1 already has a primary network configured on interface Ethernet 0, the secondary notation must be added to configure the new encapsulation type. The encapsulation type is SNAP, which is equivalent to the NetWare server's use of the Ethernet_SNAP frame type. The IPX Network number is set to 7, which is a new network number assigned to the SNAP encapsulation, since each encapsulation type is considered a separate logical network. This command must be entered from interface configuration mode, indicated by the prompt rtr1(config-if)#. The remaining answers all have invalid prompts showing that they are not in interface configuration mode.

5. **C.** Not enough time has elapsed for RIP updates to be received. This accounts for the lack of information when the SHOW IPX ROUTE command is entered. The SHOW IPX ROUTE command is entered in privileged mode. It is used to verify that IPX configuration is functioning properly by verifying that RIP is communicating with the rest of the internetwork. When the command is entered and the router has not had time to receive RIP updates, it will not display RIP routing and services information, nor will it display partial information, since some updates were received. Both RIP and SAP send out updates at 60-second intervals from an IPX router or server to its neighbors. In this manner, the RIP and SAP updates are cascaded throughout the internetwork. However, there can be a delay before a RIP or SAP table is completely updated with all the routing and services information on the internetwork.

6. **B, C.** rtr4(config)#INTERFACE ETHERNET 1.1 and rtr4(config-subif)#IPX NETWORK 8 ENCAPSULATION SAP. A subinterface is a way of defining multiple logical networks on a single physical interface. The use of subinterfaces on Ethernet ports was not added to the Cisco IOS until version 11.1*x* and later. The other method of defining multiple logical networks is by using the secondary argument notation for subsequent networks when adding a network to a physical interface, which is indicated by the prompt of rtr4(config-if)#. This contrasts with a subinterface configuration prompt of rtr4(config-subif)#.

7. **B.** rtr#SHOW IPX INTERFACE BRIEF. This command gives the basic information of the SHOW IPX INTERFACE command, but with less detail. The SHOW IPX INTERFACE command verifies the configuration of the router's IPX interfaces. It shows configured network numbers, encapsulation types, and operational status of the interface. When the SHOW IPX INTERFACE command is entered and a particular interface is not specified, all IPX interfaces and their corresponding data are output to the console. The SHOW IPX INTERFACE BRIEF command is a variant of the SHOW IPX INTERFACE command, but limits the data output details.

8. **C.** rtr1#SHOW IPX SERVERS. This privileged mode command was the one the WebSTER administrator entered. This command is used to view the SAP database of a router. This command is executed in privileged EXEC mode. Privileged EXEC mode is indicated by the prompt RTR1#. This command is entered from user EXEC mode by executing the ENABLE command. SHOW IPX SERVERS may also be entered at a user EXEC mode prompt. The SHOW IPX SERVERS command can be used to verify that the correct encapsulations are applied to the interfaces on a router. When a router interface is not using the same encapsulation as a server located on the directly connected network segment, that server will not appear in the router's SAP database.

CCNA
CISCO CERTIFIED NETWORK ASSOCIATE

Part 8

Basic Traffic Management with Access Lists

EXAM TOPICS

Standard IP Access Lists

Extended IP Access Lists

Named Access Lists

Standard IPX Access Lists

IPX SAP Filters

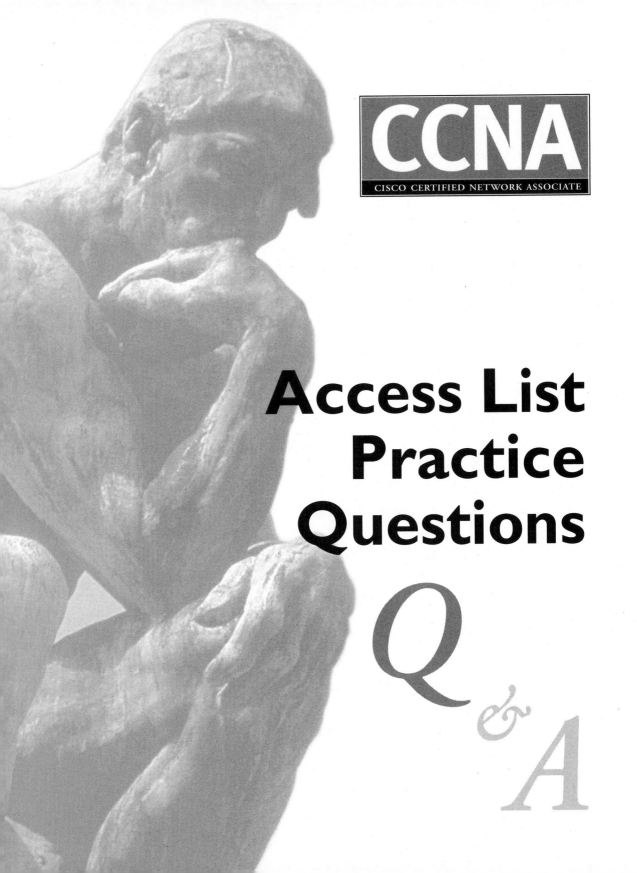

CCNA
CISCO CERTIFIED NETWORK ASSOCIATE

Access List Practice Questions

Q & A

This chapter introduces the reader to the world of traffic management and, more specifically, to managing traffic using access lists. An administrator can use access lists with Internet Protocol (IP) and Novell Internetwork Packet Exchange (Novell IPX) to filter packets and Novell server and Service Advertising Protocol (SAP) information. The questions in this chapter test your understanding of the use of access lists to set up and manage network traffic.

Standard IP Access Lists

1. Which types of IP access lists does Cisco support? (Choose all that apply.)

   A. Extended XNS
   B. Standard
   C. Dynamic
   D. Extended

2. Cisco routers process each packet in the order received against each access list statement. If the router reaches the end of the list and has found no matches, what will happen to the packet being processed?

   A. It will forward the packet to the default network.
   B. It will discard the packet and return an ICMP message.
   C. It will forward the packet back to the source as unreachable.
   D. It will send out an ICMP packet and forward the packet.

3. After an access list is created, where does the router place subsequent changes to the access list?

   A. At the beginning of the list
   B. In numeric order

C. At the end of the list

D. NVRAM

4. How do you deny all inbound Telnet sessions to the auxiliary port and allow only a trusted source?

A. You can only permit or deny traffic inbound; you cannot do both.

B. ACCESS-CLASS 41 DENY 0.0.0.0 255.255.255.255
ACCESS-CLASS 41 PERMIT 131.172.31.1
LINE AUX 0
ACCESS-CLASS 41 IN

C. You cannot Telnet to the auxiliary port.

D. ACCESS-CLASS 41 DENY 0.0.0.0 255.255.255.255
LINE AUX 0
ACCESS-CLASS 41 IN

5. Which of the following displays the wildcard bits applied to an IP access list? (Choose all that apply.)

A. WRITE TERMINAL

B. SHOW CONFIGURATION

C. SHOW ACCESS-LISTS

D. SHOW NVRAM

6. If you are not using IP accounting or any other form of authentication, how do you verify access list activity, such as matches, in real time?

A. This information is not available without IP accounting.

B. You must be running IP Lock and Key.

C. You use the SHOW INTERFACE IP command.

D. You use the SHOW IP ACCESS-LIST command.

Extended IP Access Lists

1. To further define granularity in an extended IP access list, you can define optional arguments, operator, and operand, to compare destination ports. Which protocol key words do not allow port distinctions? (Choose all that apply.)

   A. NEQ

   B. IP

   C. LT

   D. ICMP

2. What is the purpose of the keyword ESTABLISHED in an IP extended access list?

   A. To establish a connection with the access list

   B. To permit established connections to continue access

   C. To permit new connections to continue access

   D. None of the above

Named Access Lists

1. What should you consider when using named access lists? (Choose all that apply.)

   A. Access lists specified by named access lists are backward compatible.

   B. Access lists specified by name are not compatible with older releases.

   C. Not all types of access lists that accept a number will accept a name.

   D. A standard access list and an extended access list cannot have the same name.

   ### Use the Following Scenario to Answer Questions 2–10

   The following questions test your knowledge of IP access lists. ABC Corporation has a single Cisco router connecting two Ethernet segments in the home office. The LAN attached to Ethernet 0 is connected to the engineering LAN. Ethernet 1 is the general LAN for access to all devices. The questions are based on a scenario of a Cisco router with the following configuration:

```
version 11.3
!
hostname Andrews
!
boot system flash
enable password san-fran
!
ip classless
ip subnet-zero
no ip domain-lookup
!

interface Ethernet 0
 ip address 192.192.192.1 255.255.255.0
 no mop enabled
 no shutdown
!
interface Ethernet 1
 ip address 192.192.193.1 255.255.255.0
 no mop enabled
 no shutdown
!
interface Serial 0
 shutdown
!
interface Serial 1
  shutdown

router rip
network 192.192.192.0
network 192.192.193.0
!
banner motd #
           Welcome to Andrews!

!
#
!
```

```
line con 0
 exec-timeout 0 0
 password cisco
 login
line aux 0
 no exec
line vty 0 4
 password cisco
 login
 !
end
```

2. A WAN link to a remote sales office is installed on Interface Serial 0. Users will need access to the general LAN but do not require access to the engineering LAN. The remote sales office address block is 192.192.194.0 with a subnet mask of 255.255.255.0. Which of the following access lists would apply?

A. ACCESS-LIST 800 DENY EVERY

B. ACCESS-LIST 1 DENY 192.192.194.0 0.0.0.255
   ACCESS-LIST 1 PERMIT ANY

C. ACCESS-LIST 1 DENY 192.192.194.0 0.0.0.255

D. ACCESS-LIST 201 DENY EVERY HOST

3. To which interface should this access list be applied?

A. Ethernet 1

B. Serial 0

C. FDDI 0

D. Ethernet 0

4. Which of the following commands would be used to apply the access list to the interface?

A. INTERFACE ETHERNET 0
   IP ACCESS-GROUP 1 IN

B. INTERFACE ETHERNET 0
   IP ACCESS-LIST 1 IN

C. INTERFACE SERIAL 0
   IP ACCESS-GROUP 1 OUT
D. INTERFACE SERIAL 0
   IP ACCESS-LIST 1 OUT

5. Which command on the router will verify that access list 1 has been assigned to Ethernet 0 when in user mode?

A. DISPLAY IP INTERFACE

B. DISPLAY ACCESS-LIST 1

C. SHOW ACCESS-LIST 1

D. SHOW IP INTERFACE

6. A link to the Internet has been added to the router on Serial 1. Initially only e-mail traffic will be transmitted across the link. Which type of access list would be used?

A. IP standard

B. IPX extended

C. IP extended

D. IP complex

7. The IP address of ABC Corporation's SMTP server is 192.192.192.5. Which syntax would be used in the access list to allow SMTP traffic?

A. IP ACCESS-LIST 1 PERMIT SMTP

B. IP ACCESS-LIST 100 PERMIT TCP ANY HOST 192.192.192.5 EQ SMTP

C. IP ACCESS-LIST 100 DENY TCP ANY HOST 192.192.192.5 EXCEPT SMTP

D. None of the above

8. The administrator wants to expand access to now include FTP and Telnet traffic. How would this be accomplished?

A. By deleting the access list

B. By adding a new access list

C. By adding statements to the existing access list to exclude FTP and Telnet

D. By deleting the existing access list and adding a new access list to permit SMTP, FTP, and Telnet

9. The administrator has decided to change the access list from a numbered to a named access list. Which is the correct syntax for the named access list?

A. IP NAMED ACCESS-LIST *number* DENY/PERMIT *protocol* SOURCE *source_wild card source_destination name*

B. IP NAMED ACCESS-LIST *name number* DENY/PERMIT *protocol* SOURCE *source_wild card source_destination*

C. IP NAMED ACCESS-LIST [*standard/extended*] *number* DENY/PERMIT *protocol* SOURCE *source_wild card source_destination name*

D. IP ACCESS-LIST [*standard/extended*] *name* DENY/PERMIT *protocol* SOURCE *source_wild card source_destination*

10. How does the administrator verify from the router that the access list is working?

A. By using the SHOW ACCESS LIST command and checking for matches to the extended access list

B. By using the SHOW INTERFACE command

C. By using the DISPLAY ACCESS LIST command and checking for matches to the extended access list

D. None of the above

Standard IPX Access Lists

1. What makes up an IPX network address? (Choose all that apply.)

A. IPX number

B. Port number

C. Network number and node number

D. Network node

2. Which of the following may impact router performance when you enable IPX input access lists?

A. An IPX input access list may not be configured on an interface if autonomous switching is already enabled.

B. IPX autonomous switching may not be enabled on any interface where an IPX input access filter has already been configured.

C. Fast-switching performance is reduced when input filtering is configured, dependent upon the nature of the access list(s) and the traffic.

D. IPX input access lists are nonimpacting on the Cisco 12000 platforms.

3. Which configuration denies access from all nodes on Network 1 that have a source address beginning with 0000.0C?

A. ACCESS-LIST 801 DENY 1.0000.0C00.1111 0000.00FF.FFFF

B. ACCESS-LIST 799 DENY 1.0000.0C00.1111 0000.00FF.FFFF

C. ACCESS-LIST 900 DENY 1.1111.1111.1111.1111 0000.0000.0000. 2.2222.2222.2222 0000.0000.0000

D. ACCESS-LIST 801 DENY 1.1111.1111.1111.1111 0000.0000.0000. 2.2222.2222.2222 0000.0000.0000

4. Since a Cisco router does not forward any broadcast it receives, what does the router do?

A. It advertises the entire SAP table at two-minute intervals.

B. It only forwards those broadcasts that are from NetWare servers.

C. It advertises half of the SAP table every 30 seconds.

D. It advertises the entire SAP table at scheduled intervals, either configured or default.

5. Which command would you use to determine what filter rules are applied to an IPX-enabled interface?

A. SHOW IP ACCESS

B. SHOW IP INTERFACE

C. SHOW IPX TRAFFIC

D. SHOW IPX INTERFACE

ACCESS LIST
QUESTIONS

6. Extended IPX access lists can be used to filter protocol information. In which range are these numbers?

A. 700–799

B. 800–899

C. 900–999

D. 1000–1099

IPX SAP Filters

1. What does the −1 mean in a SAP filter statement?

A. It specifies that no networks are included.

B. It specifies that the following networks are included.

C. It specifies only that the −1 network is included.

D. It specifies that all networks are included.

2. Which of the following is another IPX service type supported by the SAP filter list?

A. GNA

B. GNS

C. GSA

D. GNN

3. Which command displays the interfaces that have SAP filter lists active?

A. SHOW INTERFACE

B. DISPLAY IPX INTERFACE

C. SHOW IPX INTERFACE

D. DISPLAY INTERFACE

Use the Following Scenario to Answer Questions 4–13

The following questions test your knowledge of IPX access and SAP filter lists. ABC Corporation has a single Cisco router connecting two Ethernet segments in the home office. The LAN attached to Ethernet 0 is connected

to the engineering LAN. Ethernet 1 is the general LAN for access to all
devices. The Novell file and print servers are located on the general LAN,
which is accessed by users on both LANs. The questions will be based on a
scenario of a Cisco router with the following configuration:

```
version 11.3
!
hostname Andrews
!
boot system flash
enable password san-fran
!
ipx routing
!
interface Ethernet 0
 ipx network 100
 no mop enabled
 no shutdown
!
interface Ethernet 1
 ipx network 200
 no mop enabled
 no shutdown
!
interface Serial 0
 shutdown
!
interface Serial 1
  shutdown
banner motd #
          Welcome to Andrews!
#
!
line con 0
 exec-timeout 0 0
 password cisco
 login
line aux 0
 no exec
line vty 0 4
 password cisco
 login
!
end
```

4. Server A contains employee records. Which of the following commands would be used to prevent the SAP advertisements of Server A from being advertised to users on the engineering LAN?

   A. ACCESS-LIST 800 DENY [*Novell address*]
      ACCESS-LIST 800 PERMIT ANY

   B. ACCESS-LIST 1001 DENY [*Novell address*]
      ACCESS-LIST 1001 PERMIT ANY

   C. ACCESS-LIST 1001 DENY [*Novell address*]
      ACCESS-LIST 1001 PERMIT –1

   D. ACCESS-LIST 1001 DENY [*Novell address*]
      ACCESS-LIST 1001 PERMIT –A

5. Which of the following commands correctly puts the previous SAP filter into effect?

   A. INTERFACE ETHERNET 1
      IPX OUTPUT-SAP-FILTER 1001

   B. INTERFACE ETHERNET 0
      IPX INPUT-SAP-FILTER 1001

   C. INTERFACE ETHERNET 1
      IPX-OUTPUT-SAP-FILTER 1001

   D. None of the above

6. The administrator has been requested to allow Server A's print services to be advertised to the engineering LAN. What changes to the previous SAP filter need to be made?

   A. No changes are needed.

   B. The filter needs to be changed to allow the SAP for print services to be advertised.

   C. The filter needs to be changed to allow the SAP for file services to be advertised.

   D. The filter needs to be changed to allow GNS printer services.

7. The administrator has been requested to allow Server A's print services to be advertised to the engineering LAN. Which of the following is the correct SAP filter?

A. ACCESS-LIST 1001 PERMIT [*server_a Novell address*] 7
ACCESS-LIST 1001 DENY [*server_a Novell address*] 4
ACCESS-LIST 1001 PERMIT –1

B. ACCESS-LIST 800 PERMIT [*server_a Novell address*] 7
ACCESS-LIST 800 PERMIT [*server_a Novell address*] 4
ACCESS-LIST 800 PERMIT –1

C. ACCESS-LIST 800 PERMIT [*server_a Novell address*] 7
ACCESS-LIST 800 DENY [*server_a Novell address*] 4
ACCESS-LIST 800 –1

D. ACCESS-LIST 1001 PERMIT [*server_a Novell address*] 7
ACCESS-LIST 1001 PERMIT [*server_a Novell address*] 4
ACCESS-LIST 1001 PERMIT –1

8. Users on the engineering LAN have been having intermittent periods of trouble attaching to Server B, which is located on the general LAN attached to Ethernet 1. They complain that they are not getting prompted from Server B to enter their login. What could be the source of this problem?

A. Server B is not allowing login services.

B. Server B is not accessible for users on the engineering LAN.

C. Server B is down for maintenance.

D. Other servers are responding to the client's GNS request before Server B.

9. Which syntax of the GNS filter would the administrator use?

A. ACCESS-LIST 1002 PERMIT [*server_b Novell address*]
ACCESS-LIST 1002 DENY –1

B. ACCESS-LIST 9002 PERMIT [*server_b Novell address*]
ACCESS-LIST 9002 PERMIT –1

C. ACCESS-LIST 1002 DENY [*server_b Novell address*]
ACCESS-LIST 1002 PERMIT –1

D. None of the above

10. On which interface should the administrator activate the GNS filter?

    A. Ethernet 1

    B. Ethernet 0

    C. Serial 1

    D. FDDI 0

11. Which command is used to verify which SAP filter lists are in effect?

    A. SHOW IP SERVERS

    B. SHOW IPX SERVERS

    C. SHOW IP INTERFACES

    D. SHOW IPX INTERFACES

12. After a remote office is opened and connectivity is established via Serial 0, users at the home office are not able to attach to the local server at the remote office. They are getting prompts from servers located at the home office. What can the administrator do to correct this?

    A. Shut the link

    B. Adjust GNS response on the router

    C. Activate a SAP filter to deny server access

    D. None of the above

13. Which command allows the administrator to adjust GNS response timers?

    A. IPX GNS-DELAY-RESPONSE

    B. IPX DELAY-GNS-RESPONSE

    C. IPX GNS-RESPONSE-DELAY

    D. IPX DELAY-RESPONSE-GNS

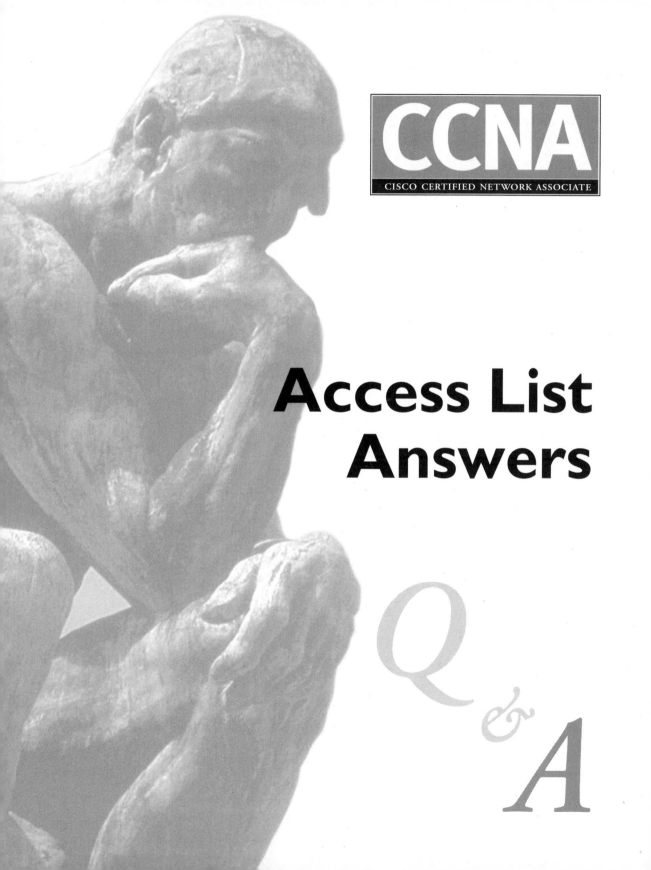

CCNA
CISCO CERTIFIED NETWORK ASSOCIATE

Access List Answers

Q & A

T he answers to the questions are in boldface, followed by a brief explanation. Some of the explanations detail the logic you should use to choose the correct answer, while others give factual reasons why the answer is correct. If you miss several questions on a similar topic, you should review the corresponding section in the *CCNA Cisco Certified Network Associate Study Guide*, Second Edition (Osborne/McGraw-Hill, 1999) before taking the CCNA Certification test.

Standard IP Access Lists

1. **B, C, D.** Standard; dynamic; and extended. Cisco currently supports these three types of access lists for IP. Access lists are numbered as follows: standard 1–99, extended 100–199. Dynamic lists are used in conjunction with extended access lists and provide Lock and Key security for specific source and destination addresses along with an authentication process.

2. **B.** It will discard the packet and return an ICMP message. For inbound access lists, after receiving a packet, the router checks the source address of the packet against the access list. If the access list permits the address, the router continues to process the packet. If the access list rejects the address, the router discards the packet and returns an ICMP host unreachable message. For outbound access lists, after receiving the packet and routing to the specific outbound interface, the router checks the source address of the packet against the access list. If the access list permits the address, the router transmits the packet. If the access list rejects the address, the router discards the packet and returns an ICMP host unreachable message. This is what is referred to as the implicit DENY. Plan your rules carefully and always remember the DENY ANY at the end.

3. **C.** At the end of the list. When an access list is created, it cannot be modified without the changes being placed at the end. You cannot selectively add or remove access list line items from a specific access list. Named access lists, however, do allow the administrator to edit existing access lists. The original numbered access list can be left as is until the

changes made while working with the named list are completed. Named access lists allow administrators to delete specific lines in the editing process.

4. **B.** ACCESS-CLASS 41 DENY 0.0.0.0 255.255.255.255
ACCESS-CLASS 41 PERMIT 131.172.31.1
LINE AUX 0
ACCESS-CLASS 41 IN

Answer B defines an access list that denies all inbound Telnet access to the auxiliary port and allows Telnet access to the router only from IP address 131.172.31.1, our trusted source. Note of caution: Because Cisco routers have no TTY lines, configuring access (on communication servers) to terminal ports 2002, 2003, 2004, and greater, could potentially provide access (on routers) to virtual terminal lines 2002, 2003, 2004, and greater To provide access only to TTY ports, you can create access lists to prevent access to VTYs. To further disable connections to the echo and discard ports, in addition to the above steps, you must disable these services completely with the global command, NO SERVICE TCP-SMALL-SERVERS.

5. **A, B, C.** WRITE TERMINAL; SHOW CONFIGURATION; and SHOW ACCESS-LISTS. While the output from WRITE TERMINAL and SHOW CONFIGURATION is very useful and you can scroll through the entire router configurations, the command SHOW ACCESS-LISTS displays all of your access lists in numerical order while displaying wildcard bits as applicable. The following is an example of output from the SHOW ACCESS-LIST command:

```
IPAccess# show access-lists
Standard IP access list 23
permit 132.72.13.0
deny   0.0.0.0, wild card bits 255.255.255.255
Standard IP access list 72
permit 132.127.31.0, wild card bits 0.0.0.255
permit 132.127.184.0, wild card bits 0.0.0.255
permit 132.127.185.0, wild card bits 0.0.0.255
permit 132.127.186.0, wild card bits 0.0.0.255
permit 132.127.187.0, wild card bits 0.0.0.255
Extended IP access list 101
permit tcp 0.0.0.0 255.255.255.255 0.0.0.0 255.255.255.255 eq 23
```

6. D. You use the SHOW IP ACCESS-LIST command. This command also displays information on how many matches have been made against the active access lists. The following is an example of the output with access list match information:

```
IPAccess#show ip access-list
Standard IP access list 77
permit 132.127.31.10
 deny any
Extended IP access list 105
deny udp any any eq 31337 (130969 matches)
```

This command can be very useful in troubleshooting access list statements to verify if the router is actually applying specific policies as configured. This is also useful in tracking down unauthorized users; however, this is a very limited debugging tool for tracking unauthorized use. See Cisco Security Configuration and Command Summary (www.cisco.com/univercd/home/home.htm) for further details on protecting your network.

Extended IP Access Lists

1. B, D. IP and ICMP. The argument operand is the decimal destination port for a specified protocol. For the TCP protocol, there is an additional keyword ESTABLISHED that does not take an argument. A match occurs if the TCP datagram has the ACK or RST bits set, indicating an established connection. The nonmatching case is that of the initial TCP datagram, where, to form a connection, the software goes on to other rules in the access list to determine whether a connection is allowed in the first place.

2. B. To permit established connections to continue access. When configuring an extended access list, you can define options to permit or deny well-known ports. This permits the administrator to narrow the definition of what is permitted to access specific network services. An established connection would be an application that once connected, would require additional connections. An example would be a Web browser opened to a home page with applications embedded that require a second program to be executed from a remote workstation. Examples of well-known ports are 23 for Telnet, 25 for SMTP, and 21 for File Transfer Protocol (FTP).

Named Access Lists

1. **B, C, D.** Access lists specified by name are not compatible with older releases; not all types of access lists that accept a number will accept a name; and a standard access list and an extended access list cannot have the same name. Named access lists are not recognized by IOS prior to Cisco release 11.2. An access list can be defined with a name instead of a number. The result of this is the capability to define more access lists than are allowed using access list numbers. When an administrator uses an access list with a name rather than a number, the mode and command syntax are slightly different. Currently, only packet and route filters can use a named list.

2. **B.** ACCESS-LIST 1 DENY 192.192.194.0 0.0.0.255
   ACCESS-LIST 1 PERMIT ANY

   This access list will deny all hosts on the 192.192.194.0 subnet from access hosts on the engineering LAN. The second part of the list is to allow any other host to access the LAN and must be used to defeat the implicit DENY ANY that is part of all IP access lists. IP standard access lists range in number from 1–99. This would make answer A incorrect, as access list 800 is an IPX standard access list. Answer C has the correct syntax of an access list, but is incorrect because it does not include the PERMIT ANY statement to defeat the implicit DENY ANY that is part of all access lists. Answer D is incorrect, because access list 201 is an Ethernet-type code access list.

3. **D.** Ethernet 0. Since access is being denied to the engineering LAN, the access list should be applied to the Ethernet interface as an outbound access list. If the access list were to be applied to Serial 0, users at the remote office would be denied access to both LANs in the home office.

4. A. INTERFACE ETHERNET 0
IP ACCESS-GROUP 1 IN

These commands correctly apply the access list to Ethernet 0 to deny the remote office traffic onto the engineering LAN. The keyword IN on the second command is needed to define the access list as inbound to the interface.

5. D. SHOW IP INTERFACE. This displays information on each of the interfaces that are configured for the IP protocol. Included in this information is whether any access lists are defined for the interface. The information covers whether the access list is inbound or outbound and also provides the access list number. The following illustration shows the information displayed by the SHOW IP INTERFACE command:

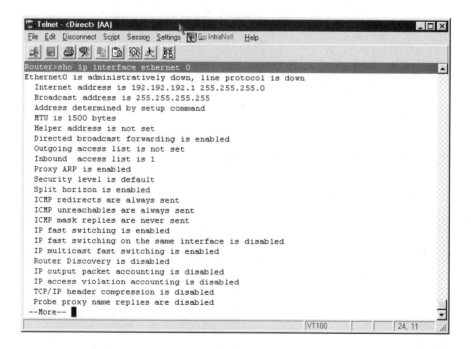

6. **C.** IP extended. When more detailed access is needed, an IP extended access is used to control packets in greater detail. Administrators can define lists by port, such as SMTP, Telnet, or FTP. Source and destination addresses are also used to provide greater detail in creating access lists.

7. **B.** IP ACCESS-LIST 100 PERMIT TCP ANY HOST 192.192.192.5 EQ SMTP. The syntax in this statement indicates that any TCP traffic that has the destination address of 192.192.192.5 will be permitted into the network if the TCP port indicates the packet is SMTP traffic. Extended access lists allow administrators to strictly define what type of traffic will be allowed in the network or over an interface.

8. **D.** By deleting the existing access list and adding a new access list to permit SMTP, FTP, and Telnet. When configuring access lists, two situations must be considered. After a list has been defined, the last statement will always be the implicit DENY ANY. Additional commands added to the access list are to be placed before the implicit DENY ANY. The last statement in all access lists is the implicit DENY ANY.

9. **D.** IP ACCESS-LIST [*standard/extended*] *name* DENY/PERMIT *protocol* SOURCE *source_wild card source_destination*

The syntax for a named access list is slightly different than a numbered access list. The administrator must include the keyword NAMED to define the name and whether the list is a standard or extended list (since numbers are not being used, the type of list has to be defined). Once the name and type of list have been defined, all other rules for IP access lists apply.

10. **A.** By using the SHOW ACCESS LIST command and checking for matches to the extended access list. The display from this command will provide information on the number of matches to the access list for each of the protocols permitted to pass the router. Standard IP access lists do not display matches to the list when the active access lists are displayed.

Standard IPX Access Lists

1. **A, D.** IPX number and network node. An IPX network number identifies a physical network. It is a 4-byte (32-bit) quantity that must be unique throughout the IPX internetwork. The network number is expressed in eight hexadecimal digits. The node number identifies a node on the network. It is a 48-bit quantity and is represented by dotted triplets of four-digit hexadecimal numbers. For example, in the address 3A.0000.0C00.32FE, 3A is the network number and 0000.0C00.32FE is the node number.

2. **D.** IPX input access lists are nonimpacting on the Cisco 12000 platforms. When setting up IPX packet filters, be cautious that filtering conditions do not result in packets being dropped. This can happen if the software is configured to advertise services on a network with access lists configured to deny these packets, or when a network is configured to advertise services on an unreachable network because routing updates are filtered out by routing update filtering. Keep these issues in mind when you configure your IPX access lists.

3. **A.** ACCESS-LIST 801 DENY 1.0000.0C00.1111 0000.00FF.FFFF. This configuration denies access from all the nodes on Network 1 that have a source beginning with 0000.0C. Access-list 799 is an incorrect number for IPX since it isn't in the range of 800–899. Answer C is an incorrect number for IPX, and in the case of answer D, while the 801 is a valid access-list number for IPX, it denies access from sources 1111.1111.111 on Network 1 to destination address 2222.2222.2222 on Network 2.

4. **D.** It advertises the entire SAP table at scheduled intervals, either configured or default. Since the Cisco router does not forward any broadcast it receives, the SAP table is sent out in scheduled intervals, at the set Cisco default of 60 seconds. Since broadcast-type traffic is bandwidth intensive, it should be

filtered across WAN links for both inbound and outbound traffic. This will assist in functionality and make your IPX network scalable.

5. **D.** SHOW IPX INTERFACE. This command allows you to view all the available types of filters that can be applied to IPX packets, routes, routers, NetBIOS packets, and SAPs. This is very useful in managing your network. As always, Cisco's command line interface is user friendly. And remember that the question mark (?) is your friend. For example: NOVELL#SHOW ? <cr>.

```
Novell# show ipx interface fddi 0/0
Fddi 0/0 is up, line protocol is up
IPX address is 1111.0000.0c01.d87a, NOVELL-ETHER [up],
RIPPQ: 0, SAPPQ: 0
  Secondary address is 2222.0000.0c01.d87a, SNAP [up]
  Incoming access list is 801
Outgoing access list is not set
IPX type 20 propagation packet forwarding is disabled
IPX SAP update interval is 1 minute(s)
IPX Helper access list is not set
SAP Input filter list is not set
SAP Output filter list is 1023
SAP Router filter list is not set
SAP GNS output filter list is not set
Input filter list is not set
Output filter list is not set
Router filter list is not set
Netbios Input host access list is not set
Netbios Input bytes access list is not set
Netbios Output host access list is not set
Netbios Output bytes access list is not set
Update time is 60 seconds
Delay of this interface, in ticks is 1
IPX Fast switching enabled
```

6. **C.** 900–999. Keep in mind that 700–799 is for XNS, 800–899 is for standard IPX access lists, and 1000–1099 is for IPX SAP access lists.

ACCESS LIST ANSWERS

IPX SAP Filters

1. **D.** It specifies that all networks are included. The −1 works in the same manner as the ANY in an IP access list statement. SAP filter lists also subscribe to the implicit DENY ALL rule for access lists.

2. **B.** GNS. The Novell Get Nearest Server request is sent by a workstation as a broadcast. The closest Novell server that is running the service will respond with a SAP indicating it has the service. If a Cisco router receives this request, it can respond with information from its SAP table on what server is running the requested service. An administrator can filter GNS requests on a Cisco router to prevent the router from responding if Novell servers are on the same LAN segment. This is accomplished with the IPX OUTPUT-GNS-FILTER command, which assigns an access list.

3. **C.** SHOW IPX INTERFACE. This command displays the interfaces that are running IPX and also lists any inbound or outbound SAP filters associated with the interface.

4. **C.** ACCESS-LIST 1001 DENY [*Novell address*]
   ACCESS-LIST 1001 PERMIT −1

   The access list is defined as a DENY of Server A's internal Novell network number and node address. The internal node number for an IPX server will always be 1. In hex this would be 0000.0000.0001. Use of the internal network address of the server will deny all services the server advertises. The second statement allows all other services to be advertised. This statement must be used to counteract the implicit DENY ALL, present in all access lists.

5. **C.** INTERFACE ETHERNET 1
   IPX-OUTPUT-SAP-FILTER 1001

   The administrator would implement this access list as an input filter on Ethernet 1. This will deny Server A's SAP advertisements as they are received on the router's Ethernet interface. The result is the services will not be placed in the router's SAP table.

6. B. The filter needs to be changed to allow the SAP for print services to be advertised. Each different SAP is identified by type. File service is identified as a type 4 SAP. Print service is identified as a type 7 SAP.

7. A. ACCESS-LIST 1001 PERMIT [*server_a Novell address*] 7
ACCESS-LIST 1001 DENY [*server_a Novell address*] 4
ACCESS-LIST 1001 PERMIT –1

This access list permits print services from Server A, denies file service from Server A, and permits all other SAP advertisements from other servers on the network. It should be noted that there are many more SAPs for printer services in the Novell architecture.

8. D. Other servers are responding to the client's GNS request before Server B. When a client sends out a GNS request, the closest server that has the service request responds. If the router sees these requests, it can respond with notification of available servers that are in its SAP table. The administrator can use a GNS filter to change the timing of GNS responses to clients.

9. A. ACCESS-LIST 1002 PERMIT [*server_b Novell address*]
ACCESS-LIST 1002 DENY –1

This access list permits SAP advertisements of Server B. The second line denies all other servers. Note: The second line is optional, as the implicit DENY ALL rule applies.

10. B. Ethernet 0. Since GNS filters are activated as an output filter, the administrator would have to activate the filter on Ethernet 0. This will deny all other servers from answering GNS requests originating from the engineering LAN.

ACCESS LIST
ANSWERS

11. D. SHOW IPX INTERFACES. This command displays IPX information for all interfaces configured for IPX. This information includes which SAP filter and GNS filter are in place. The following illustration shows the display from the SHOW IPX INTERFACE command:

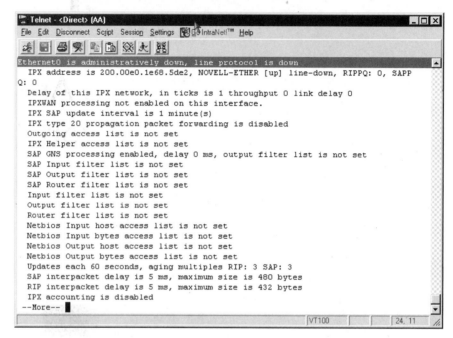

12. D. None of the above. In this case, since there are no filters on the home office router, the administrator should check the remote office router and verify there are no IPX access or SAP filter lists active that would prevent the remote office server's SAPs from being broadcast to the home office.

13. C. IPX GNS-RESPONSE-DELAY. This command will give locally attached servers priority in responding to GNS requests from clients. Note: With IOS version 11.0 and above, the router will not respond to GNS requests if there are local servers connected.

Part 9

Wide Area Networking

EXAM TOPICS

Frame Relay

X.25

X.25 over ISDN

Serial Transmission

Integrated Services Digital Network (ISDN)

Asynchronous Transfer Mode (ATM)

CISCO CERTIFIED NETWORK ASSOCIATE

Wide Area
Networking
Practice Questions

Q&A

Τhis chapter tests the reader's knowledge of wide area network (WAN) technologies such as frame relay, Integrated Services Digital Network (ISDN), X.25, Asynchronous Transfer Mode (ATM), and Point-to-Point Protocol (PPP).

ISDN provides a set of digital services that deliver voice, data, and video concurrently. X.25 is a packet-switching technology that is used in WANs. Frame relay is similar to X.25, but has no error checking feature and an excess of overheads. Frame relay networks transfer the user traffic within the frame without regard to its contents. Frame relay provides multiple independent data links to one or more destinations and is used mostly for data communications. PPP provides router-to-router and host-to-network connections over both synchronous and asynchronous circuits. ATM is a connection-oriented cell-relay technology that carries the information such as voice, video, and data in small and fixed-size cells of 53 bytes.

Frame Relay

1. What is the minimum frame relay frame size?

A. 56 bytes

B. 64 bits

C. Set by service provider in the DLCI

D. 5 bytes

2. What is the purpose of a permanent virtual circuit (PVC) in a frame relay network?

A. Protocol transmission

B. A logical connection that needs no call setup

C. Receipt of the signals from user equipment

D. None of the above

3. What is the function of the DLCI in a frame relay network?

A. Identifies the PVC locally

B. Reports congestion in the network

C. Transmits a protocol

D. None of the above

4. In a frame relay network, which of the following DLCI number ranges is valid?

A. 0–15

B. 1008–1023

C. 16–1007

D. 0–1023

5. What is the primary purpose of the signaling protocol for frame relay?

A. Call setup

B. PVC status and keepalives

C. Clocking

D. All of the above

6. Which one of the following is not a supporting signal in frame relay networks?

A. ANSI

B. ITU-T

C. ILMI

D. LMI (Cisco)

Use the Following Scenario to Answer Questions 7–11

The following illustration portrays the physical connection of the frame relay network with redundant connections to the central locations. For security purposes, all the routers are configured so that routing information will not be passed between remote routers.

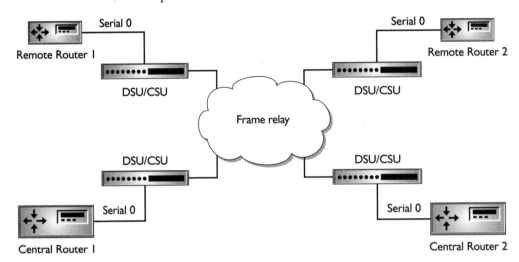

Remote Router 1

```
version 11.2
!
hostname remote-router1
!
interface Serial0
no ip address
encapsulation frame-relay
bandwidth 64
no fair-queue
!
interface Serial0.1 point-to-point
description PVC to Central Router 1
ip address 10.1.11.2 255.255.255.0
frame-relay interface-dlci 102
!
interface Serial0.2 point-to-point
description PVC to Central Router 2
ip address 10.1.12.2 255.255.255.0
frame-relay interface-dlci 103
!
end
```

Remote Router 2

```
version 11.2
!
hostname remote-router2
!
interface Serial0
no ip address
encapsulation frame-relay
bandwidth 64
no fair-queue
!
interface Serial0.1 point-to-point
description PVC to Central Router 1
ip address 10.1.11.3 255.255.255.0
frame-relay interface-dlci 202
!
interface Serial0.2 point-to-point
description PVC to Central Router 2
ip address 10.1.12.3 255.255.255.0
frame-relay interface-dlci 203
!
end
```

Central Router 1

```
hostname Central Router 1
enable secret 5
enable password cisco
!
interface Ethernet0/0
 ip address 192.157.129.254 255.255.255.0
!
interface Serial3/0
no ip address
no ip mroute-cache
encapsulation frame-relay
no ip route-cache
bandwidth 384
!
interface Serial3/0.1 multipoint
description Frame-relay T1
ip address 10.1.11.1 255.255.255.0
no ip mroute-cache
no ip route-cache
```

```
bandwidth 128
frame-relay map ip 10.1.11.2  101 broadcast
frame-relay map ip 10.1.11.3  102 broadcast
!
interface Serial3/0.2 point-to-point
description PVC for Network management
ip address 10.1.100.1 255.255.255.0
no ip route-cache
bandwidth 128
frame-relay interface-dlci 100
!
end
```

Central Router 2

```
hostname Central Router 2
!
interface Ethernet0/0
ip address 10.1.1.2 255.255.255.0
!
interface Serial3/0
no ip address
no ip mroute-cache
encapsulation frame-relay
no ip route-cache
bandwidth 384
frame-relay keepalive 20
!
interface Serial3/0.1 multipoint
description Frame-relay T1
ip address 10.1.12.1 255.255.255.0
no ip mroute-cache
no ip route-cache
bandwidth 128
frame-relay map ip 10.1.12.2 402 broadcast
frame-relay map ip 10.1.12.3 403 broadcast
!
interface Serial3/0.2 point-to-point
description PVC For Network Managment
ip address 10.1.100.2 255.255.255.0
no ip route-cache
bandwidth 128
frame-relay interface-dlci 100
!
end
```

7. Which of the following is the configuration of Remote Router 1?

    A. Point-to-point

    B. Point-to-multipoint

    C. Multipoint

    D. Point-to-point and multipoint

8. Which type of frame relay encapsulation is configured on remote and central router subinterfaces in the network?

    A. IETF

    B. One automatically provided by the frame relay network

    C. Encapsulation not configured

    D. Cisco

9. To which router does Serial 0.1 of Remote Router 1 connect?

    A. Central Router 1

    B. Central Router 2

    C. Remote Router 2

    D. Central Router 1 and Central Router 2

10. Which of the following statements is true?

    A. A single DLCI number can be used for all the mappings on the same subinterface of a serial interface configured for multilink.

    B. A DLCI number cannot be the same for all the mappings on the same subinterface, but it can be used on different subinterfaces of the serial interface.

    C. DLCI numbers have to be unique for every port.

    D. DLCI numbers have to be unique for every router.

11. Which command shows the complete frame relay mapping information and the status configured on Central Router 1?

    A. SHOW FRAME RELAY MAP

    B. SHOW FRAME RELAY PVC

    C. SHOW FRAME RELAY TRAFFIC

    D. SHOW FRAME RELAY LMI

WAN QUESTIONS

X.25

1. How is the data terminal equipment (DTE) in an X.25 network used?

    A. As a modem end point

    B. As a communication end-point device

    C. As termination of user-data equipment

    D. As data communication equipment

2. What is the DCE in an X.25 network?

    A. A modem end point

    B. Termination of user data equipment

    C. An end point of communication equipment

    D. A data communication element

3. What is a virtual circuit in an X.25 network?

    A. A bidirectional path between two DTEs

    B. A bidirectional path between a DTE and a DCE

    C. A bidirectional path between two DCEs

    D. A circuit between the user router and a DCE

4. Which layer is not spanned by X.25 in the OSI model?

    A. Physical

    B. Data-link

    C. Transport

    D. Network

X.25 over ISDN

Use the Following Configuration to Answer Question 1

```
Remote Router 1#
Interface bri0
      isdn x25 dchannel
      isdn x25 static-tei
!
interface  bri0:0
      ip address 10.1.100.10255.255.255.0
      x25 address 11110001111000
x25 map ip 10.1.100.11 11110001111001
!
end
```

1. Which of the following commands is accurate for configuring an X.25 operation on a serial interface of Remote Router 1?

   A. remote-router1(config)#ENCAPSULATION X25
   B. remote-router1(config-if)#ENCAPSULATION X25
   C. remote-router1(config)#x25 ENCAPSULATION
   D. remote-router1(config-if)#X25 ENCAPSULATION

Serial Transmission

1. How many DS-0s can a full T-1 digital signal carry?

   A. 1.544
   B. 56
   C. 24
   D. 64,000

2. How many DS-0s can a full E-1 carry?

A. 2.048

B. 24

C. 56

D. 30

Integrated Services Digital Network (ISDN)

1. Which of the following statements is true about ISDN PRI?

A. PRI consists of 2 B channels and one D channel

B. PRI consists of 23 B channels and one D Channel

C. PRI consists of 144 Kbps

D. PRI consists of 128 Kbps

Use the Following Scenario to Answer Questions 2–8

The illustration shown next and the configurations that follow it present a third scenario, where the remote routers are configured with ISDN dial backup to the dialin routers in a central location. The remote routers and the dialin routers are configured in such a way that the routing information will not be passed from or through the remote routers except through the interfaces directly connected to them. This example uses only one remote router configured for ISDN-BRI interface, subinterfaced to Dialer 0 and Dialer1. Dialin routers are AS5200s with PRI interface for multiple links to dial, as needed.

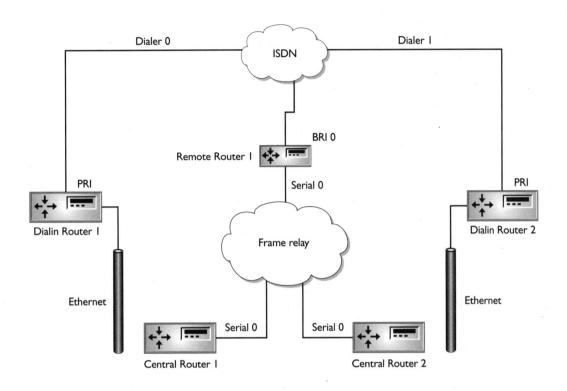

Remote Router 1

```
!
version 11.2
!
hostname remote-router1
!
enable secret
enable password
username dialin-router1 password dialin-router1
username dialin-router2 password dialin-router2
```

```
isdn switch-type basic-ni1
!
interface Ethernet0
ip address 172.24.69.2 255.255.255.128
!
interface Serial0
no ip address
encapsulation frame-relay
bandwidth 64
no fair-queue
!
interface Serial0.1 point-to-point
description PVC to Central Router 1
ip address 10.1.11.2 255.255.255.0
frame-relay interface-dlci 102
backup interface Dialer0
backup load 25 5
backup delay 10 10
!
interface BRI0
no ip address
encapsulation ppp
isdn spid1 21255512120000 5551212
dialer pool-member 1
ppp authentication chap
!
interface Dialer0
description dial backup to Dialin Router 1
ip address 10.1.101.11 255.255.255.0
encapsulation ppp
dialer remote-name Dialin-Router1
dialer string 12125551111
dialer hold-queue 30
dialer-group 1
dialer load-threshold 240
!
interface Dialer1
description dial backup to Dialin-Router2
ip address 10.1.201.11 255.255.255.0
encapsulation ppp
dialer remote-name Dialin-Router2
dialer idle-timeout 600
dialer string 12125551000
dialer hold-queue 30
dialer-group 1
dialer load-threshold 300
```

```
!
access-list 100 deny ip any host 255.255.255.255
access-list 100 permit ip any any
dialer-list 1 protocol ip list 100
!
end
```

Dialin Router 1

```
version 11.X
!
hostname Dialin Router 1
!
username Dialin-Router1 password 7 Dialin-Router1
username Remote-Router1 password 7 Remote-Router1
no ip domain-lookup
isdn switch-type primary-5ess
!
interface Dialer1
ip address 10.1.101.1 255.255.255.0
no ip mroute-cache
encapsulation ppp
no ip route-cache
no peer default ip address
dialer in-band
dialer idle-timeout 600
dialer map ip 10.1.101.11 name remote-router1
  broadcast 12125551212
dialer map ip 10.1.101.12 name remote-router2
  broadcast 5555555
ppp authentication chap
!
end
```

Dialin Router 2

```
version 11.X
!
hostname Dialin Router 2
!
username Dialin-Router2 password 7 Dialin-Router2
no ip domain-lookup
isdn switch-type primary-5ess
!
interface Dialer1
ip address 10.1.201.1 255.255.255.0
```

```
no ip mroute-cache
encapsulation ppp
no ip route-cache
no peer default ip address
dialer in-band
dialer idle-timeout 600
dialer map ip 10.1.201.11 name remote-router2
   broadcast 12125551212
dialer map ip 10.1.201.12 name remote-router3
   broadcast 5555509
ppp authentication chap
!
end
```

2. What is Remote Router 1 configured for in this configuration?

   A. Dial-on-demand routing

   B. Dial backup routing

   C. Dial-on-demand and dial backup routing

   D. A multilink router to receive calls from other routers

3. In the above configuration, what would be the result if Remote Router 1's interface S/0.1 were down?

   A. Interface Dialer 0 would become active immediately.

   B. Interface Dialer 1 would become active immediately.

   C. Interface Dialer 0 would become active after 10 seconds.

   D. Interface Dialer 0 would become active after 10 minutes.

4. In the configuration of Remote Router 1, backup load 25 5 is configured on the serial interface. What does 5 represent?

   A. Activation of the backup interface after 5 seconds of the primary failure

   B. Activation of the backup interface, if the primary interface exceeds 5 percent utilization

   C. Deactivation of the backup interface after 5 seconds

   D. Deactivation of the backup interface after an aggregate load of the primary and secondary lines returns to 5 percent or less

5. In the above ISDN, if the remote router places a call at 56 Kbps but it is delivered by the vendor network at 64 Kbps, what will happen to incoming data?

    A. It will be at 64 Kbps.

    B. It will be at 56 Kbps.

    C. The data may be corrupted.

    D. The call will be cancelled.

6. From the interface, Dialer0 of the Remote Router 1 is able to connect to Dialin Router 1, but Dialer1 of the Remote Router 1 cannot connect to Dialin Router 2. Why not?

    A. The username and password are not configured in Remote Router 1.

    B. The username and password are not configured in Dialin Router 2.

    C. The BRI Interface on Remote Router 1 is shut down.

    D. None of the above.

7. When will CHAP transactions take place?

    A. At the time the link is established

    B. After the link takes place

    C. Every few minutes during the call

    D. All of the above

8. On which devices is link-quality monitoring (LQM) enabled?

    A. Remote Router 1

    B. Dialin Router 2

    C. Dialin Router 1

    D. Not configured on any of the devices

WAN QUESTIONS

Asynchronous Transfer Mode (ATM)

1. What are two sublayers of the ATM physical layer?

A. Transmission convergence and physical medium dependent

B. ATM and SONET adaptation

C. AAL Convergence and Segmentation and Reassembly

D. None of the above

2. Which of the following is an example of a user-network interface (UNI)?

A. An interface between switches

B. An interface between a router and a switch

C. An interface between two workstations

D. All of the above

3. Which of the following is an example of a network-to-network (NNI) interface?

A. An interface between a router and a switch

B. An interface between switches

C. An interface between a switch and a workstation

D. An interface between a router and a workstation

4. What is the function of LMI (an ATM management protocol)?

A. It exchanges the status between networks performing VPI functions.

B. It provides MIB- and SNMP-based processes between UNI.

C. It sends status inquiries, reports, updates, and acknowledgements.

D. It is a switch-and-router management function.

5. What does ILMI provide as an ATM management protocol?

A. MIB- and SNMP-based processes between UNI peers

B. Status inquiries and reports, as well as updates and acknowledgements

C. An exchange of the status between networks performing VPI functions

D. None of the above

6. Which of the following statements is true about PNNI?

A. The PNNI interface is used between individuals or groups of private ATM switches.

B. PNNI is a hierarchical link-state routing protocol and works much like OSPF.

C. PNNI supports QOS routes.

D. All of the above.

7. Which is not a LAN emulation (LANE) component?

A. LAN emulation client (LEC)

B. LAN emulation configuration server (LECS)

C. LAN emulation server (LES)

D. Broadcast unknown server (BUS)

E. PNNI

8. Which of the following is a LANE service function?

A. Initialization

B. Registration

C. Address resolution

D. Data forwarding

E. All of the above

9. Which of the following is the sequence that allows the LEC to join the ATM network LANE?

A. LEC to LECS to LES to BUS

B. LEC to BUS to LECS to LES

C. LEC to LES to LECS to BUS

D. LEC to LECS to BUS to LES

Use the Following Configurations to Answer Questions 10–13

Following are the configurations for LANE on a Cisco switch and router. This is not a complete configuration but is appropriate for the questions that follow.

ATM Router 1

```
version 11.X
!
hostname Router 1
!
appletalk routing
!
decnet routing
decnet node-type area
!
ipx routing
!
interface ATM0/0/0
no ip address
no ip mroute-cache
atm pvc 1 0 5 qsaal
atm pvc 2 0 16 ilmi
hold-queue 450 in
!
interface ATM0/0/0.1 multipoint
description vlan101
ip address 10.1.1.1    255.255.255.0
lane client ethernet vlan101
ipx network
!
interface ATM0/0/0.2 multipoint
 description vlan102
 lane client ethernet vlan102
!
interface ATM0/0/0.3 multipoint
description vlan103
lane client ethernet vlan103
!
interface ATM0/0/0.10 multipoint
no ip mroute-cache
shutdown
```

```
atm pvc 4 4 88 aal5snap
map-group rfc1483
!
end
```

ATM-Database

```
hostname ATM-DATABASE
!
lane database atm-database
name vlan102 server-atm-address
          47.009181001111101011B90A01.00E0111E1441.02
name vlan102 server-atm-address
          47.009181001111106183C59401.00604747B941.02
name vlan101 server-atm-address
          47.009181001211106183C59401.00604747B941.01
name vlan101 server-atm-address
          47.009181000000001011B90A01.00E0111E1441.01
name vlan103 server-atm-address
          47.009181000000006183C59401.00604747B941.03
name vlan103 server-atm-address
          47.009181000000001011B90A01.00E0111E1441.03
!
interface ATM0
mtu 1500
atm pvc 1 0 5 qsaal
atm pvc 2 0 16 ilmi
lane config auto-config-atm-address
lane config database ATM-DATABASE
!
interface ATM0.1 multipoint
description vlan101
lane server-bus ethernet vlan101
lane client ethernet 101 vlan101
!
interface ATM0.2 multipoint
description vlan102
lane server-bus ethernet vlan102
lane client ethernet 102 vlan102
!
interface ATM0.3 multipoint
description vlan103
lane server-bus ethernet vlan103
lane client ethernet 103 vlan103
!
end
```

10. In ATM Router 1, interface ATM 0/0/0 is configured for ATM PVC 1 0 5 QSAAL. What does 1 0 5 represent in this configuration?

A. 1 is VCD, 0 is VPI, and 5 is VCI.

B. 1 is VPI, 0 is VCI, and 5 is VCD.

C. 1 is VCI, 0 is VCD, and 5 is VPI.

D. 1 is VCD, 0 is VCI, and 5 is VPI.

11. The ATM DATABASE switch is configured with the following ATM address:

47.009181001211106183C59401.00604747B941.01

Which of the following is represented in this address?

A. A 13-byte prefix

B. A 6-byte ESI

C. A 1-byte selector

D. A 5-byte header

12. What will be the result of the command SHOW LANE DEFAULT entered at the EXEC on the ATM DATABASE switch, before the fiber is connected and before the ILMI exchange takes place?

A. The complete ATM address of all the devices will be shown.

B. Only the prefix will be shown.

C. All the ESI addresses will be shown.

D. Only byte selectors will be shown.

13. Which of the following commands will show the complete LECS info, such as name, operational state, and address?

A. SHOW LANE CONFIG

B. SHOW LANE DATABASE

C. SHOW LANE DEFAULT

D. SHOW LANE CLIENT

QUESTIONS AND ANSWERS

I need an all-in-one solution for my new LAN/WAN. Cost isn't really an issue.	ATM would be an excellent solution, since it can travel over fiber and twisted-pair.
My company needs a new inexpensive solution for Internet connectivity. We have found that we need more bandwidth than an ISDN BRI interface can provide.	Try implementing Multilink PPP over two or more ISDN lines.
The average bandwidth required by my company has increased over the past six months. We have a shared T-1 line, and we don't have the extra money to get our own dedicated line.	Contact your ISP and have your committed information rate (CIR) increased to a little above the average.
We want to run classic IP over ATM. Which Cisco router would be best for a medium-sized business?	Classic IP is based on RFC 1577 and is supported in the 4000, 7000, and 7500 families. Depending on your budget, any of the three would be an excellent choice.
I need a secure method of connection and authentication for my point-to-point site. I am worried about somebody "listening" in on the line and getting access passwords. What should I use?	Use PPP encapsulation across the line with CHAP authentication. CHAP is much more secure than PAP, since passwords are never sent.
We are using software-based flow control but are having problems receiving the data correctly. What should we look at?	Some of your data might contain the strings that are used for signaling a DSR or a DTR. Either implementation of hardware flow control or ACCMs would be a good place to start.

Wide Area Networking Answers

Q
$\&$
A

T he answers to the questions are in boldface, followed by a brief explanation. Some of the explanations detail the logic you should use to choose the correct answer, while others give factual reasons why the answer is correct. If you miss several questions on a similar topic, you should review the corresponding section in the *CCNA Cisco Certified Network Associate Study Guide*, Second Edition (Osborne/McGraw-Hill, 1999) before taking the CCNA Certification test.

Frame Relay

1. **D. 5 bytes.** A frame consists of a two-byte header, a data field, and a two-byte cyclic redundancy check (CRC). The header contains the DLCI, forward explicit congestion notification (FECN), backward explicit congestion notification (BECN), DE bit, command reference (CR), and extended address (EA). The data field can be used to carry any type of information. The CRC is used to detect transmission errors and covers the header and data fields. The overall frame length ranges from 5 to 4,096 bytes. The upper-limit figure is to comply with the frame relay standards that say a device should be able to accept a frame size of at least 4,096.

2. **B. A logical connection that needs no call setup.** With frame relay, each router has a single physical connection to the frame relay network. Each of these physical connections may carry numerous logical connections called PVCs. After the PVCs are provisioned, they do not require a call setup for each use.

3. **A. Identifies the PVC locally.** DLCI is a value that specifies the PVC or switched virtual circuits (SVCs) in a frame relay network. A router differentiates the multiple PVCs that share the same physical port using the DLCI.

4. **C. 16–1007.** A 10-bit binary number represents the DLCI value. The DLCIs must be in the range of 0–1023. In practice, DLCIs 0–15 and 1008–1023 are reserved for special functions. DLCIs 0 and 1023 are reserved for local management interface (LMI) variation. DLCIs 1–15 and

DLCIs 1008–1018 are reserved. DLCIs 1019–1022 address multicast connections as defined by the industry's common specification. Therefore, DLCIs are typically chosen to be in the range of 16–1007.

5. **B.** PVC status and keepalives. The purpose of the signaling protocol is to exchange administrative information such as the addition, deletion, or failure of one or more PVC, and to exchange status information, which ensures the correct operation of each device. This exchange of signaling is known as LMI. The signaling protocol between a frame relay device and a frame relay network consists of regular, short status exchanges, typically every 10 seconds, and long status exchanges, usually every one minute.

6. **C.** ILMI. ILMI is supported in ATM networks and devices. The three common signaling protocols for frame relay are ANSI, ITU-T, and LMI (Cisco). ANSI describes frame relay signaling with T-1.617. ITU-T uses transmission standards to set frame relay signaling with Q.933 Annex A. LMI-Cisco is a consortium of Cisco, DEC, Nortel, and Stratacom.

7. **A.** Point-to-point. There are multiple PVCs configured on Remote Router 1, but they represent separate subinterfaces. The serial interface (serial 0) in Remote Router 1 is configured as two subinterfaces, serial 0.1 and serial 0.2. Serial 0.1 is configured to connect to Central Router 1. Serial 0.2 is configured to connect Central Router 2 and is represented by a separate DLCI number on each subinterface.

8. **D.** Cisco. All the routers in this scenario are configured with frame relay encapsulation. Frame relay encapsulation is configured centrally on the serial interface. If the type of encapsulation is not specified as IETF, the encapsulation type defaults to *Cisco*. Cisco encapsulation is a four-byte header divided into two bytes for DLCI and two bytes to identify the packet type.

9. **A.** Central Router 1. The IP address on Serial 0.1 of Remote Router 1 is set to IP ADDRESS 10.1.11.2, with interface DLCI 102. Central Router 1 is set to FRAME RELAY MAP IP 10.1.11.2101 BROADCAST, where 101 is

the DLCI number. The Inverse Address Resolution Protocol (Inverse ARP) is used here to dynamically map Remote Router 1 to Central Router 1.

10. **C.** DLCI numbers have to be unique for every port. The DLCI serves to distinguish the multiple PVCs that share a port. DLCIs at each end of a PVC may or may not be identical; the only restriction is that every PVC that terminates at a frame relay port must have its own DLCI that is distinct from the DLCIs associated with other PVCs at the same port.

11. **A.** SHOW FRAME RELAY MAP. This command shows all the DLCI mapping information on the router. This includes the interface number, the IP address, the DLCI number, the source of the map (static or dynamic), the encapsulation type, the bandwidth, and current status information. SHOW FRAME RELAY PVC shows the statistics information of a single PVC.

X.25

1. **C.** As termination of user-data equipment. The data terminal equipment (DTE) is the end device on the WAN link. DTE refers to any communication device that communicates directly to an end user, such as a network terminal or any other device where data terminates.

2. **C.** An end point of communication equipment. Data circuit terminating equipment (DCE) is the device at the end of the WAN provider's side. DCE primarily provides the interface of the DTE into the communication link in the WAN cloud. Here's an example showing DCEs and DTEs:

3. A. A bidirectional path between two DTEs. A virtual circuit is a logical connection created to ensure reliable communication between two network devices. A virtual circuit denotes the existence of a logical, bidirectional path from one DTE device to another across an X.25 network. Physically, the connection can pass through any number of intermediate nodes, such as data circuit-terminating equipment DCE devices and packet-switching exchanges.

4. C. Transport. X.25 spans through the first three (physical, data-link, and network) layers of the OSI model.

X.25 over ISDN

1. B. remote-router1(config-if)#ENCAPSULATION X25. The ENCAPSULATION X25 command enables the X25 encapsulation on serial interface, and this is an interface command. The default mode of operation is as DTE, and the default encapsulation method is IETF.

Serial Transmission

1. C. 24. A fractional T-1 (used primarily in North America) subrate transmission consists of multiple data-logical connections submultiplexed into a single 64 Kbps DS-0. Each DS-0 subrate supports the speed of 2,400, 4,800, and 9,600 bits, and 56 Kbps.

2. D. 30. The E-1 format is used throughout the world (except in North America) and has a speed of 2.048 Mbps. An E-1 consists of 30 DS-0s.

Integrated Services Digital Network (ISDN)

1. B. PRI consists of 23 B channels and one D channel. ISDN PRI is delivered via a T-1 circuit and is composed of 23 B channels and one D channel with

WAN ANSWERS

64 Kbps. Total speed of this PRI is 1536 Mbps (23B × 64 + 1D with 64). 8 Kbps are lost for the channelization. T-1 can also be delivered on E-1 circuits.

2. **C. Dial-on-demand and dial backup routing.** Remote Router 1 is configured for both dial-on-demand and dial-backup routing. The interface Serial 0.1 is configured with backup delay and backup load and has Specified Dialer 0 as the backup interface.

3. **C. Interface Dialer 0 will become active after 10 seconds.** The serial interface S/0.1 is configured with backup delay 10 10 and Specified Dialer 0 as backup interface. This allows the backup interface to come up after 10 seconds and will be deactivated 10 seconds after the primary link is activated.

4. **D. Deactivation of the backup interface after an aggregate load of the primary and secondary lines returns to 5 percent or less.** With backup load 25 5, the backup line will be activated if the load of the primary interface is higher than 25 percent of the primary interface bandwidth. Then the secondary line will be deactivated after an aggregate load between primary and secondary lines falls below 5 percent.

5. **C. The data may be corrupted.** When calls are made at 56 Kbps but delivered by the ISDN at 64 Kbps, the incoming data may be corrupted, even though the default-line speed is 64 Kbps. Although the call might originate at 56 Kbps, the network may improperly deliver the call to the user at a speed of 64 Kbps. This creates a speed mismatch and causes the data to be corrupted. The following commands in the receiving router will help to resolve this problem:

- ISDN NOT-END-TO-END 56 (answers all calls at 56 Kbps)
- ISDN NOT-END-TO-END 64 (answers all calls at 64 Kbps)

Enabling this command makes the router look more closely at the informational elements of the incoming call to determine a speed. On

ISDN calls, however, if the receiving side is informed that the call is not an ISDN call from end to end, it can set the line speed for the incoming call.

6. **B.** The user name and password are not configured in Dialin Router 2. Remote routers and dialin routers are configured for the Challenge Handshake Authentication Protocol (CHAP). CHAP requires configuration with username or hostname, encrypted password of routers you are connecting to, and the routers that are connecting to you. Dialin Router 2 did not have Remote Router1 username and password configured, which is required for CHAP.

7. **A.** At the time the link is established. CHAP transactions occur only at the time a link is established. The local router or access server does not request a password during the rest of the call. The local device will respond to other interface or device call requests during this call but does not need any more confirmation after the call is established.

8. **D.** Not configured on any of the devices. LQM is enabled on a serial interface using the PPP QUALITY PERCENTAGE command where percentage is calculated in both incoming and outgoing directions. This command is enabled to monitor the quality of the link. If the link quality percentage is not maintained for the specific percentage, the link will be dropped. The quality is monitored by comparing total bytes sent and received by the source and destination.

Asynchronous Transfer Mode (ATM)

**WAN
ANSWERS**

1. **A.** Transmission convergence and physical medium dependent. Cells from the ATM layer are processed into frames in the transport-convergence layer and packages 53 octet cells into a frame used in transmission, such as SONET. Physical medium dependent is the sublayer of the ATM physical

layer. This layer deals with transfer of bits between ATM network nodes and generally corresponds to DS-3, OC-3c, and others.

2. **B.** An interface between a router and a switch. UNIs are typically between the network and a single device such as a router or between user devices and a public ATM network.

3. **B.** An interface between switches. An NNI is typically between two ATM switches where both are located in either a private or public network. The difference between a UNI and an NNI cell is in the cell header structure. Although the cell size is the same in both networks, Generic Flow Control (GFC) of four bits exists in the beginning of the header of the UNI cell, whereas NNI does not have GFC and that field is occupied by a bigger virtual path identifier (VPI). This is the only field not existent in the NNI cell header.

4. **C.** It sends status inquiries, reports, updates, and acknowledgements. The LMI protocol is used across an NNI or a UNI for PVC status exchange. The LMI uses a user-defined VPI and a user-defined VCI for the cells containing the management messages. VPI-0 and VCI-31 are commonly used for the LMI protocol. There are four types of LMI messages:

   - **Status Inquiry**   Requests status information and is used as a polling mechanism
   - **Status Report**   Is sent out in response to a status inquiry message
   - **Update Status**   Is sent out to notify the status change of the connected device
   - **Update Status Ack**   Is sent out in response to an update status

5. **A.** MIB- and SNMP-based processes between UNI peers. ILMI is designed to maintain connectivity across an ATM interface. It supports the exchange

of UNI management information between UNI management entities. The MIB information for the ILMI includes the information on the physical layer, the ATM layer, the virtual path, and the virtual circuit connections.

6. D. All of the above. PNNI is a link-state routing protocol that will enable users to build multivendor, interpretable, ATM switching networks. PNNI supports QoS routes that provide connectivity over appropriate paths in order to meet individual application-bandwidth delay and other QoS requirements. The PNNI interface will be used between individuals and groups of private ATM switches. PNNI will allow different vendors' connection-management systems to communicate and provide SVC routing for switching systems that may span thousands of switches. PNNI is a hierarchical, link-state routing protocol that works much like Open Shortest Path First (OSPF).

7. E. PNNI. LANE provides four functions: initialization, registration, address resolution, and data transfer. The LEC is the entity in the end system that performs data forwarding, address resolution, and other control functions. The LECS implements the assignment of individual LESs to different emulated LANs (ELANs). The LES implements the control coordination function for the ELAN. The BUS handles data sent by a LEC to the broadcast MAC address, all multicast traffic, and initial (unknown) unicast frames that are sent by a LEC before the data-direct target ATM address has been resolved.

8. E. All of the above. LANE service functions include initialization, registration, address resolution, and data forwarding. LANE initialization obtains the ATM address of the LANE services that are available on a particular ATM network. Registration informs the other services of individual MAC addresses that the LEC represents. Address resolution obtains the ATM address representing the LES with a particular MAC address. Data forwarding moves data from the source to the destination.

9. A. LEC to LECS to LES to BUS. This is the sequence allowing LEC to join the ATM network. The following illustration explains the address registration process and the sequence.

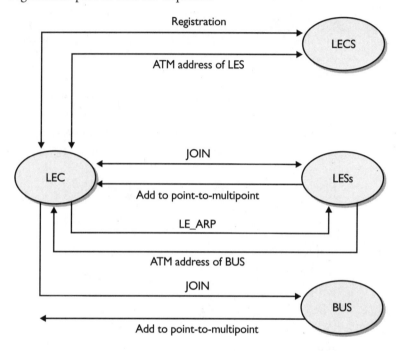

10. A. 1 is VCD, 0 is VPI, and 5 is VCI. The command for this configuration is ATM PVC VCD VPI VCI AAL-ENCAP with additional options. To create the PVC on the AIP or NPM interface card, the ATM PVC command is necessary. A VCD is a virtual circuit descriptor. A unique number per AIP or NPM identifies to the processor which VPI-VCI pair to use for a particular packet. VPI is an ATM network VPI of this PVC in the range of 0–255. The VCI is an ATM network VCI of this PVC in the range of 0–65,535.

AAL-ENCAP is the ATM adaptation layer (AAL) and encapsulation type. When aal5mux is specified, a protocol is required, such as aal34smd, for an SMDS network; aal5nlpid, for high-speed serial interfaces (HSSIs); and ATM-data exchange interfaces (DXI).

11. **A.** A 13-byte prefix. In the address 47.009181001211106183C59401.
00604747B941.01, as shown in the following table, the 13-byte prefix is
47.009181001211106183C59401, and it will be shared by all the devices
connected to the same ATM switch. The 00604747B941 portion is the
6-byte end-system identifier (ESI) address, and the 01 is the 1-byte selector.
In a Catalyst 5000, the last digit of the ESI address has meaning. If there is
a 0, it means LEC, while a 1 represents LES, a 2 represents BUS, and a 3
represents LECS.

13-Byte Prefix	6-Byte ESI	1-Byte Selector
47.009181001211106183C59401	00604747B941	01

12. **C.** All the ESI addresses will be shown. Because the signaling and ILMI
PVCs are not in place, address negotiation will not occur. This shows only
ESI addresses of the ATM address.

13. **A.** SHOW LANE CONFIG. This command shows LECS information,
such as its name, status, address, config requests, and failures. SHOW
LANE DATABASE shows ATM addresses of all the LESs entered in the
database. SHOW LANE CLIENT shows the details of the LECs, such as
the data-direct virtual circuits (VCs) and the VCs to each server and traffic.
SHOW LANE DEFAULT shows the default ATM addresses for the LANE
client, server, BUS, and config server.

Part 10

Virtual Local Area Networking

Virtual Local
Area Networking
Practice Questions

Q

&

A

This chapter introduces you to the world of virtual local area networks (VLANs). VLANs allow devices that are not located on the same physical network to be linked together as part of a larger, virtual network. VLANs do not require a change in the logical address when you move to a different segment. Dynamic Host Configuration Protocol (DHCP) allows a device to be moved from one subnet to another, but the address allocated is different. VLANs allow the device to be moved between segments with no change in configuration.

Switching and VLANs

1. With which layer of the OSI model is switching associated?

   A. Layer 1
   B. Layer 3
   C. Layer 0
   D. Layer 2

2. What is the difference between a VLAN and a physical LAN?

   A. A VLAN is a group of devices that can communicate without the need for a router or bridge.
   B. A VLAN is a group of devices that share a common physical media.
   C. A and B.
   D. None of the above.

3. What advantages do VLANs have over traditional, switched LANs? (Choose all that apply.)

   A. VLAN broadcasts are transmitted only to a specific broadcast domain.
   B. VLAN broadcasts are limited to the originating LAN media.
   C. VLAN members must be located in a central place.
   D. VLAN members are not required to be located in a central place.

4. How can VLANs assist administrators in the area of network security?

A. By allowing the administrator to define different groups

B. By allowing the administrator to define access lists

C. By allowing the administrator to define routing

D. None of the above

5. Which is the most common form of VLAN assignment?

A. MAC address

B. IP address

C. Port

D. Network address

Spanning-Tree Protocol and VLANs

1. What does the Spanning-Tree Protocol (STP) accomplish?

A. It allows for the best route to a destination.

B. It selects the interface to send traffic.

C. It permits redundant physical links but only uses one link to send traffic.

D. None of the above.

2. Which of the following bridging modes can be used for Token Ring networks?

A. Transparent source

B. Source route

C. Transparent route

D. Source transparent

3. What is the goal of STP?

A. To determine the best route to a destination

B. To link two network segments together

VIRTUAL LAN
QUESTIONS

   C. To join two WAN segments together

   D. To ensure a loop-free network topology

4. Why are switches similar to bridges?

   A. They route traffic in the same manner.

   B. They execute the STP to ensure a loop-free topology.

   C. They can do source-route bridging.

   D. None of the above.

5. Which of the following is contained in a RIF field? (Choose all that apply.)

   A. A destination IP address

   B. A bridge address

   C. A ring number

   D. A bridge number

Default VLAN Configuration

1. Which is the default VLAN for all active ports on a Catalyst switch?

   A. 1000

   B. 100

   C. 10

   D. 1

Configuring a VLAN Across a Domain

1. Which of the following is a necessary consideration when designing a VLAN?

   A. The number of users on the VLAN

   B. The number of NT servers

   C. The number of Novell servers

   D. None of the above

2. Which command is used to display VTP information on a Catalyst switch?

A. SHOW VTP STATISTICS

B. DISPLAY VTP

C. SHOW STATISTICS VTP

D. SHOW STATISTICS

3. Which command is used to display VTP domain information on a Catalyst switch?

A. SHOW VTP

B. DISPLAY VTP DOMAIN

C. SHOW VTP DOMAIN

D. DISPLAY DOMAIN

4. Which module is needed to give a Catalyst 5000 the added function of a Cisco router?

A. RSP

B. REM

C. FSP

D. RSM

5. Which of the following is supported in VTP version 2?

A. OSPF

B. Token Ring

C. X.25

D. None of the above

Grouping Switch Ports to VLANs

1. How many switch ports are available with the Catalyst 5000 24 100 Mbps Group Switching Module?

A. 16

B. 48

C. 3

D. 24

2. Which command will display the port status on a Catalyst switch?

A. DISPLAY PORTS

B. SHOW PORT INFORMATION

C. DISPLAY PORT STATUS

D. SHOW PORT STATUS

3. What occurs when a crossover cable is installed on two ports on the same switch module?

A. A network loop occurs, causing problems with the switched network.

B. Nothing occurs.

C. New routes are created.

D. None of the above.

4. When a port is in learning state, what is occuring?

A. The port is not forwarding frames, but is participating in the STP.

B. The port is in routing state.

C. The port is not forwarding frames, but is analyzing frames to gather MAC address information.

D. None of the above.

5. What does Portfast do?

A. It sets the port in fast mode to increase the speed of the port.

B. It turns on filtering to filter bad MAC addresses.

C. It sets the port to fast shutdown.

D. It allows the port to bypass listening and learning state and go directly to forwarding state.

6. Which version of Cisco software supports IEEE 802.1Q trunking protocol?

    A. IOS version 11.3

    B. Switch Code version 4.1

    C. IOS Switch Code version 5.0

    D. IOS version 12.0

Troubleshooting VLANs

1. Which command determines the port to which a workstation is connected?

    A. DISPLAY MAC TABLE

    B. SHOW MAC TABLE

    C. DISPLAY CAM

    D. SHOW CAM

VLAN Configuration

Use the Following Scenario to Answer Questions 1–17

This section follows the creation of VLANs for ABC Corporation. The corporation has three departments: Human Resources, Finance, and Engineering. These departments are spread across three floors of the ABC office building. The decision has been made to use VLANs with Cisco Catalyst 5000 series switches. VLAN 1 is designated for human resources, VLAN 2 is designated for finance, and VLAN 3 is designated for engineering. There is one Catalyst switch per floor. The LAN media is a combination of 10 Mbps and 100 Mbps Ethernet. Links between the Catalysts are 100 Mbps Ethernet. The next 17 questions will take us through the configuration and troubleshooting of these VLANs. The following illustration shows the network topology.

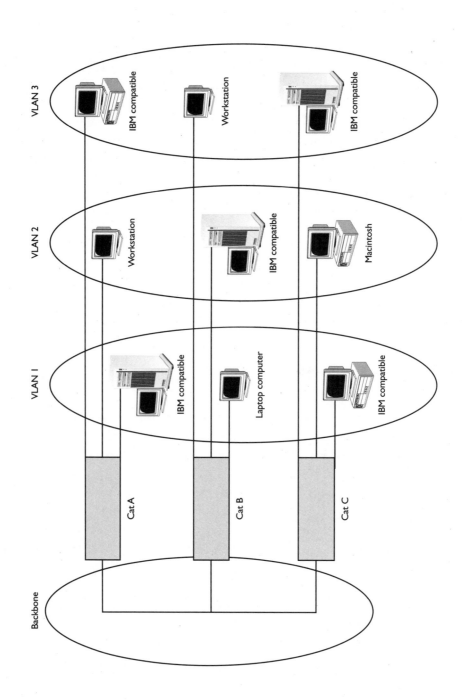

1. All three departments now use all floors of the building. A trunking protocol is needed to allow the VLANs to be spread to all floors. What needs to be configured first on all three switches?

    A. BGP

    B. ISL

    C. VTP

    D. None of the above

2. Which command do you use to verify that VTP has been enabled and is running?

    A. SHOW VTP STATISTICS

    B. SHOW VTP

    C. DISPLAY VTP INFORMATION

    D. DISPLAY VTP STATISTICS

3. Which command is used to display VTP domain information?

    A. SHOW VTP INFORMATION DOMAIN

    B. SHOW VTP DOMAIN

    C. SHOW INFORMATION VTP DOMAIN

    D. None of the above

4. Users who now occupy the second and third floors are not able to reach servers located on the first floor. What needs to be enabled on the Catalysts?

    A. BGP

    B. Port trunking

    C. ISL

    D. None of the above

5. Which command verifies that the correct VLANs have been included in the ISL trunk?

A. SHOW TRUNK INFORMATION

B. SHOW TRUNK

C. DISPLAY TRUNK

D. SHOW INFORMATION TRUNK

6. Some users on VLAN 3 are reporting that they are not able to reach other VLAN 3 servers and workstations located on the same floor. The network interface cards (NICs) on the workstations are set to 10 Mbps. What needs to be checked on the Catalysts?

A. The cabling, to make sure there are no crossover cables installed

B. The routing, to make sure it is turned on

C. The ports, to verify that the correct port speed has been set

D. The ports, to verify that they have transceivers connected

7. You discover that the ports in question are set for 100 Mbps port speed. Which of the following can be used to correct this problem?

A. Set the port speed to 10 Kbps.

B. Set the port speed to 10 Mbps.

C. Set the port Ethernet routing to On.

D. Set the port Token Ring routing to On.

8. Users on VLAN 2 are reporting that they are not getting IP address assignments from the Dynamic Host Control Protocol (DHCP) server. You confirm that the VLAN is operating normally. Users are still reporting problems. What is your next step?

A. Enable Portfast on the Catalyst.

B. Enable routing on the Catalyst.

C. Enable DHCP on the Catalyst.

D. None of the above.

9. A Cisco 7500 router has been purchased to provide an Internet connection for VLAN 3. The router has been equipped with Fast Ethernet ports. How does the router need to be connected?

   A. The router must be connected to all VLANs to provide the connectivity.

   B. The router must be connected to VLANs 1 and 2. VLAN 3 can already communicate with VLAN 1.

   C. The router must be connected to VLAN 3.

   D. None of the above.

10. Users on VLAN 1 and VLAN 2 need access to the others servers and workstations, as well as access to the Internet, but access must be denied for VLAN 3. Which of the following accomplishes this?

   A. Routing VLANs 1 and 2 together

   B. Bridging traffic between VLANs 1 and 3

   C. Routing traffic between VLANs 1 and 3

   D. Connect VLANs 1 and 2 to the router.

   E. Connect VLANs 1 and 2 to the router and use an access list to deny VLAN 3.

   F. Use a bridge DENY list to deny VLAN 3.

   G. Use a firewall.

   H. None of the above

11. ABC Corporation has purchased a competitor that is located in the same building and on the third floor. The company is using a 16 Mbps Token Ring network to connect its workstations and servers. Which is the best solution for connecting the new company?

   A. Use PNNI to connect to two networks.

   B. Use a serial link to connect the two networks.

   C. Add a Token Ring module to the Catalyst on the third floor.

   D. Convert the new company to Ethernet.

12. When the Token Ring is connected to the Catalyst, the ring starts beaconing. Further investigation indicates that the problem is with the Token Ring module on the Catalyst. How do you stop the beaconing?

A. Check the Token Ring module speed setting.
B. Make sure bridging is turned on.
C. Confirm that Token Ring routing is working.
D. None of the above.

13. The ring has stopped beaconing, but users are still having problems with connectivity. Which of the following should be checked?

A. IP routing, to see that it is enabled
B. RIP, to see that it is enabled
C. The duplex setting, to confirm that it is set correctly
D. None of the above

14. Due to personnel changes, VLAN 3 needs additional port capacity. How can you accomplish this?

A. By adding more hubs
B. By deleting VLAN 2
C. By adding more routers
D. By adding more ports to VLAN 3

15. The company is exploring the possibility of adding another vendor's switch to the network as part of a network expansion project. What change is needed to allow the Catalysts currently in the network to communicate with the other vendor's switch?

A. The switch translator needs to be added.
B. A crossover cable is needed.
C. The IEEE 802.1Q trunking protocol needs to be used.
D. None of the above.

16. Which command does ABC Corporation's network administrator use to verify that 802.1Q trunking is available?

A. DISPLAY SOFTWARE VERSION

B. SHOW SOFTWARE VERSION

C. SHOW VERSION

D. SHOW SOFTWARE

CISCO CERTIFIED NETWORK ASSOCIATE

Virtual Local
Area Networking
Answers

Q

&

A

The answers to the questions are in boldface, followed by a brief explanation. Some of the explanations detail the logic you should use to choose the correct answer, while others give factual reasons why the answer is correct. If you miss several questions on a similar topic, you should review the corresponding section in the *CCNA Cisco Certified Network Associate Study Guide*, Second Edition (Osborne/McGraw-Hill, 1999) before taking the CCNA Certification test.

Switching and VLANs

1. **D. Layer 2.** Since switching is based on MAC addresses and is associated with forwarding Ethernet and Token Ring frames, Layer 2, the data-link layer, is the point where switching takes place.

2. **A.** A VLAN is a group of devices that can communicate without the need for a router or bridge. A physical LAN is defined as a group of devices that share a common physical media and can be bounded by a router or bridge, although a bridge or router is not necessary. Since a VLAN is not bounded by a router or bridge, but includes the router or bridge as part of a larger, virtual network, devices do not have to be on the same physical media to be able to communicate. An example would be a company campus that has both Ethernet and Token Ring LANs in separate buildings. A VLAN would combine both network topologies with a switch that handles the translation of Ethernet packet to Token Ring and vice versa, with some type of connection (FDDI or ATM) between the buildings.

3. **A, D.** VLAN broadcasts are transmitted only to a specific broadcast domain, and VLAN members are not required to be located in a central place. In a traditional, switched LAN environment, broadcast traffic is sent to every port on the switch, regardless of type. In a VLAN environment, domains are established to handle the broadcast traffic, which allows the administrator to control the ports in which this traffic is transmitted. The result is an increase in network performance brought about by a reduction in the amount of broadcast traffic. Because VLAN members are not required to be located

in a central location, they allow the network to be extended as far as is necessary to allow users to be located where they are needed while retaining the ability to connect to the network without changing the configuration of the workstation. Traditional, switched LANs would require the user to change the workstation configuration to meet the requirement of the remote LAN.

4. A. By allowing the administrator to define different groups. Defining groups allows the administrator to control which data is available to each group. Personnel data should only be available to the human resources group and financial data should only be available to the accounting group. By defining groups that have access to certain types of data, a major part of a larger network security strategy is created. Since VLANs are individual broadcast domains, they need the assistance of a router to allow traffic between different VLANs. If this access is needed, the router would provide security through the use of access lists to prevent access to sensitive data. Switches do not allow traffic from different VLANs to travel between VLANs.

5. C. Port. Administrators can assign multiple ports to different VLANs. This allows users in different locations, whether on different floors, in different buildings, or in different cities, to be part of a VLAN. VLANs can be assigned to either individual ports or multiple ports simultaneously. They can also be assigned across different switches. A trunking protocol allows switches to communicate VLAN information to each other.

Spanning-Tree Protocol and VLANs

1. C. It permits redundant physical links but only uses one link to send traffic. When multiple links are in use, STP notes the multiple links but only uses one link to send traffic. Other links are placed in blocking state to prevent traffic from being sent from the redundant link. When topology changes occur, Spanning-Tree recalculates the links to determine which link will carry traffic and which link will be placed in blocking state.

2. B. Source route. The responsibility for locating a device on the Token Ring is placed on the sending device. A test packet is sent out on the ring to determine what destination device is on the ring. If no response is received, an explorer frame is then sent to determine the location of the destination. As the frame moves across networks, the ring and bridge numbers are placed in the RIF field of the frame.

3. D. To ensure a loop-free network topology. This is done by noting the redundant links in the network, setting those links in blocking state, and allowing traffic to use one link.

4. B. They execute the STP to ensure a loop-free topology. STP provides a loop-free network, blocking redundant links. STP should be enabled on switches to prevent loops when new devices are introduced on the network.

5. C, D. A ring number and a bridge number. In source-route bridging, Token Ring frames contain a RIF field. The ring numbers and bridge numbers are contained in this field. As the frame moves across the network, the appropriate ring and bridge numbers are added to this field. When the frame reaches the destination, the device reads the RIF field and is able to get a clear picture of where to send the return data.

Default VLAN Configuration

1. D. 1. Most Catalyst switches have VLAN 1 set as default for all active ports on the switch. There are also VLANs (1002–1005) set for both Token Ring and FDDI networks on Catalysts equipped with FDDI and Token Ring modules. These VLANs cannot be removed, as they are part of the Catalyst's default configuration. The following illustration shows the display of the default VLANs on a Catalyst switch.

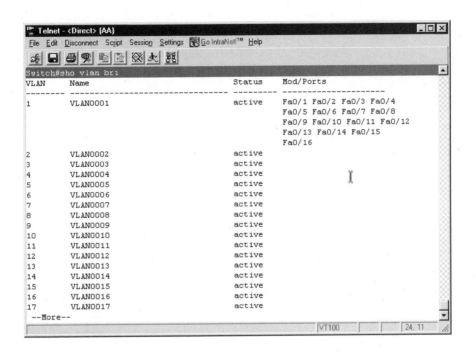

Configuring a VLAN Across a Domain

I. A. The number of users on the VLAN. This number should not be based solely on the number of individuals, but on a combination of users, servers, and other devices using the network without causing problems, such as congestion or slow response. This should include room for expansion of the VLAN for additional users or devices. Determining the number of users, servers, and other devices on a traditional LAN presented different problems. The number of users is even more critical in LAN design because the size of the LAN is more closely based on the physical location of the users. (Remember that VLANs are not limited by physical media or location.)

2. A. SHOW VTP STATISTICS. This command displays information that includes the links that are in the trunk group, advertisement counters, and configuration errors.

3. C. SHOW VTP DOMAIN. This command displays information for the domain. Information includes the domain name, the domain index, the VTP version, the mode VTP is running, the total number of VLANs in the domain, the maximum number of VLANs allowed in the domain, Simple Network Management Protocol (SNMP) notification, and pruning details.

4. D. RSM. The RSM module provides a full-function Cisco router that gives the Catalyst 5000 level-3 routing capability. The RSM runs the IOS software and is configured using the same commands as a Cisco router. The RSM has 128KB of NVRAM and has onboard Flash as well as a PCMCIA slot for additional flash memory in which to store the IOS software. The PCMCIA flash can be formatted either by the RSM module or by an RSP 2 card found on Cisco 7500 series routers.

5. B. Token Ring. VTP version 2 can allow the switch administrator to create a Token Ring switched network through the Token Ring bridge relay function. This function serves to interconnect several Token Ring VLANs. For source routing, the Catalyst will appear to be a bridge between the logical rings of the network.

Grouping Switch Ports to VLANs

1. C. 3. The are three switch ports available on the Catalyst 5000 24 100 Mbps Group Switching Module. The 24 user ports on the module are divided equally between the three switch ports. User ports 1–8 are set for switch port 1, user ports 9–16 are set for switch port 2, and user ports 17–24 are set for switch port 3. This gives a maximum of three VLANs that can be configured on the module.

2. **D.** SHOW PORT STATUS. The SHOW PORT STATUS command displays information on each port such as status, VLAN, speed of the port, and type of port in use. The following shows the information display by command.

```
Cat5000> (enable) show port status
Port  Name     Status      Vlan    Level   Duplex  Speed  Type
-------------------------------------------------------------------------
1/1            connected   1       normal  full    100    100BaseTX
1/2            connected   trunk   normal  full    155    OC3 MMF ATM
```

3. **A.** A network loop occurs, causing problems with the switched network. This happens when the switch recognizes a new link and adjusts the network topology appropriately. The switch runs STP to add the new link, recognizes that a loop has been introduced, and takes the steps necessary to eliminate the loop.

4. **C.** The port is not forwarding frames, but is analyzing frames to gather MAC address information. This state prepares the port to begin forwarding frames and also prepares the port to enter forwarding state.

5. **D.** It allows the port to bypass listening and learning state and go directly to forwarding state. Portfast allows the port to move more quickly to forwarding to cut down on the time workstations and other devices are not able to see other devices on the VLAN. Note that this command should be used for ports that are connected to one host. The PORTFAST command should not be used for ports with hubs, concentrators, bridges, or routers connected, as it can cause spanning-tree loops.

6. **B.** Switch Code version 4.1. This version of switch code allows Cisco switches to communicate with other vendor switches. Versions older than 4.1 do not support 802.1Q trunking. Verify which releases of hardware (specifically hardware that employs ASIC chips) support 802.1Q trunking. To verify that the switch's port can support 802.1Q trunking, use the SHOW PORT CAPABILITIES command.

Troubleshooting VLANs

1. **D. SHOW CAM.** When used with the MAC address of a workstation, this command provides information such as the VLAN in which the device is located and the port off of which the device is located. Other options are available for the SHOW CAM command; however, most network administrators do not track MAC addresses as a normal practice. Here are the other options:

   ■ **count,** which displays only the number of content-addressable memory (CAM) entries

   ■ **dynamic,** which displays the dynamic CAM entries

   ■ **static,** which displays static CAM entries

   ■ **permanent,** which displays permanent entries

   ■ **system,** which displays system entries

VLAN Configuration

1. **C. VTP.** Virtual Trunk Protocol (VTP) will allow all three switches to exchange VLAN information. Since the three VLANs now have connections on all three switches, they need to communicate information to allow connectivity. To configure VTP on the switches, use the following commands in enable mode on the Catalyst:

   ■ **SET VTP DOMAIN** *name*   This defines the VTP domain that is used.

   ■ **SET VLAN** *vlan_number*   This defines the VLAN for the backbone 100 Mbps Ethernet.

2. **A. SHOW VTP STATISTICS.** This command displays information on various advertisements that are transmitted and received, pruning statistics (if enabled), and the trunks that are configured for VTP.

3. B. SHOW VTP DOMAIN. This command displays domain information including the domain name, the mode VTP is running (server, client, or transparent), the number of VLANs that are currently configured on the switch, and information on which switch sent the last update.

4. C. ISL. Inter-Switch Link (ISL) was developed as a trunking protocol between Catalyst switches. ISL is able to send Ethernet and Token Ring frames between switches. To configure a switch to use ISL trunking protocol, use the following commands:

SET TRUNK mod_num/port_num ON
SET TRUNK *mod_num/port_num vlan_num*

The SET TRUNK *mod_num/port_num* commands sets the specified port as the ISL trunk. The SET TRUNK *mod_num/port_num vlan_num* adds the VLAN specified to the trunk.

5. B. SHOW TRUNK. This command displays trunk information, which includes the ports that are configured as trunks, the trunking mode, the encapsulation, the current trunk status, and the VLANs that are allowed to use the trunk. This information will allow the administrator to verify whether the trunk has been configured correctly and is passing frames.

6. C. The ports, to verify that the correct port speed has been set. This can be accomplished via the SHOW PORT command along with the port number in question. This command, along with the port number, provides information on individual ports, including port speed, port status, to which VLAN the port has been assigned, security, and whether or not the port has been shutdown.

7. B. Set the port speed to 10 Mbps. This is done by using the SET PORT SPEED command for the port in question. The default for all switching ports on the 10/100 switching module is autosense. It is a well-known fact that the autosense setting is not reliable. It is better to manually set the port speed to match what is connected to avoid any possible connectivity problems. Here is the syntax of the SET PORT SPEED command:

SET PORT SPEED *mod_num/port_num* 10

This will set the speed for the specified port to 10 Mbps.

8. **A.** Enable Portfast on the Catalyst. Portfast enables ports on the Catalyst to immediately begin forwarding frames. If Portfast is disabled on a Catalyst, it could cause problems for devices directly connected, such as making it impossible to reach DHCP servers. To enable Portfast on a Catalyst switch port, use the following command:

SET SPANTREE PORTFAST *mod_num/port_num* ENABLE

Note that Portfast should be enabled only for ports that are connected to individual workstations or PCs. Ports that are connected to hubs or concentrators should not have Portfast enabled.

9. **C.** The router must be connected to VLAN 3. Since there has been no requirement for the VLANs to communicate with each other, devices on the same VLAN can communicate with each other without the need for a router. The Catalyst is acting like a bridge, a level-2 device; but if devices need to communicate with the devices outside the VLAN, the Catalyst will need help with level-3 routing since devices outside the VLAN will not see broadcasts from devices within VLAN. The Cisco 7500 will need to be connected to VLAN 3 to provide the level-3 routing decisions.

10. **E.** Connect VLANs 1 and 2 to the router and use an access list to deny VLAN 3. Since the router is handling level-3 routing, an access list is used to deny VLAN 3 traffic on VLANs 1 and 2.

11. **C.** Add a Token Ring module to the Catalyst on the third floor. Since ABC Corporation is using Catalyst 5000 series switches, a Token Ring module can be added to provide the connectivity required. Since VLAN 1003 is already configured for Token Ring (part of the default configuration), all that is needed is to assign the proper port to the VLAN. This is accomplished with the command SET VLAN 1003 *mod_num/port_num*. Doing so assigns VLAN 1003 on the correct Token Ring module and port and will activate the VLAN. You will also need to add a Token Ring card to the Cisco 7500 router to translate the Token Ring packets into Ethernet and vice versa.

12. **A.** Check the Token Ring module speed setting. Token Rings operate at either 4 or 16 Mbps. If a device enters the ring and the ring speed is not set correctly, the result will be beaconing on the ring. To set the ring speed on a Token Ring module, use the SET PORT SPEED command to set the ring speed to either 4 or 16 Mbps. The default setting for the Token Ring module is autosense; it is recommended not to use autosense and set the port speed to either 4 or 16 Mbps. Note that you must stop and restart the port so the Catalyst can reenter the ring at the correct speed.

13. **C.** The duplex setting, to confirm that it is set correctly. If the Catalyst is connected to a multistation access unit (MAU), the Token Ring port needs to be set for half-duplex concentrator port. In this mode the port will function like any other device attached to the Token Ring. Here is the command to set the mode to half-duplex concentrator port:

SET TOKENRING PORTMODE *mod_num/port_num* HDXCPORT

14. **D.** By adding more ports to VLAN 3. Since the Catalyst 5000 series switch is modular, adding port capacity is as simple as adding a module to the chassis and assigning a VLAN to those ports. The SET VLAN command is used to define which ports are to be assigned to a VLAN.

15. **C.** The IEEE 802.1Q trunking protocol needs to be used. Catalyst switches are able to communicate with other vendors' switches. IEEE 802.1Q is a trunking protocol that has been developed to allow interoperability between switches of different vendors. Currently the three Catalysts are using ISL as the trunking protocol to communicate. If another vendor's switch is introduced to the network, 802.1Q trunking will have to be enabled.

Catalyst 5000 series switches can support both ISL and 802.1Q trunking. Since the network consists of Catalyst 4000 switches, only 802.1Q trunking is supported.

16. C. SHOW VERSION. This command displays the version of software that is in use on the switch. Information such as the type of hardware, the Bootstrap version, memory in use, and what hardware modules are installed, is displayed. The software version that Cisco Catalyst 5000 series switches need to support 802.1Q trunking is version 4.1 of the Catalyst switch code. The hardware must also be using ASIC-based chips to use the 802.1Q trunking.

Part 11

Test Yourself:
Practice Exam 1

Test Yourself:
Practice Exam 1
Questions

Q
&
A

Before you call to register for the actual exam, take the following test and see how you make out. Set a timer for 90 minutes—the time you'll have to take the live CCNA Certification exam—and answer the following 70 questions in the time allotted. Once you've finished, turn to the Practice Exam I Answers section and check your score to see if you passed! Good luck!

Practice Exam I Questions

1. When using an IP standard access list, if you do not define the wildcard mask for an IP host-address access list specification, what would the mask be?

   A. 255.255.255.255

   B. 0.0.0.255

   C. 0.0.0.0

   D. 255.255.255.252

2. The Acme Co. has acquired Widget, Inc. and is now merging with it. As shown in Figure 11-1, the management plans to open 22 new sales branches. The Acme Co. had two major offices with 500 employees in London and 1,000 in New York. Widget, Inc., had three major offices with 2,000 employees in Phoenix, 500 employees in Los Angeles, and 1,200 employees in Salt Lake City. Fourteen of the 22 sales offices will connect to Phoenix. Four sales branches will connect to the London office. Four sales branches will connect to the New York office. The newly merged IT department has hired you to assist them in selecting and assigning IP addresses.

   The IT department head states that the company is already using IP on the Acme portion of the network, but IPX on the Widget network. He says that two addresses have been assigned to their router, including a new IP address from Acme, but he cannot remember which of these addresses is the IP address and he is not sure if he has written the IP address correctly. He is sure that it is one of the following four addresses. Which of the following is most likely to be both the address and the correct address class?

| FIGURE 11-1 | Acme and Widget Merger |

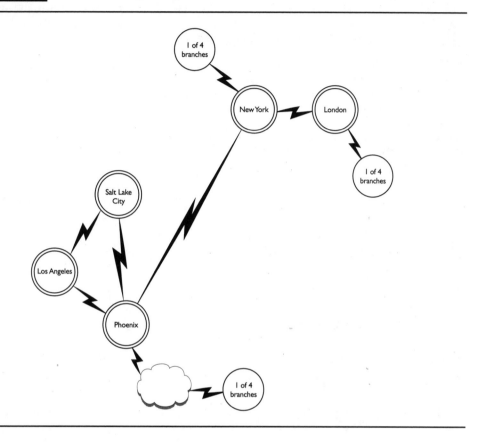

A. 2c.0000.8af3.715a.064d, Class A

B. 198.116.288.2, Class C

C. 127.0.0.1, Class B

D. 155.55.88.118, Class B

3. When typing on a command line, which keystroke should you use to go to the beginning of the line?

A. CTRL-B

B. CTRL-A

C. ESC-B

D. ESC-A

4. Refer to Figure 11-2 to choose the command that adds a basic security option to each packet leaving interface Ethernet 1 of the Boston router:

A. IP SECURITY ETHERNET E1
B. ADD IP SECURITY
C. IP SECURITY ADD
D. None of the above

Network diagram

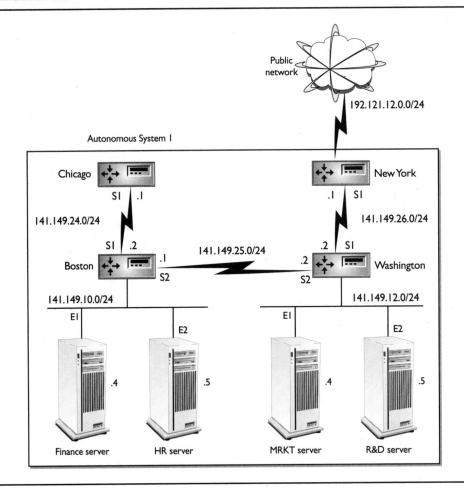

5. Packet filtering can assist network administrators with controlling packet movement throughout the network. What other purposes do access lists serve? (Choose all that apply.)

A. They control transmission of packets on an interface.

B. They restrict contents of routing updates.

C. They control virtual terminal line access.

D. They limit IP path MTU discovery.

6. What is the decimal value of the subnet portion of a Class B address 144.25.98.150 with a subnet mask of 255.255.255.128?

A. 144.25.98.150

B. 144.25.98.128

C. 144.25.150.98

D. 144.25.255.128

7. What occurs when there is a change in topology in a Layer 2 network?

A. The bridge reboots.

B. The bridge goes into blocking state.

C. The bridge sends out a BPDU.

D. The router sends out a BDPU.

8. Which address does the media access control (MAC) provide?

A. Logical address

B. IP address

C. Data address

D. Hardware address

9. What command in UNIX will show the workstation's routing table?

A. NETSTAT

B. RLOGIN

C. PING

D. WINIPCFG

10. What happens to data at the sending station as it passes down through the layers of the OSI model?

   A. The data is broken down into smaller units that can be handled by the next layer.

   B. The data is examined by each layer and discarded if it does not contain proper instructions for that layer.

   C. The data is broken down into smaller units and encapsulated, adding a new header to the unit.

   D. The data is transmitted directly to the corresponding OSI layer at the receiving station.

11. When entering a password to access privileged mode, what do you see?

   A. Nothing is shown on your screen.

   B. Your password is shown in encrypted text.

   C. xxxxxxx

   D. ********

12. When you create a standard or extended access list that has not been applied to an interface, how does the router process the packets coming in and out of the interface?

   A. It denies all traffic, with implicit DENY.

   B. It permits all traffic.

   C. It permits only traffic within your own network.

   D. It restricts only inbound traffic for your Ethernet port.

13. Following are the configurations for LANE on a Cisco switch and router. This is not a complete configuration, but is appropriate for the question that follows.

ATM Router I

```
version 11.X
!
hostname Router 1
!
appletalk routing
!
decnet routing
decnet node-type area
!
ipx routing
!
interface ATM0/0/0
no ip address
no ip mroute-cache
atm pvc 1 0 5 qsaal
atm pvc 2 0 16 ilmi
hold-queue 450 in
!
interface ATM0/0/0.1 multipoint
description vlan101
ip address 10.1.1.1     255.255.255.0
lane client ethernet vlan101
ipx network
!
interface ATM0/0/0.2 multipoint
 description vlan102
 lane client ethernet vlan102
!
interface ATM0/0/0.3 multipoint
description vlan103
lane client ethernet vlan103
!
interface ATM0/0/0.10 multipoint
no ip mroute-cache
shutdown
atm pvc 4 4 88 aal5snap
map-group rfc1483
!
end
```

ATM-Database

```
hostname ATM-DATABASE
!
lane database atm-database
name vlan102 server-atm-address 47.009181001111101011B90A01.00E0111E1441.02
name vlan102 server-atm-address 47.009181001111106183C59401.00604747B941.02
name vlan101 server-atm-address 47.009181001211106183C59401.00604747B941.01
name vlan101 server-atm-address 47.009181000000001011B90A01.00E0111E1441.01
name vlan103 server-atm-address 47.009181000000006183C59401.00604747B941.03
name vlan103 server-atm-address 47.009181000000001011B90A01.00E0111E1441.03
!
interface ATM0
mtu 1500
atm pvc 1 0 5 qsaal
atm pvc 2 0 16 ilmi
lane config auto-config-atm-address
lane config database ATM-DATABASE
!
interface ATM0.1 multipoint
description vlan101
lane server-bus ethernet vlan101
lane client ethernet 101 vlan101
!
interface ATM0.2 multipoint
description vlan102
lane server-bus ethernet vlan102
lane client ethernet 102 vlan102
!
interface ATM0.3 multipoint
description vlan103
lane server-bus ethernet vlan103
lane client ethernet 103 vlan103
!
end
```

The ATM DATABASE switch is configured with ATM address
47.009181001211106183C59401.00604747B941.01. Which of the
following are represented in this address?

A. A 13-byte prefix

B. A 6-byte ESI

C. A 1-byte selector

D. A 5-byte header

14. How would you change the rate of CDP packets sent from the default to one every 50 seconds?

A. CDP TIMER 50

B. SET TIMER 50

C. SET CDP 50

D. SET CDP TIMER 500

15. Company XYZ has 50,000 employees in locations around the world. The corporate headquarters is in London, the North American headquarters is in Washington D.C., and the Asian headquarters is in Singapore. All three headquarters are connected via T-1s. Each regional location manages its own network system. Each of the three networks has IP, IPX, and AppleTalk running. RIP is the dominant routing protocol in use. Cisco routers are used throughout the entire wide area network (WAN). You have been asked to install and configure a router in each regional area. Upon investigation, you find that each network has been set up a little differently. In the corporate headquarters, there is a TFTP server that has a configuration for the router already set up. You will need to install router A in London and access the TFTP server for the configuration files. The configuration file to be loaded is named config-1_2.P. The address of the TFTP server is 151.176.21.5. The IOS image is located in ROM. Router B is to be installed in Washington D.C. You find out from the engineer shipping the router that it has been preconfigured in a lab. You need only install the router and bring it up. The configuration has been saved in the router's NVRAM. The IOS image is located in flash. Singapore will be the location of new router C. This router does not have a configuration completed. You want to initially bring the router up and complete the configuration on the fly. Which type of ports does 10BaseT use?

A. RJ-11

B. RJ-12

C. RJ-45

D. RJ-48

16. Which portion of the configuration register makes up the Boot field?

A. The most significant four bits

B. The most significant two bits

C. The least significant four bits

D. The least significant two bits

17. According to Figure 11-2 (shown earlier), which of the following commands defines a neighboring router for Boston with which to exchange routing information (assuming that this is a nonbroadcast network)? (Choose all that apply.)

A. NEIGHBOR 141.149.24.1

B. NEIGHBOR 141.149.25.2

C. NEIGHBOR 141.149.24.0

D. NEIGHBOR 141.149.25.0

18. WebSTER Services is a new World Wide Web corporation dedicated to providing Internet connectivity. Because of the amount of incoming traffic, WebSTER plans to install multiple routers and LAN segments to separate the service traffic from corporate data traffic. There will be four segments, each separated by routers. WebSTER will have a NetWare server (Svr2) running both IP and IPX placed on Network 4. This NetWare server's internal network number will be 5. WebSTER also will have a NetWare server (Svr1) running only IPX placed on Network 1 with an internal network number 6. Corporate client computers may attach directly to either Network 1 or Network 2. The following illustration depicts the future WebSTER network.

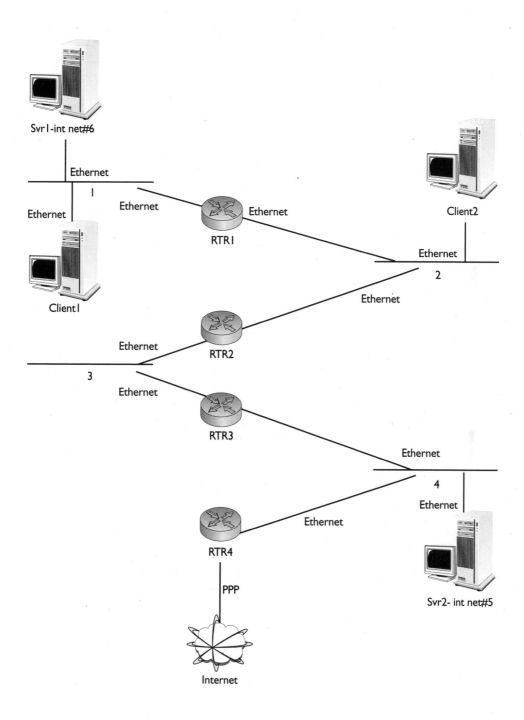

When configuring RTR4, which of the following commands must be entered to enable IPX?

A. rtr4(config)#IPX ROUTING

B. rtr4(config-if)#IPX ENABLE

C. rtr4(config-if)#IPX ROUTING

D. rtr4#IPX ENABLE

19. What tool is used to transmit files?

A. DNS

B. FTP

C. CDR

D. TRACERT

20. Which of the following does auto-installation accomplish?

A. Automatic rebooting of the router if the system fails

B. Automatic configuration of the router by an IPX server on your network

C. Automatic configuration of the router from a TFTP server on your network

D. The router never having power failure

21. What happens to the encapsulation that is added at the data-link layer of the sending machine when it reaches the physical layer on the destination machine?

A. It is discarded.

B. It is interpreted.

C. The physical layer encapsulates it with its own header and trailer.

D. Nothing happens.

22. According to the following configuration, which command is accurate to configure X.25 operation on a serial interface of Remote Router 1?

```
Remote Router 1#
Interface bri0
        isdn x25 dchannel
        isdn x25 static-tei
!
interface  bri0:0
        ip address 10.1.100.10  255.255.255.0
        x25 address 11110001111000
x25 map ip 10.1.100.11 11110001111001
!
end
```

A. remote-router1(config)#ENCAPSULATION X25

B. remote-router1(config-if)#ENCAPSULATION X25

C. remote-router1(config)#x25 ENCAPSULATION

D. remote-router1(config-if)#X25 ENCAPSULATION

23. According to Figure 11-2 (shown earlier), which of the following commands should be used to set up the Boston router as a default gateway to provide a route for employees off the Chicago network to communicate with the HR server when IP routing is disabled?

A. IP DEFAULT-GATEWAY 141.149.24.2

B. IP DEFAULT-NETWORK 141.149.10.0

C. DEFAULT-GATEWAY 141.149.10.2

D. IP DEFAULT-GATEWAY 141.149.10.0

24. Which of the following sends out updates of the routing table every 60 seconds?

    A. SAP

    B. RIP

    C. NCP

    D. SPX

25. Which of the following are purposes of the Logical Link Control (LLC)? (Choose all that apply.)

    A. Error correction

    B. Management of network device connections

    C. Flow control

    D. Communication with the physical layer

26. For which of the following situations is frame relay best suited?

    A. Applications with bursty data traffic

    B. Videoconferencing

    C. Traffic with voice, data, and video

    D. None of the above

27. Referring to the following illustration, select the encapsulation for the host node to use across all routers to contact Host_1 without changing encapsulation types.

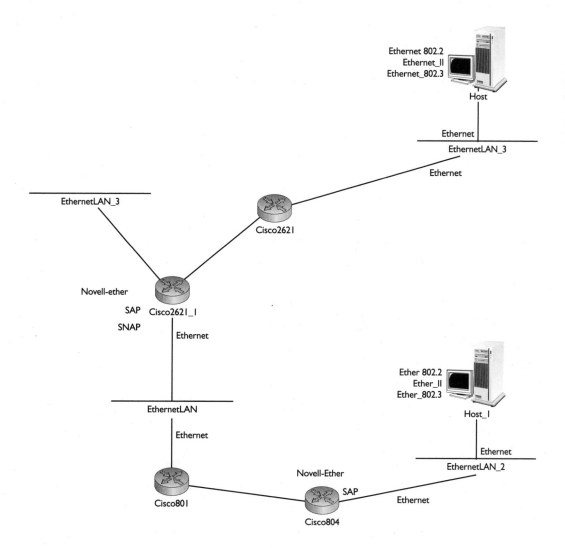

A. Arpa

B. SNAP

C. Novell-Ether

D. SAP

E. None of the above

28. What is indicated by the !!!!! result after entering the Packet Internet Groper (PING) command?

A. Successful echo responses were received

B. Timed out waiting for responses

C. Destination unreachable

D. Time to live exceeded

29. Which of the following provides a way for servers and routers to announce their services to the internetwork?

A. NCP

B. NetBIOS

C. IPX

D. SAP

30. How long is an ATM cell header (Q 41 and 40)?

A. 53 bytes

B. 48 bytes

C. 5 bytes

D. 8 bytes

31. Which of the following is the line rate for T3, or digital signal level 3 (DS-3)?

A. 155.5 Mbps

B. 44.7 Mbps

C. 34.3 Mbps

D. 1.544 Mbps

32. Referring to Figure 11-2 (shown earlier), from the enable mode in a Cisco router, what are the necessary steps needed to enter into the global configuration mode?

A. Type **en** to get into the enable mode of the router and then enter the password.

B. Log out of the router and log in as **root**.

C. Type **configure terminal**.

D. Log out of the router and log in with the global configuration password.

33. A&A is migrating its existing NetBEUI network to TCP/IP. A&A has 150 network nodes and has noticed that performance is greatly degraded since it was originally installed with 10 nodes. The move to TCP/IP will also be accompanied by the installation of routers and several directly connected networks, in order to isolate some of the network traffic. All new hardware and cabling will be replacing the existing infrastructure. There are four departments in A&A: Marketing, Administration, Sales, and Service. The Marketing and Sales departments share a significant amount of data. The Administration department, however, has a subdepartment, Payroll, which will require a significant level of security. A&A is a fairly stable company. It has experienced 25 percent or less growth in the number of employees in a 10-year period. A&A has an outside field force of 2,500 independent, commission-based agents. The company has decided to enable remote access to the network so the agents can check their sales status. Since they are not planning on connecting to the Internet, A&A has decided to implement a Class B address 172.10.0.0 with a subnet mask of 255.255.252.0. What is the address range of the first available subnet?

A. 172.10.253.1–172.10.253.255

B. 172.10.4.1–172.10.7.254

C. 172.10.8.1–172.10.15.254

D. 172.10.4.1–172.10.4.255

34. What is encapsulation?

    A. The process of moving data from one network to another in capsules or packets

    B. The placement of upper-layer protocol data segments within lower-layer protocol data segments

    C. The calculation of hops and ticks from one route on an Ethernet network to another on a Token Ring network

    D. The synchronous serial network inclusion of a clocking mechanism in the data stream

35. The following illustration portrays the physical connection of the frame relay network with redundant connections to the central locations. All the routers are configured so that routing information will not be passed between remote routers, for security purposes. Which of the routers in the illustration is configured for LMI?

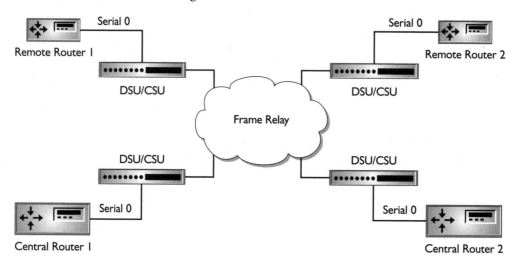

Remote Router 1

```
version 11.2
!
hostname remote-router1
!
interface Serial0
no ip address
```

```
encapsulation frame-relay
bandwidth 64
no fair-queue
!
interface Serial0.1 point-to-point
description PVC to Central Router1
ip address 10.1.11.2 255.255.255.0
frame-relay interface-dlci 102
!
interface Serial0.2 point-to-point
description PVC to Central Router2
ip address 10.1.12.2 255.255.255.0
frame-relay interface-dlci 103
!
end
```

Remote Router 2

```
version 11.2
!
hostname remote-router2
!
interface Serial0
no ip address
encapsulation frame-relay
bandwidth 64
no fair-queue
!
interface Serial0.1 point-to-point
description PVC to Central Router 1
ip address 10.1.11.3 255.255.255.0
frame-relay interface-dlci 202
!
interface Serial0.2 point-to-point
description PVC to Central Router2
ip address 10.1.12.3 255.255.255.0
frame-relay interface-dlci 203
!
end
```

Central Router I

```
hostname Central Router1
enable secret 5
enable password cisco
!
```

```
interface Ethernet0/0
 ip address 192.157.129.254 255.255.255.0
!
interface Serial3/0
no ip address
no ip mroute-cache
encapsulation frame-relay
no ip route-cache
bandwidth 384
!
interface Serial3/0.1 multipoint
description Frame-relay T1
ip address 10.1.11.1 255.255.255.0
no ip mroute-cache
no ip route-cache
bandwidth 128
frame-relay map ip 10.1.11.2  101 broadcast
frame-relay map ip 10.1.11.3  102 broadcast
!
interface Serial3/0.2 point-to-point
description PVC for Network management
ip address 10.1.100.1 255.255.255.0
no ip route-cache
bandwidth 128
frame-relay interface-dlci 100
!
end
```

Central Router 2

```
hostname Central Router 2
!
interface Ethernet0/0
ip address 10.1.1.2 255.255.255.0
!
interface Serial3/0
no ip address
no ip mroute-cache
encapsulation frame-relay
no ip route-cache
bandwidth 384
frame-relay keepalive 20
!
```

```
interface Serial3/0.1 multipoint
description Frame-relay T1
ip address 10.1.12.1 255.255.255.0
no ip mroute-cache
no ip route-cache
bandwidth 128
frame-relay map ip 10.1.12.2 402 broadcast
frame-relay map ip 10.1.12.3 403 broadcast
!
interface Serial3/0.2 point-to-point
description PVC For Network Managment
ip address 10.1.100.2 255.255.255.0
no ip route-cache
bandwidth 128
frame-relay interface-dlci 100
!
end
```

A. Central Router 1

B. Central Router 2

C. Client Router 1 and Client Router 2

D. All of the above

36. Which of the following is an advantage that VLANs give administrators?

A. They require the use of a single media.

B. They allow them to add routers as needed.

C. They allow them to create workgroups based on function rather than media.

D. They allow them to run RIP.

37. Which of the following describes blocking state?

A. The port is not forwarding, but is participating in STP.

B. The port is not forwarding and not participating in STP.

C. The port is not forwarding, but is analyzing frames to gather MAC address information.

D. The port is forwarding and participating in STP.

38. Match the following Novell frame types to their Cisco encapsulations:

A. Ethernet_II	1. Novell-Ether
B. Token_Ring_SNAP	2. SAP
C. Ethernet_802.2	3. Arpa
D. Ethernet_802.3	4. SNAP

39. The R&D employees in New York need a static route to the 141.149.12.0 network in order to access the R&D server. According to Figure 11-2 (shown earlier), which command configures that route in the New York router?

A. IP ROUTE 141.149.12.0 255.255.255.0 141.149.26.2

B. IP ROUTE 141.149.12.0 141.149.26.2

C. IP ROUTE 141.149.12.0 255.255.255.0 141.149.26.1

D. ROUTE 141.149.12.0 255.255.255.0 141.149.26.2

40. What is the primary function of the packet assembler/disassembler (PAD)?

A. Buffers packets sent to or from DTE

B. Assembles packets

C. Disassembles packets

D. All of the above

41. What is the purpose of sliding windows?

A. To enable TCP to operate on different architectures

B. To more effectively use network bandwidth

C. To maintain data transmission integrity

D. To provide a mechanism for network management

42. At which layer of the OSI reference model do bridges and switches operate?

A. Application

B. Presentation

C. Session

D. Transport

E. Network

F. Data-link

G. Physical

43. Company XYZ has 50,000 employees in locations around the world. The corporate headquarters is in London, the North American headquarters is in Washington D.C., and the Asian headquarters is in Singapore. All three headquarters are connected via T-1s. Each regional location manages its own network system. Each of the three networks has IP, IPX, and AppleTalk running. RIP (Routing Information Protocol) is the dominant routing protocol in use. Cisco routers are used throughout the entire wide area network (WAN). You have been asked to install and configure a router in each regional area. Upon investigation, you find that each network has been set up a little differently. In the corporate headquarters, there is a TFTP server that has a configuration for the router already set up. You will need to install router A in London and access the TFTP server for the configuration files. The configuration file to be loaded is named config-1_2.P. The address of the TFTP server is 151.176.21.5. The IOS image is located in ROM. Router B is to be installed in Washington D.C. You find out from the engineer shipping the router that it has been preconfigured in a lab. You need only install the router and bring it up. The configuration has been saved in the router's NVRAM. The IOS image is located in flash. Singapore will be the location of new router C. This router does not have a configuration completed. You want to initially bring the router up and complete the configuration on the fly. What is the size of the header in a RIP packet?

A. 32 bytes

B. 16 bytes

C. 8 bytes

D. 24 bytes

44. Chloe is the new network administrator of MacGuire Enterprises. The former administrator created an IP addressing scheme using multiple Class B addresses and applied it to every node on the internetwork. Chloe discovers that the Class B addresses are not assigned to MacGuire Enterprises by InterNIC. Her boss has asked her to establish a connection to the Internet. What should Chloe do to establish the connection?

A. She should change the Class B addresses to Class D addresses in order to take advantage of Internet multicasting.

B. She should supernet the Class B addresses together and change the mask on each host.

C. She should have a new address assigned to MacGuire Enterprises by InterNIC and make changes to the rest of the addressing scheme.

D. She does not need to do anything.

45. How large is the configuration register?

A. 8 bits

B. 16 bits

C. 32 bits

D. 8 bytes

46. This scenario follows the creation of VLANs for ABC Corporation. The corporation has three departments: Human Resources, Finance, and Engineering. They are spread across three floors of their office building. The decision has been made to use VLANs with Cisco Catalyst 5000 series switches. VLAN 1 is designated for human resources, VLAN 2 is designated for finance, and VLAN 3 is designated for engineering. There is one Catalyst switch per floor. The LAN media is a combination of 10 Mbps and 100 Mbps Ethernet. Links between the Catalysts are 100 Mbps Ethernet. The following illustration shows the network topology.

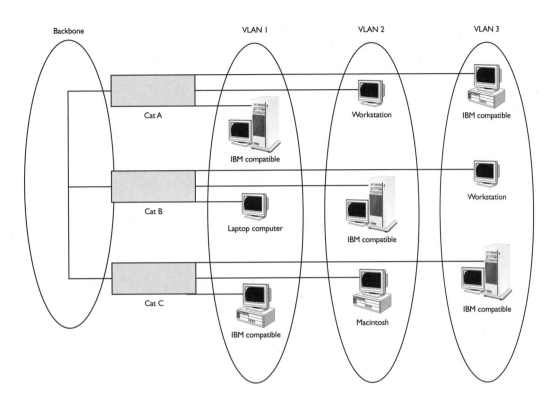

Due to expansion, it has been decided to use space on the second and third floors of the building. The VLANs must be expanded to these floors. There already are 100Mbps Ethernet connections between the three Catalysts. How must the VLANs be expanded to these floors?

A. By installing new routers

B. By enabling OSPF

C. By installing new hubs

D. By configuring ports for the three VLANs

47. Which of the following is a correct classification for OSPF?

A. Distance vector routing protocol

B. Link-state routing protocol

C. Static routing protocol

D. None of the above

48. What needs to be configured on Catalyst switches to allow for automatic VLAN information exchange?

   A. VRIP
   B. ISL
   C. OSPF
   D. VTP

49. Which function occurs at the network layer?

   A. Fragmentation
   B. Electrically converting 1s and 0s to pulses
   C. Error correction
   D. Security

50. Which IP configuration command removes an IP address from an interface?

   A. NO ADDRESS-IP
   B. NO IP-ADDRESS *IP-address mask*
   C. REMOVE IP-ADDRESS *IP-address mask*
   D. None of the above

51. What is a remote procedure call?

   A. A new protocol
   B. A programming technique
   C. An application-layer tool
   D. A client-server computing technique

52. After installing your router, what do you use to gain login access to the router? (Choose all that apply.)

   A. Server access
   B. Telnet
   C. Console
   D. Login port

53. What is the standard measurement used by routing protocols to help determine the path to a destination?

A. MED

B. Metric

C. Hop count

D. Route

54. How many layers do the respective protocol layers contain?

A. TCP/IP, 2; OSI, 7

B. TCP/IP, 4; OSI, 4

C. TCP/IP, 4; OSI, 7

D. TCP/IP, 7; OSI, 7

55. Router A is connected to Router B via Serial 1. Router A also has a connection to the Internet via port Serial 0. The following listings show the network layout.

Router A

```
hostname RouterA
!
interface Ethernet 0
 ip address 192.168.1.1 255.255.255.0
  no mop enabled
 no shutdown
!
interface Serial 0
 description Serial Link to the Internet
 encapsulation hdlc
  ip address 204.59.144.3 255.255.255.252
 no shutdown
!
interface Serial 1
 description Serial Link to Router B
 ip address 172.16.10.3 255.255.255.252
 encapsulation hdlc
 no shutdown
 network 192.168.0.0
 network 172.16.0.0
 !
 ip route 0.0.0.0 0.0.0.0 204.59.144.2
```

Router B

```
hostname RouterB
!
interface Ethernet 0
 ip address 192.168.10.2 255.255.0.0
  no shutdown
!
interface Serial 0
   ip address 172.16.10.2 255.255.255.252
encapsulation hdlc
no shutdown
!
router rip
network 128.129.0.0
network 192.168.0.0
```

RIP network updates from Router A are not being received by Router B because of a congested link. This is causing routes from Router A to be declared invalid. What do the administrators of the routers need to do?

A. They need to install a new link.

B. They need to adjust the Invalid timer within RIP.

C. They need to change routing protocols.

D. They need to install more routers.

56. To ensure automatic redistribution of IGRP into EIGRP, which of the following must happen?

A. The metrics must be equal.

B. The autonomous system AS numbers must agree.

C. RIP must be enabled.

D. None of the above.

57. What is the difference between a hub and a switch?

A. A hub handles a frame by examining the destination MAC address and saving this information, while a switch copies and transmits the frame to all ports.

    B. A hub copies a frame and transmits it based on the MAC address, while a switch examines the destination MAC address and saves this information.

    C. A hub copies and transmits a frame to all ports, while a switch examines the source MAC address and stores this information in its switching table to build a list of all MAC address locations.

    D. None of the above.

58. Why does the Simple Network Management Protocol (SNMP) use the User Datagram Protocol (UDP) to communicate?

    A. There are no other protocols that support SNMP's requirements.

    B. UDP is reliable enough for network management.

    C. It would be inefficient to use TCP for network management.

    D. SNMP uses RPCs, not UDP, for communication.

59. The Acme Co. has acquired Widget, Inc., and is now merging with it. The management plans to open 22 new sales branches. The Acme Co. had two major offices with 500 employees in London and 1,000 in New York. Widget, Inc. had three major offices with 2,000 employees in Phoenix, 500 employees in Los Angeles and 1,200 employees in Salt Lake City. Fourteen of the 22 sales offices will connect to Phoenix. Four sales branches will connect to the London office. Four sales branches will connect to the New York office. The newly merged IT department has hired you to assist them in selecting and assigning IP addresses. See Figure 11-1 (shown earlier).

    Acme/Widget would like to know what class of IP address to use to service all of its end users. Assume that there is a maximum of 5,500 nodes on the entire internetwork. Which class of address is best?

    A. Class A

    B. Class B

    C. Class C

    D. Class D

    E. Class E

    F. Class F

    G. None of the above

60. Suppose you have a network connected to the Internet, and you want any host on a Fast Ethernet network to be able to form TCP connections to any host on the Internet. However, you do not want IP hosts to be able to form TCP connections to hosts on the Fast Ethernet side except to a dedicated mail host such as Simple Mail Transfer Protocol (SMTP). SMTP uses TCP port 25 on one end of the connection and a random port number on the other end. Your network address is 131.72.0.0, and the address of the mail host is 131.72.1.2. Which of the following would you use to control the flow of traffic on this interface?

A. ACCESS-LIST 103 PERMIT TCP ANY131.72.0.0 0.0.255.255 ESTABLISHED
   ACCESS-LIST 103 PERMIT TCP ANY131.72.1.2 0.0.0.0 EQ SMTP
   INTERFACE FASTETHERNET 0/0/0
   ACCESS-GROUP 103 IN

B. ACCESS-LIST 103 PERMIT NLSP ANY131.72.1.2 0.0.0.0 EQ SMTP
   ACCESS-LIST 103 PERMIT NLSP ANY131.72.0.0 0.0.255.255 ESTABLISHED

C. INTERFACE FASTETHERNET 0/0/0
   ACCESS-GROUP 103 IN

D. ACCESS-LIST 103 PERMIT UDP ANY131.72.0.0 0.0.255.255 ESTABLISHED
   ACCESS-LIST 103 PERMIT UDP ANY131.72.1.2 0.0.0.0 EQ SMTP
   INTERFACE FASTETHERNET 0/0/0
   ACCESS-GROUP 103 IN

E. ACCESS-LIST 103 PERMIT UDP ANY131.72.1.2 0.0.0.0 EQ SMTP
   ACCESS-LIST 103 PERMIT UDP ANY131.72.0.0 0.0.255.255 ESTABLISHED
   INTERFACE FASTETHERNET 0/0/0
   ACCESS-GROUP 103 IN

61. Which layers of the OSI reference model are considered the upper-layer protocols?

A. Application, presentation
B. Application, presentation, session
C. Application, presentation, session, transport
D. Transport, network, data-link, physical
E. Network, data-link, physical
F. Data-link, physical

62. Which command starts the RIP routing process in a router?

A. RIP ROUTER

B. ROUTER RIP

C. RIP ON

D. IP ROUTER RIP

E. None of the above

63. How much bandwidth is used by EIGRP on an interface?

A. 25 percent

B. 75 percent

C. 20 percent

D. 50 percent

64. What types of access lists can IPX filter?

A. SAP access lists

B. Extended access lists

C. Standard access lists

D. IPX NetBIOS access lists

E. All of the above

65. What is the default VLAN for all active ports on a Catalyst switch?

A. 1000

B. 100

C. 10

D. 1

66. What types of algorithms are used by IP routing protocols?

A. OSPF and RIP

B. Static and dynamic

C. Distance vector and link-state

D. None of the above

67. Standard IPX access lists are numbered 800–899. On what do they filter?

A. Source and destination

B. Destination mask

C. Novell destination network

D. Source Mask

68. Which of the following network-layer protocols are correctly matched to their function? (Choose all that apply.)

A. RIP, updates routing tables dynamically

B. NCP, provides core services for NetWare

C. IPX, is a connectionless, unreliable datagram service

D. SAP, advertises services for servers and routers

69. A&A is migrating their existing NetBEUI network to TCP/IP. A&A has 150 network nodes and has noticed that performance is greatly degraded since it was originally installed with 10 nodes. The move to TCP/IP will also be accompanied by the installation of routers and several directly connected networks, in order to isolate some of the network traffic. All new hardware and cabling will be replacing the existing infrastructure. There are four departments in A&A: Marketing, Administration, Sales, and Service. The Marketing and Sales departments share a significant amount of data. The Administration department, however, has a subdepartment, Payroll, that will require a significant level of security. A&A is a fairly stable company. They have experienced 25 percent or less growth in the number of employees in a 10-year period. A&A tries a Class B address with a subnet mask of 255.255.224.0. In which range of addresses is 172.10.99.220?

A. 172.10.99.1–172.10.99.255

B. 172.10.96.1–172.10.127.254

C. 172.10.64.1–172.10.128.254

D. 172.10.72.1–172.10.100.254

70. The following tests your knowledge of IP access lists. ABC Corporation has a single Cisco router connecting two Ethernet segments in the home office. The LAN attached to Ethernet 0 is connected to the engineering LAN. Ethernet 1 is the general LAN for access to all devices.

```
version 11.3
!
hostname Andrews
!
boot system flash
enable password san-fran
!
ip classless
ip subnet-zero
no ip domain-lookup
!

interface Ethernet 0
 ip address 192.192.192.1 255.255.255.0
 no mop enabled
 no shutdown
!
interface Ethernet 1
 ip address 192.192.193.1 255.255.255.0
 no mop enabled
 no shutdown
!
interface Serial 0
 shutdown
!
interface Serial1
  shutdown

router rip
network 192.192.192.0
network 192.192.193.0
!
banner motd #
          Welcome to Andrews!
```

```
#
!
line con 0
 exec-timeout 0 0
 password cisco
 login
line aux 0
 no exec
line vty 0 4
 password cisco
 login
!
end
```

What type of access list is in effect at this time?

A. IP standard

B. IP standard/extended

C. IP extended/standard

D. None of the above

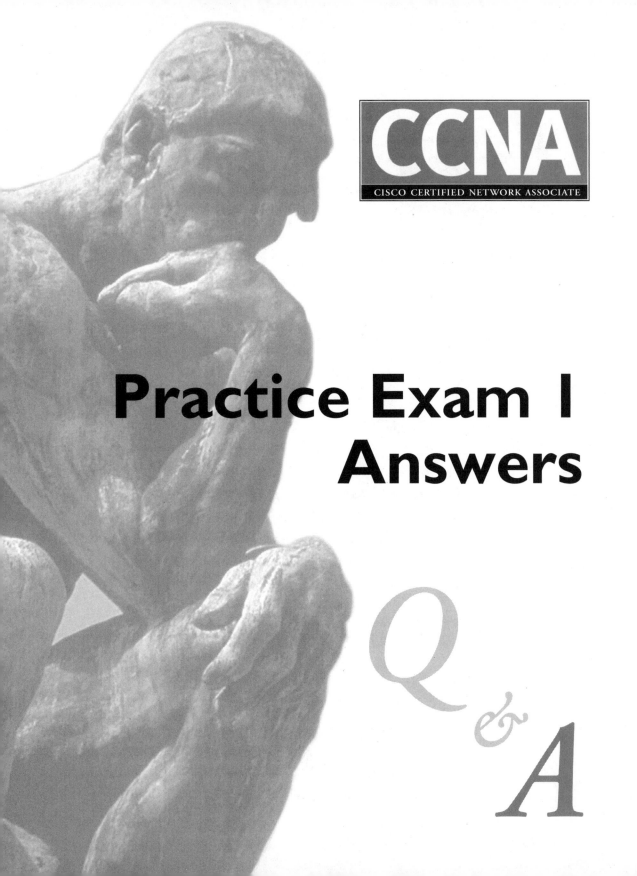

Threhe answers to the questions are in boldface, followed by a brief explanation. Some of the explanations detail the logic you should use to choose the correct answer, while others give factual reasons why the answer is correct. If you miss several questions on a similar topic, you should review the corresponding section in the *CCNA Cisco Certified Network Associate Study Guide*, Second Edition (Osborne/McGraw-Hill, 1999) before taking the CCNA Certification test.

Practice Exam I Answers

1. **C. 0.0.0.0.** IP standard access lists contain implicit masks. For instance, if you omit the mask from an associated IP host-address access list specification, 0.0.0.0 is assumed to be the mask. Consider the following example:

   ```
   access-list 4 permit 0.0.0.
   access-list 4 permit 131.72.0.
   access-list 4 deny 0.0.0.0 255.255.255.255
   ```

   For the preceding example, the following masks are implied in the first two lines:

   ```
   access-list 4 permit 0.0.0.0 0.0.0.0
   access-list 4 permit 131.72.0.0 0.0.0.0
   ```

   The last line in the configuration (with the DENY keyword) can be left off, because IP access lists implicitly deny all other access. This is equivalent to finishing the access list with the following command statement:

   ```
   access-list 4 deny 0.0.0.0 255.255.255.255
   ```

2. **D. 155.55.88.118, Class B.** Since Acme is already using IP, and has a few thousand hosts, it is likely that Acme already uses a Class B address. Class B addresses are in the range of 128.*x.x.x* to 191.*x.x.x*, to which 155.55.88.118 belongs. Widget is migrating an IPX network to IP and has no IP addresses. So of the four addresses that the IT head wrote down, answer A is an IPX address. Answer B is not an IP address, since the third octet is greater than 255, the maximum number in any one of the octets. Answer C is neither a Class B address nor an option for the address assigned to Acme since it is known as a loopback address. Loopback addresses are in the 127.*x.x.x* range of addresses and are used to test a local host's configuration.

3. **B.** CTRL-A. This is useful because sometimes the commands will be very long. Being able to move around on the command line is known as enhanced editing. Other enhanced editing features include CTRL-E, which allows you to go the end of the line, CTRL-B, which allows you to go back one character at a time, CTRL-F, which allows you to go forward one character at a time, ESC-B, which allows you to go back one word at a time, and ESC-F, which allows you to go forward one word at a time. These editing commands come from EMACS. Of course, also use the BACKSPACE or DELETE keys to change characters if you make a mistake. Depending upon the terminal type you are using, you may also be able to use the arrow keys to navigate along the line. In the answer choices, ESC-A has no meaning, and is not used as an enhanced editing feature.

4. **C.** IP SECURITY ADD. Since there is no reference to a particular interface in the answer, the command must be used in the interface configuration mode of a particular interface. This option activates, or adds, the security option to all outgoing packets. If an outgoing packet does not have a security option present, this interface configuration command adds one as the first IP option. The security label added to the Option field is the label that was computed for this packet when it first entered the router. Because this action is performed after all the security tests have been passed, this label is the same as, or falls within, the range of the interface. According to RFC 1108, this basic security option identifies the U.S. classification level at which the datagram is to be protected and the authorities whose protection rules apply to each datagram. Furthermore, this command validates the datagram for transmission from the source and delivery to the destination, and ensures that the route taken by the datagram is at the protected level required by all authorities indicated on the datagram. The DoD Basic Security option must be copied on fragmentation. This option appears at most once in a datagram. Some security systems require this as the first option if more than one option is carried in the IP header, but this is not a general requirement of this specification.

5. **A, B, C.** They control transmission of packets on an interface; they restrict contents of routing updates; and they control virtual terminal line access.

Packet filtering helps control the packet movement throughout the network and helps control the amount of traffic and restrict network use by certain users and/or devices. Access lists define the actual traffic that will be permitted or denied, while an access group applies an access list definition to an interface. Access lists can be used to deny conditions that are known security risks and then permit all other connections, or to permit only those connections that are acceptable and deny all the rest.

6. **B.** 144.25.98.128. The subnet mask translates to 11111111.11111111. |11111111.1|0000000 in binary. The address itself translates to 10010000.00011001.|01100010.1|0010110. The subnet portion is 01100010.1 which is equivalent to 98.128

7. **C.** The bridge sends out a BPDU. A Bridge Protocol Data Unit (BPDU) is a packet that is sent to the root bridge in the network. This packet announces that a change has occurred in the topology and that a recalculation of the topology is required to determine which links will forward traffic and which links will be placed in blocking state to prevent loops. Devices in a transparent bridge environment use the BPDU to handle topology changes.

8. **D.** Hardware address. The MAC provides the hardware address of the device, or, as it is more commonly known, the MAC address. This is usually provided by the vendor but can sometimes be applied using software. The addresses consist of 12 hexadecimal digits. The Institute of Electrical and Electronics Engineers (IEEE) assigns the first six digits to the vendor. These are called the organizational unique identifier. The remaining six digits are assigned by the vendor to each individual card.

9. **A.** NETSTAT. The following table shows other useful UNIX commands.

Command	Function
PING	Verifies configurations and tests connectivity
FINGER	Retrieves system information from a remote computer that supports the TCP/IP FINGER service
ARP	Displays cache of locally resolved IP addresses to MAC (media access control) addresses
IPCONFIG	Displays the current TCP/IP configuration
TRACERT	Displays the path a packet takes to a destination host
NETSTAT	Displays the TCP/IP protocol session information
ROUTE	Displays or modifies the local routing table

10. **C.** The data is broken down into smaller units and encapsulated, adding a new header to the unit. Each layer in the OSI model performs a specific function, which may include breaking the data into smaller units for the next layer to process. Encapsulation also takes place to provide information that will be used to help reconstruct the original data. Some layers are not used, and simply pass data through. These include the presentation layer, which often has no function to perform on data.

11. **A.** Nothing is shown on your screen. This is an added security system. Answers B, C, and D are nonsense. Passwords are stored in the router's configuration file. You can, however, configure your router to refer to an authentication server instead. To have minimal security on your router you should set passwords for the console and the auxiliary line, and set a VTY, and, of course, an ENABLE password. By default, no passwords are required for the console or auxiliary lines. If you do choose to set up passwords for the console and auxiliary lines you will also have to configure a login as well. Cisco also offers encryption service for passwords. Instead of seeing the password in text in your configuration files, you will see it as encrypted. This will ensure that anyone able to access your configuration files will not also have the password to change configurations. Cisco also recommends that you avoid the Cisco encryption techniques. There are ways to crack simple password encryption in the Cisco router. The ENABLE SECRET PASSWORD command should be used in router configuration mode, not the ENABLE PASSWORD. This password employs the MD6 hashing algorithm, which currently cannot be cracked.

12. **B.** It permits all traffic. When an access list has not been applied to an interface, the interface will accept all packets. By default, no access lists are defined, all addresses are accepted and it is the default for all interfaces.

13. **A.** A 13-byte prefix. In the address 47.009181001211106183C59401. 00604747B941.01, as shown in the following table, 47.009181001211106183C59401 is the13-byte prefix, which will be shared by all the devices connected to the same ATM switch. 00604747B941 is the 6-byte end-system identifier (ESI) address and 01 represents the 1-byte selector. In a Catalyst 5000, the last digit of the ESI address has meaning. If there is a 0, it means LEC, while a 1 represents LES, a 2 represents BUS, and a 3 represents LECS.

13-Byte Prefix	6-Byte ESI	1-Byte Selector
47.009181001211106183C59401	00604747B941	01

14. **A.** CDP TIMER 50. The syntax for this command is CDP TIMER *<#ofseconds>*. This command must be done in config mode. To set it back to default, use the NO form of this command, NO CDP TIMER. CDP multicasts are usually sent every 60 seconds by default. The hold time is 180 seconds by default. The hold time is the amount of time the entry will be in the router's CDP table, if advertisements from the neighbor stop.

15. **C.** RJ-45. It is a female jack that accepts an 8-wire male. It is similar to a phone jack, but wider in size, and can accommodate eight wires instead of

six. The RJ-45 cables that connect to the ports may either be straight-through or crossover cables depending on what is connected. If you are directly connecting two pieces of hardware, and neither has an uplink port for crossover, then you will need a crossover cable. Likewise, you may need one when you are connecting a router to a hub that doesn't have an uplink port.

16. **C.** The least significant four bits. The least significant bits are bits 0–bits 3. The configuration register as a whole is made up of 16 bits. You can change the configuration register number using the CONFIG-REGISTER *<value>* command, but to get the changes to take place you will need to reload the router. Other boot commands include BOOT SYSTEM, which specifies the image to load. BOOT BOOTSTRAP is used to configure a file used to boot the bootstrap image. Use the NO form of these commands to disable. Be sure to check that there is an image to boot, before issuing the command.

17. **A, B.** NEIGHBOR 141.149.24.1 and NEIGHBOR 141.149.25.2. Both the Chicago router (141.149.24.1) and Washington router (141.149.25.2) are neighbors of the Boston router. Defining this command in the Boston router exchanges routing information with neighbors. The other answers are incorrect. Answers C and D refer to a network number instead of an IP address.

18. **A.** rtr4(config)#IPX ROUTING. This command must be entered on the RTR4 console in global configuration mode in order to enable IPX on the router. The IPX ROUTING command enables IPX on the router, which means all interfaces are ready for IPX configuration, if needed. The IPX ROUTING command only needs to be entered once in global configuration mode. To enter global configuration mode, the user must go through two steps: First, from User EXEC mode, which is indicated by the RTR4> prompt, the command ENABLE must be typed. ENABLE brings the router to privileged EXEC mode, indicated by the RTR4# prompt. From privileged EXEC mode, the command CONFIGURE TERMINAL must be typed to enter global configuration mode, which is indicated by the rtr4(config)# prompt.

19. **B.** FTP. The File Transfer Protocol (FTP) was documented in RFC 959 and is one of the oldest Internet protocols still in widespread use. FTP is implemented using TCP. FTP uses separate command and data connections. The Protocol Interpreter (PI) implements the FTP protocol itself, while the Data Transfer Process (DTP) actually performs data transfer. The FTP protocol and the data transfer use entirely separate TCP sessions. FTP servers listen on port 21. Data connections are initiated by the server from its port 20 to a port on the client identified in a PORT command. DNS is used to resolve mnemonic hostnames to IP addresses, and has no capability to transmit files. CDP is used to learn about neighboring Cisco routers and switches on a network. TRACERT is used for tracing routes.

20. **C.** Automatic configuration of the router from a TFTP server on your network. The TFTP server will have the configuration files on it so that when the router is connected to the network via serial links, you are able to access the server. To configure the router from the TFTP server, issue the COPY RUN START command after you boot the router. The COPY RUN START command copies the running configuration to NVRAM. This allows the correct configuration to be running on your router, even if it is re-booted. The startup CONFIG is the name of the configuration stored in NVRAM.

21. **D.** Nothing happens. The only layer that uses the encapsulation from the sending machine's data-link layer would be the receiving machine's data-link layer. Each layer in the OSI model on the sending machine communicates data with its corresponding layer on the destination machine in a peer-to-peer communication. For a bridge to work, it must take the data from the physical layer and then interpret the MAC address that it contains.

22. **B.** remote-router1(config-if)#ENCAPSULATION X25. The ENCAPSULATION X25 command enables the X25 encapsulation on serial interface and this is an interface command. The default mode of operation is as DTE, and the default encapsulation method is IETF.

23. **A.** IP DEFAULT-GATEWAY 141.149.24.2. Since there is no IP routing for the network, the Chicago employees need a way to communicate with the HR server. Specifying a default gateway in the Boston router provides a route between the HR server and the Chicago router. In this implementation, Boston is the next-hop router interface with an IP address of 141.149.24.2 that provides the connectivity. Since there is no routing for the network, the HR server needs a way to transmit information outbound. Specifying a default gateway, the HR server has a path outside its network. Data is forwarded out the Boston router via interface E2, IP address 141.149.10.2. The router sends any packets that need the assistance of a gateway to the address specified. If another gateway has a better route to the requested host, the default gateway sends an ICMP redirect message to the router. The ICMP redirect message indicates which local router the router should use. The other answers are either incorrect or incomplete. In answer B, the command is incorrect, you must specify gateway and use the IP address associated with that router. Essentially, a router is synonymous with gateway; they perform some similar tasks. Answer C is incomplete and needs reference to IP. Answer D refers to a network and not a particular outbound IP address.

24. **B.** RIP. Servers and routers running the Routing Information Protocol (RIP) broadcast the contents of their routing tables to their neighbors every 60 seconds. SAP sends updates every 60 seconds, but does not affect the routing tables. NCP and SPX do not send out any routing table updates. RIP is used to propagate dynamic IPX routing information. IPX routers send RIP broadcasts to advertise the IPX networks to which they know routes. Each router advertises directly connected networks, as well as routes

to networks it has learned from other routers. To avoid routing loops, a router will never advertise a learned route back onto the network from which it learned the route. This is the split-horizon principle.

25. **B, C, D.** Management of network device connections; flow control; and communication with the physical layer. Error correction is not a part of the LLC, but error detection can be. The main purpose of the LLC layer is to identify which protocol (IP, IPX, AppleTalk) to which the data should be passed in the network layer. The LLC manages network device connections. This management is done through communication with the physical layer and flow control. It also tries to prevent buffer overflows when receiving data. This helps reduce the chance that errors will occur because of the local hardware.

26. **A.** Applications with bursty data traffic. The frame relay network provides a guarantee of throughput service to the application's users, such as workstations and servers. This guarantee applies as long as the data rate into the frame relay network is below some established committed information rate (CIR). If the data exceeds CIR for a period of time, the frame relay switch sets the discard eligibility (DE) indicator bit. This bit is used to indicate to the network that a frame may be discarded in case of congestion. Frame relay may discard the traffic beyond the CIR limit if bandwidth is not available, but traffic over the CIR will not necessarily be discarded as long as there is available bandwidth in the frame relay network.

27. **C.** Novell-Ether. The Host node can communicate with the Host_1 node using the Ethernet_802.3 frame type, which is the same as the Novell-Ether encapsulation and uses that same encapsulation across all routers. In the diagram, both nodes are using three frame types, Ethernet_802.2, Ethernet_II, and Ethernet_802.3. Since Ethernet_802.2 = SAP, Ethernet_II = Arpa, and Ethernet_802.3 = Novell-Ether, SNAP is excluded as a possible encapsulation. The first router encountered, Cisco2621, uses Novell-Ether and Arpa. This excludes the SAP encapsulation or Ethernet_802.2 frame type. The second router encountered, Cisco2621_1, uses Novell-Ether, SAP,

and SNAP, but does not use Arpa, so the only remaining possible encapsulation is Novell-Ether. Novell-Ether is used on both Cisco801 and Cisco804, so Novell-Ether, Ethernet_802.3, is the only encapsulation that can be used across the entire internetwork from Host to Host_1.

28. **A.** Successful echo responses were received. The !!!!! result indicates that successful echo responses were received from the host to which PING was sending echo requests. PING is a utility that employs Internet Control Message Protocol (ICMP) echo requests and responses. PING can be used with either a host name or an IP address. When the command PING 155.55.23.12 is issued, the possible responses are listed here:

Response Symbol	Meaning of Symbol
! (exclamation point)	Successful echo
. (period)	Timed out waiting
U	Destination unreachable
& (ampersand)	Time to Live exceeded

29. **D.** SAP. The Service Advertising Protocol (SAP) enables servers and routers to advertise services to the internetwork. Servers and routers use SAP to announce file, print and other services to the internetwork. At the same time, servers and routers collect the SAP announcements in internal databases. A client sends a SAP request to any server to locate services available on the internetwork. Answer A, NCP, manages connections and is used for access to files and printers. Answer B, NetBIOS, is an emulation that runs over IPX allowing NetBIOS applications to run. Answer C, IPX is used to provide the network-layer routing and addressing and a connectionless unreliable datagram service.

30. **C.** 5 bytes. The ATM cell header is five bytes (byte1–byte 5) and the data portion is 48 bytes (byte 6–byte 53). The 5-byte header is distributed with the information about GFC, VPI, virtual channel identifier (VCI), payload type (PT), cell loss priority (CLP), and the header error control (HEC). The remaining 48 bytes represent the cell payload.

Byte 1	GFC	VPI	
Byte 2	VPI	VCI	
Byte 3	VCI		
Byte 4	VCI	PT	CLP
Byte 5	HEC		
Bytes 6 to 53	CELL PAY LOAD		

31. **B.** 44.7 Mbps. The T3 line, which is also referred to as DS-3, transmits formatted digital signals at the rate of 44.7 Mbps. The channelized T3 can multiplex 28 T-1 interfaces together into a single circuit or can isolate them into 673 individual 64 kbps channels.

32. **C.** Type **configure terminal**. In order to configure a router, it is important for you to understand in what mode the configuration takes place. Generally, there are at least three modes of operation in a router: the user mode, enable mode and the configuration mode. All IOS changes are done in the global configuration mode. In order to navigate to the global configuration mode you must first have access to the enable mode. The enable mode provides an interface to the global configuration mode. Simply typing **config t** or **configure terminal** in the enable mode will get you into the global configuration mode. Of the other choices, answer A only gives you access to the enable mode, assuming you are in the user mode of the router. Therefore, typing **enable** simply repeats the login process for the enable mode. As for answers B and D, there is no such thing as a root password for Cisco products or a global configuration password.

33. **B.** 172.10.4.1–172.10.7.254. The subnet mask 255.255.252.0 translates to 11111111.11111111.|111111|00.00000000 in binary format. In order to determine the first available subnet, the lowest bit of the subnet section should be a 1 bit. This value is a four. The lowest host number is 1. So the first range of addresses starts at 172.10.4.1. The highest address in this range would still have the same subnet bit. The host portion would change with only the final bit set at 0. This makes the host portion |11.11111110. When added to the subnet the result is .|000001|11.11111110, which makes the final two octets 7.254. The final address in the first range is then 172.10.7.254.

34. **B.** The placement of upper-layer protocol data packets within lower-layer protocol data segments. The IPX protocol stack defines the upper-five layers of the OSI protocol stack as network, transport, session, presentation, and application. This enables IPX to be largely media independent through encapsulation. The network-layer IPX and datagram are received by the MAC layer. The MAC layer then places the datagram within the data portion MAC frame, enclosing, or encapsulating it with the MAC header and frame-check sequence segments.

35. **D.** All of the above. All the routers are enabled for LMI. LMI is automatically enabled on the routers after configuring for frame relay encapsulation. Frame relay keepalive is manually set for 20 seconds on Serial interface 3/0 of Central Router 2. The keepalive interval has to be less than the interval set on the switch. The default keepalive interval is 10 seconds.

36. **C.** They allow them to create workgroups based on function rather than media. In a traditional LAN environment, users are required to be on the same physical wire to access a server or other workstations in the workgroup. In a VLAN environment, this is not a requirement. Users can be in different locations, or servers can be clustered together without an interruption in service. Administrators can add, change, or create new segments without having to physically move users or change LAN media.

37. **B.** The port is not forwarding and not participating in STP. When a switch is first powered on, all ports are in blocking state. Blocking state is the default setting for all ports on a Catalyst switch at startup.

38. **A–3, B–4, C–2, D–1.** Ethernet_II with Arpa; Token_Ring_SNAP with SNAP; Ethernet_802.2 with SAP; Ethernet_802.3 with Novell-Ether. Only the description names differ for Novell's implementation of encapsulation and Cisco's implementation of encapsulation. The following table maps many of the Novell frame types to Cisco encapsulation types.

Novell Frame Type	Cisco Encapsulation
Ethernet_II	Arpa
Ethernet_802.3 (sometimes called Ethernet_raw)	Novell-Ether
Ethernet_802.2	SAP
Ethernet_SNAP	SNAP
Token_Ring	SAP
Token_Ring_SNAP	SNAP
FDDI_802.3 (sometimes called FDDI_raw)	Novell-FDDI
FDDI_802.2	SAP
FDDI_SNAP	SNAP

39. **A.** IP ROUTE 141.149.12.0 255.255.255.0 141.149.26.2. In this scenario a static route is needed for users in New York to access a resource behind the Washington net. This implementation implies that the New York net has no direct route to the Washington net. The network (141.149.12.0) behind the Washington net is not being propagated to the New York router. Issuing a static route requires manually adding a route to a specific network, which essentially may be the only route to that particular network. Using static routes often reduces the overhead associated with route and distance calculations performed by the router. Static routes are always known, which helps reduce the number of places where faults can lie.

The other answer answers are either incomplete or incorrect. The format for this command is specification of the IP address and address mask of the destination network and the IP address of the interface to that network. Answer B is a legal command; however, it does not specify the mask of the destination network. Without the referencing a mask, the router assumes the entire Class B network is out the serial port. There is only one Class B used in the following illustration. The mask is needed in case there is a particular subnet of the Class B in question. Answer C specifies the incorrect IP address of the interface. Answer D specifies the wrong IP address interface and an incomplete command.

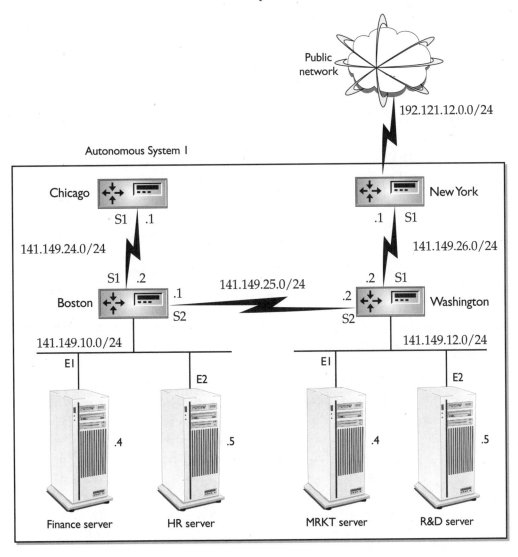

Public network

192.121.12.0.0/24

Autonomous System I

Chicago   S1   .1

141.149.24.0/24

.1   S1   New York

141.149.26.0/24

S1   .2   141.149.25.0/24   .2   S1

Boston   .1   .2   Washington

S2   S2

141.149.10.0/24   141.149.12.0/24

E1   E2   E1   E2

.4   .5   .4   .5

Finance server   HR server   MRKT server   R&D server

40. D. All of the above. The PAD is a device commonly found in X.25 networks. PADs are used when a DTE device, such as a character-mode terminal, is too simple to implement the full X.25 functionality. The PAD is located between a DTE device and a DCE device. It performs three primary functions:

- **Buffering** The PAD buffers data sent to or from the DTE device.
- **Packet assembly** The PAD assembles outgoing data into packets and forwards them to the DCE device (This includes adding an X.25 header).
- **Packet disassembly** The PAD disassembles incoming packets before forwarding the data to the DTE. (This includes removing the X.25 header.)

41. B. To more effectively use network bandwidth. Because TCP requires an acknowledgement for all data transmitted, it is not efficient to simply send one packet, and then wait for the recipient's reply. Sliding window algorithms are a method of flow control for network data transfers. A sliding window algorithm places a buffer between the application program and the network data flow. For TCP, the buffer is typically in the operating system kernel, but this is more of an implementation detail than a hard and fast requirement. Data received from the network is stored in the buffer, from which the application can read it at its own pace. As the application reads data, buffer space is freed up to accept more input from the network. The window is the amount of data that can be read ahead; that is, the size of the buffer, less the amount of valid data stored in it. Window announcements are used to inform the remote host of the current window size. If the local application can't process data fast enough, the window size will drop to zero and the remote host will stop sending data. After the local application has processed some of the queued data, the window size grows, and the remote host starts transmitting again. On the other hand, if the local application can process data at the rate it's being transferred, sliding window still gives us an advantage. If the window size is larger than the packet size, then multiple packets can be outstanding in the network, since the sender knows that buffer space is available on the receiver to hold all of them. Keeping a series of data packets in transit ensures the efficient use of network resources.

42. **F.** Data-link. Bridges and switches examine the MAC address of the packet to determine if it exists on one of the segments that are connected to it. If the address is know by the bridge or switch, the packet is only forwarded onto the segment on which the address exists. If the address is not known by the switch, the packet is forwarded to all segments. Switching has grown in popularity since it can reduce network traffic by diminishing the number of packets sent out across the whole network. As they are seen by every machine, the number of collisions is also diminished. Switching is also popular on networks that use non-routable protocols such as LAT.

43. **D.** 24 bytes. A RIP packet is broken down into the following segments:

- Command, which identifies the packet as a request or response (one byte)
- Version number, which indicates the version of RIP (one byte)
- Zero, unused at this time (two bytes)
- Address Family Identifier (AFI), the family of addresses used for Internet traffic (four bytes)
- Family Identifier (two bytes)
- Address (four bytes), an IP address for the Internet
- Metric, two octets must be set to zero and are not used at this time (eight bytes) and the metric segment which shows the distance (hop count) to the destination (four bytes)

This information makes up the RIP header. The information that follows the header is routing table information.

44. **C.** She should have a new address assigned to MacGuire Enterprises by InterNIC and make changes to the rest of the addressing scheme. A new address assignment is needed because each address on the Internet must be unique. The InterNIC registers addresses for networks that connect to the

Internet in order to maintain IP address uniqueness. The former administrator had arbitrarily used Class B addresses that are probably already assigned to other networks, rendering them non-unique and unusable. Once the new addresses are assigned to the network, each host will need to have a new address assigned to it so that they are not using the non-unique Class B addresses any longer. Answer A is incorrect, since Class D addresses are not assigned to hosts for Internet access. Answer B is incorrect, since supernetting will not render the addresses unique on the Internet. Answer D is incorrect, since not taking action will create problems for MacGuire Enterprises.

45. **B.** 16 bits. All Cisco routers have 16-bit configuration registers. The registers are stored in NVRAM. It enables functions such as booting from a TFTP server, loading operating software from ROM, selecting a boot source, and selecting a default boot filename. Depending upon the Boot field value in these registers, the IOS image is located and loaded. If the Boot field value were 0x0 then the router would enter ROM Monitor mode. If the Boot field value is 0x1, then the router would enter RXBoot mode. If the Boot field value were 0x2 to 0xF, then the router would go through the normal booting sequence. The router would check the configuration for BOOT SYSTEM commands, telling it where to go to boot the IOS image. If this fails, it goes to flash to find the first file. If this fails, it goes to the TFTP server for a default file name. If this fails, it goes to ROM (RXBoot mode).

46. **D.** By configuring ports for the three VLANs. Since the switches are already connected via 100 Mb Ethernet, all that is needed is to assign ports for the VLANs on each of the other two switches. This is accomplished by using the SET VLAN command and assigning ports to each VLAN. You will also need to enable trunking on the three switches. Depending on the model of Catalyst being used, you can either enable ISL or 802.1Q trunking on the switches.

47. **B.** Link-state routing protocol. OSPF uses the link-state algorithm based on the SPF algorithm to build its routing table. Link-state protocols will only

advertise changes to the routing table as opposed to distance vector routing protocols, which send their entire routing table. OSPF builds a topological database of all the links in the network and builds a routing table based on those links. Changes in the network are noted and the routing table is adjusted based on the LSAs, which are received from other routers in the network.

48. **D.** VTP. The VLAN Trunk Protocol (VTP) is used by Catalyst switches to exchange VLAN information across trunk ports automatically. This information is in the form of advertisements that are sent to each VLAN neighbor. The information includes active VLANs, the revision number, and the domain. The advantage of VTP is the ability of a network administrator to control the addition, deletion, and changes to the VLAN topology. VTP pruning would be used to prevent unnecessary traffic from being sent to devices that are not using VTP. The administrator can limit the amount of VTP traffic by manually configuring which devices will receive this information. Unfortunately this will require manual configuration of all the switches that will participate.

49. **A.** Fragmentation. At the network layer or the Internet layer, one of the protocols used is the Internet Protocol (IP). IP is a connectionless internetwork service that includes provisions for addressing, fragmentation and reassembly, type of service support, and security. IP packets or datagrams can be transported over multiple physical networks and copied by intermediate systems, such as IP routers, from one network to another. IP addresses are independent of the underlying hardware addressing scheme (MAC address). This allows IP addresses to be used in any network and provides a level of abstraction which enables Internet communication to take place over multiple subnetworks.

50. **B.** NO IP-ADDRESS *IP-address mask*. This is somewhat similar to configuring an IP address and address mask; however, you must use both the IP and mask to remove the address from the interface of the router. A NO is used in front of the format to signify the IOS to remove the IP address from the router. The remaining answers are either incomplete or incorrect.

51.   D. A client-server computing technique. Programs that communicate over a network need a method for communication. Using remote-procedure calls (RPCs), a client communicates with a server. In this process, the client first initiates a procedure to send some type of request to the server. When the packet containing the request arrives at the server (via the network), the server initiates a dispatch routine, performs the service requested, sends back the reply back to the dispatch routine, and the procedure results return to the client.

52.   B, C. Telnet and console. You gain login access to a router through a Telnet session and through its console port connection. You also gain access through its auxiliary port. Login and passwords should be configured in each of these login cases. This is for added security. Each router has five virtual terminal lines to accept incoming Telnet sessions. All five can be configured. Here is an example command sequence to accomplish this:

```
line vty 0 4
password <password>
login
```

53.   B. Metric. Each routing protocol defines the metric by a different name. For example, the metric for RIP is hop count. Every IP Routing protocol uses the information gathered by the routing algorithm to determine the metric for each destination and the information is placed in the router's IP routing table.

54.   C. TCP/IP, 4; OSI, 7. The four TCP/IP layers map into the seven-layer OSI model. There are several differences among them, however. In the TCP/IP protocols, a given protocol can be used by other protocols within the same layer, where in the OSI model, two separate layers would be defined. Examples of such horizontal dependencies are File Transfer

Protocol (FTP), which uses the same common representation as TELNET on the application layer, and Internet Control Message Protocol (CMP), which uses IP for sending its datagrams on the internetwork layer. The OSI norms tend to be prescriptive; for instance, a layer N must go through *all layers below it.* The TCP/IP protocols are descriptive, and leave the most freedom for the implementers. One of the advantages of the TCP/IP approach is that each particular implementation can use operating system-dependent features, which generally results in greater efficiency, such as fewer CPU cycles and more throughput for similar functions, while still ensuring interoperability with other implementations.

55. B. They need to adjust the Invalid timer within RIP. In normal operation, RIP will declare a route unusable if an update has not been received in 180 seconds. If the link between Router A and Router B is congested, then the possibility exists that updates will not be received within the default length of time.

The solution is to adjust the Invalid timer to deal with the congested link. The administrator of each router can adjust the timer to the optimal setting for both routers. There are five different timers that can be adjusted in RIP. They are the Update, Invalid, Holddown, Flush, and Sleeptime. To adjust the Invalid timer on the router, use the following command in router configuration mode:

```
router(config)# ROUTER RIP
router(config)# TIMERS BASIC update invalid holddown flush sleeptime
```

In this situation the other timer settings can suffice, so the command will look something like this:

```
router(config)# TIMERS BASIC 30 240 180 240 300
```

56. B. The autonomous system AS numbers must agree.

57. C. A hub copies and transmits a frame to all ports, while a switch examines the source MAC address and stores this information in its switching table to build a list of all MAC address locations. A hub is really a repeater. This means that each frame that is received by the hub is copied and transmitted to all ports in use. A switch is more intelligent. When a frame is received, the switch takes the source MAC address and places it in its switching table. A switching table, contains information about the location of MAC addresses connected to its ports, much as a routing table contains information of address blocks and which interface to route the data.

58. **C.** It would be inefficient to use TCP for network management. This is because TCP uses a three-way handshake to set up its communications path. Therefore, one would be, in effect, checking the connectivity to a device at least twice for availability. Normally, network management applications will re-query a device if the packet has been lost through the less reliable, but more efficient, UDP transport.

59. **B.** Class B. The Class B address will provide at least 5,500 IP addresses and service all of Acme/Widget's end users. Each IP address must be unique on the internetwork in order for data to be routed to the correct hosts. Acme/Widget needs an IP address class that can provide at least one IP address to each host on the network and a Class B address has the maximum capacity of 65,534 nodes, or hosts, per address. A Class A address would also work, since it has the capacity of 16,777,206 hosts, but that would be far more addresses than this internetwork needs. The Class C address does not have enough addresses available for hosts, since a single Class C address supports only 254 hosts. The Class D address is specified for multicasting and cannot be used. The Class E address is an experimental address set and also cannot be used for host addressing. There is no such thing as a Class F address.

60. **A.** ACCESS-LIST 103 PERMIT TCP ANY131.72.0.0 0.0.255.255
ESTABLISHED
ACCESS-LIST 103 PERMIT TCP ANY131.72.1.2 0.0.0.0 EQ SMTP
INTERFACE FASTETHERNET 0/0/0
ACCESS-GROUP 103 IN

The Fast Ethernet address is a Class B 131.172.0.0, and the mail host's address is 131.172.1.2. The keyword ESTABLISHED is used only for the TCP protocol to indicate an established connection. A match occurs if the TCP datagram has the ACK or RST bits set, which indicate that the packet belongs to the existing condition. In answers B and D (answer D, of course, being the wrong protocol) the order in which the access lines are listed will deny SMTP. The router reads the access list in sequential order.

61. **B.** Application, presentation, session. Upper-layer protocols are usually implemented in software rather than hardware. They deal with application-related issues such as encryption, data formatting, and file transfer.

62. **B.** ROUTER RIP. The enabling of RIP is performed at the global level by entering ROUTER RIP. This notifies the IOS that you want to initialize the RIP process for routing. This process is needed to run RIP on the network. The other answers are either incorrect or incomplete. In answer A, the router reference belongs before the RIP reference. Answers C and D are both incorrect commands.

63. **D.** 50 percent. EIGRP will use a maximum of 50 percent of the bandwidth of a given interface as set by the command BANDWIDTH INTERFACE CONFIGURATION. This setting is adjustable through the use of the IP BANDWIDTH-PERCENTAGE EIGRP command. This command, when used in interface configuration mode, will allow the administrator to adjust the bandwidth used by EIGRP to fit his or her needs.

64. **E.** All of the above. SAP access lists restrict traffic based on the IPX Service Advertisement Protocol (SAP) type. These lists are used for SAP filters and GNS response filters. SAP access lists numbers are 1,000–1,999. Extended access lists restrict traffic based on the IPX protocol type. You can further restrict traffic by specifying source/destination addresses and address masks, and source and destination sockets. Extended IPX access lists numbers are 900–999. Standard access lists restrict traffic based upon the source network number. Further restrictions can be made by specifying a destination address and a source and destination address mask. Standard IPX access lists numbers are 800–899. IPX NetBIOS access lists restrict IPX NetBIOS traffic based upon NETBIOS names, not numbers.

65. D. 1. Most Catalyst switches have VLAN 1 set as default for all active ports on the switch. There are also VLANs (1002–1005) set for both Token Ring and FDDI networks on Catalysts equipped with FDDI and Token Ring modules. These VLANs cannot be removed, as they are part of the Catalyst's default configuration. The following illustration displays the default VLANs on a Catalyst switch.

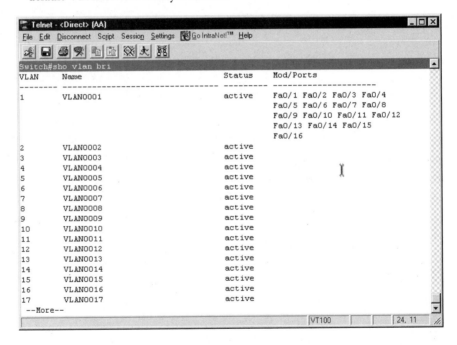

66. C. Distance vector and link-state. Distance vector algorithms, which are based on the Bellman-Ford algorithm, are used in protocols such as RIP or IGRP. Distance vector protocol routers communicate by sending their entire routing table to their neighbors. This can be a disadvantage since the convergence time is longer and makes the routes more prone to loops. Moreover, metrics used by distance vector protocols sometimes limit accessibility. RIP, for example, has a maximum hop count of 15 and anything beyond 15 is deemed unreachable. Link-state routing protocols are based on the link-state algorithm. Protocols such as OSPF and IS-IS use the link-state algorithm to communicate with their neighbors. Instead of sending the entire routing table to the neighbor, a link-state protocol will only send updated information based on link-state advertisements (LSAs) received from all of its neighbors.

67. **A.** Source and destination. IPX access lists (800–899) filter on the source and destination address only. The only required argument for Standard IPX access lists is the Novell IXP source network. The rest of the parameters are optional; however, the source and/or destination address masks are present only if the corresponding source and/or destination address was entered.

68. **A, C.** RIP, updates routing tables dynamically; and IPX, is a connectionless, unreliable datagram service. This is a trick question and is similar to some that appear on the CCNA test. The testing candidate must be able to discern not only which protocols are correctly matched to their function, but also which are at the network layer. In this question all of the answers are protocols that are correctly matched to their function. However, only answers A and C, Routing Information Protocol (RIP) and Internetwork Packet eXchange (IPX), are network-layer protocols. Answer B, NetWare Core Protocol (NCP) is an upper-layer (application- and presentation-layer) protocol. Answer D, Service Advertising Protocol (SAP) is a session-layer protocol.

69. **B.** 172.10.96.1–172.10.127.254. The subnet mask 255.255.224.0 shows that in the binary format 11111111.11111111.|111|00000.0000000 only three bits are used for subnetting. The address 172.10.99.220 translates to the binary as 10101100.00001010.|011|00011.11011100. The range can be determined from just the final two octets. The subnet portion never changes, but the host portion starts from a single 1 bit in the lowest bit value, so the start of the range is .|011|00000.00000001, and the end of the range is all 1s and a 0 in the lowest bit value: .|011|11111.11111110. This makes the range 172.10.96.1–172.10.127.254.

70. D. None of the above. In the example configuration, there are no access lists defined. With the router in this state, there are no access restrictions and any device is allowed to access the router.

CISCO CERTIFIED NETWORK ASSOCIATE

Part 12

Test Yourself:
Practice Exam 2

Test Yourself:
Practice Exam 2
Questions

Q

&

A

Before you call to register for the actual exam, take the following test and see how you make out. Set a timer for 90 minutes—the time you'll have to take the live CCNA Certification exam—and answer the following 70 questions in the time allotted. Once you've finished, turn to the Practice Exam 2 Answers section and check your score to see if you passed! Good luck!

Practice Exam 2 Questions

I. Which of the following are trunking protocols? (Choose all that apply.)

A. TCO

B. ISL

C. IEEE 802.1Q

D. BGP

2. The following illustration portrays the physical connection of the frame relay network with redundant connections to the central locations. All the routers are configured so that routing information will not be passed between remote routers, for security purposes. Which type of frame relay encapsulation is configured on remote and central router subinterfaces in the network?

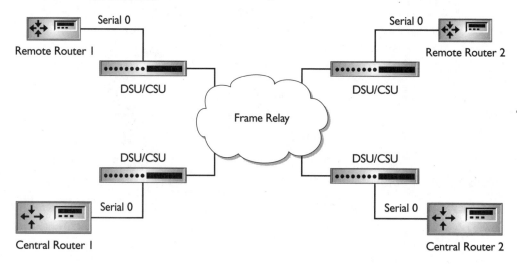

Remote Router 1

```
version 11.2
!
hostname remote-router1
!
interface Serial0
no ip address
encapsulation frame-relay
bandwidth 64
no fair-queue
!
interface Serial0.1 point-to-point
description PVC to Central Router1
ip address 10.1.11.2 255.255.255.0
frame-relay interface-dlci 102
!
interface Serial0.2 point-to-point
description PVC to Central Router2
ip address 10.1.12.2 255.255.255.0
frame-relay interface-dlci 103
!
end
```

Remote Router 2

```
version 11.2
!
hostname remote-router2
!
interface Serial0
no ip address
encapsulation frame-relay
bandwidth 64
no fair-queue
!
interface Serial0.1 point-to-point
description PVC to Central Router 1
ip address 10.1.11.3 255.255.255.0
frame-relay interface-dlci 202
!
interface Serial0.2 point-to-point
description PVC to Central Router2
ip address 10.1.12.3 255.255.255.0
frame-relay interface-dlci 203
```

```
!
end
```

Central Router 1

```
hostname Central Router1
enable secret 5
enable password cisco
!
interface Ethernet0/0
 ip address 192.157.129.254 255.255.255.0
!
interface Serial3/0
no ip address
no ip mroute-cache
encapsulation frame-relay
no ip route-cache
bandwidth 384
!
interface Serial3/0.1 multipoint
description Frame-relay T1
ip address 10.1.11.1 255.255.255.0
no ip mroute-cache
no ip route-cache
bandwidth 128
frame-relay map ip 10.1.11.2  101 broadcast
frame-relay map ip 10.1.11.3  102 broadcast
!
interface Serial3/0.2 point-to-point
description PVC for Network management
ip address 10.1.100.1 255.255.255.0
no ip route-cache
bandwidth 128
frame-relay interface-dlci 100
!
end
```

Central Router 2

```
hostname Central Router 2
!
interface Ethernet0/0
ip address 10.1.1.2 255.255.255.0
!
interface Serial3/0
```

```
no ip address
no ip mroute-cache
encapsulation frame-relay
no ip route-cache
bandwidth 384
frame-relay keepalive 20
!
interface Serial3/0.1 multipoint
description Frame-relay T1
ip address 10.1.12.1 255.255.255.0
no ip mroute-cache
no ip route-cache
bandwidth 128
frame-relay map ip 10.1.12.2 402 broadcast
frame-relay map ip 10.1.12.3 403 broadcast
!
interface Serial3/0.2 point-to-point
description PVC For Network Managment
ip address 10.1.100.2 255.255.255.0
no ip route-cache
bandwidth 128
frame-relay interface-dlci 100
!
end
```

A. IETF

B. One automatically provided by the frame-relay network

C. Encapsulation not configured

D. Cisco

3. Why is IPX security and traffic optimization improved in Cisco IOS 11.1 software? (Choose all that apply.)

A. IPX filters can only be inbound or outbound.

B. It builds more secure IPX networks by moving the filter process from the outgoing to the incoming interface.

C. Input access lists can validate user information at the borders of the network and build more sophisticated firewalls.

D. It provides the capability of filtering traffic at the originating end of GRE-tunneled networks.

4. Given the following configuration, how does TCP ensure reliable delivery of data?

```
Remote Router 1#
Interface bri0
      isdn x25 dchannel
      isdn x25 static-tei
!
interface  bri0:0
      ip address 10.1.100.10   255.255.255.0
      x25 address 11110001111000
x25 map ip 10.1.100.11 11110001111001
  !
end
```

A. TCP requires a dedicated data connection.

B. TCP uses application software to verify data integrity.

C. TCP sends acknowledgements for every transmitted packet or group of packets.

D. TCP checks its loopback for every transmitted packet or group of packets.

5. What is the maximum number of VPIs that can be configured for UNI?

A. 4,096

B. 65,535

C. 1,048

D. 256

6. The Acme Co. has acquired Widget, Inc., and is now merging with it. The management plans to open 22 new sales branches. The Acme Co. had two major offices with 500 employees in London and 1,000 in New York. Widget, Inc., had three major offices with 2,000 employees in Phoenix, 500 employees in Los Angeles, and 1,200 employees in Salt Lake City. Fourteen of the 22 sales offices will connect to Phoenix. Four sales branches will connect to the London office. Four sales branches will connect to the New York office. The newly merged IT department has hired you to assist them in selecting and assigning IP addresses. Refer to Figure 12-1 to answer the following question.

FIGURE 12-1 Acme and Widget Merger

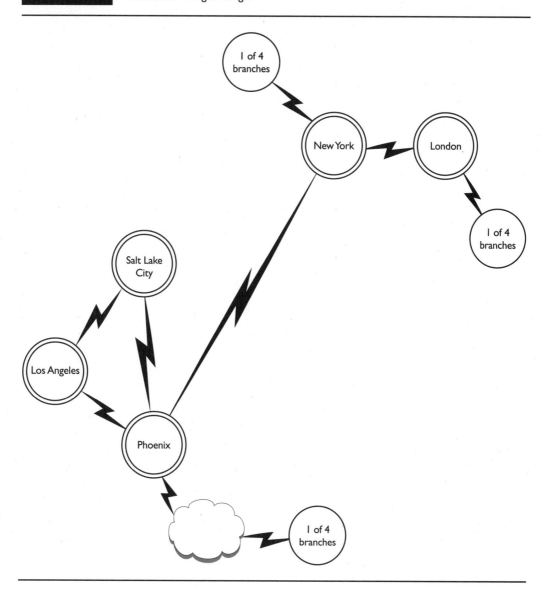

As final verification of their newfound skill, the IT department asks you to translate the following two addresses and tell them what type or class of address they are. They write down the following: 10010010.11110000. 11111111.11111111 and 11011100.00001011.10111000.000s00011. What types of addresses are they?

A. 189.222.225.225, a Class B address; and 220.12.199.3, a Class C address

B. 164.240.255.225, a Class B address; and 220.11.188.3, a Class C address

C. 146.240.255.255, a directed broadcast to a Class B network; and 220.11.184.3, a Class C address

D. 146.240.225.255, a local broadcast address to a Class B network; and 220.11.184.3, a class D multicast address

7. Below are the configurations for LANE on a Cisco switch and router. This is not a complete configuration. In ATM Router 1, interface ATM 0/0/0 is configured for ATM PVC 1 0 5 QSAAL. What does 1 0 5 represent in these configurations?

ATM Router I

```
version 11.X
!
hostname Router 1
!
appletalk routing
!
decnet routing
decnet node-type area
!
ipx routing
!
interface ATM0/0/0
no ip address
no ip mroute-cache
atm pvc 1 0 5 qsaal
```

```
atm pvc 2 0 16 ilmi
hold-queue 450 in
!
interface ATM0/0/0.1 multipoint
description vlan101
ip address 10.1.1.1      255.255.255.0
lane client ethernet vlan101
ipx network
!
interface ATM0/0/0.2 multipoint
 description vlan102
 lane client ethernet vlan102
!
interface ATM0/0/0.3 multipoint
description vlan103
lane client ethernet vlan103
!
interface ATM0/0/0.10 multipoint
no ip mroute-cache
shutdown
atm pvc 4 4 88 aal5snap
map-group rfc1483
!
end
```

ATM-Database

```
hostname ATM-DATABASE
!
lane database atm-database
name vlan102 server-atm-address
47.009181001111101011B90A01.00E0111E1441.02
name vlan102 server-atm-address
47.009181001111106183C59401.00604747B941.02
name vlan101 server-atm-address
47.009181001211106183C59401.00604747B941.01
name vlan101 server-atm-address
47.009181000000001011B90A01.00E0111E1441.01
name vlan103 server-atm-address
47.009181000000006183C59401.00604747B941.03
name vlan103 server-atm-address
47.009181000000001011B90A01.00E0111E1441.03
```

```
!
interface ATM0
mtu 1500
atm pvc 1 0 5 qsaal
atm pvc 2 0 16 ilmi
lane config auto-config-atm-address
lane config database ATM-DATABASE
!
interface ATM0.1 multipoint
description vlan101
lane server-bus ethernet vlan101
lane client ethernet 101 vlan101
!
interface ATM0.2 multipoint
description vlan102
lane server-bus ethernet vlan102
lane client ethernet 102 vlan102
!
interface ATM0.3 multipoint
description vlan103
lane server-bus ethernet vlan103
lane client ethernet 103 vlan103
!
end
```

A. 1 is VCD, 0 is VPI, and 5 is VCI.

B. 1 is VPI, 0 is VCI, and 5 is VCD

C. 1 is VCI, 0 is VCD, and 5 is VPI

D. 1 is VCD, 0 is VCI, and 5 is VPI

8. Within which range of addresses does a 177.77.89.200 with a subnet mask of 255.255.255.192 fall?

A. 77.77.89.193–177.77.89.254

B. 177.77.89.1–177.77.89.254

C. 177.77.64.1–177.77.95.254

D. 177.77.89.129–177.77.89.223

9. Which of the following commands is used to define a static host name–to–address mapping in the host cache?

A. IP HOST *name IP-address*

B. IP *name* HOST

C. IP HOSTNAME

D. IP HOSTS *name*

E. None of the above

10. Which of the following configuration commands should be used to define blue.com as the default domain name?

A. NETWORK.COM DOMAIN-NAME

B. IP DOMAIN-NAME BLUE.COM

C. DOMAIN-NAME NETWORK.COM

D. IP NETWORK.COM DOMAIN-NAME

11. What is a traceroute?

A. A tool to set up routers

B. A network management tool

C. An application based on IGMP

D. A utility to examine and follow the path of a packet through the network

12. Which of the following is a characteristic of a connectionless protocol?

A. Efficient

B. Reliable

C. Guaranteed

D. Secure

13. What is Winsock?

    A. A Microsoft port

    B. Windows-based network management

    C. A Microsoft application programming interface

    D. An enabler of routing on servers

14. Which command determines the port to which a workstation is connected?

    A. DISPLAY MAC TABLE

    B. SHOW MAC TABLE

    C. DISPLAY CAM

    D. SHOW CAM

15. Why is there a three-way handshake at the beginning of a TCP transmission?

    A. TCP double checks the connection.

    B. TCP establishes three channels for communication.

    C. TCP establishes two channels for communication.

    D. TCP sends a test packet to determine network latency.

16. What is the key value of using Inverse ARP with frame relay?

    A. The DLCI number is made logically significant.

    B. The discovery of the DLCI number is automated.

    C. It assigns an IP address to the DLCI.

    D. None of the above.

17. Which layer is responsible for routing functions?

    A. Layer 2

    B. Layer 3

    C. Layer 4

    D. Layer 5

18. Which command displays the Windows IP address provided by DHCP?

    A. NETSTAT

    B. PING

    C. RLOGIN

    D. WINIPCFG

19. What are the most common methods of transmitting traffic through a switch? (Choose all that apply.)

    A. Store and forward

    B. Store-through

    C. Cut-and-forward

    D. Cut-through

20. Which of the following bridging modes are used for Ethernet networks?

    A. Transparent

    B. Transparent source

    C. Source route

    D. Transparent route

21. What are two characteristics of Ethernet?

    A. It uses CSMA/CA.

    B. It uses CSMA/CD.

    C. It is a broadcast system.

    D. It is connection-oriented.

22. This scenario follows the creation of VLANs for ABC Corporation. The corporation has three departments: Human Resources, Finance, and Engineering. They are spread across three floors of ABC's office building. The decision has been made to use VLANs with Cisco Catalyst 5000 series switches. VLAN 1 is designated for human resources, VLAN 2 is designated for finance, and VLAN 3 is designated for engineering. There is one Catalyst switch per floor. The LAN media is a combination of 10 Mbps and 100 Mbps Ethernet. Links between the Catalysts are 100 Mbps Ethernet. Figure 12-2 shows the network topology. A user on VLAN 2 reports she is unable to reach any servers or other workstations. You are not able to identify to which port the user is connected. She does provide the MAC address of her workstation. How can you identify the port to which the workstation is connected?

A. Use the SHOW CAM command.

B. Use the DISPLAY MAC ADDRESS command.

C. Ping the workstation.

D. Use the TRACEROUTE command.

FIGURE 12-2   The network topology of ABC Corporation

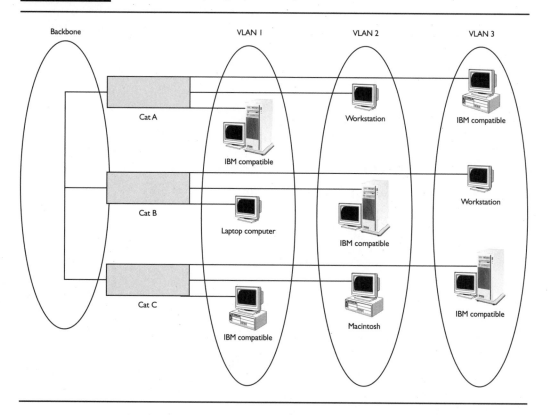

23. Which of the following are features of the transport layer? (Choose all that apply.)

A. Provides connection-oriented data delivery

B. Provides connectionless data delivery

C. Encryption

D. Transport-layer addressing

E. Data formatting

24. What may take place at the presentation layer?

A. File transfer

B. Data compression

C. Flow control

D. Establishing and maintaining sessions between two network nodes

25. You are installing a 10BaseT network with 100 network nodes. You want to provide guaranteed 10 Mbps connectivity for each node, but it may be cost prohibitive. The network will be connected to the Internet and will require some security. Which type of hardware will you use to provide shared bandwidth to each node?

A. Repeater

B. Hub

C. Switch

D. Router

26. When you switch the power on, what does a Cisco switch or hub do?

A. It waits for a password.

B. It floods the network.

C. It does a power on self-test.

D. It begins forwarding data.

27. Which command do you use to disable the enhanced editing feature?

    A. TERMINAL EDITING

    B. DISABLE EDITING

    C. TERMINAL NO EDITING

    D. EDITING DISABLE

28. Which mode are you in when accessing configuration modes and making configuration changes to your router?

    A. User EXEC mode

    B. User enhanced mode

    C. Privileged enhanced mode

    D. Privileged EXEC mode

29. Which of the following evolved into today's Internet?

    A. ARPANET

    B. ATM

    C. IEEE 802 standards

    D. ALOHANET

30. In which mode must DEBUG commands be run?

    A. User EXEC mode

    B. Privileged EXEC mode

    C. Both A and B

    D. None of the above

31. You are responsible for maintaining the network for Company ABC, which has 6,000 users. There are three primary sites, with the remaining employees located in two smaller branch offices. The company decides to go with Cisco routers in its network. There are currently two backbone routers in each primary site and one smaller router in each branch office. T1 lines

connect the three primary sites. The branch offices are connected to the closest primary site by a 56 Kbps line.

Your network only runs Internet Protocol (IP). IP is being routed with Routing Information Protocol (RIP) and Open Shortest Path First (OSPF) in different areas of your network. You have a complaint that network response is slow. Upon investigation, you narrow the problem to be in a backbone router in one of the primary buildings. You find that the router processor is currently running at 80 percent. Your Fast Ethernet connection to the backbone is also dropping a lot of packets. You determine that a server on your segment is sending out multicast packets and the router is viewing the multicast packets as broadcasts. This is resulting in a broadcast storm. You go to the server and eliminate the multicasts, so the processor utilization drops to four percent.

Just when you think things are quieting down, you receive another trouble report. Employees in a branch office are unable to access the server on segment 141.154.20.65. You go to the router on which the segment originated and you find there has been an access list configured to deny forwarding this segment. You fix the access list and employees are now able to access the server on this segment. Since you telecommute from home, all of these changes were done remotely by Telnetting into the routers. You have done an excellent job!

In the scenario, how many routing tables are there?

A. 1

B. 2

C. 3

D. None

32. Which command would you use to view the routing table to see if the 141.154.0.0 is included?

A. SHOW IP ROUTE

B. SHOW IP TABLE

C. VIEW IP TABLE

D. SHOW TABLE

33. Company XYZ has 50,000 employees in locations around the world. The corporate headquarters is in London, the North American headquarters is in Washington D.C., and the Asian headquarters is in Singapore. All three headquarters are connected via T-1s. Each regional location manages its own network system. Each of the three networks has IP, IPX, and AppleTalk running. RIP is the dominant routing protocol in use. Cisco routers are used throughout the entire wide area network (WAN). You have been asked to install and configure a router in each regional area. Upon investigation you find that each network has been set up a little differently. There is a TFTP server that has a configuration for the router already set up in the corporate headquarters. You will need to install Router A in London and access the TFTP server for the configuration files. The configuration file to be loaded is named config-1_2.P. The address of the TFTP server is 151.176.21.5. The IOS image is located in ROM. Router B is to be installed in Washington D.C. You find out from the engineer shipping the router that it has been preconfigured in a lab. You need only to install the router and bring it up. The configuration has been saved in the router's NVRAM. The IOS image is located in flash. Singapore will be the location of new router C. This router does not have a configuration completed. You want to initially bring the router up and complete the configuration on the fly. Which is a valid Boot field value for Router A?

    A. 0x0

    B. 0x1

    C. 0x2

    D. 2x0

34. How would you apply an access list to a Cisco IOS rev. 9.21 or earlier, that does not support input access lists to deny spoofing attacks? Your internal address is 131.72.31.0/24.

    A. ACCESS-LIST 101 DENY IP 131.72.31.0 0.0.0.255 ANY

    B. ACCESS-LIST 101 PERMIT IP 131.72.31.0 0.0.0.255 ANY

    C. ACCESS-LIST 102 PERMIT IP 131.72.0.0 0.0.0.255 ANY

    D. ACCESS-LIST 102 DENY IP 131.72.0.0 0.0.0.255 ANY

35. In which layer of the OSI reference model does IP routing occur?

    A. Layer 1

    B. Layer 4

    C. Layer 3

    D. Layer 2

36. Which version of RIP is the latest version?

    A. Version 5

    B. Version 2

    C. Version 4

    D. Version 3

37. Which of the following does OSPF use to determine the best path to a destination?

    A. Hop count

    B. MED

    C. Database

    D. Cost

38. When defining OSPF areas, which of the following is true?

    A. Each router must have the same Area ID.

    B. Each interface must have the same Area ID.

    C. Each network defined must have an Area ID.

    D. None of the above.

39. Router A is connected to Router B via Ethernet 0. Router A also has a connection to the Internet via port Serial 0. The following listings show the network topology as reflected in the router configurations.

Router A

```
hostname RouterA
!
interface Ethernet 0
 ip address 192.168.1.1 255.255.255.0
  no mop enabled
 no shutdown
!
interface Serial 0
 description Serial Link to the Internet
 encapsulation hdlc
  ip address 204.59.144.3 255.255.255.252
 no shutdown
!
interface Serial 1
shutdown
!
router igrp 200
network 192.168.1.0
!
ip route 0.0.0.0 0.0.0.0 204.59.144.2
```

Router B

```
hostname RouterB
!
interface Ethernet 0
 ip address 192.168.1.2 255.255.0.0
  no shutdown
!
interface Ethernet 1
 ip address 192.168.10.2 255.255.255.0
  no shutdown
!
interface Serial 0
  ip address 172.16.10.2 255.255.255.252
encapsulation hdlc
no shutdown
!
router igrp 200
```

```
network 172.16.10.0
network 192.168.10.
```

Which of the following is true?

A. Split-horizon is enabled by default for IGRP on an Ethernet interface.

B. Split-horizon is enabled by default for IGRP on a serial interface with frame relay encapsulation.

C. Split-horizon is enabled by default for IGRP on a serial interface with X.25 encapsulation.

D. None of the above.

40. Router A's administrator determines that the router is susceptible to unauthorized access to gain routing information. Which of the following is true?

A. IGRP supports authentication.

B. IGRP routing information is encrypted.

C. IGRP does not support authentication, so Router A needs to upgrade to EIGRP.

D. None of the above.

41. Which of the following RFCs defines BGP-4?

A. RFC 1000

B. RFC 1771

C. RFC 1200

D. RFC 2154

42. Which of the following is needed for external neighbors to be configured?

A. They must have the same AS number.

B. They must be adjacent and have different subnets.

C. They must be adjacent and share a network subnet.

D. None of the above.

Use to Figure 12-3 to Answer Questions 43 and 44

FIGURE 12-3   Network diagram

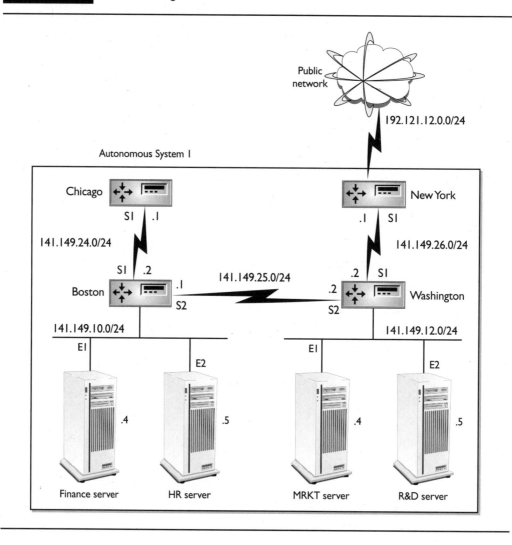

43. In order to set up the Washington router as a default gateway for the MRKT server for traffic with a New York destination when IP routing is disabled, which of the following commands should be used?

A. DEFAULT-GATEWAY 141.149.12.1
B. IP DEFAULT-GW 141.149.12.0
C. IP DEFAULT-GATEWAY 141.149.26.1
D. IP DEFAULT-GATEWAY 141.149.12.0

44. Which of the following commands associates Boston's directly connected interfaces with the RIP routing process:

A. NETWORK 141.149.25.0
B. NETWORK 141.149.26.0
C. IP 141.149.0.0
D. NETWORK 141.149.0.0

45. Which syntax do you use to define a standard access list using a name?

A. IP ACCESS-LIST STANDARD [*name*]
B. IP ACCESS-LIST [*name*]
C. IP ACCESS-LIST 99 [*name*]
D. IP ACCESS-LIST 101 [*name*]

46. According to Figure 12-3 (shown earlier), which command configures a secondary IP address of 141.151.12.1/24 for Washington's interface E1?

A. IP ADDRESS 141.151.12.0 255.255.255.0 SECONDARY
B. IP ADDRESS 141.151.12.1 255.255.254.0 SECONDARY
C. IP ADDRESS 141.151.12.1 255.255.255.0 SECONDARY
D. None of the above

47. Which of the OSI layer information do the commands ISDN DEBUG Q931 and ISDN DEBUG Q921 show?

A. Both commands monitor the same layers.

B. Q931 shows the network layer, and Q921 shows the data-link layer.

C. Q931 shows the data-link layer, and Q921 shows the physical layer.

D. None of the above.

48. Which of the following do you use to remove the Class B network from the RIP process? (Refer to Figure 12-3, shown earlier.)

A. NO ROUTER RIP 141.149.26.0 255.255.255.0

B. NO NETWORK 141.149.0.0

C. NO NETWORK 141.149.24.1

D. NO ROUTER RIP 141.149.24.0

49. Which of the following commands allows you to set a default metric for RIP?

A. DEFAULT-METRIC *number*

B. DEFAULT-METRIC *time*

C. DEFAULT-METRICS *number*

D. DEFAULT-METRICS *time*

50. This section follows the creation of VLANs for ABC Corporation. The corporation has three departments: Human Resources, Finance, and Engineering. They are spread across three floors of ABC's office building. The decision has been made to use VLANs with Cisco Catalyst 5000 series switches. VLAN 1 is designated for Human Resources, VLAN 2 is designated for Finance, and VLAN 3 is designated for Engineering. There is one Catalyst switch per floor. The LAN media is a combination of 10 Mbps and 100 Mbps Ethernet. Links between the Catalysts are 100 Mbps

Ethernet. Figure 12-2 (shown earlier) illustrates the network topology. Which command would be used to define each VLAN?

A. SET VLAN

B. CONFIGURE VLAN

C. ENABLE VLAN

D. None of the above

51. When an IP address is being subnetted, to what are bits added?

A. To the default subnet mask

B. To the network portion of the IP address

C. To the host portion of the IP address

D. To the MAC address

52. A&A is migrating its existing NetBEUI network to TCP/IP. A&A has 150 network nodes and has noticed that performance is greatly degraded since it was originally installed with 10 nodes. The move to TCP/IP will also be accompanied by the installation of routers and several directly connected networks, in order to isolate some of the network traffic. All new hardware and cabling will be replacing the existing infrastructure. There are four departments in A&A: Marketing, Administration, Sales, and Service. The Marketing and Sales departments share a significant amount of data. The Administration department, however, has a subdepartment, Payroll, that will require a significant level of security. A&A is a fairly stable company. They have experienced 25 percent or less growth in the number of employees in a 10-year period. If A&A registers a Class C address, which subnet mask will give them the greatest number of subnets?

A. 255.255.255.0

B. 255.255.255.248

C. 255.255.255.254

D. 255.255.255.252

53. Whitestone Co.'s network has just been connected to Cableview Co.'s network in order to have Whitestone data entry clerks begin to Telnet to an application on a UNIX server at the Cableview network. The server is named MAIN and has the IP address 194.5.5.83 and the subnet mask 255.255.255.192. Which command will add MAIN to the Whitestone router's host cache for name-to-address mapping?

A. router#IP ADDRESS 194.5.5.83 255.255.255.192
B. router>IP DOMAIN-NAME MAIN
C. router(config)#IP NAME-SERVER MAIN 194.5.5.83
D. router(config)#IP HOST MAIN 194.5.5.83

54. A router processes each access list statement in sequence against each packet. How does the router differentiate between the access lists types? (Choose all that apply.)

A. IP standard access lists examine source addresses.
B. Dynamic extended access lists grant access based on destination on a per-user basis not using any other authentication process.
C. IP extended access lists examine both source and destination addresses for filtering.
D. It advertises a NetWare-type service.

55. Which of the following protocols is responsible for dynamically updating routing information tables?

A. RIP
B. SAP
C. NCP
D. SPX

56. On which of the following specifications is the IPX protocol stack based?

A. AFP

B. XNS

C. IP

D. DIX

57. At which layer of the OSI reference model does encapsulation-into-frames take place?

A. Presentation

B. Physical

C. Network

D. Data-link

58. Which of the following protocols provides similar services to IP?

A. NCP

B. SAP

C. IPX

D. SPX

59. What determines if a protocol is routable?

A. If it can be bridged

B. If it supports transport-layer addressing

C. If it supports network-layer addressing

D. If it supports data-link–layer addressing

60. On which network route(s) in the following illustration will Router 1 broadcast RIP updates to Router 2?

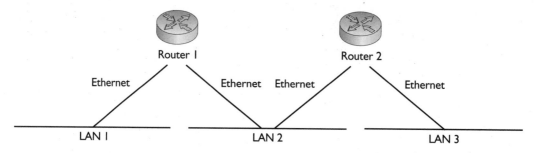

    A. LAN 1

    B. LAN 1 and LAN 2

    C. LAN 2

    D. LAN 2 and LAN 3

61. How do you allow ICMP for error message response?

    A. ACCESS-LIST 101 PERMIT TCP ANY ANY

    B. ACCESS-LIST 101 PERMIT ICMP ANY ANY

    C. ACCESS-LIST 52 PERMIT ICMP ANY ANY

    D. ACCESS-LIST 52 DENY ICMP ANY ANY

62. Which of the following RIP packet fields are only valid in RIP responses? (Choose all that apply.)

    A. Packet-Type

    B. Network-Number

    C. Hops Away

    D. Ticks Away

63. WebSTER Services is a new World Wide Web corporation dedicated to providing Internet connectivity. Because of the amount of incoming traffic, WebSTER plans to install multiple routers and LAN segments to separate the service traffic from corporate data traffic. There will be four segments, each separated by routers. WebSTER will have a NetWare server (Svr2) running both IP and IPX placed on Network 4. This NetWare server's internal network number will be 5. WebSTER also will have a NetWare server (Svr1) running only IPX placed on Network 1 with an internal network number 6. Corporate client computers may attach directly to

either Network 1 or Network 2. The following illustration depicts the
future WebSTER network.

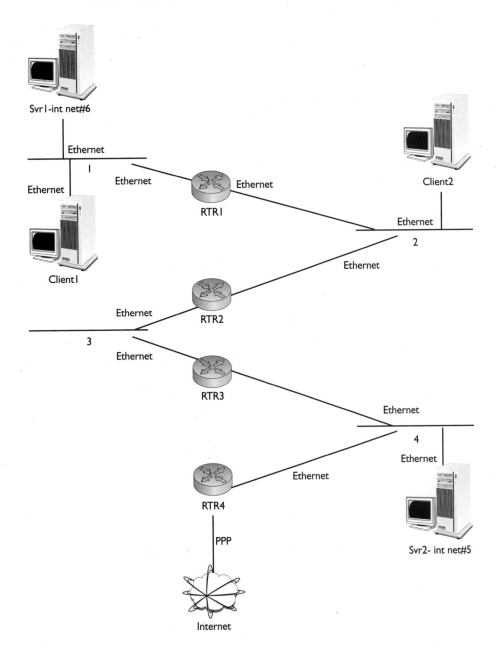

Due to some high-traffic expectations, WebSTER wants to know if it can install another router between Network 4 and Network 3 so that there are multiple redundant equal-cost paths available. Which command executed on RTR2 will enable redundant routes to the same Network 4?

A. rtr2>IPX REDUNDANT ROUTING

B. rtr2#IPX ROUTING MULTIPLE

C. rtr2(config)#IPX MULTIPLE NETWORKS 2

D. rtr2(config)#IPX MAXIMUM-PATHS 2

64. Which of the following statements is true?

A. Cisco routers forward every broadcast they receive.

B. Cisco routers forward only server advertisements.

C. Cisco routers do not forward any broadcasts they receive.

D. None of the above.

65. Which range of access list numbers are reserved for SAP filters on a Cisco router?

A. 1000–1099

B. 250–500

C. 900–999

D. 1001–1099

66. In Central Router 2 for subinterface, serial 3/0.1 is configured in the following way. What do 402 and 403 represent in this command?

```
frame-relay map ip 10.1.12.2 402 broadcast
frame-relay map ip 10.1.12.3 403 broadcast
```

A. VPI numbers

B. VCI numbers

C. PVC numbers

D. DLCI numbers

67. At which layer of the OSI model is CDP?

    A. Layer 1

    B. Layer 2

    C. Layer 3

    D. Layer 5

68. Which is the subnet mask for an address of 148.20.240.12/24?

    A. 255.255.0.0

    B. 255.0.0.0

    C. 255.255.255.0

    D. 255.255.240.0

69. Which of the following are steps to configure a domain name on a Catalyst switch? (Choose all that apply.)

    A. Set the domain name.

    B. Enable VTP version 1.

    C. Set the VTP mode to server.

    D. Configure a VTP password.

70. The Acme Co. has acquired Widget, Inc., and is now merging with it. The management plans to open 22 new sales branches. The Acme Co. had two major offices with 500 employees in London and 1,000 in New York. Widget, Inc., had three major offices with 2,000 employees in Phoenix, 500 employees in Los Angeles, and 1,200 employees in Salt Lake City. Fourteen of the 22 sales offices will connect to Phoenix. Four sales branches will connect to the London office. Four sales branches will connect to the New York office. The newly merged IT department has hired you to assist it in selecting and assigning IP addresses. Refer to Figure 12-1 (shown earlier) to answer the following question.

    The IT department has set up a sales branch office that has 24 workers with its own server. The department has temporarily used an ISP to connect the network to the Internet. The ISP has assigned 199.222.25.0 to the network. What class of address is this?

A. Class A

B. Class B

C. Class C

D. Class D

E. Class E

F. Class F

G. None of the above

CISCO CERTIFIED NETWORK ASSOCIATE

Practice Exam 2
Answers

Thee answers to the questions are in boldface, followed by a brief explanation. Some of the explanations detail the logic you should use to choose the correct answer, while others give factual reasons why the answer is correct. If you miss several questions on a similar topic, you should review the corresponding section in the *CCNA Cisco Certified Network Associate Study Guide,* Second Edition (Osborne/McGraw-Hill, 1999) before taking the CCNA Certification test.

Practice Exam 2 Answers

1. **B, C.** ISL and IEEE 802.1Q. Both Inter-Switch Link (ISL) and 802.1Q are trunking protocols that switches use to communicate VLAN information. This information is sent to all links that are configured in the trunk. IEEE 802.1Q is an industry-standard trunking protocol that allows for communication between different vendor switches. ISL is a trunking protocol developed by Cisco that allows for communication between Cisco Catalyst switches. ISL also allows switches to route between VLANs, thus eliminating the need for a router between the switches.

2. **D.** Cisco. All the routers in the example are configured with frame relay encapsulation. Frame relay encapsulation is configured centrally on the serial interface. If the type of encapsulation is not specified as IETF, the encapsulation type defaults to *Cisco*. Cisco encapsulation is a four-byte header divided into two bytes for DLCI, and two bytes to identify the packet type.

3. **A, B, C, D.** IPX filters can only be inbound or outbound; it builds more secure IPX networks by moving the filter process from the outgoing to the incoming interface; input access lists can validate user information at the borders of the network and build more sophisticated firewalls; and it provides the capability of filtering traffic at the originating end of the GRE-tunneled networks.

   By building a more secure IPX network, you are moving the filter process from the outgoing interface to the incoming interface. Input access lists can validate user information at the borders of the actual network and assist in the building of a more complex firewall system. By reducing the overhead (of processing a packet), the inbound access list rule, if applied, will drop the packets before they transit the router.

4. **C.** TCP sends acknowledgements for every transmitted packet or group of packets. The TCP protocol was developed to withstand the effects of a devastating network catastrophe. The TCP requires positive acknowledgement of the arrival of every packet of data it sends. Remember, because of sliding windows, TCP can also adjust the number of packets sent before requiring an acknowledgement.

5. **D.** 256. UNI and NNI cell headers differ in the number of addressable PVCs that may terminate on one interface. For UNI, the maximum number of VPIs and VCIs that can be configured are 256 and 65,535 respectively. So the total number of PVCs that can be configured is 16,776,960 for UNI. For NNI, the maximum number of VPIs and VCIs are 4096 and 65,535 respectively. So the total number of PVCs that can be configured is 268,431,360 for NNI. VCIs 0–15 have been reserved by the ITU-T, and VCIs 16–30 have been reserved by the ATM forum for management and signaling messages. The number of VCs per VP can change accordingly with the hardware. On the Cisco 7000 AIP, valid values are 32, 64, 128, 256, 512, 1024, 2048, or 4096. On the Cisco 4500 NPM, valid values are 32, 64, 128, 256, 512, 1024, 2048, 4096, or 8192. The default is 1024. To set the maximum number of VCIs per VPI, use the ATM VC-PER-VP interface configuration command.

6. **C.** 146.240.255.255, a directed broadcast to a Class B network; and 220.11.184.3, a Class C address. A directed broadcast address, also called an *all-hosts broadcast,* is one that is directed to all hosts on a particular network. The one denoted here is a Class B address. Class B addresses begin with the bit pattern of 10*xxxxxx* in the first octet. The range of Class B addresses is 128–191. The second address begins with the bit pattern 110*xxxxx,* and is a Class C address. Class C addresses have a range of 192–223. The binary-to-decimal translation associates the decimal value to each bit of the four octets. If this were presented in table format for the first octet of the

first address (**10010010**.11110000.11111111.11111111, or 146.240.255.255), it would look like this:

Value	1	0	0	1	0	0	1	0	Result
128	128								128
64		0							0
32			0						0
16				16					16
8					0				0
4						0			0
2							2		2
1								0	0
Total									146

7. **A.** 1 is VCD, 0 is VPI, and 5 is VCI. The command for this configuration is ATM PVC VCD VPI VCI AAL-ENCAP with additional options. To create the PVC on the AIP or NPM interface card, the ATM PVC command is necessary. A VCD is a virtual circuit descriptor. A unique number per AIP or NPM identifies to the processor which VPI-VCI pair to use for a particular packet. VPI is an ATM network VPI of this PVC in the range of 0–255. The VCI is an ATM network VCI of this PVC in the range of 0–65,535. AAL-ENCAP is the ATM adaptation layer (AAL) and encapsulation type. When Aal5mux is specified, a protocol is required, such as Aal34smd, for an SMDS network, and Aal5nlpid, for high-speed serial interfaces (HSSIs) and ATM-data exchange interfaces (DXI).

8. **A.** 177.77.89.193–177.77.89.254. The subnet mask 255.255.255.192 crosses octet boundaries of a Class B subnet mask. It translates to 11111111.11111111.|11111111.11|000000 in binary. The address 177.77.89.200 is 10110001.01001101.|01011001.11|001000 in binary. The range in binary is 10110001.01001101.|01011001.11|000001– 10110001.01001101.|01011001.11|111110, which is 177.77.89.193– 177.77.89.254.

9. **A.** IP HOST *name IP-address*. This command defines a static host, where *name* refers to the name of the host and *IP-address* refers to the host IP address. The first character of the host can be either a letter or a number, but if you use a number, the operations you can perform, such as packet Internet groper (ping), are limited. The other answers are incorrect. In order to configure the process in the global configuration mode of the router, the right commands must be used in its proper implementation. Somewhat like Domain Name System (DNS), each host name has an IP address associated with it.

10. **B.** IP DOMAIN-NAME BLUE.COM. Use the IP domain-name global configuration command to define a default domain name that the router uses to complete unqualified host names (names without a dotted-decimal domain name). The name in the command specifies a default domain name used to complete unqualified host names. Do not include the initial period that separates an unqualified name from the domain name. In this example blue.com is defined as the default domain name. The correct format should be IP DOMAIN-NAME *name*. The IOS allows DNS configuration, providing the capability to dynamically look up host name-to-address mapping. This is used for connectivity with devices in networks where you don't control the name assignments.

11. **D.** A utility to examine and follow the path of a packet through the network. The traceroute program can be useful for debugging purposes. It enables an administrator to determine the route that IP datagrams follow from host to host. Cisco's ConfigMaker Application configures routers, but traceroute does not. It can be used as a network troubleshooting tool, but it is not intended to be a network management tool. Traceroute is based upon ICMP, not Internet Group Management Protocol (IGMP). It sends an IP datagram with a Time to Live (TTL) of 1 to the destination host. The first router to see the datagram will decrement the TTL to 0 and return an ICMP Time Exceeded message as well as discarding the datagram. In this way, the first router in the path is identified. This process can be repeated with successively larger TTL values in order to identify the series of routers in the path to the destination host. Traceroute actually sends UDP datagrams to the destination host that references a port number outside the normally used range. This enables traceroute to determine when the destination host has been reached that is, when an ICMP Port Unreachable message is received.

12. **A. Efficient.** A connectionless protocol can be compared to a postal service for letters. There is no call setup, and packets may travel by whatever route makes the most use of the network to the end receiver. Packets may be lost or duplicated. The network makes its best effort to deliver the packet, but does not guarantee its delivery.

13. **C. A Microsoft application programming interface.** The Windows Sockets specification defines a network-programming interface for Microsoft Windows, based on the Berkeley socket definition. It includes a set of Microsoft Windows-specific extensions designed to allow the programmer to take advantage of the message-driven nature of Microsoft Windows.

14. **D. SHOW CAM.** When used with the MAC address of a workstation, this command provides information such as the VLAN in which the device is located, and the port off of which the device is located. Other options are available for the SHOW CAM command; however, most network administrators do not track MAC addresses as a normal practice. The other options are listed here:

- count, which displays only the number of content-addressable memory (CAM) entries
- dynamic, which displays the dynamic CAM entries
- static, which displays static CAM entries
- permanent, which displays permanent entries
- system, which displays system entries

15. **C.** TCP establishes two channels for communication. No matter what the particular application, TCP almost always operates full duplex. The transmissions operate in both directions, in an almost completely independent manner. It's sometimes useful to think of a TCP session as two independent byte streams, traveling in opposite directions. No TCP mechanism exists to associate data in the forward and reverse byte streams. Only during connection start and close sequences can TCP exhibit asymmetric behavior (data transfer in the forward direction, but not in the reverse, or vice versa).

16. **B.** The discovery of the DLCI number is automated. Inverse ARP is used to create DLCI mapping dynamically. Dynamic address mapping uses frame relay Inverse ARP to request the next hop protocol address for a specific connection, given its known DLCI. Inverse ARP is enabled by default for all protocols it supports on a physical interface.

17. **C.** Layer 4. The transport layer provides the connectivity and route selection between two end systems. It is responsible for the establishment and termination of a network-wide connection between two transport-layer entities. It includes addressing and network routing. While Layer 3, the network layer, provides logical addressing, the router depends on other applications to learn about the best path through the network.

18. **D.** WINIPCFG. This application will display the DHCP assigned IP address to that particular workstation. It will also allow you to release your address and request another.

19. **A, D.** Store and forward and cut-through. A store-and-forward switch receives the entire frame (store) and then transmits it out the appropriate port (forward), so frames that are invalid are not transmitted, which cuts down on network overhead and enables the administrator to manage traffic more efficiently. However, these benefits come at the cost of higher network latency. A cut-through switch begins to forward a frame as soon as it receives enough of the frame to read the destination MAC addresses and determines to which port to forward the frame. This method has a lower latency than store and forward, but at the cost of reduced management and control of traffic.

20. **A.** Transparent. Since Ethernet packets do not contain a Routing Information Field (RIF), devices on an Ethernet network send packets and assume they will reach the destination device. The bridge looks at the destination MAC address of the packet and compares it to entries in its bridge table. If a match is found, the packet is sent out the appropriate port. If no match is found, then the packet is sent out all ports except the originating port.

21. **B, C.** It uses CSMA/CD, and it is a broadcast system. Carrier sense multiple access/collision detection is the method by which Ethernet gains access to the network. This method allows any node to use the network, but before a node may begin transmitting, it must listen to see if the network is in use by another node. If it is not, then it will begin transmitting. If the network is in use, the node will wait until it is available.

    Ethernet is also a broadcast system. This means that every node on the network sees all of the data that is being transmitted. In normal operations, the node will discard any data that is not meant for that node. This is determined by looking at the MAC address to which the packet is directed. A node can be placed in promiscuous mode if you have the right software, in which case the node can view all data. This is how packet sniffing works.

22. **A.** Use the SHOW CAM command. This command will display information that is contained in the switch's CAM table. This table contains the MAC addresses of all connected devices. This information is gained when the Catalyst is powered on and stored in the CAM table. The switch needs this information to be able to forward frames to the correct port. The SHOW CAM command (used with either the workstation MAC address, or with the dynamic option) will display which port the device is connected to.

23. **A, B.** Provides connection-oriented data delivery, and provides connectionless data delivery. Connection-oriented protocols are considered reliable. They require the receiving end to send an acknowledgement to the sender that the data was received. This allows the sender to know the status of their data communications. Connectionless data delivery does not provide any guarantees to the sender that the data was ever received.

24. **B.** Data compression. Data compression can take place at the presentation layer of the OSI reference model. It can also take place at other layers, such as the data-link layer using PPP with STAC. The presentation layer includes most items that deal with reformatting of data. This also includes encryption and data format conversion. Some common formats used on the Internet include GIF, ASCII text, and MPEG.

Data compression allows for less bandwidth to be consumed when using a network. This is especially important when you have a low bandwidth connection such as a modem. Various methods of compression are used depending on what type of data is compressed.

25. **B.** Hub. To provide each node with shared bandwidth, you would use hubs. Hubs redistribute data onto all ports without analyzing any addressing. Though still very common, hubs are slowly being replaced with switches in some organizations. Hubs still provide adequate service for most networks and save some money.

26. **C.** It does a power on self-test. A power on self-test (POST) is identified by all of the port lights illuminating and then turning off. It verifies that the hardware does not have any failures in the circuitry. Each card that is installed has its own POST that occurs whenever the card is reset or the components are power cycled.

27. **C.** TERMINAL NO EDITING will disable the enhanced editing features in your router. To enable them, use TERMINAL EDITING. Notice that to disable enhanced editing mode, you do not use the NO form of the enable command. This is an exception. The NO form of a command is often used to disable features in the IOS command set. Exceptions such as this make this a good area to watch carefully during the exam, so be sure to take the time to familiarize yourself with those exceptions. The commands DISABLE EDITING and EDITING DISABLE have no meaning. To enable enhanced editing mode for a particular line, use EDITING. To disable for a line, you use the NO form of the command, NO EDITING.

28. **D.** Privileged EXEC mode. This mode is commonly referred to as privileged mode. To enter privileged mode, you must type **enable** at the user prompt. The user prompt is Router>. After typing ENABLE and supplying a password if needed, your prompt is Router#. The Router# prompt indicates that you are in privileged mode and now able to access configuration modes and make changes if needed. Some configuration modes are global, interface, line, router, and controller modes. To view the commands that can be executed at a prompt type ?. A display of all valid commands will appear on your screen. Before taking the test it will be a good idea to view the commands available at the user mode prompt and the privileged mode prompt and compare the two. This will give you an indication of what commands can be issued at which level.

29. **A.** ARPANET. The Internet's inception is a result of the ARPANET project run by the Defense Advanced Research Projects Agency (DARPA). The project's mission was to develop methods to link geographically remote computers. In January of 1969, the firm of Bolt, Baranek, and Newman was awarded the contract to develop this project. By the end of that year, the four initial nodes for the network were in place and operational. Government offices and universities then continually added nodes to ARPANET until it grew into what is now known as the Internet. In recent years, businesses and individuals have also added their presence to the network.

30. **B.** Privileged EXEC mode. To view available debug options, go into privileged mode and type **debug ?**. This will allow you to view all DEBUG commands. These commands are a useful troubleshooting tool. You can view what packets are sent and received from your router. Be sure to remember that the DEBUG command has the potential to lock up your router. If your router is already running at 50 percent, then you may not want to run a DEBUG command locally. Instead you may want to Telnet to the router and run DEBUG from a remote console. To turn off all debugging use the command U AL (un-debug all). Some examples of debugging options are listed here:

DEBUG ARP	DEBUG PPP
DEBUG DECNET	DEBUG SERIAL
DEBUG DHCP	DEBUG SNA
DEBUG EIGRP	DEBUG SPANNING
DEBUG IP	DEBUG TOKEN
DEBUG IPX	DEBUG TUNNEL
DEBUG LANE	DEBUG VLAN
DEBUG MODEM	DEBUG X25
DEBUG PACKET	

Please note that these are just available options, not syntax. Familiarize yourself with the syntax and arguments associated with these commands before using them. It's also possible to send the output of your DEBUG command to a server for later viewing.

31. **A.** 1. Note that the network is running both RIP and OSPF. Routes that are discovered by each of the routing protocols will be added to the single routing table. The router will also maintain a separate routing table for each routed protocol, such as IPX or AppleTalk. Routing protocols are used to determine the best path to an end node. Two types are distance vector protocols and link-state protocols. Distance vector protocols are very simple; however, their disadvantage is that the metrics used by the various protocols do not take into account the speed of the link, making a faster link look the same as a slower one. Link-state routing protocols, however, look at the bandwidth as part of a larger set of variables to determine the best path. This makes link-state protocols very efficient. Convergence is also quicker in a link-state network.

32. **A.** SHOW IP ROUTE. The syntax of this command is as follows:

> SHOW IP ROUTE [*address*[*mask*][*longer-prefixes*]]|
> [*protocol*[*process-id*]]

The *address* argument represents the choice of address you want displayed; *mask* is the subnet mask for that address; *longer-prefixes* is the address and mask pair in which all matches of the pair will be displayed; *protocols* are RIP, OSPF, EIGRP; and the *process id* is the number used to identify the protocol process. All of these arguments are optional. When viewing the routing table you will see what protocol has found the network and what networks are directly connected to your interface. If you expect to see a network that is not there, check to be sure that network is being forwarded and not blocked by any distribution filters on another router.

33. **B.** 0x1. If the Boot field value is 0x1, then the router will boot from the IOS image in ROM. 0x1 in hex is 0000 0000 0000 0001. The configuration register Boot field is a section of the configuration register. This portion of the register tells the router from what location, if anywhere, to load the IOS image. The last four, least significant, bits make up the Boot field. Use the SHOW VERSION command to view the configuration value. You will also be able to see the value used at the next reboot. If the Boot field value were 0x0 then the router would enter ROM monitor mode. If the Boot field value were 0x2 to 0xF, then the router would go through the normal booting sequence commands. The router would check the configuration for BOOT SYSTEM commands, telling it where to go to boot the IOS image. If this fails, it goes to flash to find the first file. If this fails, it goes to the TFTP server for a default file name. If this fails, it goes to ROM (RXBoot mode).

34. **A.** ACCESS-LIST 101 DENY IP 131.72.31.0 0.0.0.255 ANY. This illustrates how to deny traffic from a user attempting to spoof any of your internal addresses from the outside world. This would be placed on your router interface to the outside world using the ACCESS-GROUP command in interface configuration mode. Additional lines would be needed to permit other traffic into the router from the outside world and to defeat the implicit DENY ANY.

35. **C.** Layer 3. Routing occurs at Layer 3, the network layer, as opposed to bridging, which occurs at Layer 2, the data-link layer. While both get information from source to destination, they differ in the way they do this. Routed data will follow a path that is discovered via a routing protocol from the source to the destination. In a bridged environment, if the destination address is not on an originating segment, the data is sent via other interfaces. For routing to occur, it's necessary to have a path from the source to the destination and a means of transport for the information. The optimal path is determined by a routing protocol that uses various algorithms. Bridging does not select an optimal path as it uses data-link-layer information to transfer information from one internetwork to another.

36. **B.** Version 2. This version was first described in RFC 1088, which was developed in 1988. When additional data space was needed to support areas such as authentication, RFC 1723 and then RFC 2453 were adopted to provide the extra message space needed for routers to provide the additional data.

37. **D.** Cost. OSPF calculates cost as the metric determining the best path to the destination. Cost is defined to be the overhead required to transmit packets across a given interface. The cost of an interface is inversely proportional to its bandwidth. For example, a 10Mbps Ethernet: the cost is calculated using the formula $10^8 \div$ bandwidth = cost, so the cost of the 10Mbps Ethernet would be $10^8 \div 10,000,000$, or 10.

38. C. Each network defined must have an Area ID. If a network doesn't have an Area ID, it will not be advertised by OSPF. The defined network also determines which interfaces are to be included in the area.

39. A. Split-horizon is enabled by default for IGRP on an Ethernet interface. Split-horizon is a mechanism to block the advertisement of information from a router in which the information originated. This was put into place to prevent routing loops. Split-horizon is sometimes not needed in the case of nonbroadcast networks such as SMDS and frame relay. On Cisco routers with frame relay or Switched Multimegabit Data Service (SMDS), split-horizon is disabled by default.

40. C. IGRP does not support authentication, so Router A needs to upgrade to EIGRP. Authentication is used to deter the unauthorized access to routing information. Router A would best benefit by transitioning to and configuring EIGRP to take advantage of authentication in order to prevent unauthorized access.

41. B. RFC 1771. This RFC was authored in 1995. Changes incorporated in version 4 include support for CIDR and the advertising of IP prefixes.

42. C. They must be adjacent and share a network subnet. When external BGP neighbors are configured, they must have an adjacent connection and have different AS numbers. If the AS were the same, communications would be considered internal.

43. C. IP DEFAULT-GATEWAY 141.149.26.1. Since there is no routing for the network, the MRKT server needs a way to transmit information outbound. Specifying a default gateway, the MRKT server has a path outside its network. Data are forwarded out the Washington router via interface E1, IP address 141.149.12.1. The router sends any packets that need the assistance of a gateway to the address specified. If another gateway has a better route to the requested host, the default gateway sends an

Internet Control Message Protocol (ICMP) redirect message to the router. The ICMP redirect message indicates which local router the router should use. The other answers are either incorrect or incomplete. In answer A, the command is incorrect, since you must make reference to IP. Answer B is incorrect, since the word gateway, instead of GW, is necessary. Answer D refers to a network and not a particular outbound IP address.

44. D. NETWORK 141.149.0.0. In this scenario, Boston is directly connected to both the Chicago router and the Washington router. In order to route packets to either of these routers via RIP, the network (141.149.0.0) must be defined in the Boston router. It simply routes the Class B address, since the network is using one Class B to address the entire network. This ensures that anything coming from or through the Boston router destined for either Chicago or Washington knows how to properly route the information. Each router should have the network 141.149.0.0 defined for the RIP process. Defining the network allows adjacent routers to share routing information about that network's directly connected interfaces and routes to other nodes on the network. The RIP protocol is somewhat old, but it is still deployed in many network infrastructures today. RIP has its limitations, which are causing network administrators to resort to other solutions for network routing. Of late, many corporations are migrating to OSPF. Familiarize yourself with all the routing protocols for preparation for the CCNA Certification examination.

45. A. IP ACCESS-LIST STANDARD [*name*]. In configuration mode, you define a standard access list using a name with this syntax, followed by PERMIT/DENY rules. For extended access lists using names, the following syntax applies: IP ACCESS-LIST EXTENDED [*name*], followed by PERMIT/DENY rules. For example:

> STANDARD: *ip access-list standard Internet_Rules*
> PERMIT 131.72.31.2
> DENY ANY
> EXTENDED: *ip access-list extended Finance_Dept*
> PERMIT TCP ANY 131.72.0.0 0.0.255.255 EQ TELNET
> DENY TCP ANY ANY

Now, applied to an interface:

```
INTERFACE FASTETHERNET 0/0/0
IP ACCESS-GROUP INTERNET_RULES OUT
IP ACCESS-GROUP FINANCE_DEPT OUT
```

46. C. IP ADDRESS 141.151.12.1 255.255.255.0 SECONDARY. Keep in mind that each router that is attached to the same physical subnet as the one that has the secondary address also needs a secondary address on that same subnet to ensure that each packet can reach its destination. So, it makes sense to implement the scheme in each router attached to the same physical interface to provide the reliability and scalability needed for routing across the network. The formats of the other answers are invalid. Use the same command for creating the primary IP address of an interface and add SECONDARY at the end of the configuration command.

47. B. Q931 shows the network layer, and Q921 shows the data-link layer. Following are some commands that show activity at different layers in an ISDN:

Layer 1 (Physical Layer of the BRI)	Layer 2 (Data-link Layer)	Layer 3 (Network Layer)
SHOW CONTROLLERS BRI #	DEBUG Q921	DEBUG ISDN EVENTS
		DEBUG DIALER
		SHOW DIALER

48. B. NO NETWORK 141.149.0.0. This removes the entire Class B network 141.149.0.0 from the RIP process of a router. At this point RIP is turned off. The other answers refer to specific subnets and router interface that are not directly related to the RIP process. Whenever you are configuring any routing protocol (RIP, IGRP, or OSPF, for example) you must use the network number to associate the network with the routing process. If no network is specified, the routing process is not configured for that particular router.

49. **A.** DEFAULT-METRIC *number.* This command sets and assigns a metric value for RIP. Use the default-metric statement to set the metric for the redistributed routes. Because metrics for different protocols cannot be directly compared, you must specify the default metric in order to designate the cost of the redistributed route used in RIP updates. All routes that are redistributed use the default metric. The other answers are either incorrect or incomplete.

50. **A.** SET VLAN. This command defines the VLAN. With optional commands you can determine which ports are to be assigned with each VLAN. An example would be to set VLAN 1 on ports 3/1–24, 4/1–24, and 5/1–24 as SET VLAN 1 3/1–24, 4/1–24, 5/1–24.

51. **A.** To the default subnet mask. When the bits are added, the result is that more bits are used for the network portion of the address and fewer bits are used for the host portion. The result is that multiple subnets are created with fewer host addresses available on each of the new subnets. Answer B is incorrect because the network portion of the IP address is not determined until the subnet mask is applied. Answer C is incorrect because the host portion of the IP address is not determined until the subnet mask is applied. Also, adding bits to the end of the host portion will make the IP address longer than 32 bits, generating an invalid address. Answer D is incorrect since the MAC address does not participate in subnets. A MAC address is defined at Layer 2 (the data-link layer), IP addresses are defined at Layer 3 (the network layer).

52. **D.** 255.255.255.252. In binary format, this 255.255.255.252 is 11111111.11111111.11111111.|111111|00. The number of subnets that is created from this is $2^6 - 2 = 62$ subnets. There can only be two hosts on each subnet, so this configuration would allow 124 network nodes. Answer A is incorrect since it is the default subnet mask without any added bits. Answers B and C do not create as many subnets as answer D.

53. D. router(config)#IP HOST MAIN 194.5.5.83. The IP HOST *name ip_address* is the global configuration command that is used to add a mapping entry to the router's host cache. To add the MAIN server's name-to-address mapping, the prompt and command are router(config)#IP HOST MAIN 194.5.5.83. Mapping a host name to an address helps route data when a host name is known and the address is not. Domain Name System (DNS) is a special type of server that maps names to addresses for an entire network. If domain name servers are not used, routers and servers need to be able to map names to addresses. UNIX servers typically use a hosts file that lists the host name and the address of any hosts that need to be found. Cisco routers use the IP HOST *name ip_address* command in global configuration mode to do the same type of name-to-address mapping. Each host name and address must be input manually on each router.

54. A, C. IP standard access lists examine source addresses, and IP extended access lists examine both source and destination addresses for filtering. Further defining protocol type on an extended access list provides a more granular method of controlling traffic. While dynamic extended access lists do grant access based upon destination and on a per-user basis, these types of lists must be used with another form of authentication.

55. A. RIP. Routing Information Protocol (RIP) is responsible for dynamically updating routing information tables. RIP is a distance vector protocol in the IPX protocol stack that bases its choices on the number of hops (distance) and the direction to the router, or vector. Hops represents the number of routers a packet must cross before it reaches the destination network. The maximum number of hops is 15. An additional metric that RIP uses is called ticks. Ticks are approximately $1/18^{th}$ of a second and are used to measure the time it takes for a packet to reach a destination network. RIP uses the hops and ticks information to update routing table information on routers and servers. The selection criteria for any particular path are based on the lowest number of ticks and the lowest number of hops. RIP updates are sent every 60 seconds and consist of the entire routing table sent to neighboring routers.

56. **B.** XNS. The IPX protocol stack was developed using the Xerox Network Systems (XNS) protocol stack as a basis. Xerox Corporation created XNS, a client/server architecture, in the late 1970s. The client server architecture is where a client requests a service from a server, which then fulfills the request. Novell developed NetWare in the early 1980s and used the IPX protocol stack derived from XNS as the core architecture of the NOS. NetWare provides many services on the internetwork, including transparent file and printer access.

57. **D.** Data-link. This layer contains the MAC sublayer. The NetWare IPX protocol stack specifies the following layers that can be mapped to the OSI protocol reference model: network, transport, session, presentation, application. Therefore, none of these layers is a candidate for encapsulating the upper-layer protocol data into media-dependent frames. Instead, they encapsulate it into other packet types, such as into datagrams at the network layer. The missing layers from the IPX protocol stack are the data-link and physical layers. The physical layer handles bitstream-data transmission, electrical signaling, and media specifications. The remaining layer is the data-link layer that consists of the LLC (Logical Link Control) and MAC (Media Access Control) sublayers. The MAC layer is the sublayer that handles the encapsulation-into-frames by encapsulating network-layer datagrams within MAC-layer frames.

58. **C.** IPX. This is the network-layer protocol in the TCP/IP protocol stack and provides addressing and routing on the internetwork. IPX is the NetWare network-layer protocol that provides addressing and routing of packets through the internetwork. All the remaining answer choices are part of the IPX protocol stack, but at different layers and providing different services than IP. Answer A, NCP, is an upper-layer protocol which is used for managing connections. Answer B, SAP, is a session-layer protocol used to advertise services. Answer D, SPX, is a transport-layer protocol that provides a connection-oriented, reliable service.

59. **C.** If it supports network-layer addressing. Protocols such as AppleTalk, IP, and IPX are all routable. Each one supports a different type of routable address, but the router understands them all. This is because the Internet uses IP addressing to create a hierarchical structure.

The network administrator can assign AppleTalk, IP, and IPX addresses at his or her own choosing. If a connection to the Internet or any shared network is desired, IP addressing must be obtained from a controlling body, the American Registry for Internet Numbers (ARIN) in the United States. It is often the case that your ISP will have addresses already and will provide the IP address for a network. If you have no desire to be on the Internet, you can use private addressing as described in RFC 918 or any addressing scheme you desire.

60. **A.** LAN 1. Using RIP with its default behavior of split-horizon, Router 1 will only broadcast the route to LAN 1 on the LAN 2 network to which Router 2 is connected. Split-horizon is an algorithm used by RIP that prevents it from broadcasting any routes back to the network from which they were learned. This is used to prevent routing loops, and prevent transmission of information that is already known. In the diagram, Router 1 will know of three routes:

- LAN 1 (directly connected) learned from interface Ethernet 0
- LAN 2 (directly connected) learned from interface Ethernet 1
- LAN 3 (one hop via Router 2) learned from interface Ethernet 1

Since Router1 has two interfaces, Ethernet 0 connected to LAN 1, and Ethernet 1 connected to LAN2, it will not broadcast any routes learned from Ethernet 1 back onto Ethernet 1. This means that the only network that Router1 will broadcast to Router 2 via RIP is LAN 1.

61. **B.** ACCESS-LIST 101 PERMIT ICMP ANY ANY. Extended IP access lists use source and destination addresses for matching operations, and optional protocol type information for finer granularity of control. Standard IP access lists only use source addresses for matching operations.

62. C, D. Hops Away and Ticks Away. Workstations and other nodes use the RIP request packet to find a route to a destination-IPX network. The RIP response packet is used by routers to reply to a request with the information needed. The format of the RIP request and response packets is identical. The content of the RIP request packet differs from the RIP response packet in the two fields of Hops Away and Ticks Away. In these fields a RIP request packet, since it is sent by a workstation or other node, does not yet know how many hops or how many ticks it takes to reach the destination network. Therefore, in the RIP request packet, these fields are not valid and have a value of 0xFFFF.

63. D. rtr2(config)#IPX MAXIMUM-PATHS 2. The global configuration command IPX MAXIMUM-PATHS *n* will enable RTR2 to use two redundant paths to the same network. By default, Cisco IOS will instruct RTR2 to forward IPX packets along the least-cost route to a destination network. If there are multiple paths of equal cost, the router will keep one route in the routing table and discard all others. All traffic to the network is then forwarded along this one path. The IPX MAXIMUM-PATHS *n* command can configure the Cisco IOS to maintain up to a maximum of whatever number has been entered as part of the command equal-cost paths to a destination network. When multiple paths to a destination do exist, traffic is distributed among the paths in a round robin fashion. Answers A through C are incorrect commands that do not exist in the Cisco IOS. Answer D is correct for this command in that it uses the global configuration mode prompt rtr2(config)#, and the correct command, IPX MAXIMUM-PATHS 2. Any number 2 or higher would have satisfied this command's requirements to use multiple redundant paths of equal cost.

64. C. Cisco routers do not forward any broadcasts they receive. If this were not the case, the router would waste resources and, depending on the size of the Novell network, bog the router down trying to keep up with all of the broadcasts. Instead, Cisco routers send out the entire SAP table at regular intervals. The default is 60 seconds. Like a Novell server, a Cisco router listens to broadcasts that originate from other Novell servers and routers and builds an internal SAP table.

65. A. 1000–1099. SAP filters are numbered from 1000–1099 on a Cisco router.

66. D. DLCI numbers. Frame relay mappings are configured to the remote locations on this subinterface. This subinterface serial 3/0.1 is configured for multipoint connectivity. 402 and 403 are the DLCI numbers in this command. The EXEC command for this is FRAME RELAY MAP IP [*address*] DLCI [*broadcast*] [CISCO | IETF]. This FRAME RELAY MAP command is used to define the mapping between a next hop protocol address and the DLCI used to connect to the address.

67. B. Layer 2. CDP works at Layer 2 and is media and protocol independent. CDP works on the MAC layer, each device configured for CDP sends out messages to a MAC-layer multicast address. These messages include information about its originator. Information about the software version and device capabilities is included. To see information on neighboring devices use the SHOW CDP NEIGHBOR command. CDP runs on all Cisco equipment, including switches and access servers. Because CDP works at Layer 2, the devices do not need any network protocols configured in order to be discovered; however, if addresses are configured on the devices, CDP will discover the address as well.

68. C. 255.255.255.0. The "/24" portion of the notation in the address is a different way of stating the subnet mask that is being used. This states that 24 bits are used for a subnet mask. When the decimal format is changed to binary, it can easily be seen that 11111111.11111111.11111111.00000000 offers 24 1 bits for a subnet address. This is translated to 255.255.255.0. Answer A is incorrect, although it does denote the default subnet mask for a Class B address. Answer B is incorrect since it is the default subnet mask for a Class A address. Answer D is incorrect since it shows only 20 bits being used for the subnet mask, instead of the 24 the notation states.

69. **A, C, D.** Set the domain name, set the VTP mode to server, and configure a VTP password. These steps, in conjunction with commands to set pruning, are used to configure a domain name for a VLAN. Once logged in, the administrator would follow these steps to configure a domain name:

1. Set the VTP to version 2.
2. Define the VTP domain name.
3. Enable VTP pruning. (This is optional.)
4. Set a password. (This is optional.)
5. Create the VLAN, map the name to the VLAN, and activate.

70. **C.** Class C. The Class C network address 199.222.25.0 has been assigned to the sales branch office by the ISP. The range of addresses for a Class C network address is 192.*x.x.x* to 223.*x.x.x*. A Class C network address can be discerned from other classes by noting the leading bits. Class C addresses begin with 110 in the first octet. The address 199.222.25.0 has the leading octet bits 11000111, and the first three bits are clearly 110. A Class A network address has as its range 0–126 and the leading bit of the first octet is always 0. A Class B network address has as its range 128–191 and the leading bits of the first octet are always 10. A Class D network address, which is used for multicasting, has as its range 224–239 and has the first four leading bits of 1110. A Class E network address, which is used for research, has as its range 240–254 and has the first four leading bits of 1111. There is no such thing as a Class F address.

Part 13

Test Yourself:
Practice Exam 3

CISCO CERTIFIED NETWORK ASSOCIATE

Test Yourself:
Practice Exam 3
Questions

Q

&

A

B efore you call to register for the actual exam, take the following test and see how you make out. Set a timer for 90 minutes—the time you'll have to take the live CCNA Certification exam—and answer the following 70 questions in the time allotted. Once you've finished, turn to the Practice Exam 3 Answers section and check your score to see if you passed! Good luck!

Practice Exam 3 Questions

1. Which of the following transport-layer protocols is correctly matched with its function?

   A. Transmission Control Protocol, provides network and node addressing and uses a subnet mask

   B. Internet Protocol, provides network and node addressing and uses a subnet mask

   C. User Datagram Protocol, provides a connectionless transport service

   D. Telnet, provides a remote control host session

2. When data passes from an upper-layer protocol to a lower-layer protocol, what happens to the packet?

   A. It is segmented into smaller packets and, if necessary, each packet is encapsulated in the lower layer's header and checksum and passed on to the next layer.

   B. The header is stripped from the packet, and the packets are reassembled into larger data segments.

   C. The checksum is recalculated, and the packet is forwarded on.

   D. Nothing happens. The data packet simply passes onto the bitstream.

3. Which of the following are portions of Layer 2?

   A. TCP/IP

   B. IEEE and DIX

   C. IPX/SPX

   D. LLC/MAC

4. When two workstations attempt to access the Ethernet-network segment at the same time, what mechanism prevents a second collision?

A. CSMA/CD

B. A backoff algorithm

C. CSMA/CA

D. Wrapping

5. What mechanism does IEEE 802.5 use to notify stations of a network fault?

A. Beaconing

B. MAU

C. Autoreconfiguration

D. Encapsulation

6. Which of the following physical/data-link topologies specifies a dual-ring topology?

A. IEEE 802.5

B. Token Ring

C. FDDI

D. Ethernet

7. Which of the following is an ISDN interface?

A. BRI

B. HSSI

C. EIA/TIA-232

D. V.35

8. General Companies, Inc., will be adding three remote sales offices with six users each to its network, which already consists of two main offices connected via a T1 line. Connectivity will be for electronic messaging and sharing of sales information data. The bandwidth utilization is expected to be very small. The president of General Companies, Inc., is interested in using ISDN with at least 512 Kbps of bandwidth open on the link between the remote office and the existing network. The main office contains all of the servers and messaging systems. The HQ office contains only executives and desktop equipment. The General Companies has an objective of causing the least amount of traffic utilization on the Main-to-HQ T1 line. Which of the following will provide connectivity to the network, use ISDN with speeds of 512 Kbps or greater, and cause little or no traffic on the Main-HQ T1 line?

A. PPP links using T1 lines between each remote office and the main office
B. BRI links from each remote office to the HQ office
C. PRI links from each remote office to the HQ office
D. PRI links from each remote office to the main office

9. Gerald is configuring frame relay between New York and East Rutherford on his network. When his provider told him the Data-link Connection Identifier (DLCI) numbers, Gerald wrote them down but did not remember to write down which number was meant for New York and which for East Rutherford. Gerald arbitrarily uses one number for New York and the other for East Rutherford. What will happen if these are not the correctly assigned numbers?

A. The link will be established but will suffer instability, because the DTE will transmit the wrong DLCI number through the PVC.
B. The link will not be able to be established, because the DTE will not recognize the DLCI number.
C. The DLCI numbers will reconfigure themselves correctly, so there will be no appreciable error.
D. Nothing. DLCI numbers represent the link and will be identical for the DTEs.

10. Which of the following uses cell-switching technology?

A. Frame relay
B. SLIP
C. X.25
D. ATM

11. Which of the following routing protocols is correctly matched with its function?

    A. Internet Protocol, provides addressing and routing at the network layer

    B. RIP, uses distance vector methods to maintain the routing table

    C. OSPF, provides dynamic route table maintenance through distance vector technology

    D. EIGRP, provides data formatting and encryption services

12. When Bart walks up to a console attached to the router, he presses a key to be prompted for a password. He types the password. What does he see?

    A. *******

    B. #######

    C. ......

    D. Nothing

13. Jeannette walks up to a router console that Bart has just left. She determines that Bart was in privileged EXEC mode. What would indicate to Jeannette which mode Bart was in?

    A. When in privileged EXEC mode, the router states *privilege* at the top of the screen.

    B. When in privileged EXEC mode, the router prompt is displayed as router>.

    C. When in privileged EXEC mode, the router prompt is displayed as router#.

    D. When in privileged EXEC mode, the screen changes to reverse colors.

14. Which of the following commands will exit privileged EXEC mode?

    A. router>LOGOUT

    B. router>EXIT

    C. router#ENABLE

    D. router#DISABLE

PRACTICE EXAM 3 QUESTIONS

15. What command will display *lock login logout* on the router console?

   A. HELP L

   B. COMMANDS L?

   C. LO?

   D. LIST ALL LO?

16. Which of the following keystroke sequences will go to the beginning of the line on the router console?

   A. CTRL-A

   B. CTRL-E

   C. CTRL-B

   D. ESC-B

17. Wilma has entered twelve commands into the router since logging into privileged EXEC mode. Wilma wants to reuse the fifth command that she has entered, but cannot remember the exact syntax. Which command would display the commands Wilma has entered?

   A. TERMINAL HISTORY

   B. TERMINAL EDITING

   C. SHOW HISTORY

   D. SHOW EDITING

18. Which of the following is not a router memory component?

   A. RAM

   B. Flash

   C. DROM

   D. NVRAM

19. Which command is used to enter global configuration mode?

    A. router>ENABLE

    B. router#ENABLE

    C. router>CONFIGURE TERMINAL

    D. router#CONFIGURE TERMINAL

20. Jack decided to enforce a new naming convention for routers on his internetwork. Each router is named after the IATA code for the nearest airport and a numeric sequence number. Additionally, backbone routers are named with a B following the sequence number. Jack is renaming router LARTR to LAX02. Which command will Jack enter to execute this?

    A. lartr>HOSTNAME LAX02

    B. lax02#HOSTNAME LARTR

    C. lartr(config-if)#HOSTNAME LARTR

    D. lartr(config)#HOSTNAME LAX02

21. Which of the following commands will exit from global configuration mode to privileged EXEC mode?

    A. router(config)#DROPCONFIG

    B. router#EXIT

    C. router(config)#EXIT

    D. router>LOGOUT

22. Which of the following commands will display the router configuration running in RAM?

    A. SHOW RUNNING-CONFIG

    B. SHOW STARTUP-CONFIG

    C. SHOW FLASH

    D. SHOW BUFFERS

23. Marci is adding a new Cisco router to the JKL & Associates' internetwork, which uses TCP/IP exclusively. The router has not been configured with an IP address. What command will display other network routers?

A. SHOW ROUTERS

B. SHOW CDP ROUTERS

C. SHOW CDP NEIGHBOR

D. None. Marci must configure the IP address before the router will see other routers on the internetwork.

24. Which of the following is an output of a successful PING command?

A. .....

B. !!!!!

C. #####

D. *****

25. Which of the following commands will have the router startup using a configuration file on a TFTP server?

A. router>BOOT SYSTEM FLASH TFTP 111.111.111.111

B. router#BOOT SYSTEM ROM 123.45.6.78

C. router(config)#BOOT SYSTEM TFTP BOOT.ME 123.45.6.78

D. router(config-if)#BOOT SYSTEM IOS 123.45.6.78

26. Which command will copy the configuration file from NVRAM to a TFTP server?

A. COPY TFTP RUNNING-CONFIG

B. COPY RUNNING-CONFIG TFTP

C. COPY TFTP STARTUP-CONFIG

D. COPY STARTUP-CONFIG TFTP

27. Which of the following is a valid Class A address?

    A. 124.253.3.2

    B. 127.0.0.1

    C. 128.9.22.5

    D. 129.3.2.1

28. Which of the following is a reserved IP address?

    A. 2.255.255.254

    B. 127.2.5.8

    C. 35.0.0.253

    D. 1.0.255.3

29. Select the network address that will provide 254 hosts if you are using the default subnet mask for that address class.

    A. 128.5.0.0

    B. 124.0.0.0

    C. 191.253.0.0

    D. 192.3.8.0

30. Gargantuan Networks hired a new network administrator. The administrator learned that Gargantuan will need 500 IP addresses distributed across 16 different network segments. Which class of IP address will best provide this?

    A. Class A

    B. Class B

    C. Class C

    D. Class D

    E. Class E

PRACTICE EXAM 3 QUESTIONS

31. Gargantuan Networks decides on using multiple Class C addresses to provide the 16 subnets with 500 hosts. The largest network segment has 45 hosts. All other segments have fewer than 45 hosts. How many Class C addresses will Gargantuan need if they all use the same subnet mask?

A. 8

B. 6

C. 7

D. 5

32. A consultant is hired by Belker, Inc., to review the network of a recently acquired subsidiary. The network administrator has left the subsidiary, and there is no existing documentation. The consultant finds that the subsidiary network consists of two network segments with 48 hosts on each. One of the hosts on Segment 1 has the address 193.5.51.72 with a subnet mask of 255.255.255.192. What is the range of addresses for this subnet on Segment 1?

A. 193.5.51.65–193.5.51.126

B. 193.5.51.1–193.5.51.127

C. 193.5.51.32–193.5.51.96

D. 193.5.51.48–193.5.51.72

33. Jens Co. has implemented a new IP address scheme. One of the hosts has an address of 194.8.201.1 with a subnet mask of 255.255.252.0. What type of scheme is this?

A. Variable-length subnet masking

B. Subnetting

C. Supernetting

D. Complex subnetting

34. Which of the following commands will configure the IP address as 192.3.5.88 with its default subnet mask for a Cisco router interface?

 A. router>IP ADDRESS 192.3.5.88 255.255.255.192
 B. router#IP ADDRESS 193.2.5.88 255.255.0.0
 C. router(config)#IP ADDRESS 192.3.5.88 255.255.255.0
 D. router(config-if)#IP ADDRESS 192.3.5.88 255.255.255.0

35. The TCP/IP-based network of Tracers, Inc., uses the domain name tracers.com for all of its IP hosts. The administrator wants to set the routers so that they will automatically fully qualify host names with the tracers.com domain name. Which of the following commands can perform this function?

 A. router(config)#IP DOMAIN-NAME TRACERS.COM
 B. router#IP NAME-SERVER TRACERS.COM
 C. router>IP HOST TRACERS.COM
 D. router(config)#IP NETMASK-FORMAT TRACERS.COM

36. Which of the following commands will discover the IP routers in the route to a destination IP address of 123.45.6.78?

 A. PING 123.45.6.78
 B. TRACE 123.45.6.78
 C. TELNET 123.45.6.78
 D. ROUTE 123.45.6.78

37. Select the session-layer protocol that is matched correctly with its function.

 A. RPC, makes remote procedures appear as though executed locally
 B. FTP, transfers files between a local and remote host
 C. UDP, provides an unreliable connectionless service
 D. IP, establishes addresses for networks and hosts

38. Which of the following is the port that Telnet uses?

A. TCP 80

B. TCP 21

C. TCP 23

D. TCP 25

39. Gardens, Inc.'s network configuration is shown in the following illustration. Select the commands that would configure Router A's interface connected to Network 2.

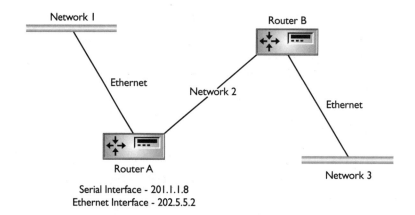

A. INTERFACE ETHERNET0
   IP ADDRESS 201.1.1.8 255.255.255.0

B. INTERFACE SERIAL0
   IP ADDRESS 202.5.5.2 255.255.0.0

C. INTERFACE ETHERNET0
   IP ADDRESS 202.5.5.2 255.255.255.0

D. INTERFACE SERIAL0
   IP ADDRESS 201.1.1.8 255.255.255.0

40. SCN's network administrator has just added a router with an ISDN connection from a remote branch office. This network is Ethernet3 in the following illustration. The network administrator wants all traffic to automatically be sent to the NETRTR from the Ethernet3 network if it is not traffic that is local to the Ethernet3 network segment. Which command sequence will provide this functionality?

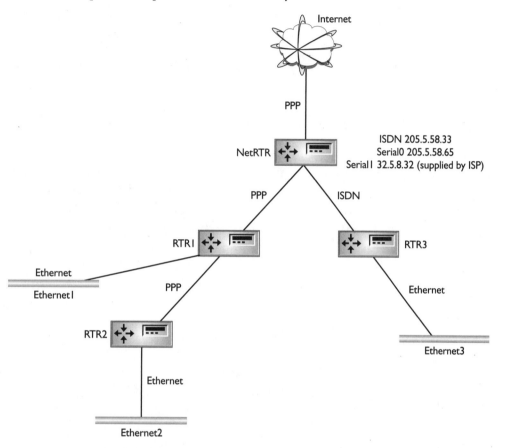

A. netrtr>IP DEFAULT ROUTER

B. rtr3(config)#IP DEFAULT-NETWORK 205.5.58.32 255.255.255.224

C. rtr3#IP DEFAULT ROUTER 205.5.58.33

D. netrtr(config)#IP DEFAULT-NETWORK 205.5.58.32 255.255.255.224

41. Which routing protocol from the following list uses split horizon?

A. NLSP

B. OSPF

C. RIP

D. NetBEUI

42. Which of the following routing protocols uses a hello packet?

A. IP

B. OSPF

C. RIP

D. UDP

43. The MCR network, shown in the following illustration, has three routers, RTR1, RTR3 and NetRTR, which are connected so that there is a redundant ISDN connection if one of the point-to-point WAN connections fails. The network administrator configures RIP on NetRTR. Which set of commands did the administrator execute?

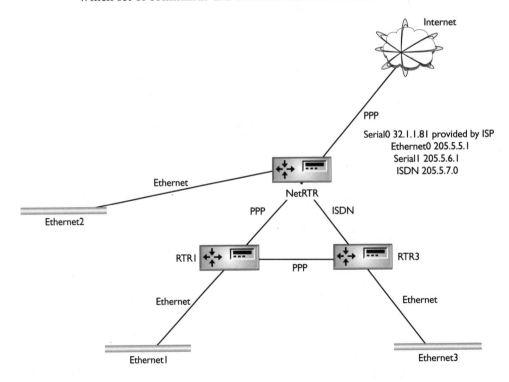

A. ROUTER IGRP 1
   NETWORK 32.0.0.0
   NETWORK 205.5.5.0
   NETWORK 205.5.6.0
   NETWORK 205.5.7.0
B. ROUTER RIP
   NETWORK 205.5.5.0
   NETWORK 205.5.6.0
   NETWORK 205.5.7.0
C. ROUTER RIP
   NETWORK 32.0.0.0
   NETWORK 205.5.5.0
   NETWORK 205.5.6.0
   NETWORK 205.5.7.0
D. ROUTER RIP
   NETWORK 205.5.0.0

44. The following illustration displays a simple internetwork with two Ethernet
segments and a WAN connection between two routers. The administrator
does not want to use an entire IP subnet on the WAN connection. Which
command will let the administrator configure RTR1 so that it does not
need an IP address for the WAN link?

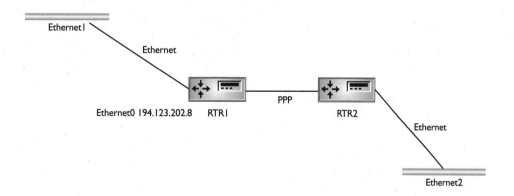

    A. INTERFACE ETHERNET0
       IP ADDRESS 194.123.202.8
       INTERFACE SERIAL0
       IP ADDRESS 194.123.202.8
    B. INTERFACE ETHERNET0
       IP UNNUMBERED ETHERNET0
    C. INTERFACE ETHERNET0
       IP ADDRESS 194.123.202.8
       INTERFACE SERIAL0
       IP ADDRESS UNNUMBERED ETHERNET0
    D. INTERFACE SERIAL0 UNNUMBERED

45. There are some legacy UNIX hosts on a segment in Grace's network that use BOOTP. Grace decides to move the BOOTP server to a backbone segment to change the traffic patterns on the network. When Grace moves the server so that a router is now between it and the legacy UNIX hosts, its employees can no longer boot. What can Grace do to enable BOOTP while keeping the server on the backbone?

    A. Nothing. Once the server was moved, the connection permanently damaged the legacy UNIX hosts.

    B. It can move the server back to its original place.

    C. It can invoke the IP HELPER-ADDRESS command on the router between the server and the equipment.

    D. It can execute a reboot of the server.

46. Which of the following is the IPX network portion of the address a210.0000.c002.ab13.452?

    A. a210

    B. a210.0000

    C. 452

    D. 0000.c002.ab13

47. Which of the following addresses represents a router that can use NLSP?

    A. 123.5.8.9

    B. 199.55.235.1

    C. 0x00.abk3.0001

    D. 1.0000.4582.000a.4

48. What does the address 20.0000.0000.0001 represent?

    A. It represents a dynamic IPX address.

    B. It represents an internal network address of 20.

    C. It represents a network address of 20 and a node address of 1.

    D. Nothing. It is an invalid address.

49. Select the Cisco encapsulation type that is correctly matched to the NetWare frame type.

    A. Arpa, Ethernet_SNAP

    B. SAP, Ethernet_II

    C. Novell-ether, Ethernet_802.3

    D. SNAP, Ethernet_802.2

PRACTICE EXAM 3
QUESTIONS

50. The servers in the following illustration are configured with the displayed frame types. The routers use the displayed encapsulations. Which servers can SVR2 "see" on the internetwork?

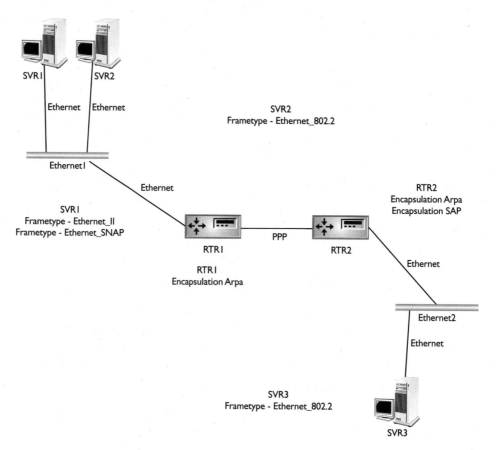

A. SVR1

B. SVR3

C. SVR1 and SVR3

D. Neither

51. Which of the following commands enables IPX on a Cisco router?

   A. IPX ENABLE

   B. IPX ROUTING

   C. RIP ROUTING

   D. IPX START

52. Server A is configured to use the Ethernet_II frame type for network 400. A router is added to the segment that contains Server A. In order for the router to be able to route Server A's IPX traffic, which of the following commands should be executed on the router?

   A. router(config-if)#IPX NETWORK 401 ENCAPSULATION SNAP

   B. router(config-if)#IPX NETWORK 402 ENCAPSULATION SAP

   C. router(config-if)#IPX NETWORK 400 ENCAPSULATION ARPA

   D. router(config-if)#IPX NETWORK 400 ENCAPSULATION NOVELL-ETHER

53. Greta wants to verify that IPX is configured correctly on Rtr1. Which of the following commands will display the IPX configuration information?

   A. rtr1>SHOW VERSION

   B. rtr1#SHOW IPX TRAFFIC

   C. rtr1#SHOW IPX INTERFACE BRIEF

   D. rtr1#IPX INTERFACE BRIEF

54. Which of the following commands will deny all traffic except that from network 10.10.10.0?

   A. ACCESS-LIST 801 PERMIT 10.10.10.0

   B. ACCESS-LIST 3 PERMIT 10.10.10.0 DENY 255.255.255.255

   C. ACCESS-LIST 301 PERMIT 10.10.10.0 DENY ALL

   D. ACCESS-LIST 23 PERMIT 10.10.10.0 0.0.0.255

55. Select the protocol that is correctly matched with its access list number range.

A. Novell SAP, 800–899

B. Standard Novell, 900–999

C. IP, 1–99

D. Extended IP, 300–399

56. Access list 10 has a single rule of permit 190.1.1.0. This access list is applied to a router interface. That router interface receives a packet from 191.2.1.0. What happens with this packet?

A. It is allowed to pass.

B. The router broadcasts the packet to all interfaces.

C. The router forwards the packet to a different interface.

D. The packet is dropped.

57. Which of the following protocols is used by a NetWare server to advertise its services on the internetwork?

A. IPX

B. SAP

C. RIP

D. SPX

58. What does the following line actually permit?

```
access-list 101 permit ip any host 199.2.25.13
```

A. It permits IP traffic to host 199.2.25.13 from any host.

B. It permits IP traffic from host 199.2.25.13 to any host.

C. Nothing. It is an invalid access-list number.

D. It permits IP traffic either to or from host 199.2.25.13

59. Which of the following commands configures the Challenge Handshake Authentication Protocol for the Point-to-Point Protocol encapsulation?

    A. PPP ENCAPSULATION CHALLENGE

    B. PPP AUTHENTICATION CHALLENGE

    C. PPP AUTHENTICATION CHAP

    D. PPP ENCAPSULATION CHAP

60. Select the ISDN command that configures the service profile identifier.

    A. DIALER-GROUP 2

    B. INTERFACE BRI0

    C. ISDN SPID1 1882228880 5551212

    D. DIALER MAP IP 199.9.9.88 NAME RTR1 SPEED 56 BROADCAST 6025551234

61. RtrA is a Cisco router that will be connecting to a non-Cisco router via frame relay. Which is a command that will enable this connection?

    A. FRAME RELAY INTERFACE-DLCI 7 BROADCAST

    B. ENCAPSULATION FRAME-RELAY IETF

    C. FRAME RELAY INTERFACE ENCAPSULATION

    D. ENCAPSULATION FRAME RELAY

62. What OSI reference model layer does a VLAN operate at?

    A. Physical

    B. Data-link

    C. Network

    D. Transport

63. What protocol enables Catalyst switches to share VLAN list information?

    A. VTP

    B. Source Routing

    C. ISL

    D. IEEE 802.1Q

64. Which protocol is used to avoid loops in Catalyst Ethernet bridging?

A. Split horizon

B. Poison reverse

C. IEEE 802.1D Spanning-Tree Protocol

D. DEC Spanning-Tree Protocol

65. Which command creates a new VLAN on a Cisco Catalyst switch?

A. DEFINE VLAN 3

B. SET VLAN 3

C. ENABLE VLAN 3

D. VLAN 3

66. Which of the following is the protocol that Cisco created to trunk between switches?

A. ISL

B. VLAN

C. STP

D. 8021Q

67. What is the decimal value of the binary IP address 01001111.10111001.00011001.00001001?

A. 79.129.33.9

B. 79.142.38.5

C. 79.185.38.5

D. 79.185.25.9

68. Select the binary value for the number 219.

A. 11011011

B. 11001011

C. 11010011

D. 10111011

69. How many hosts are allowed on each subnet if 6 bits are added to a Class B subnet mask?

   A. 512

   B. 510

   C. 1,022

   D. 1,024

70. Which of the following commands will assign a secondary IP address of 155.155.155.12 with a mask of 255.255.0.0 to a router interface?

   A. router>IP ADDRESS 155.155.155.12

   B. router#IP ADDRESS 155.155.155.12 SECOND

   C. router(config-if)#IP ADDRESS 155.155.155.12 255.255.0.0 SECONDARY

   D. router(config-if)#IP SECONDARY ADDRESS 155.155.155.12 255.255.0.0

CCNA
CISCO CERTIFIED NETWORK ASSOCIATE

Practice Exam 3
Answers

Q & A

The answers to the questions are in boldface, followed by a brief explanation. Some of the explanations detail the logic you should use to choose the correct answer, while others give factual reasons why the answer is correct. If you miss several questions on a similar topic, you should review the corresponding section in the *CCNA Cisco Certified Network Associate Study Guide*, Second Edition (Osborne/McGraw-Hill, 1999) before taking the CCNA Certification test.

Practice Exam 3 Answers

1. **C.** User Datagram Protocol, provides a connectionless transport service. User Datagram Protocol (UDP) is a protocol in the TCP/IP protocol stack. UDP runs at the same layer as TCP, but is a simpler protocol. UDP does not provide the reliability functions that TCP does. The UDP header is concerned only with the source service port, the destination service port and the checksum of the packet. As a result, those services that do not require reliability, such as Trivial File Transport Protocol (TFTP), use UDP as the transport-layer protocol. Without the extra overhead of reliability functions, the performance of those services is improved.

2. **A.** It is segmented into smaller packets and, if necessary, each packet is encapsulated in the lower-layer's header and checksum and passed on to the next layer. As a data packet is passed from an upper-layer protocol to a lower-layer protocol, it is first broken into smaller packets if the protocol requires it. Then the smaller packets are given a new header for the lower layer and a checksum is calculated. Each of the new smaller packets is then passed onto the next layer for further processing. This process is called *encapsulation* or *wrapping* the data.

3. **D.** LLC/MAC. Layer 2 is the data-link layer of the OSI reference model. This protocol layer has two defined sublayers, as shown in the following illustration. These layers are Logical Link Control (LLC) and Media Access Control (MAC). The MAC layer specifies the media access method, the

topology, and the physical address of the network node. The LLC layer handles connection services.

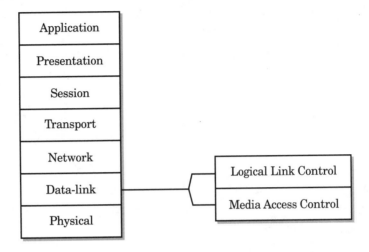

4. B. A backoff algorithm. Backoff algorithms prevent secondary collisions between the same two workstations on an Ethernet network. Ethernet uses the CSMA/CD (Carrier Sense Multiple Access/Collision Detection) method of media access. This method enables nodes to access the network media at any time they have data to send. When two nodes transmit simultaneously, collisions occur. The collision ruins both transmissions and the nodes must retransmit the data. To avoid a second collision, each node uses the backoff algorithm to create a random wait time for retransmission. The random time staggers the retransmissions so that a collision is prevented.

5. A. Beaconing. This is the method IEEE 802.5 uses to notify stations of a network fault. Whenever a station detects a fault in the network, it sends a specially formatted frame, called a *beacon* frame onto the network. The frame specifies the sending station, the network area that failed and the nearest active upstream neighbor. Beaconing will initiate the network's autoreconfiguration. This process is effective when using a MAU, since it simply blocks a port that fails on the ring, bypasses it and reestablishes a ring by which the remaining ports and stations can transmit data.

6. **C.** FDDI. Fiber Distributed Data Interface (FDDI) is a physical topology that specifies a dual ring. FDDI uses token passing over a dual-ring topology using fiber-optic cable. FDDI uses one of the rings as a primary ring, but retains the other ring for backup purposes in case of cable failure. This effectively provides redundancy so that stations can restore service through the backup ring.

7. **A.** BRI. Basic Rate Interface (BRI) is an ISDN interface and is one of the two most common ISDN interface types. The other is Primary Rate Interface (PRI). BRI offers two B channels and one D channel. A B channel is 64 Kbps and a D channel is 16 Kbps. According to the BRI standard specification, the B channels are used for data transmission and the D channel is used for transmission of framing control, signaling, and other overhead data.

8. **D.** PRI links from each remote office to the main office. These will provide connectivity to General Companies' network, use ISDN, provide speeds greater than 512 Kbps, and cause little or no traffic overhead on the Main-HQ T1 link. The PRI link is the Primary Rate Interface ISDN specification that provides speeds approximating those of a T1 line at 1.544 Mbps. Since all servers and messaging systems exist at the main office, the traffic added to the network should be concentrated on the link between each remote office and the main office. By ensuring that the HQ office is not included on a link between any remote office and the main office, the link will cause little or no effect on the Main-HQ T1 line.

9. **B.** The link will not be able to be established, because the DTE will not recognize the DLCI number. This is a local identifier and is used by the DTE to refer to the connection between two DTEs. The DLCI is local and can be different for two DTEs even when they are referring to the same link.

10. **D.** ATM. Asynchronous Transfer Mode (ATM) uses cell switching technology. Cell switching is an improvement on packet switching because its small, fixed-length packet, called a cell, provides a more effective and efficient data transmission. The small size of the ATM packet, a mere 53 bytes, can be switched at the hardware level so that the ATM switch has little processing overhead. ATM provides speeds of up to 622 Mbps and can utilize multiple media types from UTP to fiber-optic cable.

11. **B.** RIP, uses distance vector methods to maintain the routing table. Routing Information Protocol (RIP) is the only protocol that is both a routing protocol and matched correctly with its function. RIP is available in the TCP/IP protocol stack and a similar RIP is available in the IPX/SPX protocol stack. Distance vector routing protocols use a distance metric and a direction (vector) to select routes.

12. **D.** Nothing. Bart will see nothing on the screen when he types his password. When Bart walked up to the console, he had to press the ENTER key before he was prompted for the password. When a router has been idle for sometime, the router's console will display the message to press ENTER to get started. The router initially enters user EXEC mode.

13. **C.** When in privileged EXEC mode, the router prompt is displayed as router#. A user EXEC mode prompt is displayed as router>. The router console does not display any color reversal for any mode, nor does the router console display a message explaining which mode the user is in.

14. **D.** router#DISABLE. Additionally, the commands LOGOUT and EXIT will exit the console completely and log out of the Cisco IOS. These commands would exit privileged EXEC mode if entered into the console while the router was in privileged EXEC mode. However, for answers A and B, the router was in user EXEC mode, as indicated by the prompt, and is not an answer for this question.

15. **C.** LO?. The keystroke sequence LO? will display all commands that begin with the letters lo. These commands are LOCK, LOGIN, and LOGOUT. None of the remaining answers for this question represents valid keystroke sequences or commands in the Cisco IOS.

16. **A.** CTRL-A. This is one of several enhanced editing commands available in the Cisco IOS. The CTRL-E keystroke sequence will move the cursor to the end of the line. The CTRL-B keystroke sequence will move the cursor back one character. The ESC-B keystroke sequence will move the cursor back to the beginning of the previous word.

17. **C.** SHOW HISTORY. The default for the router is to retain the last 10 commands that were entered. If Wilma wanted to retain more than 10 commands in the buffer, she would use the TERMINAL HISTORY SIZE ### command to change the default, where ### is replaced with the number of commands to retain in the buffer.

18. **C.** DROM. There are four types of router memory:

- **RAM**   Stores the running configuration
- **Flash**   Stores the internetwork operating system software image
- **NVRAM**   Stores the startup configuration
- **ROM**   Stores the first IOS version used to boot the router

19. **D.** router#CONFIGURE TERMINAL. The privileged EXEC mode is indicated by the router# prompt. Answer A displays the router prompt for user EXEC mode, and the command to enter privileged EXEC mode. Answer B is invalid, because the command is used to enter privileged EXEC mode, and the prompt shows that the router is already in privileged EXEC mode. Answer C is invalid because the router cannot move directly from user EXEC mode (as indicated by the router> prompt) to global configuration mode.

20. **D.** lartr(config)#HOSTNAME LAX02. Answer A is incorrect because the prompt lartr> indicates that the router is in user EXEC mode. Answer B is incorrect because the prompt lax02# shows that the router is already named LAX02 and is in privileged EXEC mode. Answer C is incorrect since the command will rename the router to LARTR. Additionally, the command

HOSTNAME should be executed from global configuration mode, not interface configuration mode as indicated by the prompt lartr(config-if)#.

21. **C.** router(config)#EXIT. Answer A is incorrect because there is no DROPCONFIG command. Answer B is incorrect because the router# prompt indicates that the router is already in privileged EXEC mode. Answer D is incorrect because the router> prompt shows that the router is in user EXEC mode.

22. **A.** SHOW RUNNING-CONFIG. Answer B, SHOW STARTUP-CONFIG, will display the configuration that is stored in nonvolatile RAM, which is the default startup configuration file. Answer C, SHOW FLASH, will display the name of the IOS image in flash memory. Answer D, SHOW BUFFERS, will display buffer memory pool statistics for the router.

23. **C.** SHOW CDP NEIGHBOR. This command will display the contents of the Cisco Discovery Protocol (CDP) table. The CDP table stores information about other Cisco routers on the internetwork. It uses a MAC-layer multicast address and does not require a network-layer address in order to work. The SHOW CDP NEIGHBOR DETAIL command will display the network-layer configuration of the neighboring router's advertised interface.

24. **B.** !!!!!. The series of five exclamation points (!!!!!) indicates that a successful PING command has been executed.

25. **C.** router(config)#BOOT SYSTEM TFTP BOOT.ME 123.45.6.78. When entered in global configuration mode, this command boots the system from a file called BOOT.ME on a TFTP server with the address of 123.45.6.78. Global configuration mode is indicated by the prompt router(config)#. There can be multiple BOOT SYSTEM TFTP commands entered, if redundant TFTP servers are available for configuration file storage. The

BOOT SYSTEM commands are executed in the order in which they are entered. For this reason, the commands should be carefully configured.

26. **D.** COPY STARTUP-CONFIG TFTP. Answer A, COPY TFTP RUNNING-CONFIG, will configure the router immediately by copying a configuration file from a TFTP server to the configuration in RAM. Answer B, COPY RUNNING-CONFIG TFTP, will copy the configuration currently running to a TFTP server. Answer C, COPY TFTP STARTUP-CONFIG, will copy a file from a TFTP server to the startup configuration stored in NVRAM.

27. **A.** 124.253.3.2. Class A addresses are those that have the first octet value between 1 and 126. There are only 126 networks available for Class A addresses, but each of these networks can have up to 16,777,213 hosts. Answer B is incorrect, because the value of 127 for the first octet is reserved for loopback function. Answers C and D are both Class B addresses. The following table describes the various IP address classes.

Address Class	Value of First Octet	Bit Pattern of First Octet (Binary)	Number of Networks	Number of Hosts per Network
Class A	1–126	0xxxxxxx	126	16,777,213
Class B	128–191	10xxxxxx	16,383	65,533
Class C	192–223	110xxxxx	2,097,151	254
Class D	224–239	1110xxxx	N/A	N/A
Class E	240–254	1111xxxx	N/A	N/A

28. **B.** 127.2.5.8. There are three reserved IP addresses. They are 0.*x.x.x*, 127.*x.x.x*, and 255.*x.x.x*. The 0.*x.x.x* address is reserved for use when indicating a host that exists on the current network. The 127.*x.x.x* is reserved for use in loopback functions, indicating the local host. The 255.*x.x.x* is used for broadcasting.

29. D. 192.3.8.0. This address is a Class C address. Class C addresses have a first octet value of 192–223. The Class C address using a default subnet mask will provide 254 hosts on a single network. Answer A and answer C are both Class B addresses that provide 65,533 hosts on a single network. Answer B is a Class A address and provides 16,777,213 hosts on a single network.

30. B. Class B. The Class B address actually provides 65,533 hosts on a single network segment. However, using a subnet mask of 255.255.248.0 will provide 30 subnets with 2,046 hosts per segment. Answer A, a Class A address, will provide more IP addresses than are necessary. Answer C, a Class C address, will provide only 254 hosts on a network segment and is insufficient. Answer D, a Class D address, is used for multicasting and is not valid for use as an IP address scheme for hosts. Answer E, a Class E address, is used for research and is not valid for use as an IP address scheme for hosts.

31. A. 8. Gargantuan Networks will require each Class C address subnet to provide enough addresses for 45 hosts or more. This means that the subnet mask will be 255.255.255.192. This subnet mask provides 62 hosts per network and two subnets per address. With 16 subnets required, the result is that eight Class C addresses are needed because they will each provide two subnets.

32. A. 193.5.51.65–193.5.51.126. The subnet mask 255.255.255.192 will enable two subnets. The two bits that make up the final octet value of 192 are 128 and 64. The only valid subnets are when one of these bits is a one and the other a zero, since subnet bits cannot be all ones or all zeroes. That means that one of the subnets will have the final octet start at 65 (193.5.51.65), which is the smallest subnet bit (64) plus the smallest host bit (1). The other possible subnet will have the final octet start at 129 (193.5.51.129), which is the other subnet bit (128) plus the smallest host bit (1). The address of the host is 193.5.51.72, which is greater than 193.5.51.65 and less than 193.5.51.129. This means that the beginning of the address range will be 193.5.51.65. The end of the address range will be

193.5.51.126. The end of the address range is calculated by adding all the highest bits of the host address except the one bit with the subnet bit value for the octet. This would be 32 + 16 + 8 + 4 + 2 + 64 = 126.

33. **C.** Supernetting. The Jens Co. IP address given, 194.8.201.1, is a Class C address. A Class C address has a default subnet mask of 255.255.255.0. However, the subnet mask given was 255.255.252.0. This mask has fewer bits than the default. Supernetting takes multiple contiguous Class C addresses and "adds" them together so that they can be used like a Class B subnetted address. Supernetting manages to "add" Class C addresses by subtracting bits from the subnet mask.

34. **D.** router(config-if)#IP ADDRESS 192.3.5.88 255.255.255.0. This command must be entered during interface configuration mode. Interface configuration mode is indicated by the router(config-if)# prompt. The address, 193.3.5.88, is a Class C address and has a default subnet mask of 255.255.255.0. Answer A is incorrect because the prompt indicates that the router is in user EXEC mode and the mask is not the default subnet mask for a Class C address. Answer B is incorrect because the prompt indicates that the router is in Privileged EXEC mode, the address itself is incorrect, and the subnet mask is the default for a Class B address. Answer C is incorrect because the prompt indicates that the router is in global configuration mode.

35. **A.** router(config)#IP DOMAIN-NAME TRACERS.COM. When entered in global configuration mode, this command specifies tracers.com to be the default domain name to use for unqualified host names. A fully qualified domain name (FQDN) for a host named myhost on the tracers.com network is myhost.tracers.com. Cisco's IOS can make administration easier by not requiring the FQDN to be used for any hosts on the tracers.com domain, limiting that use only to the host name itself. This command must be entered when requiring a default domain name for appending to hostnames.

36. **B.** TRACE 123.45.6.78. This command can be used from user EXEC or privileged EXEC mode to discover the routers on the path to the destination address of 123.45.6.78. The default TRACE command will send out three test probes to discover the routers in the path. The output of the TRACE command lists the IP address of each router, the hostname of each router (if the hostname can be resolved) and the return times for the three probes.

37. **A.** RPC, makes remote procedures appear as though executed locally. Remote procedure calls (RPCs) act at the session layer. Answer B is incorrect because File Transfer Protocol (FTP) functions at the application layer. Answer C is incorrect because User Datagram Protocol (UDP) is a transport-layer protocol. Answer D is incorrect because Internet Protocol (IP) is a network-layer protocol.

38. **C.** TCP 23. Both TCP and UDP use *ports* to identify the service connection between two computers. The source and destination ports identify the point where a service is accessed. A *socket* is an IP address plus the service port. Answer A, TCP 80, is the port for Hypertext Transfer Protocol (HTTP). Answer B, TCP 21, is the port for File Transfer Protocol (FTP). Answer D, TCP 25, is the port for Simple Mail Transport Protocol (SMTP).

39. **D.** INTERFACE SERIAL0
    IP ADDRESS 201.1.1.8 255.255.255.0

Router A on Gardens, Inc.'s internetwork has two interfaces. One interface is Ethernet, which can only be connected to the Ethernet Network 1 segment. The other interface is serial, which can only be connected to the WAN Network 2 segment. The serial interface is assigned the address 201.1.1.8. This is a Class C address and has a default subnet mask of 255.255.255.0. The configuration command to configure the serial interface is INTERFACE SERIAL0. The subsequent command of IP ADDRESS 201.1.1.8 255.255.255.0 will configure the serial interface's IP address to be 201.1.1.8 using a default subnet mask of 255.255.255.0.

40. B. rtr3(config)#IP DEFAULT-NETWORK 205.5.58.32 255.255.255.224. Entering this command in global configuration mode on RTR3 will configure a default route to the 205.5.58.32 subnet. The NetRTR router is in a perfect position to be configured as a smart router, which contains the routing information for all of SCN's internetwork and a default route to the Internet.

41. C. RIP. Routing Information Protocol (RIP) is a distance vector routing protocol. Distance vector routing protocols use split horizon or poison reverse to mitigate the problems of routing loops. Split horizon is a method that filters updates sent to neighboring routers so that it omits references to networks learned from the interface to which it is sending the current updates. Poison reverse is a modified version of split horizon that sends the updates but marks as unreachable those that are being sent through the interface from which they were learned. Answers A and B, NLSP and OSPF, are both link-state routing protocols and do not use split horizon. Answer D, NetBEUI, is not a routing protocol.

42. B. OSPF. Open Shortest Path First (OSPF) is a link-state routing protocol. Link-state routing protocols use a hello packet when the link-state router comes online in order to learn about neighboring routers. Answer A, Internet Protocol (IP), is not a routing protocol. IP is the network-layer protocol in the TCP/IP stack that provides network and node addresses. Answer C, RIP, is a distance vector routing protocol and does not use hello packets. Answer D, User Datagram Protocol (UDP), is not a routing protocol. It is a transport-layer protocol in the TCP/IP stack that provides a connectionless, unreliable service.

43. B. ROUTER RIP
    NETWORK 205.5.5.0
    NETWORK 205.5.6.0
    NETWORK 205.5.7.0

This command sequence will enable RIP on the router. Then it will add RIP routing updates to be sent on the interfaces connected to the 205.5.5.0, 205.5.6.0, and 205.5.7.0 networks. RIP updates should not be exchanged with the Internet. Instead, the network administrator should use a default route to the Internet connection so that any traffic not designated for the standard network can be sent automatically to the Internet.

44. C. INTERFACE ETHERNET0
IP ADDRESS 194.123.202.8
INTERFACE SERIAL0
IP ADDRESS UNNUMBERED ETHERNET0

The administrator can use the IP UNNUMBERED capability of the Cisco IOS to eliminate the need for an IP address on the WAN link.

45. C. It can invoke the IP HELPER-ADDRESS command on the router between the server and the equipment. This will ensure that BOOTP packets are forwarded and will enable the legacy UNIX hosts to boot. BOOTP uses UDP as its underlying transport-layer protocol. UDP is not automatically forwarded from one network to the next. The IP HELPER-ADDRESS *host address* command will forward selected protocols received on that interface to the specified IP host address.

46. A. a210. The node address portion is 0000.c002.ab13. The socket portion of the address is 452.

47. D. 1.0000.4582.000a.4. This address represents a router that can use NLSP. It is an IPX address, and NLSP is an IPX routing protocol. Answers A and B are not correct since they are IP addresses and may not represent routers that are configured for IPX. Answer C is not correct since the IPX address is hexadecimal. Hexadecimal addresses do not use any characters other than 0–9 and a–f. Answer C includes an *x* and a *k*.

48. B. It represents an internal network address of 20. The server is always designated as node 0000.0000.0001 on its internal network.

49. C. Novell-Ether, Ethernet_802.3. Novell-Ether is the same as the NetWare frame type of Ethernet_802.3. Encapsulation types are mapped according to the following table:

Cisco Encapsulation	NetWare Frame Type
Arpa	Ethernet_II
Novell-Ether	Ethernet_802.3
SAP	Ethernet_802.2
SNAP	Ethernet_SNAP

50. D. Neither. SVR2 would not be able to see either SVR1 or SVR3 in the displayed configuration. SVR2 would not see SVR1 on the same network link, because the use of different frame types effectively places SVR1 onto two different, separate, logical IPX networks. SVR2 would not be able to see SVR3 because the next router, RTR1, does not use an encapsulation equivalent to the Ethernet_802.2 frame type used on SVR2. As a result, SVR2 does not see any other servers.

51. B. IPX ROUTING. This command is executed when the router is in global configuration mode. To enter global configuration mode, the command CONFIGURE TERMINAL is executed while the router is in privileged EXEC mode.

52. C. router(config-if)#IPX NETWORK 400 ENCAPSULATION ARPA. This will enable the router to begin routing traffic for Server 1. It is entered in interface configuration mode, which is indicated by the router(config-if)# prompt. The router should be configured to participate in the same network that Server 1 participates in. Each frame type configured for a server represents a different logical IPX network. In this case, the frame type used is Ethernet_II configured for network 400. To participate in this network, the router must use the Cisco encapsulation type for Arpa.

53. C. rtr1#SHOW IPX INTERFACE BRIEF. This command will display a listing of each interface on the router with its IPX configuration. This command should be executed in privileged EXEC mode. Answer A will not provide this type of information. Answer B will show the IPX packets sent and received by the router. Answer D is not a valid Cisco IOS command.

54. D. ACCESS-LIST 23 PERMIT 10.10.10.0 0.0.0.255. This command will permit the traffic from 10.10.10.0. This command implies a DENY ALL command after the permit statement, which effectively permits the one network address, but denies all other traffic. An IP access list must be numbered between 1 and 99, or an extended IP access list can be numbered between 100 and 199. Answer A is incorrect since the access list number is 801, which is an IPX access list number. Answer B is incorrect because of its syntax. Answer C is incorrect because its access list number is 301, which is a DECnet access list number, and because of its syntax.

55. C. IP, 1–99. Cisco uses a strict numbering scheme to define access lists for certain protocols. The IP access list range is any number between 1 and 99. Answer A is incorrect, since Novell SAP uses the range of 1000–1099. Answer B is incorrect, since Standard Novell uses the range of 800–899. Answer D is incorrect, since Extended IP access lists use the range of 100–199.

56. D. The packet is dropped. When the router interface receives the packet, it checks it against the rules of the applied access list. When the router does not find a rule that matches the packet, it drops the packet.

57. B. SAP. The Service Advertising Protocol (SAP) is the protocol in the IPX protocol stack that advertises services on the internetwork. SAP can be filtered on a Cisco router using the Novell SAP access list.

58. **A.** It permits IP traffic to host 199.2.25.13 from any host. The argument ANY stands for any source network. The HOST argument is the same as using a mask of 0.0.0.0 for the 199.2.25.13 address.

59. **C.** PPP AUTHENTICATION CHAP. This command establishes the Challenge Handshake Authentication Protocol. It is used when a Point-to-Point Protocol connection has been established using the ENCAPSULATION PPP command.

60. **C.** ISDN SPID1 18822288880 5551212. The service profile identifier (SPID) is the number that the telephone company assigns to the ISDN connection equipment. The SPID is much like a telephone number.

61. **B.** ENCAPSULATION FRAME-RELAY IETF. This command will enable frame relay to work between a Cisco router and a non-Cisco router. The Internet Engineering Task Force (IETF) argument changes the encapsulation type from the default Cisco version to the IETF standard.

62. **B.** Data-link. In order for VLANs to communicate with other VLANs, they must use a router or a type of Layer 3 switch. Both routers and Layer 3 switches operate at the network layer of the OSI reference model.

63. **A.** VTP. The VLAN Trunk Protocol (VTP) allows Catalyst switches to exchange their list of VLANs. Answer B, Source Routing, is a Token Ring switching method. Answer C, ISL, is a trunking protocol for Ethernet media. It allows the Ethernet link to be used by multiple VLANs. Answer D, IEEE 802.1Q, is a trunking protocol for 100 Mbps and Gbps Ethernet links.

64. **C.** IEEE 802.1D Spanning-Tree Protocol. This protocol is used to avoid loops in Catalyst switches and in Cisco routers running transparent bridging. Answers A and B are distance vector routing protocol loop avoidance techniques. Answer D is a transparent bridging loop avoidance protocol used only by Cisco Routers. It is not used by Catalyst switches.

65. B. SET VLAN 3. This command would create a VLAN numbered 3. By default, a Cisco Catalyst switch contains a defined VLAN 1 to which all ports are assigned, and VLANS 1002–1005 for use with FDDI and Token Ring.

66. A. ISL. The Inter-Switch Link (ISL) protocol was developed by Cisco as a trunking protocol for switches. ISL is used to reduce the ports required on routers to route between VLANs. A Cisco router running ISL only requires a single port to route between two VLANs on a switch.

67. D. 79.185.25.9. Although the router works in binary, the decimal value of an IP address is typically used. The decimal value is the one that is actually configured on the router.

68. A. 11011011. The way to translate between binary and decimal is to determine the bit value, as a power of 2, for each bit and add them up until the number is the same as the decimal value. For 219, the bits are 128 + 64 + 0 + 16 + 8 + 0 + 2 + 1. If manually converting to binary, it is helpful to subtract each bit value and place a 1 value for any bit that can be subtracted from the decimal value. Place a 0 value for any bit that cannot be subtracted from the decimal value. For example, with 219 the first bit value to subtract is 128. Since 219 is larger than 128, 128 can be subtracted and the 128 bit value is set as a 1. Repeat this for 64, 32, 16, 8, 4, 2, and finally 1. The result is again 11011011.

69. C. 1,022. If 6 bits are allocated to the subnet mask, 10 bits are left for host addresses. The 10 bits establish a host range of 0–1,023. However, the first address of the host range cannot be used for host addresses. The range becomes 1–1,023.

70. C. router(config-if)#IP ADDRESS 155.155.155.12 255.255.0.0 SECONDARY. Answer A is in user EXEC mode, not interface configuration mode and does not use the secondary argument. Answer B is in privileged EXEC mode, not interface configuration mode, and uses the wrong syntax for the command. Answer D places the argument secondary in the wrong order for the command.

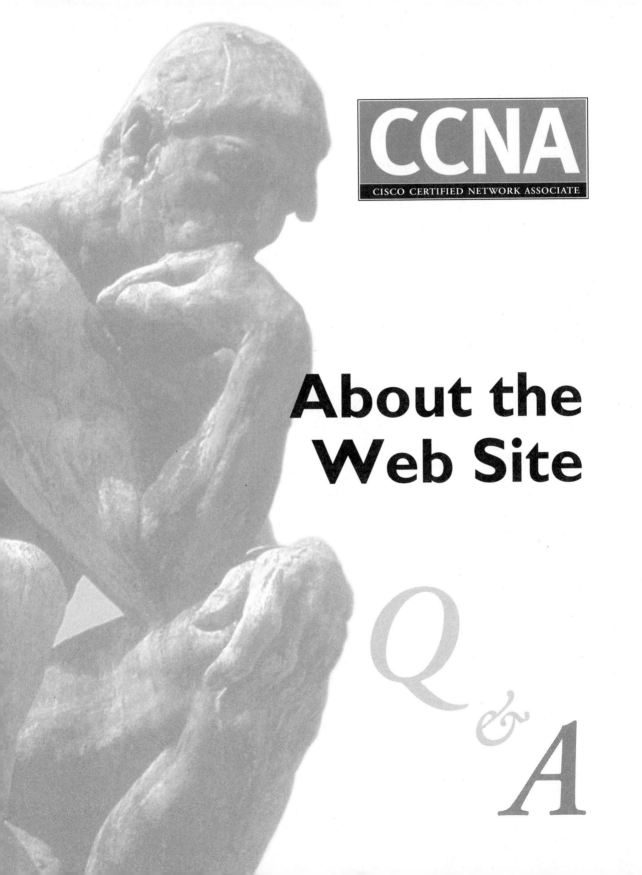

CCNA
CISCO CERTIFIED NETWORK ASSOCIATE

About the Web Site

Q & A

Access Global Knowledge

As you know by now, Global Knowledge is the largest independent IT training company in the world. Just by purchasing this book, you have also secured a free subscription to the Global Knowledge Web site and its many resources. You can find it at http://access.globalknowledge.com.

You can log on directly at the Global Knowledge site, and you will be e-mailed a new, secure password immediately upon registering.

What You'll Find There. . .

The wealth of useful information at the Global Knowledge site falls into three categories:

Skills Gap Analysis

Global Knowledge offers several ways for you to analyze your networking skills and discover where they may be lacking. Using Global Knowledge's trademarked Competence Key Tool, you can do a skills gap analysis and get recommendations for where you may need to do some more studying. (Sorry, it just might not end with this book!)

Networking

You'll also gain valuable access to another asset: people. At the Access Global site, you'll find threaded discussions, as well as live discussions. Talk to other CCNA candidates, get advice from folks who have already taken the exams, and get access to instructors and CCSIs.

Product Offerings

Of course, Global Knowledge also offers its products on the Web site, and you may find some valuable items for purchase—CBTs, books, or courses. Browse freely and see if there's something that could help you take that next step in career enhancement.

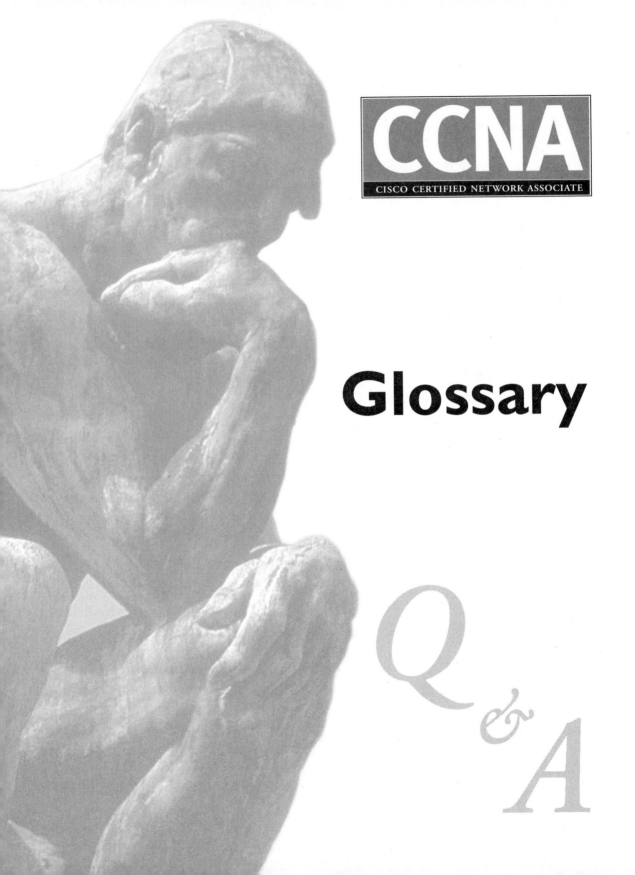

CCNA
CISCO CERTIFIED NETWORK ASSOCIATE

Glossary

Q & A

10BASE2   An Ethernet specification using 50-ohm thin coaxial cable and a signaling rate of 10 Mbps baseband.

10BASE5   An Ethernet specification using standard (thick) 50-ohm baseband coaxial cable and a signaling rate of 10 Mbps baseband.

10BASEFL   An Ethernet specification using fiber-optic cabling and a signaling rate of 10 Mbps baseband, and FOIRL.

10BASET   An Ethernet specification using two pairs of twisted-pair cabling (Category 3, 4, or 5): one pair for transmitting data and the other for receiving data, and a signaling rate of 10 Mbps baseband.

10BROAD36   An Ethernet specification using broadband coaxial cable and a signaling rate of 10 Mbps.

100BASEFX   A Fast Ethernet specification using two strands of multimode fiber-optic cable per link and a signaling rate of 100 Mbps baseband. A 100BaseFXlink cannot exceed 400 meters in length.

100BASET   A Fast Ethernet specification using UTP wiring and a signaling rate of 100 Mbps baseband. 100BaseT sends link pulses out on the wire when there is no data traffic present.

100BASET4   A Fast Ethernet specification using four pairs of Category 3, 4, or 5 UTP wiring and a signaling rate of 100 Mbps baseband. The maximum length of a 100BaseT4 segment is 100 meters.

100BASETX   A Fast Ethernet specification using two pairs of UTP or STP wiring and 100 Mbps baseband signaling. One pair of wires is used to receive data; the other is used to transmit. A 100BaseTX segment cannot exceed 100 meters in length.

100BASEX   A 100 Mbps baseband Fast Ethernet specification based on the IEEE 802.3 standard. 100BaseX refers to the 100BaseFX and 100BaseTX standards for Fast Ethernet over fiber-optic cabling.

AAL (ATM ADAPTATION LAYER)   A service-dependent sublayer of the data-link layer. The function of the AAL is to accept data from different applications and present it to the ATM layer in 48-byte ATM segments.

AARP (APPLETALK ADDRESS RESOLUTION PROTOCOL)
The protocol that maps a data-link address to an AppleTalk network address.

ABR (AREA BORDER ROUTER)   A router located on the border of an OSPF area, which connects that area to the backbone network. An ABR would be a member of both the OSPF backbone and the attached area. It maintains routing tables describing both the backbone topology and the topology of the other area.

ACCESS LIST   A sequential list of statements in a router configuration that identify network traffic for various purposes, including traffic and route filtering.

ACKNOWLEDGMENT   Notification sent from one network device to another to acknowledge that a message or group of messages has been received. Sometimes abbreviated ACK. Opposite of NAK.

ACTIVE HUB   A multiport device that repeats and amplifies LAN signals at the physical layer.

ACTIVE MONITOR   A network device on a Token Ring that is responsible for managing ring operations. The active monitor ensures that tokens are not lost, and that frames do not circulate indefinitely on the ring.

ADDRESS   A numbering convention used to identify a unique entity or location on a network.

ADDRESS MAPPING A technique that allows different protocols to operate together by associating addresses from one format with those of another.

ADDRESS MASK A string of bits, which, when combined with an address, describes which portion of an address refers to the network or subnet and which part refers to the host. *See also* subnet mask.

ADDRESS RESOLUTION A technique for resolving differences between computer addressing schemes. Address resolution most often specifies a method for mapping network-layer addresses to data-link layer addresses. *See also* address mapping.

ADDRESS RESOLUTION PROTOCOL *See* ARP.

ADMINISTRATIVE DISTANCE A rating of the preferability of a routing information source. Administrative distance is expressed as a value between 0 and 255. The higher the value, the lower the preference.

ADVERTISING A process in which a router sends routing or service updates at frequent intervals so that other routers on the network can maintain lists of usable routes or services.

ALGORITHM A specific process for arriving at a solution to a problem.

AMI (ALTERNATE MARK INVERSION) The line-code type that is used on T1 and E1 circuits. In this code, zeros are represented by 01 during each bit cell, and ones are represented by 11 or 00, alternately, during each bit cell.

ANSI (AMERICAN NATIONAL STANDARDS INSTITUTE) An organization of representatives of corporate, government, and other entities that coordinates standards-related activities, approves U.S. national standards, and develops positions for the United States in international standards organizations.

APPLETALK A suite of communications protocols developed by Apple Computer for allowing communication among their devices over a network.

APPLICATION LAYER   Layer 7 of the OSI reference model. This layer provides services to end-user application processes such as electronic mail, file transfer, and terminal emulation.

ARP (ADDRESS RESOLUTION PROTOCOL)   An Internet protocol used to map an IP address to a MAC address.

ASBR (AUTONOMOUS SYSTEM BOUNDARY ROUTER)   An ABR connecting an OSPF autonomous system to a non-OSPF network. ASBRs run two protocols: OSPF and another routing protocol. ASBRs must be located in a nonstub OSPF area.

ASYNCHRONOUS TRANSMISSION   A method of transmission in which digital signals are transmitted without precise clocking or synchronization.

ATM (ASYNCHRONOUS TRANSFER MODE)   An international standard for cell relay suitable for carrying multiple service types (such as voice, video, or data) in fixed-length (53-byte) cells. Fixed-length cells allow cell processing to occur in hardware, thereby reducing latency.

ATM ADAPTATION LAYER   *See* AAL.

ATM FORUM   An international organization founded in 1991 by Cisco Systems, NET/ADAPTIVE, Northern Telecom, and Sprint to develop and promote standards-based implementation agreements for ATM technology.

AUI (ATTACHMENT UNIT INTERFACE)   An interface between a MAU and a NIC (network interface card) described in the IEEE 802.3 specification. AUI often refers to the physical port to which an AUI cable attaches.

AUTONOMOUS SYSTEM   A group of networks under a common administration that share in a common routing strategy. Sometimes abbreviated AS.

B8ZS (BINARY 8-ZERO SUBSTITUTION) The line-code type used on T1 and E1 circuits. With B8ZS, a special code is substituted whenever eight consecutive zeros are sent over the link. This code is then interpreted at the remote end of the connection.

BACKOFF The retransmission delay used by contention-based MAC protocols such as Ethernet, after a network node determines that the physical medium is already in use.

BANDWIDTH The difference between the highest and lowest frequencies available for network signals. The term may also describe the throughput capacity of a network link or segment.

BASEBAND A network technology in which a single carrier frequency is used. Ethernet is a common example of a baseband network technology.

BAUD A unit of signaling speed equal to the number of separate signal elements transmitted in one second. Baud is synonymous with bits per second (bps), as long as each signal element represents exactly one bit.

B CHANNEL (BEARER CHANNEL) An ISDN term meaning a full-duplex, 64 Kbps channel used to send user data.

BEARER CHANNEL *See* B channel.

BECN Backward explicit congestion notification. A frame relay network facility that allows switches in the network to advise DTE devices of congestion. The BECN bit is set in frames traveling in the opposite direction of frames encountering a congested path.

BEST-EFFORT DELIVERY A network system that does not use a system of acknowledgment to guarantee reliable delivery of information.

BGP (BORDER GATEWAY PROTOCOL)   An interdomain path vector routing protocol. BGP exchanges reachability information with other BGP systems. It is defined in RFC 1163.

BINARY   A numbering system in which there are only two digits, ones and zeros.

BNC CONNECTOR   A standard connector used to connect coaxial cable to a MAU or line card.

BOOTP (BOOTSTRAP PROTOCOL)   Part of the TCP/IP suite of protocols, used by a network node to determine the IP address of its Ethernet interfaces in order to boot from a network server.

BPS   Bits per second.

BRI (BASIC RATE INTERFACE)   An ISDN interface consisting of two B channels and one D channel for circuit-switched communication. ISDN BRI can carry voice, video, and data.

BRIDGE   A device that connects and forwards packets between two network segments that use the same data-link communications protocol. Bridges operate at the data-link layer of the OSI reference model. A bridge will filter, forward, or flood an incoming frame based on the MAC address of the frame.

BROADBAND   A data transmission system that multiplexes multiple independent signals onto one cable. Also, in telecommunications, any channel with a bandwidth greater than 4 KHz. In LAN terminology, a coaxial cable using analog signaling.

BROADCAST   A data packet addressed to all nodes on a network. Broadcasts are identified by a broadcast address that matches all addresses on the network.

BROADCAST ADDRESS A special address reserved for sending a message to all stations. At the data-link layer, a broadcast address is a MAC destination address of all 1s.

BROADCAST DOMAIN The group of all devices that will receive the same broadcast frame originating from any device within the group. Because routers do not forward broadcast frames, broadcast domains are typically bounded by routers.

BUFFER A memory storage area used for handling data in transit. Buffers are used in internetworking to compensate for differences in processing speed between network devices or signaling rates of segments. Bursts of packets can be stored in buffers until they can be handled by slower devices.

BUS A common physical path composed of wires or other media, across which signals are sent from one part of a computer to another.

BUS TOPOLOGY A topology used in LANs. Transmissions from network stations propagate the length of the medium and are then received by all other stations.

BYTE A series of consecutive binary digits that are operated on as a unit, usually eight bits.

CABLE A transmission medium of copper wire or optical fiber wrapped in a protective cover.

CABLE RANGE A range of network numbers on an extended AppleTalk network. The cable range value can be a single network number or a contiguous sequence of several network numbers. Nodes assign addresses within the cable range values provided.

CAM Content-addressable memory.

CARRIER An electromagnetic wave or alternating current of a single frequency, suitable for modulation by another, data-bearing signal.

CARRIER DETECT *See* CD.

CARRIER SENSE MULTIPLE ACCESS WITH COLLISION DETECTION *See* CSMA/CD.

CATEGORY 5 CABLING One of five grades of UTP cabling described in the EIA/TIA-586 standard. Category 5 cabling can transmit data at speeds up to 100 Mbps.

CCITT (CONSULTATIVE COMMITTEE FOR INTERNATIONAL TELEGRAPHY AND TELEPHONY) An international organization responsible for the development of communications standards. Now called the ITU-T. See ITU-T.

CD (CARRIER DETECT) A signal that indicates whether an interface is active.

CDDI (COPPER DISTRIBUTED DATA INTERFACE) The implementation of FDDI protocols over STP and UTP cabling. CDDI transmits over distances of approximately 100 meters, providing data rates of 100 Mbps. CDDI uses a dual-ring architecture to provide redundancy.

CELL The basic data unit for ATM switching and multiplexing. A cell consists of a 5-byte header and 48 bytes of payload. Cells contain fields in their headers that identify the data stream to which they belong.

CHAP (CHALLENGE HANDSHAKE AUTHENTICATION PROTOCOL) A security feature used with PPP encapsulation, which prevents unauthorized access by identifying the remote end. The router or access server determines whether that user is allowed access.

CHECKSUM A method for checking the integrity of transmitted data. A checksum is an integer value computed from a sequence of octets taken through a series of arithmetic operations. The value is recomputed at the receiving end and compared for verification.

CIDR (CLASSLESS INTERDOMAIN ROUTING)   A technique supported by BGP4 and based on route aggregation. CIDR allows routers to group routes together in order to cut down on the quantity of routing information carried by the core routers. With CIDR, several IP networks appear to networks outside the group as a single, larger entity. With CIDR, IP addresses and their subnet masks are written as four octets, separated by periods, followed by a forward slash and a two-digit number that represents the subnet mask.

CIR (COMMITTED INFORMATION RATE)   The rate at which a frame relay network agrees to transfer information under normal conditions, averaged over a minimum increment of time. CIR, measured in bits per second, is one of the key negotiated tariff metrics.

CIRCUIT SWITCHING   A system in which a dedicated physical path must exist between sender and receiver for the entire duration of a call. Used heavily in telephone networks.

CLIENT   A node or software program, or front-end device, that requests services from a server.

CLNS (CONNECTIONLESS NETWORK SERVICE)   An OSI network layer service for which no circuit need be established before data can be transmitted. Routing of messages to their destinations is independent of other messages.

COLLISION   In Ethernet, the result of two nodes transmitting simultaneously. The frames from each device cause an increase in voltage when they meet on the physical media, and are damaged.

CONGESTION   Traffic in excess of network capacity.

CONNECTIONLESS   A term used to describe data transfer without the prior existence of a circuit.

CONSOLE   A DTE device, usually consisting of a keyboard and display unit, through which users interact with a host.

CONTENTION   An access method in which network devices compete for permission to access the physical medium. Compare with circuit switching and token passing.

COST   A value, typically based on media bandwidth or other measures, that is assigned by a network administrator and used by routing protocols to compare various paths through an internetwork environment. Cost values are used to determine the most favorable path to a particular destination—the lower the cost, the better the path.

COUNT TO INFINITY   A condition in which routers continuously increment the hop count to particular networks. Often occurs in routing algorithms that are slow to converge. Usually, an arbitrary hop count ceiling is imposed to limit the extent of this problem.

CPE (CUSTOMER PREMISES EQUIPMENT)   Terminating equipment, such as terminals, telephones, and modems, installed at customer sites and connected to the telephone company network.

CRC (CYCLIC REDUNDANCY CHECK)   An error-checking technique in which the receiving device performs a calculation on the frame contents and compares the calculated number to a value stored in the frame by the sending node.

CSMA/CD (CARRIER SENSE MULTIPLE ACCESS/COLLISION DETECTION)   A media-access mechanism used by Ethernet and IEEE 802.3. Devices use CSMA/CD to check the channel for a carrier before transmitting data. If no carrier is sensed, the device transmits. If two devices transmit at the same time, the collision is detected by all colliding devices. Collisions delay retransmissions from those devices for a randomly chosen length of time.

CSU (CHANNEL SERVICE UNIT)   A digital interface device that connects end-user equipment to the local digital telephone loop. Often referred to together with DSU, as CSU/DSU.

DATAGRAM   A logical unit of information sent as a network layer unit over a transmission medium without prior establishment of a circuit.

DATA-LINK LAYER   Layer 2 of the OSI reference model. This layer provides reliable transit of data across a physical link. The data-link layer is concerned with physical addressing, network topology, access to the network medium, error detection, sequential delivery of frames, and flow control. The data-link layer is divided into two sublayers: the MAC sublayer and the LLC sublayer.

DCE (DATA CIRCUIT-TERMINATING EQUIPMENT)   The devices and connections of a communications network that represent the network end of the user-to-network interface. The DCE provides a physical connection to the network and provides a clocking signal used to synchronize transmission between DCE and DTE devices. Modems and interface cards are examples of DCE devices.

D CHANNEL   A data channel. Full-duplex, 16 Kbps (BRI) or 64 Kbps (PRI) ISDN channel.

DDR (DIAL-ON-DEMAND ROUTING)   A technique whereby a router can automatically initiate and close a circuit-switched session as transmitting stations demand. The router spoofs keepalives so that end stations treat the session as active. DDR permits routing over ISDN and telephone lines using an external ISDN terminal adapter or modem.

DECNET   A group of communications products (including a protocol suite) developed and supported by Digital Equipment Corporation. DECnet/OSI (also called DECnet Phase V) is the most recent iteration and supports both OSI protocols and proprietary Digital protocols. Phase IV Prime supports inherent MAC addresses that allow DECnet nodes to coexist with systems running other protocols that have MAC address restrictions. *See also* DNA.

DEDICATED LINE   A communications line that is indefinitely reserved for transmissions, rather than switched as transmission is required. *See also* leased line.

DE FACTO STANDARD   A standard that exists because of its widespread use.

DEFAULT ROUTE   A routing table entry that is used to direct packets when there is no explicit route present in the routing table.

DE JURE STANDARD   A standard that exists because of its development or approval by an official standards body.

DELAY   The time between the initiation of a transaction by a sender and the first response received by the sender. Also, the time required to move a packet from source to destination over a network path.

DEMARC   The demarcation point between telephone carrier equipment and CPE.

DEMULTIPLEXING   The separating of multiple streams of data that have been multiplexed into a common physical signal for transmission, back into multiple output streams. The opposite of multiplexing.

DESTINATION ADDRESS   The address of a network device to receive data.

DHCP (DYNAMIC HOST CONFIGURATION PROTOCOL)   A protocol that provides a mechanism for allocating IP addresses dynamically so that addresses can be reassigned instead of belonging to only one host.

DISCOVERY MODE   A method by which an AppleTalk router acquires information about an attached network from an operational router and then uses the information to configure its own addressing information.

DISTANCE VECTOR ROUTING ALGORITHM   A class of routing algorithms that use the number of hops in a route to find a shortest path to a destination network. Distance vector routing algorithms call for each router to send its entire routing table in each update to each of its neighbors. Also called a Bellman-Ford routing algorithm.

DLCI (DATA-LINK CONNECTION IDENTIFIER)   A value that specifies a virtual circuit in a frame relay network.

DNA (DIGITAL NETWORK ARCHITECTURE)   A network architecture that was developed by Digital Equipment Corporation. DECnet is the collective term for the products that comprise DNA (including communications protocols).

DNIC (DATA NETWORK IDENTIFICATION CODE)   Part of an X.121 address. DNICs are divided into two parts: the first specifying the country in which the addressed PSN is located and the second specifying the PSN itself. *See also* X.121.

DNS (DOMAIN NAME SYSTEM)   A system used on the Internet for translating names of network nodes into addresses.

DSP (DOMAIN SPECIFIC PART)   Part of an ATM address. A DSP is comprised of an area identifier, a station identifier, and a selector byte.

DTE (DATA TERMINAL EQUIPMENT)   A device at the user end of a user-network interface that serves as a data source, destination, or both. DTE connects to a data network through a DCE device (for example, a modem) and typically uses clocking signals generated by the DCE. DTE includes such devices as computers, routers, and multiplexers.

DUAL (DIFFUSING UPDATE ALGORITHM)   A convergence algorithm used in EIGRP. DUAL provides constant loop-free operation throughout a route computation by allowing routers involved in a topology change to synchronize at the same time, without involving routers that are unaffected by the change.

DVMRP (DISTANCE VECTOR MULTICAST ROUTING PROTOCOL)   An internetwork gateway protocol that implements a typical dense mode IP multicast scheme. Using IGMP, DVMRP exchanges routing datagrams with its neighbors.

DYNAMIC ROUTING   Routing that adjusts automatically to changes in network topology or traffic patterns.

E1   A wide area digital transmission scheme used in Europe that carries data at a rate of 2.048 Mbps.

EIA/TIA-232   A common physical-layer interface standard, developed by EIA and TIA, that supports unbalanced circuits at signal speeds of up to 64 Kbps. Formerly known as RS-232.

ENCAPSULATION   The process of attaching a particular protocol header to a unit of data prior to transmission on the network. For example, a frame of Ethernet data is given a specific Ethernet header before network transit.

END POINT   A device at which a virtual circuit or virtual path begins or ends.

ENTERPRISE NETWORK   A privately maintained network connecting most major points in a company or other organization. Usually spans a large geographic area and supports multiple protocols and services.

ENTITY   Generally, an individual, manageable network device. Sometimes called an alias.

ERROR CONTROL   A technique for detecting and correcting errors in data transmissions.

ETHERNET   A baseband LAN specification invented by Xerox Corporation and developed jointly by Xerox, Intel, and Digital Equipment Corporation. Ethernet networks use the CSMA/CD method of media access control and run over a variety of cable types at 10 Mbps. Ethernet is similar to the IEEE 802.3 series of standards.

ETHERTALK   Apple Computer's data-link product that allows an AppleTalk network to be connected by Ethernet cable.

EXPLORER PACKET   A packet generated by an end station trying to find its way through a SRB network. It gathers a hop-by-hop description of a path through the network by being marked (updated) by each bridge that it traverses, thereby creating a complete topological map.

FAST ETHERNET   Any of a number of 100 Mbps Ethernet specifications. Fast Ethernet offers a speed increase ten times that of the 10BaseT Ethernet specification, while preserving such qualities as frame format, MAC mechanisms, and MTU. Such similarities allow the use of existing 10BaseT applications and network management tools on Fast Ethernet networks. Based on an extension to the IEEE 802.3 specification. Compare with Ethernet. *See also* 100BaseFX; 100BaseT; 100BaseT4; 100BaseTX; 100BaseX; IEEE 802.3.

FDDI (FIBER DISTRIBUTED DATA INTERFACE)   A LAN standard, defined by ANSI X3T9.5, specifying a 100 Mbps token-passing network using fiber-optic cable, with transmission distances of up to 2 km. FDDI uses a dual-ring architecture to provide redundancy. Compare with CDDI.

FECN (FORWARD EXPLICIT CONGESTION NOTIFICATION)
A facility in a frame relay network to inform DTE receiving the frame that congestion was experienced in the path from source to destination. DTE receiving frames with the FECN bit set can request that higher-level protocols take flow-control action as appropriate.

FILE TRANSFER   A category of popular network applications that features movement of files from one network device to another.

FILTER   Generally, a process or device that screens network traffic for certain characteristics, such as source address, destination address, or protocol, and determines whether to forward or discard that traffic or routes based on the established criteria.

FIREWALL   A router or other computer designated as a buffer between public networks and a private network. A firewall router uses access lists and other methods to ensure the security of the private network.

FLASH MEMORY   Nonvolatile storage that can be electrically erased and reprogrammed as necessary.

FLASH UPDATE   A routing update sent asynchronously when a change in the network topology occurs.

FLAT ADDRESSING   A system of addressing that does not incorporate a hierarchy to determine location.

FLOODING   A traffic-passing technique used by switches and bridges in which traffic received on an interface is sent out all of the interfaces of that device except the interface on which the information was originally received.

FLOW CONTROL   A technique for ensuring that a transmitting device, such as a modem, does not overwhelm a receiving device with data. When the buffers on the receiving device are full, a message is sent to the sending device to suspend transmission until it has processed the data in the buffers.

FORWARDING   The process of sending a frame or packet toward its destination.

FRAGMENT   A piece of a larger packet that has been broken down to smaller units.

FRAGMENTATION   The process of breaking a packet into smaller units when transmitting over a network medium that is unable to support a transmission unit the original size of the packet.

FRAME   The logical grouping of information sent as a data-link layer unit over a transmission medium. Sometimes refers to the header and trailer, used for synchronization and error control, which surround the user data contained in the unit. The terms cell, datagram, message, packet, and segment are also used to describe logical information groupings at various layers of the OSI reference model and in various technology circles.

FRAME RELAY   An industry-standard, switched data-link layer protocol that handles multiple virtual circuits over a single physical interface. Frame relay is more efficient than X.25, for which it is generally considered a replacement.

FREQUENCY   The number of cycles, measured in hertz, of an alternating current signal per unit of time.

FTP (FILE TRANSFER PROTOCOL)   An application protocol, part of the TCP/IP protocol stack, used for transferring files between hosts on a network.

FULL DUPLEX   The capability for simultaneous data transmission and receipt of data between two devices.

FULL MESH   A network topology in which each network node has either a physical circuit or a virtual circuit connecting it to every other network node.

GATEWAY   In the IP community, an older term referring to a routing device. Today, the term router is used to describe devices that perform this function, and gateway refers to a special-purpose device that performs an application-layer conversion of information from one protocol stack to another.

GB   A gigabyte. Approximately 1,000,000,000 bytes.

GBps   Gigabytes per second.

Gb   A gigabit. Approximately 1,000,000,000 bits.

Gbps   Gigabits per second.

GNS (GET NEAREST SERVER)   A request packet sent by a client on an IPX network to locate the nearest active server of a particular type. An IPX network client issues a GNS request to solicit either a direct response from a connected server or a response from a router that tells it where on the internetwork the service can be located. GNS is part of the IPX SAP.

HALF DUPLEX   The capability for data transmission in only one direction at a time between a sending station and a receiving station.

HANDSHAKE   A sequence of messages exchanged between two or more network devices to ensure transmission synchronization.

HARDWARE ADDRESS   *See* MAC address.

HDLC (HIGH-LEVEL DATA LINK CONTROL)   A bit-oriented synchronous data-link layer protocol developed by ISO and derived from SDLC. HDLC specifies a data encapsulation method for synchronous serial links and includes frame characters and checksums in its headers.

HEADER   Control information placed before data when encapsulating that data for network transmission.

HELLO PACKET   A multicast packet that is used by routers for neighbor discovery and recovery. Hello packets also indicate that a client is still operating on the network.

HELLO PROTOCOL   A protocol used by OSPF and other routing protocols for establishing and maintaining neighbor relationships.

HIERARCHICAL ADDRESSING   A scheme of addressing that uses a logical hierarchy to determine location. For example, IP addresses consist of network numbers, subnet numbers, and host numbers, which IP routing algorithms use to route the packet to the appropriate location.

HOLDDOWN   The state of a routing table entry in which routers will neither advertise the route nor accept advertisements about the route for a specific length of time (known as the holddown period).

HOP   A term describing the passage of a data packet between two network nodes (for example, between two routers). *See also* hop count.

HOP COUNT   A routing metric used to measure the distance between a source and a destination. RIP uses hop count as its metric.

HOST   A computer system on a network. Similar to the term *node* except that *host* usually implies a computer system, whereas *node* can refer to any networked system, including routers.

HOST NUMBER   Part of an IP address that designates which node is being addressed. Also called a host address.

HUB   A term used to describe a device that serves as the center of a star topology network; or, an Ethernet multiport repeater, sometimes referred to as a concentrator.

ICMP (INTERNET CONTROL MESSAGE PROTOCOL)   A network-layer Internet protocol that provides reports of errors and other information about IP packet processing. ICMP is documented in RFC 792.

IEEE (INSTITUTE OF ELECTRICAL AND ELECTRONICS ENGINEERS)　A professional organization among whose activities are the development of communications and networking standards. IEEE LAN standards are the most common LAN standards today.

IEEE 802.3　An IEEE LAN protocol for the implementation of the physical layer and the MAC sublayer of the data-link layer. IEEE 802.3 uses CSMA/CD access at various speeds over various physical media.

IEEE 802.5　An IEEE LAN protocol for the implementation of the physical layer and MAC sublayer of the data-link layer. Similar to Token Ring, IEEE 802.5 uses token passing access over STP cabling.

IGP (INTERIOR GATEWAY PROTOCOL)　A generic term for an Internet routing protocol used to exchange routing information within an autonomous system. Examples of common Internet IGPs include IGRP, OSPF, and RIP.

INTERFACE　A connection between two systems or devices; or in routing terminology, a network connection.

INTERNET　A term used to refer to the global internetwork that evolved from the ARPANET, that now connects tens of thousands of networks worldwide.

INTERNET PROTOCOL　Any protocol that is part of the TCP/IP protocol stack. *See* TCP/IP.

INTERNETWORK　A collection of networks interconnected by routers and other devices that functions (generally) as a single network.

INTERNETWORKING　A general term used to refer to the industry that has arisen for the purpose of connecting networks together. The term may be used to refer to products, procedures, and technologies.

INVERSE ARP (INVERSE ADDRESS RESOLUTION PROTOCOL) A method of building dynamic address mappings in a frame relay network. Allows a device to discover the network address of a device associated with a virtual circuit.

IP (INTERNET PROTOCOL)   A network-layer protocol in the TCP/IP stack offering a connectionless datagram service. IP provides features for addressing, type-of-service specification, fragmentation and reassembly, and security. Documented in RFC 791.

IP ADDRESS   A 32-bit address assigned to hosts using the TCP/IP suite of protocols. An IP address is written as four octets separated by dots (dotted decimal format). Each address consists of a network number, an optional subnetwork number, and a host number. The network and subnetwork numbers together are used for routing, while the host number is used to address an individual host within the network or subnetwork. A subnet mask is often used with the address to extract network and subnetwork information from the IP address.

IPX (INTERNETWORK PACKET EXCHANGE)   A NetWare network layer (Layer 3) protocol used for transferring data from servers to workstations. IPX is similar to IP in that it is a connectionless datagram service.

IPXCP (IPX CONTROL PROTOCOL)   The protocol that establishes and configures IPX over PPP.

IPXWAN   A protocol that negotiates end-to-end options for new links on startup. When a link comes up, the first IPX packets sent across are IPXWAN packets negotiating the options for the link. When the IPXWAN options have been successfully determined, normal IPX transmission begins, and no more IPXWAN packets are sent. Defined in RFC 1362.

ISDN (INTEGRATED SERVICES DIGITAL NETWORK)   A communication protocol, offered by telephone companies, that permits telephone networks to carry data, voice, and other source traffic.

ITU-T (INTERNATIONAL TELECOMMUNICATION UNION TELECOMMUNICATION STANDARDIZATION SECTOR)   An international body dedicated to the development of worldwide standards for telecommunications technologies. ITU-T is the successor to CCITT.

KB   A kilobyte. Approximately 1,000 bytes.

Kb A kilobit. Approximately 1,000 bits.

KBps Kilobytes per second.

Kbps Kilobits per second.

KEEPALIVE INTERVAL A period of time between keepalive messages sent by a network device.

KEEPALIVE MESSAGE A message sent by one network device to inform another network device that it is still active.

LAN (LOCAL AREA NETWORK) A high-speed, low-error data network covering a relatively small geographic area. LANs connect workstations, peripherals, terminals, and other devices in a single building or other geographically limited area. LAN standards specify cabling and signaling at the physical and data-link layers of the OSI model. Ethernet, FDDI, and Token Ring are the most widely used LAN technologies.

LANE (LAN EMULATION) A technology that allows an ATM network to function as a LAN backbone. In this situation LANE provides multicast and broadcast support, address mapping (MAC-to-ATM), and virtual circuit management.

LAPB (LINK ACCESS PROCEDURE, BALANCED) The data-link layer protocol in the X.25 protocol stack. LAPB is a bit-oriented protocol derived from HDLC.

LAPD (LINK ACCESS PROCEDURE ON THE D CHANNEL) An ISDN data-link-layer protocol for the D channel. LAPD was derived from the LAPB protocol and is designed to satisfy the signaling requirements of basic ISDN access. Defined by ITU-T recommendations Q.920 and Q.921.

LATENCY The amount of time elapsed between the time a device requests access to a network and the time it is allowed to transmit; or, the amount of time between the point at which a device receives a frame and the time that frame is forwarded out the destination port.

LCP (LINK CONTROL PROTOCOL)   A protocol used with PPP that establishes, configures, and tests data-link connections.

LEASED LINE   A transmission line reserved by a communications carrier for the private use of a customer. A leased line is a type of dedicated line.

LINK   A network communications channel consisting of a circuit or transmission path and all related equipment between a sender and a receiver. Most often used to refer to a WAN connection. Sometimes called a line or a transmission link.

LINK-STATE ROUTING ALGORITHM   A routing algorithm in which each router broadcasts or multicasts information regarding the cost of reaching each of its neighbors to all nodes in the internetwork. Link-state algorithms require that routers maintain a consistent view of the network and are therefore not prone to routing loops.

LLC (LOGICAL LINK CONTROL)   The higher of two data-link layer sublayers defined by the IEEE. The LLC sublayer handles error control, flow control, framing, and MAC-sublayer addressing. The most common LLC protocol is IEEE 802.2, which includes both connectionless and connection-oriented types.

LMI (LOCAL MANAGEMENT INTERFACE)   A set of enhancements to the basic frame relay specification. LMI includes support for keepalives, a multicast mechanism, global addressing, and a status mechanism.

LOAD BALANCING   In routing, the ability of a router to distribute traffic over all its network ports that are the same distance from the destination address. Load balancing increases the utilization of network segments, thus increasing total effective network bandwidth.

LOCAL LOOP   A line from the premises of a telephone subscriber to the telephone company central office.

LOCALTALK   Apple Computer's proprietary baseband protocol that operates at the data-link and physical layers of the OSI reference model. LocalTalk uses CSMA/CA and supports transmissions at speeds of 230.4 Kbps.

LOOP   A situation in which packets never reach their destination, but are forwarded in a cycle repeatedly through a group of network nodes.

MAC (MEDIA ACCESS CONTROL)   The lower of the two sublayers of the data-link layer defined by the IEEE. The MAC sublayer handles access to shared media.

MAC ADDRESS   A standardized data-link layer address that is required for every port or device that connects to a LAN. Other devices in the network use these addresses to locate specific ports in the network and to create and update routing tables and data structures. MAC addresses are 48 bits long and are controlled by the IEEE. Also known as a hardware address, a MAC-layer address, or a physical address.

MAN (METROPOLITAN AREA NETWORK)   A network that spans a metropolitan area. Generally, a MAN spans a larger geographic area than a LAN, but a smaller geographic area than a WAN.

MAU   See MSAU.

Mb   A megabit. Approximately 1,000,000 bits.

Mbps   Megabits per second.

MEDIA   The various physical environments through which transmission signals pass. Common network media include cable (twisted-pair, coaxial, and fiber optic) and the atmosphere through which microwave, laser, and infrared transmission occur. Sometimes referred to as physical media.

MEDIA ACCESS CONTROL   *See* MAC.

MESH   A network topology in which devices are organized in a segmented manner with redundant interconnections strategically placed between network nodes.

MESSAGE   An application-layer logical grouping of information, often composed of a number of lower-layer logical groupings such as packets.

MSAU (MULTISTATION ACCESS UNIT) A wiring concentrator to which all end stations in a Token Ring network connect. Sometimes abbreviated MAU.

MULTIACCESS NETWORK A network that allows multiple devices to connect and communicate by sharing the same medium, such as a LAN.

MULTICAST A single packet copied by the network and sent to a specific subset of network addresses. These addresses are specified in the Destination Address field.

MULTICAST ADDRESS A single address that refers to multiple network devices. Sometimes called a group address.

MULTIPLEXING A technique that allows multiple logical signals to be transmitted simultaneously across a single physical channel.

MUX A multiplexing device. A mux combines multiple input signals for transmission over a single line. The signals are demultiplexed, or separated, before they are used at the receiving end.

NAK (NEGATIVE ACKNOWLEDGMENT) A response sent from a receiving device to a sending device indicating that the information received contained errors.

NAME RESOLUTION The process of associating a symbolic name with a network location or address.

NAT (NETWORK ADDRESS TRANSLATION) A technique for reducing the need for globally unique IP addresses. NAT allows an organization with addresses that may conflict with others in the IP address space to connect to the Internet by translating those addresses into unique ones within the globally routable address space.

NBMA (NONBROADCAST MULTIACCESS) A term describing a multiaccess network that either does not support broadcasting (such as X.25) or one in which broadcasting is not feasible.

NBP (NAME BINDING PROTOCOL)   An AppleTalk transport-level protocol that translates a character string name into the DDP address of the corresponding socket client.

NCP (NETWORK CONTROL PROTOCOL)   A protocol that establishes and configures various network-layer protocols. Used for AppleTalk over PPP.

NETBIOS (NETWORK BASIC INPUT/OUTPUT SYSTEM)   An application programming interface used by applications on an IBM LAN to request services from lower-level network processes such as session establishment and termination, and information transfer.

NETWARE   A network operating system developed by Novell that provides remote file access, print services, and numerous other distributed network services.

NETWORK   A collection of computers, printers, routers, switches, and other devices that are able to communicate with each other over some transmission medium.

NETWORK INTERFACE   A border between a carrier network and a privately owned installation.

NETWORK LAYER   Layer 3 of the OSI reference model. This layer provides connectivity and path selection between two end systems. The network layer is the layer at which routing takes place.

NLSP (NETWARE LINK SERVICES PROTOCOL)   A link-state routing protocol for IPX based on IS-IS.

NODE   The endpoint of a network connection or a junction common to two or more lines in a network. Nodes can be processors, controllers, or workstations. Nodes, which vary in their functional capabilities, can be interconnected by links and serve as control points in the network.

NVRAM (NONVOLATILE RAM)   RAM that retains its contents when a device is powered off.

OSI REFERENCE MODEL (OPEN SYSTEMS INTERCONNECTION REFERENCE MODEL)   A network architectural framework developed by the International Organization for Standardization (ISO) and ITU-T. The model describes seven layers, each of which specifies a particular network. The lowest layer, called the physical layer, is closest to the media technology. The highest layer, the application layer, is closest to the user. The OSI reference model is widely used as a way of understanding network functionality.

OSPF (OPEN SHORTEST PATH FIRST)   A link-state, hierarchical IGP routing algorithm that includes features such as least-cost routing, multipath routing, and load balancing. OSPF is based on an early version of the IS-IS protocol.

OUT-OF-BAND SIGNALING   Transmission using frequencies or channels outside the frequencies or channels used for transfer of normal data. Out-of-band signaling is often used for error reporting when normal channels are unusable for communicating with network devices.

PACKET   A logical grouping of information that includes a header containing control information and (usually) user data. Packets are most often used to refer to network-layer units of data. The terms datagram, frame, message, and segment are also used to describe logical information groupings at various layers of the OSI reference model and in various technology circles. *See also* PDU.

PAP   The Password Authentication Protocol. An authentication protocol that allows PPP peers to authenticate one another. The remote router attempting to connect to the local router is required to send an authentication request. Unlike CHAP, PAP passes the password and host name or username in the clear (unencrypted). PAP does not itself prevent unauthorized access, but merely identifies the remote end. The router or access server then determines if that user is allowed access. PAP is supported only on PPP lines.

PARTIAL MESH   A term describing a network in which devices are organized in a mesh topology, with some network nodes organized in a full mesh, but with others that are only connected to one or two other nodes in the network. A partial mesh does not provide the level of redundancy of a full mesh topology, but is less expensive to implement. Partial mesh topologies are generally used in the peripheral networks that connect to a fully meshed backbone. *See also* full mesh; mesh.

PDU (PROTOCOL DATA UNIT)   The OSI term for a packet.

PHYSICAL LAYER   Layer 1 of the OSI reference model; it corresponds with the physical control layer in the SNA model. The physical layer defines the specifications for activating, maintaining, and deactivating the physical link between end systems.

PING (PACKET INTERNET GROPER)   An ICMP echo message and its reply. Often used in IP networks to test the reachability of a network device.

POISON REVERSE UPDATES   Routing updates that explicitly indicate that a network or subnet is unreachable, rather than implying that a network is unreachable by not including it in updates. Poison reverse updates are sent to defeat large routing loops.

PORT   1. An interface on an internetworking device (such as a router). 2. In IP terminology, an upper-layer process that receives information from lower layers. Ports are numbered, and each numbered port is associated with a specific process. For example, SMTP is associated with port 25. A port number is also known as a well-known address. 3. To rewrite software or microcode so that it will run on a different hardware platform or in a different software environment than that for which it was originally designed.

PPP (POINT-TO-POINT PROTOCOL)   A successor to SLIP that provides router-to-router and host-to-network connections over synchronous and asynchronous circuits. Whereas SLIP was designed to work with IP, PPP was designed to work with several network-layer protocols, such as IP, IPX, and ARA. PPP also has built-in security mechanisms, such as CHAP and PAP. PPP relies on two protocols: LCP and NCP. *See also* CHAP; LCP; NCP; PAP; SLIP.

PRESENTATION LAYER   Layer 6 of the OSI reference model. This layer ensures that information sent by the application layer of one system will be readable by the application layer of another. The presentation layer is also concerned with the data structures used by programs and therefore negotiates data transfer syntax for the application layer.

PRI (PRIMARY RATE INTERFACE)   An ISDN interface to primary rate access. Primary rate access consists of a single 64 Kbps D channel plus 23 (T1) or 30 (E1) B channels for voice or data. Compare with BRI.

PROTOCOL   A formal description of a set of rules and conventions that govern how devices on a network exchange information.

PROTOCOL STACK   A set of related communications protocols that operate together and, as a group, address communication at some or all of the seven layers of the OSI reference model. Not every protocol stack covers each layer of the model, and often a single protocol in the stack will address a number of layers at once. TCP/IP is a typical protocol stack.

PROXY ARP (PROXY ADDRESS RESOLUTION PROTOCOL)   A variation of the ARP protocol in which an intermediate device (for example, a router) sends an ARP response on behalf of an end node to the requesting host. Proxy ARP can lessen bandwidth use on slow-speed WAN links. *See also* ARP.

PVC (PERMANENT VIRTUAL CIRCUIT)   Permanently established virtual circuits save bandwidth in situations where certain virtual circuits must exist all the time, such as during circuit establishment and tear down.

QUERY   A message used to inquire about the value of some variable or set of variables.

QUEUE   A backlog of packets stored in buffers and waiting to be forwarded over a router interface.

RAM   Random-access memory. Volatile memory that can be read and written by a computer.

REASSEMBLY   The putting back together of an IP datagram at the destination after it has been fragmented either at the source or at an intermediate node. *See also* fragmentation.

RELOAD   The event of a Cisco router rebooting, or the command that causes the router to reboot.

RFC (REQUEST FOR COMMENTS)   A document series used as the primary means for communicating information about the Internet. Some RFCs are designated by the IAB as Internet standards.

RING   The connection of two or more stations in a logically circular topology. Information is passed sequentially between active stations. Token Ring, FDDI, and CDDI are based on this topology.

RING TOPOLOGY   A network topology that consists of a series of repeaters connected to one another by unidirectional transmission links to form a single closed loop. Each station on the network connects to the network at a repeater.

RIP (ROUTING INFORMATION PROTOCOL)   A routing protocol for TCP/IP networks. The most common routing protocol in the Internet. RIP uses hop count as a routing metric.

ROM (READ-ONLY MEMORY)   Nonvolatile memory that can be read, but not written, by the computer.

ROUTED PROTOCOL   A protocol that carries user data so it can be routed by a router. A router must be able to interpret the logical internetwork as specified by that routed protocol. Examples of routed protocols include AppleTalk, DECnet, and IP.

ROUTER   A network-layer device that uses one or more metrics to determine the optimal path along which network traffic should be forwarded. Routers forward packets from one network to another based on network-layer information.

ROUTING   A process of finding a path to a destination host.

ROUTING METRIC   A method by which a routing algorithm determines preferability of one route over another. This information is stored in routing tables.

Metrics include bandwidth, communication cost, delay, hop count, load, MTU, path cost, and reliability. Sometimes referred to simply as a metric.

ROUTING PROTOCOL   A protocol that accomplishes routing through the implementation of a specific routing algorithm. Examples of routing protocols include IGRP, OSPF, and RIP.

ROUTING TABLE   A table stored in a router or some other internetworking device that keeps track of routes to particular network destinations and, in some cases, metrics associated with those routes.

ROUTING UPDATE   A message sent from a router to indicate network reachability and associated cost information. Routing updates are typically sent at regular intervals and after a change in network topology. Compare with flash update.

RSRB (REMOTE SOURCE-ROUTE BRIDGING)   Equivalent to an SRB over WAN links.

SAP (SERVICE ACCESS POINT)   1. A field defined by the IEEE 802.2 specification that is part of an address specification. Thus, the destination plus the DSAP define the recipient of a packet. The same applies to the SSAP. 2. The Service Advertising Protocol, an IPX protocol that provides a means of informing network routers and servers of the location of available network resources and services.

SEGMENT   1. A section of a network that is bounded by bridges, routers, or switches. 2. In a LAN using a bus topology, a continuous electrical circuit that is often connected to other such segments with repeaters. 3. A term used in the TCP specification to describe a single transport-layer unit of information.

SERIAL TRANSMISSION   A method of data transmission in which the bits of a data character are transmitted sequentially over a single channel.

SESSION   1. A related set of communications transactions between two or more network devices. 2. In SNA, a logical connection that enables two NAUs to communicate.

SESSION LAYER   Layer 5 of the OSI reference model. This layer establishes, manages, and terminates sessions between applications and manages data exchange between presentation-layer entities. Corresponds to the data flow control layer of the SNA model. *See also* application layer; data-link layer; network layer; physical layer; presentation layer; transport layer.

SLIDING WINDOW FLOW CONTROL   A method of flow control in which a receiver gives a transmitter permission to transmit data until a window is full. When the window is full, the transmitter must stop transmitting until the receiver acknowledges some of the data or advertises a larger window. TCP, other transport protocols, and several data-link layer protocols use this method of flow control.

SLIP (SERIAL LINE INTERNET PROTOCOL)   A protocol that uses a variation of TCP/IP to make point-to-point serial connections. Succeeded by PPP.

SNAP (SUBNETWORK ACCESS PROTOCOL)   An Internet protocol that operates between a network entity in the subnetwork and a network entity in the end system. SNAP specifies a standard method of encapsulating IP datagrams and ARP messages on IEEE networks.

SNMP (SIMPLE NETWORK MANAGEMENT PROTOCOL)   A network management protocol used almost exclusively in TCP/IP networks. SNMP provides a means to monitor and control network devices, and to manage configurations, statistics collection, performance, and security.

SOCKET   A software structure operating as a communications end point within a network device.

SONET (SYNCHRONOUS OPTICAL NETWORK)   A high-speed synchronous network specification developed by Bellcore and designed to run on optical fiber.

SOURCE ADDRESS   An address of a network device that is sending data.

SPANNING TREE   A loop-free subset of a network topology. *See also* Spanning-Tree Protocol.

SPANNING-TREE PROTOCOL   A protocol developed to eliminate loops in the network. The Spanning-Tree Protocol ensures a loop-free path by placing one of the bridge ports in "blocking mode," preventing the forwarding of packets.

SPF (SHORTEST PATH FIRST ALGORITHM)   A routing algorithm that sorts routes by length of path to determine a shortest-path spanning tree. Commonly used in link-state routing algorithms. Sometimes called Dijkstra's algorithm.

SPLIT-HORIZON UPDATES   A routing technique in which information about routes is prevented from being advertised out the router interface through which that information was received. Split-horizon updates are used to prevent routing loops.

SPX (SEQUENCED PACKET EXCHANGE)   A reliable, connection-oriented protocol at the transport layer that supplements the datagram service provided by IPX.

SRB (SOURCE-ROUTE BRIDGING)   A method of bridging in Token Ring networks. In an SRB network, before data is sent to a destination, the entire route to that destination is predetermined in real time.

SRT (SOURCE-ROUTE TRANSPARENT BRIDGING)   IBM's merging of SRB and transparent bridging into one bridging scheme that requires no translation between bridging protocols.

SR/TLB (SOURCE-ROUTE TRANSLATIONAL BRIDGING)   A method of bridging that allows source-route stations to communicate with transparent bridge stations using an intermediate bridge that translates between the two bridge protocols.

STANDARD   A set of rules or procedures that are either widely used or officially specified.

STAR TOPOLOGY   A LAN topology in which end points on a network are connected to a common central switch by point-to-point links. A ring topology that is organized as a star implements a unidirectional closed-loop star, instead of point-to-point links. Compare with bus topology, ring topology, and tree topology.

STATIC ROUTE   A route that is explicitly configured and entered into the routing table. Static routes take precedence over routes chosen by dynamic routing protocols.

SUBINTERFACE   A virtual interface defined as a logical subdivision of a physical interface.

SUBNET ADDRESS   A portion of an IP address that is specified as the subnetwork by the subnet mask. *See also* IP address; subnet mask; subnetwork.

SUBNET MASK   A 32-bit address mask used in IP to indicate the bits of an IP address that are being used for the subnet address. Sometimes referred to simply as a mask. *See also* address mask; IP address.

SUBNETWORK   1. In IP networks, a network sharing a particular subnet address. 2. Networks arbitrarily segmented by a network administrator in order to provide a multilevel, hierarchical routing structure while shielding the subnetwork from the addressing complexity of attached networks. Sometimes called a subnet.

SVC (SWITCHED VIRTUAL CIRCUIT)   A virtual circuit that can be established dynamically on demand and that is torn down after a transmission is complete. SVCs are used when data transmission is sporadic.

SWITCH   1. A network device that filters, forwards, and floods frames based on the destination address of each frame. The switch operates at the data-link layer of the OSI model. 2. A general term applied to an electronic or mechanical device that allows a connection to be established as necessary and terminated when there is no longer a session to support.

T1   A digital WAN carrier facility. T1 transmits DS-1-formatted data at 1.544 Mbps through the telephone-switching network, using AMI or B8ZS coding. Compare with E1. *See also* AMI; B8ZS.

TCP (TRANSMISSION CONTROL PROTOCOL)   A connection-oriented transport-layer protocol that provides reliable full-duplex data transmission. TCP is part of the TCP/IP protocol stack.

TCP/IP (TRANSMISSION CONTROL PROTOCOL/INTERNET PROTOCOL)   The common name for the suite of protocols developed by the U.S. DoD in the 1970s to support the construction of worldwide internetworks. TCP and IP are the two best-known protocols in the suite.

THROUGHPUT   The rate of information arriving at, and possibly passing through, a particular point in a network system.

TIMEOUT   An event that occurs when one network device expects to hear from another network device within a specified period of time but does not. A timeout usually results in a retransmission of information or the termination of the session between the two devices.

TOKEN   A frame that contains only control information. Possession of the token allows a network device to transmit data onto the network. *See also* token passing.

TOKEN PASSING   A method by which network devices access the physical medium based on possession of a small frame called a token. Compare this method to circuit switching and contention.

TOKEN RING   A token-passing LAN developed and supported by IBM. Token Ring runs at 4 or 16 Mbps over a ring topology. Similar to IEEE 802.5. *See also* IEEE 802.5; ring topology; token passing.

TOKENTALK   Apple Computer's data-link product that allows an AppleTalk network to be connected by Token Ring cables.

TRANSPARENT BRIDGING A bridging scheme used in Ethernet and IEEE 802.3 networks that allow bridges to pass frames along one hop at a time, based on tables that associate end nodes with bridge ports. Bridges are transparent to network end nodes.

TRANSPORT LAYER Layer 4 of the OSI reference model. This layer is responsible for reliable network communication between end nodes. The transport layer provides mechanisms for the establishment, maintenance, and termination of virtual circuits, transport fault detection and recovery, and information flow control.

TREE TOPOLOGY A LAN topology that resembles a bus topology. Tree networks can contain branches with multiple nodes. In a tree topology, transmissions from a station propagate the length of the physical medium and are received by all other stations.

TWISTED-PAIR A relatively low-speed transmission medium consisting of two insulated wires arranged in a regular spiral pattern. The wires can be shielded or unshielded. Twisted-pair is common in telephony applications and is increasingly common in data networks.

UDP (USER DATAGRAM PROTOCOL) A connectionless transport-layer protocol in the TCP/IP protocol stack. UDP is a simple protocol that exchanges datagrams without acknowledgments or guaranteed delivery, requiring that error processing and retransmission be handled by other protocols. UDP is defined in RFC 768.

UTP (UNSHIELDED TWISTED-PAIR) A four-pair wire medium used in a variety of networks. UTP does not require the fixed spacing between connections that is necessary with coaxial-type connections.

VIRTUAL CIRCUIT A logical circuit created to ensure reliable communication between two network devices. A virtual circuit is defined by a VPI/VCI pair, and can be either permanent or switched. Virtual circuits are used in frame relay and X.25. In ATM, a virtual circuit is called a virtual channel. Sometimes abbreviated VC.

VLAN (VIRTUAL LAN)   A group of devices on one or more LANs that are configured (using management software) so that they can communicate as if they were attached to the same wire, when in fact they are located on a number of different LAN segments. Because VLANs are based on logical instead of physical connections, they are extremely flexible.

VLSM (VARIABLE-LENGTH SUBNET MASKING)   The ability to specify a different length subnet mask for the same network number at different locations in the network. VLSM can help optimize available address space.

WAN (WIDE AREA NETWORK)   A data communications network that serves users across a broad geographic area and often uses transmission devices provided by common carriers. Frame relay, SMDS, and X.25 are examples of WANs. Compare with LAN and MAN.

WILDCARD MASK   A 32-bit quantity used in conjunction with an IP address to determine which bits in an IP address should be matched and ignored when comparing that address with another IP address. A wildcard mask is specified when defining access list statements.

X.121   An ITU-T standard describing an addressing scheme used in X.25 networks. X.121 addresses are sometimes called IDNs (International Data Numbers).

X.21   An ITU-T standard for serial communications over synchronous digital lines. The X.21 protocol is used primarily in Europe and Japan.

X.25   An ITU-T standard that defines how connections between DTE and DCE are maintained for remote terminal access and computer communications in public data networks. X.25 specifies LAPB, a data-link layer protocol, and PLP, a network-layer protocol. Frame relay has to some degree superseded X.25.

ZONE   In AppleTalk, a logical group of network devices.

Custom Corporate Network Training

Train on Cutting Edge Technology   We can bring the best in skill-based training to your facility to create a real-world hands-on training experience. Global Knowledge has invested millions of dollars in network hardware and software to train our students on the same equipment they will work with on the job. Our relationships with vendors allow us to incorporate the latest equipment and platforms into your on-site labs.

Maximize Your Training Budget   Global Knowledge provides experienced instructors, comprehensive course materials, and all the networking equipment needed to deliver high quality training. You provide the students; we provide the knowledge.

Avoid Travel Expenses   On-site courses allow you to schedule technical training at your convenience, saving time, expense, and the opportunity cost of travel away from the workplace.

Discuss Confidential Topics   Private on-site training permits the open discussion of sensitive issues such as security, access, and network design. We can work with your existing network's proprietary files while demonstrating the latest technologies.

Customize Course Content   Global Knowledge can tailor your courses to include the technologies and the topics which have the greatest impact on your business. We can complement your internal training efforts or provide a total solution to your training needs.

Corporate Pass   The Corporate Pass Discount Program rewards our best network training customers with preferred pricing on public courses, discounts on multimedia training packages, and an array of career planning services.

Global Knowledge Training Lifecycle   Supporting the Dynamic and Specialized Training Requirements of Information Technology Professionals

- Define Profile
- Assess Skills
- Design Training
- Deliver Training
- Test Knowledge
- Update Profile
- Use New Skills

College Credit Recommendation Program   The American Council on Education's CREDIT program recommends 53 Global Knowledge courses for college credit. Now our network training can help you earn your college degree while you learn the technical skills needed for your job. When you attend an ACE-certified Global Knowledge course and pass the associated exam, you earn college credit recommendations for that course. Global Knowledge can establish a transcript record for you with ACE, which you can use to gain credit at a college or as a written record of your professional training that you can attach to your resume.

Registration Information

COURSE FEE: The fee covers course tuition, refreshments, and all course materials. Any parking expenses that may be incurred are not included. Payment or government training form must be received six business days prior to the course date. We will also accept Visa/MasterCard and American Express. For non-U.S. credit card users, charges will be in U.S. funds and will be converted by your credit card company. Checks drawn on Canadian banks in Canadian funds are acceptable.

COURSE SCHEDULE: Registration is at 8:00 a.m. on the first day. The program begins at 8:30 a.m. and concludes at 4:30 p.m. each day.

CANCELLATION POLICY: Cancellation and full refund will be allowed if written cancellation is received in our office at least six business days prior to the course start date. Registrants who do not attend the course or do not cancel more than six business days in advance are responsible for the full registration fee; you may transfer to a later date provided the course fee has been paid in full. Substitutions may be made at any time. If Global Knowledge must cancel a course for any reason, liability is limited to the registration fee only.

GLOBAL KNOWLEDGE: Global Knowledge programs are developed and presented by industry professionals with "real-world" experience. Designed to help professionals meet today's interconnectivity and interoperability challenges, most of our programs feature hands-on labs that incorporate state-of-the-art communication components and equipment.

ON-SITE TEAM TRAINING: Bring Global Knowledge's powerful training programs to your company. At Global Knowledge, we will custom design courses to meet your specific network requirements. Call 1 (919) 461-8686 for more information.

YOUR GUARANTEE: Global Knowledge believes its courses offer the best possible training in this field. If during the first day you are not satisfied and wish to withdraw from the course, simply notify the instructor, return all course materials, and receive a 100% refund.

In the US:

CALL: 1 (888) 762-4442

FAX: 1 (919) 469-7070

VISIT OUR WEBSITE:

www.globalknowledge.com

MAIL CHECK AND THIS FORM TO:

Global Knowledge

Suite 200

114 Edinburgh South

P.O. Box 1187

Cary, NC 27512

In Canada:

CALL: 1 (800) 465-2226

FAX: 1 (613) 567-3899

VISIT OUR WEBSITE:

www.globalknowledge.com.ca

MAIL CHECK AND THIS FORM TO:

Global Knowledge

Suite 1601

393 University Ave.

Toronto, ON M5G 1E6

REGISTRATION INFORMATION:

Course title _____

Course location _____ Course date _____

Name/title _____ Company _____

Name/title _____ Company _____

Name/title _____ Company _____

Address _____ Telephone _____ Fax _____

City _____ State/Province _____ Zip/Postal Code _____

Credit card _____ Card # _____ Expiration date _____

Signature _____

Notes

Notes

Notes